Sociology

Introductory Readings

Fourth Edition

Edited by

Anthony Giddens
and
Philip W. Sutton

KT-529-882

polity

Copyright © this collection and editorial summaries Polity Press 2022

First edition published in 1997 by Polity Press
This fourth edition first published in 2022 by Polity Press

Polity Press
65 Bridge Street
Cambridge CB2 1UR, UK

Polity Press
101 Station Landing
Suite 300
Medford, MA 02155, USA

All rights reserved. Except for the quotation of short passages for the purpose of criticism and review, no part of this publication may be reproduced, stored in a retrieval system or transmitted, in any form or by any means, electronic, mechanical, photocopying, recording or otherwise, without the prior permission of the publisher.

ISBN-13: 978-1-5095-4912-2
ISBN-13: 978-1-5095-4913-9 (pb)

A catalogue record for this book is available from the British Library.

Typeset in 10 on 12.5pt Galliard by
Servis Filmsetting Ltd, Stockport, Cheshire
Printed and bound in by Great Britain by TJ Books Ltd,
Padstow, Cornwall

The publisher has used its best endeavours to ensure that the URLs for external websites referred to in this book are correct and active at the time of going to press. However, the publisher has no responsibility for the websites and can make no guarantee that a site will remain live or that the content is or will remain appropriate.

Every effort has been made to trace all copyright holders, but if any have been overlooked the publisher will be pleased to include any necessary credits in any subsequent reprint or edition.

For further information on Polity, visit our website:
politybooks.com

Contents

Acknowledgements

Typographical errors identified in original materials have been corrected. Language and referencing style have been left as in the originals, with one exception in Reading 48.

We are grateful to the following for permission to reproduce copyright material:

Extracts from 'The Study of the Negro Problems' by W.E.B. Du Bois from *Annals of the American Academy of Political and Social Science*, Vol 11(1): 1–23, 11/01/1898, copyright © 1898. Reprinted by permission of SAGE Publications, Inc.; Extracts from *The Sociological Imagination* by C. Wright-Mills, Oxford University Press, copyright © 1959, 2000. Reprinted with permission of the Licensor through PLSclear; Extracts from 'Decolonizing Sociology' by Raewyn Connell from *Contemporary Sociology*, Vol 47(4): 399–407, 2018, copyright © 2018. Reprinted by permission of SAGE Publications, Inc.; Extracts from *Thinking Sociologically, 3rd edition* by Zygmunt Bauman and Tim May, John Wiley & Sons Inc., 2019, copyright © 2019, John Wiley & Sons Ltd. Reprinted by permission of the publisher; Extracts from *Distinction – RC, 1st edition* by Pierre Bourdieu, Routledge, copyright © 1984, 2010, the President and Fellows of Harvard College and Routledge. Reprinted by arrangement with Taylor & Francis Group; Extracts from 'Learning From the Outsider Within: The Sociological Significance of Black Feminist Thought' by Patricia Hill Collins from *Social Problems*, Vol 33(6): S14–S32, 01/12/1986, copyright © 1986, Society for the Study of Social Problems, Inc. Reprinted by permission of Oxford University Press; Extracts from 'Sociology and Postcolonialism: Another 'Missing' Revolution?' by Gurminder K. Bhambra from *Sociology*, Vol 41(5): 871–84, 01/10/2007, copyright © 2007. Reprinted by permission of SAGE Publications, Inc.; Extracts from *The Rules of Sociological Method* by Emile Durkheim, edited by George E.G. Catlin, translated by Sarah A. Solovay and John H. Mueller, The Free Press, 1966, copyright © 1966, renewed. Reprinted by permission of Curtis Brown, Ltd. All rights reserved; Extracts from 'Paralympic Broadcasting and Social Change: An Integrated Mixed Method Approach to Understanding the Paralympic Audience in the UK' by Emma Pullen, Daniel Jackson and Michael Silk, *Television and New Media*, 1–21, 24/03/2007, copyright © 2007, SAGE Publications, Inc. Creative Commons licence, CC. 4.0; Extracts from *Contemporary Feminist Research from Theory to Practice* by Patricia Leavy and Anne Harris, The Guilford Press, 2019, copyright © 2019, The Guilford Press. Permission conveyed through Copyright Clearance Center, Inc.; Extracts from "The Metropolis and Mental Life" by Georg Simmel and translated by Edward A. Shils, from *Georg Simmel on Individuality and Social Forms*, edited by Donald N. Levine, pp.334–332, published by The University of Chicago Press, copyright © 1971, The University of Chicago. All rights reserved. Reprinted with permission; Extracts from 'The White Space' by Elijah Anderson from *Sociology of Race and Ethnicity*, Vol 1(1): 10–21, 01/01/2015, copyright © 2007. Reprinted by permission of SAGE Publications, Inc.; Extracts

x

Extracts from "'A monstrous threat': how a state of exception turns into a 'new normal'" by Jens O. Zinn, *Journal of Risk Research*, Vol 23(7–8): 1083–91, 27/04/2020. Reprinted by permission of Taylor and Francis Group Ltd; Extracts from *Outsiders: Studies in the Sociology of Deviance* by Howard S. Becker, The Free Press, copyright © 1963, The Free Press, renewed 1991 by Howard S. Becker. Reprinted with the permission of The Free Press, a division of Simon & Schuster, Inc. All rights reserved; Extracts from 'Editorial: Punishment and Society Today' by David Garland, *Punishment and Society*, Vol 1(1): 5–10, 01/07/1999, copyright © 1999. Reprinted by permission of SAGE Publications, Inc.; Extracts from 'Race as Civic Felony' by Loïc Wacquant, *International Social Science Journal*, Vol 57(183): 127–42, 23/05/2005. Reprinted by permission of John Wiley & Sons, Inc.; Extracts from *Banished: The New Social Control in Urban America* by Katherine Beckett and Steve Herbert, Oxford University Press, 2010. Reprinted with permission of the Licensor through PLSclear; Extracts from *Power: A Radical View, 2nd edition* by Steven Lukes, Palgrave Macmillan, 2005. Reprinted with permission of the Licensor through PLSclear; Extracts from *The Dark Side of Democracy:*

Explaining Ethnic Cleansing by Michael Mann, Cambridge University Press, 2005. Reprinted with permission of the Licensor through PLSclear; Extracts from 'Ethno-Nationalist Populism and the Mobilization of Collective Resentment' by Bart Bonikowski from *The British Journal of Sociology*, Vol 68(S1): S181–S213, 08/11/2017, copyright © 2017, London School of Economics and Political Science. Reprinted by permission of John Wiley & Sons, Inc.; Extracts from 'Disrupting or Reconfiguring Racist Narratives about Muslims? The Representation of British Muslims During the Covid Crisis' by Elizabeth Poole and Milly Williamson from *Journalism*, 02/07/2021, copyright © 2021. Reprinted by permission of SAGE Publications, Inc.; and extracts from 'Scaling Social Movements Through Social Media: The Case of Black Lives Matter' by Marcia Mundt, Karen Ross and Charla M. Burnett from *Social Media + Society*, Vol 4(4): 1–14, 01/11/2018, copyright © 2018. Reprinted by permission of SAGE Publications, Inc.

In some instances we have been unable to trace the owners of copyright material, and we would appreciate any information that would enable us to do so.

from 'Anthropocene: A Cautious Welcome From Environmental Sociology?' by Rolf Lidskog and Claire Waterton from *Environmental Sociology*, Vol 2(4): 395–406, Taylor & Francis, 11/01/2016. Creative Commons CC BY license; Extracts from *The Protestant Ethic and the Spirit of Capitalism* by Max Weber, translated by Talcott Parsons, copyright © 1967. Reprinted by permission of Taylor and Francis Group LLC, a division of Informa plc; Extracts from *Assembling Women: The Feminization of Global Manufacturing* by Teri L. Caraway, an ILR Press book published by Cornell University Press, copyright © 2007, Cornell University. Reprinted by permission of the publisher; Extracts from ''Structure Liberates?': Mixing for Mobility and the Cultural Transformation of Urban Children in a London Academy' by Christy Kulz from *Ethnic and Racial Studies*, Vol 37(4): 685–701, 18/07/2013. Reprinted by permission of Taylor and Francis Group Ltd; Extracts from *The Age of Surveillance Capitalism: The Fight for a Human Future at the New Frontier of Power* by Shoshana Zuboff, Profile Books Ltd, 2019, copyright © 2019, Shoshana Zuboff. Reprinted by permission of Profile Books; Extracts from 'Mapping the Margins: Intersectionality, Identity Politics, and Violence Against Women of Color' by Kimberle Crenshaw, *Stanford Law Review*, Vol 43(6): 1241–99, July 1991, copyright © 1991. Permission conveyed through Copyright Clearance Center, Inc.; Extracts from *Contours of Ableism: The Production of Disability and Abledness* by Fiona K. Campbell, Palgrave Macmillan, 2009, copyright © 2009, Fiona Kumari Campbell. Reprinted with permission of the Licensor through PLSclear; Extracts and 2 figures from *Capital in the Twenty-First Century* by Thomas Piketty, translated by Arthur Goldhammer, Cambridge, Mass.: The Belknap Press of Harvard University Press, copyright © 2014 by the President and Fellows of Harvard College. Used by permission. All rights reserved; Extracts from *What We Now Know About Race and Ethnicity* by Michael Banton, Berghahn, 2015. Reprinted by permission of Berghahn Books Inc.; Extracts from 'Sharing the Load? Partners' Relative Earnings and the Division of Domestic Labour' by Clare Lyonette and Rosemary Crompton from *Work, Employment and Society*, Vol 29(1): 23–40, 10/06/2014, copyright © 2015. Reprinted by permission of SAGE Publications, Inc.; Extracts from *Mind, Self, and Society* by George Herbert Mead, University of Chicago Press, copyright © 1934, 2015, The University of Chicago Press, Ltd. Permission conveyed through Copyright Clearance Center, Inc.; Extracts from *The Life Course: A Sociological Introduction*, 2nd edition by Stephen J. Hunt, Palgrave Macmillan, 2017, copyright © 2005, 2017, Stephen J. Hunt. Reprinted with permission of the Licensor through PLSclear; Extracts from *The Presentation of Self in Everyday Life* by Erving Goffman, published by Anchor Books 1959, Penguin Press 1969, Pelican Books 1971, Penguin Books 1990, copyright © 1959, Erving Goffman. Reprinted by permission of Penguin Books Limited; Extracts from *Violence: A Micro-sociological Theory* by Randall Collins, Princeton University Press, 2008, copyright © 2008, Princeton University Press. Permission conveyed through Copyright Clearance Center, Inc.; Extracts from *Beauty and Misogyny*, 2nd edition by Sheila Jeffreys, Routledge, copyright © 2015, Sheila Jeffreys. Reprinted by arrangement with Taylor & Francis Group; Extracts from 'Post–Truth Society? An Eliasian Sociological Analysis of Knowledge in the 21st Century' by Dominic Malcolm, from *Sociology*, pp.1–17, 26/03/2021, copyright © 2021, Dominic Malcolm. Reprinted by permission of SAGE Publications, Inc.; Extracts from *The Medicalization of Society: On the Transformation of Human Conditions into Treatable Disorders* by Peter Conrad, Johns Hopkins University Press, 2007, copyright © 2007, The Johns Hopkins University Press. Reprinted with permission; Extracts from *The Spirit Level* by Kate Pickett & Richard Wilkinson, Penguin Books, copyright © 2009, 2010, Richard Wilkinson and Kate Pickett. Reprinted by permission of Penguin Books Limited;

Introduction:
The Sociological Perspective

The third edition of *Sociology: Introductory Readings* was published in 2010, and, as the COVID-19 pandemic dramatically proves, a lot has happened since then. Hence, this fourth edition is all new for the 2020s, with many contemporary readings that reflect important shifts in sociological theories and empirical research over the last decade. However, as with previous editions, we have sought to find a judicious combination of the classical statements of sociology and more recent work to provide readers with a broad overview of contemporary sociology.

The book is designed as a stand-alone text that can be used with any sociology textbook. However, the ten-part structure is based on key themes – from theories and methods to the environment and political sociology – which mirror our companion volume, *Essential Concepts in Sociology* (3rd edn, 2021). This enables students who use both books to cross-reference concepts and readings more easily. Each of the ten parts is introduced with a brief essay that acts as a means of orientation to the theme and our selected readings.

The reader takes in longstanding debates on the scientific status of sociology, which methods are appropriate for the discipline and what we should expect from sociological studies. It also covers more recent critical work on postcolonialism and how sociology might be 'decolonized', as well as studies that examine how the digital revolution is changing sociological practice 'in the field'.

We have incorporated readings on topical subjects such as continuing globalization, COVID-19, political populism, climate change, intersectional inequalities, love and sexuality, violence and ethnic cleansing, Black Lives Matter activism and Islamophobia. These are included alongside the classical sociological subjects of stratification and social class, capitalism, health inequalities, social solidarity, the nature of power, deviance and crime, theories of self-formation and identity, and religion. Overall, the book is a concise yet comprehensive resource that teachers, students and anyone interested in sociology will find useful as a guide to the discipline. For those who already have or use our main textbook, *Sociology* (9th edn, 2021), a guide to the relevant chapters and sections in that book is provided at the end of each section, together with recommendations for further reading.

Sociology today is more diverse than ever before, theoretically, methodologically and in terms of its subject matter. Older sociological staples are still evident – education, work, organizations, urban life, inequality, families and religion – but now alongside new subjects such as climate change, cybercrime, digital surveillance and social media, body modification and global migration. To maintain its role as a vital and wide-ranging academic enterprise into the twenty-first century, as our readings clearly illustrate, sociology continues to adapt and change as it strives to keep pace with the social world.

Our Introduction contains five readings on the basic questions 'What is sociology?' and 'What should we expect of it?' A simple, though insufficient answer is that sociology is the systematic study of human societies, which helps us understand them better. Yet there are different ways in which this study might be approached, and the readings explore various aspects of the sociological mission.

One of the most debated and contentious questions is whether sociology is, or could ever be, a scientific discipline. Can people and social life really be studied in a scientific manner, or should sociologists accept that their discipline is more akin to the humanities, where definitive conclusions are more elusive? The extract from W. E. B Du Bois' late nineteenth-century study in the USA is a very clear rejection of the latter position. For Du Bois, the urgent social problems associated with urban poverty, racial injustice and inequality demand to be rooted in empirical evidence. This means that sociologists have to approach their work in a systematic way, carefully collecting data from the people whose lives they study. Du Bois also shows that sociology must adopt an historical approach to contemporary problems if it is properly to understand how those problems developed. But he is keenly aware of the dangers posed when sociologists allow their own biases and prejudices to interfere with their scientific work. He proposes that, ultimately, sociology must involve the pursuit of the truth as the basis for tackling the most serious issues of the day. Given the recent emergence of 'fake news' and 'post-truth' politics, Du Bois provides an excellent reminder of why 'the truth' remains a goal worth pursuing.

Charles Wright Mills's book *The Sociological Imagination* (1959) has been read by all aspiring sociologists and remains a classic text whose main argument is remarkably contemporary. Wright Mills argues that sociology should combine an interest in the personal troubles of individual people with broader public issues that are of concern to governments. This means that sociology must study the 'intersections' of biography and history, and the reading offers several illustrations of this perspective, from divorce and its impact on partners, children and government policy to unemployment and even war. In each case the intertwining of individual actions, structural conditions and institutional change provides the subject matter for sociologists. One of the key tasks is to bring together personal troubles and public issues to provide reliable evidence for policy-makers. But sociological studies also provide the information to help individuals to understand their own lives and social situations better.

The findings arrived at through scientific study are often in conflict with common-sense beliefs and ideas and with moral standpoints and politically committed positions. In this way, science challenges people to reconsider their most cherished ideals. In Reading 3, Norbert Elias discusses the way that sociology, like all the sciences, challenges our fixed, often traditional beliefs and superstitions about the world. In particular, he takes aim at the widespread assumption that 'society' is merely the name given to large aggregations of individual human beings. For Elias, this assumption is simply wrong. A more accurate way to think about social life is in terms of figurations of people who live their lives together and the reading explores the consequences of abandoning the concept of the 'sovereign individual' as the unit of analysis. He argues that it can be difficult to accept that social life is not explicable purely in terms of the intentions of individuals but, rather, is the outcome of the actions of millions of people who never meet one another. It is the most urgent task of sociologists to investigate and understand this impersonal, largely unplanned social order.

One of the most significant challenges to 'business as usual' in sociology has been the development of postcolonial theories that take issue with mainstream sociology for its relative neglect of colonialism. Conventional theories of modernity, for example, tend to discuss this in the context of the relatively wealthy, 'developed' economies of the Global North, ignoring those of the South. They also underplay or fail to build in the long-term impact of colonial regimes on the colonized societies and their prospects for development. In order to rectify this, it is suggested that sociology (and other disciplines) needs to be thoroughly 'decolonized'. Raewyn Connell argues that this process should tackle all aspects of knowledge production, including the teaching curriculum, research funding and access to academic journals, to incorporate and embed research and theorizing in the Global South, which has been sidelined for far too long. In a globalizing world, this task has become ever more urgent if sociology is to be relevant long into the future.

In the final reading in this section, Zygmunt Bauman and Tim May address the thorny problem of agency and structure, or, to what extent do individuals really have free will to live life as they please? And to what extent are their apparently free choices actually constrained by social structures? They note that, despite the focus on 'free will', in fact much more than ideas are required. For instance, resources can both limit and enable the extent of the individual's freedom to achieve their goals. Resources can be the financial means to pay for healthcare or education, but they can also be markers of status or easy access to influential or powerful social networks. Similarly, sociological studies have provided a wealth of evidence which shows that race and ethnicity, gender, social class and disability heavily influence the life chances of individual members of society. This so-called structure–agency debate remains one of the central dilemmas of sociology today.

1. Sociology as the Science of Social Life*

W. E. B. Du Bois

The present period in the development of socio-logical study is a trying one; it is the period of observation, research and comparison – work always wearisome, often aimless, without well-settled principles and guiding lines, and subject ever to the pertinent criticism: What, after all, has been accomplished? To this the one positive answer which years of research and speculation have been able to return is that the phenomena of society are worth the most careful and system-atic study, and whether or not this study may eventually lead to a systematic body of knowl-edge deserving the name of science, it cannot in any case fail to give the world a mass of truth worth the knowing.

Being then in a period of observation and com-parison, we must confess to ourselves that the sociologists of few nations have so good an oppor-tunity for observing the growth and evolution of society as those of the United States. The rapid rise of a young country, the vast social changes, the wonderful economic development, the bold political experiments, and the contact of varying moral standards – all these make for American students crucial tests of social action, microcosmic reproductions of long centuries of world history, and rapid – even violent – repetitions of social problems. Here is a field for the sociologist – a field rich, but little worked, and full of great possi-bilities. European scholars envy our opportunities

and it must be said to our credit that great interest in the observation of phenomena has been aroused in the last decade – an interest of which much is ephemeral and superficial, but which opens the way for broad scholarship and scientific effort.

In one field, however, – and a field perhaps larger than any other single domain of social phenomena, there does not seem to have been awakened as yet a fitting realization of the oppor-tunities for scientific inquiry. This is the group of social phenomena arising from the presence in this land of eight million persons of African descent.

It is my purpose in this paper to discuss cer-tain considerations concerning the study of the social problems affecting American Negroes; first, as to the historical development of these prob-lems; then as to the necessity for their careful systematic study at the present time; thirdly, as to results of scientific study of the Negro up to this time; fourthly, as to the scope and method which future scientific inquiry should take, and, lastly, regarding the agencies by which this work can best be carried out.

[. . .]

In the latter part of the seventeenth and early in the eighteenth centuries, the central and all-absorbing economic need of America was the creation of a proper labor supply to develop American wealth. This question had been answered in the West Indies by enslaving Indians and Negroes. In the colonies of the mainland it was answered by the importation of Negroes and indented servants. Immediately then there arose

* From Du Bois, W. E. B. (1898) 'The Study of the Negro Problems', *Annals of the American Academy of Political and Social Science*, Jan, 11: 1–23. Extracts from pp. 1–2, 3–6, 16–17, 21–23.

the question of the legal status of these slaves and servants; and dozens of enactments, from Massachusetts to Georgia, were made "for the proper regulation of slaves and servants." Such statutes sought to solve problems of labor and not of race or color. Two circumstances, however, soon began to differentiate in the problem of labor, problems which concerned slaves for life from those which concerned servants for limited periods; and these circumstances were the economic superiority of the slave system, and the fact that the slaves were neither of the same race, language nor religion as the servants and their masters. In laboring classes thus widely separated there naturally arose a difference in legal and social standing. Colonial statutes soon ceased to embrace the regulations applying to slaves and servants in one chapter, and laws were passed for servants on the one hand and for Negro slaves on the other.

As slave labor, under the peculiar conditions of colonial life, increased in value and efficiency, the importations of Africans increased, while those of indented servants decreased; this gave rise to new social problems, namely, those of protecting a feeble civilization against an influx of barbarism and heathenism. Between 1750 and 1800 an increasing number of laws began to form a peculiar and systematic slave code based on a distinct idea of social caste. Even, as this slave code was developing, new social conditions changed the aspect of the problems. The laws hitherto had been made to fit a class distinguished by its condition more than by its race or color. There arose now, however, a class of English-speaking Negroes born on American soil, and members of Christian churches; there sprang from illicit intercourse and considerable intermarriage with indented servants, a number of persons of mixed blood; there was also created by emancipation and the birth of black sons of white women a new class of free Negroes: all these developments led to a distinct beginning of group life among Negroes. Repeated attempts at organized insurrection were made; wholesale running away, like that which established the exiles in Florida, was

resorted to; and a class of black landholders and voters arose. Such social movements brought the colonists face to face with new serious problems; which they sought at first to settle in curious ways, denying the rite of baptism, establishing the legal presumption that all Negroes and mulattoes were slaves, and finally changing the Slave Code into a Black Code, replacing a caste of condition by a caste of race, harshly stopping legal sexual intercourse, and seeking to prevent further complications by restricting and even suppressing the slave-trade.

This concerted and determined action again changed the character of the Negro problems, but they did not cease to be grave. The inability of the Negro to escape from a servile caste into political freedom turned the problems of the group into problems of family life. On the separated plantations and in households the Negro became a constituent member of the family, speaking its language, worshiping in its churches, sharing its traditions, bearing its name, and sometimes sharing its blood; the talented slaves found large freedom in the intimate intercourse with the family which they enjoyed; they lost many traditions of their fatherland, and their ideals blended with the ideals of their new country. Some men began to see in this development a physical, economic and moral danger to the land, and they busied themselves with questions as to how they might provide for the development of white and black without demoralizing the one or amalgamating with the other. The solution of these difficulties was sought in a widespread attempt to eliminate the Negro from the family as he had formerly been eliminated from the state, by a process of emancipation that made him and his sons not even half-free, with the indefinite notion of colonizing the anomalous serfs thus created. This policy was carried out until one-half the land and one-sixth of the Negroes were quasi-freemen.

Just as the nation was on the point of realizing the futility of colonization, one of those strange incalculable world movements began to be felt throughout civilized states – a movement so vast that we call it the economic revolution of the nineteenth century. A world demand for crops peculiarly suited to the South, substituted in Europe the factory system for the house industry, and in America the large plantation slave system for the family patriarchy; slavery became an industrial system and not a training school for serfdom; the Black Codes underwent a sudden transformation which hardened the lot of the slave, facilitated the slave trade, hindered further emancipation and rendered the condition of the free Negro unbearable. The question of race and color in America assumed a new and peculiar importance when it thus lay at the basis of some of the world's greatest industries.

The change in industrial conditions, however, not only affected the demands of a world market, but so increased the efficiency of labor, that a labor system, which was eminently successful, soon became under the altered conditions of 1850 not only an economic monstrosity, but a political menace, and so rapidly did the crisis develop that the whole evolution of the nation came to a standstill, and the settlement of our social problems had to be left to the clumsy method of brute force.

So far as the Negro race is concerned, the Civil War simply left us face to face with the same sort of problems of social condition and caste which were beginning to face the nation a century ago. It is these problems that we are to-day somewhat helplessly – not to say carelessly – facing, forgetful that they are living, growing social questions whose progeny will survive to curse the nation, unless we grapple with them manfully and intelligently.

[. . .]

The scope of any social study is first of all limited by the general attitude of public opinion toward truth and truth-seeking. If in regard to any social problem there is for any reason a persistent refusal on the part of the people to allow the truth to be known, then manifestly that problem cannot be studied. Undoubtedly much of the unsatisfactory work already done with regard to

the Negro is due to this cause; the intense feeling that preceded and followed the war made a calm balanced research next to impossible. Even to-day there are certain phases of this question which we cannot hope to be allowed to study dispassionately and thoroughly, and these phases, too, are naturally those uppermost in the public mind. For instance, it is extremely doubtful if any satisfactory study of Negro crime and lynching can be made for a generation or more, in the present condition of the public mind, which renders it almost impossible to get at the facts and real conditions. On the other hand, public opinion has in the last decade become sufficiently liberal to open a broad field of investigation to students, and here lies the chance for effective work.

The right to enter this field undisturbed and untrammeled will depend largely on the attitude of science itself. Students must be careful to insist that science as such – be it physics, chemistry, psychology, or sociology – has but one simple aim: the discovery of truth. Its results lie open for the use of all men – merchants, physicians, men of letters, and philanthropists, but the aim of science itself is simple truth. Any attempt to give it a double aim, to make social reform the immediate instead of the mediate object of a search for truth, will inevitably tend to defeat both objects. The frequent alliance of sociological research with various panaceas and particular schemes of reform, has resulted in closely connecting social investigation with a good deal of groundless assumption and humbug in the popular mind. There will be at first some difficulty in bringing the Southern people, both black and white, to conceive of an earnest, careful study of the Negro problem which has not back of it some scheme of race amalgamation, political jobbery, or deportation to Africa. The new study of the American Negro must avoid such misapprehensions from the outset, by insisting that historical and statistical research has but one object, the ascertainment of the facts as to the social forces and conditions of one-eighth of the inhabitants of the land. Only by such rigid adherence to the true object of the scholar, can statesmen and philanthropists of all shades of belief be put into possession of a reliable body of truth which may guide their efforts to the best and largest success.

In the next place, a study of the Negro, like the study of any subject, must start out with certain generally admitted postulates. We must admit, for instance, that the field of study is large and varying, and that what is true of the Negro in Massachusetts is not necessarily true of the Negro in Louisiana; that what was true of the Negro in 1850 was not necessarily true in 1750; and that there are many distinct social problems affecting the Negro. Finally, if we would rally to this common ground of scientific inquiry all partisans and advocates, we must explicitly admit what all implicitly postulate – namely, that the Negro is a member of the human race, and as one who, in the light of history and experience, is capable to a degree of improvement and culture, is entitled to have his interests considered according to his numbers in all conclusions as to the common weal.

[. . .]

For simple, definite inquiries carried out periodically on a broad scale we should depend on the national and state governments. The decennial census properly organized under civil service rules should be the greatest single agency for collecting general information as to the Negro. If, however, the present Congress cannot be induced to organize a census bureau under proper Civil Service rules, and in accordance with the best expert advice, we must continue for many years more to depend on clumsy and ignorant methods of measurement in matters demanding accuracy and trained technique. It is possible also for the different national bureaus and for the state governments to study certain aspects of the Negro question over wide areas. A conspicuous example of this is the valuable educational statistics collected by Commissioner Harris, and the series of economic studies just instituted by the Bureau of Labor.

On the whole it may be laid down as axiomatic that government activity in the study of this problem should confine itself mainly to the ascertainment of simple facts covering a broad field. For the study of these social problems in their more complicated aspects, where the desideratum is intensive study, by trained minds, according to the best methods, the only competent agency is the university. Indeed, in no better way could the American university repay the unusual munificence of its benefactors than by placing before the nation a body of scientific truth in the light of which they could solve some of their most vexing social problems.

It is to the credit of the University of Pennsylvania that she has been the first to recognize her duty in this respect, and in so far as restricted means and opportunity allowed, has attempted to study the Negro problems in a single definite locality. This work needs to be extended to other groups, and carried out with larger system; and here it would seem is the opportunity of the Southern Negro college. We hear much of higher Negro education, and all candid people know there does not exist to-day in the centre of Negro population a single first-class fully equipped institution devoted to the higher education of Negroes; not more than three Negro institutions in the South deserve the name of *college* at all; and yet what is a Negro college but a vast college settlement for the study of a particular set of peculiarly baffling problems? What more effective or suitable agency could be found in which to focus the scientific efforts of the great universities of the North and East, than an institution situated in the very heart of these social problems, and made the centre of careful historical and statistical research? Without doubt the first effective step toward the solving of the Negro question will be the endowment of a Negro college which is not merely a teaching body, but a centre of sociological research, in close connection and co-operation with Harvard, Columbia, Johns Hopkins and the University of Pennsylvania.

In this direction the Negro conferences of Tuskegee and Hampton are tending; and there is already inaugurated an actual beginning of work at Atlanta University. In 1896 this university brought into correspondence about one hundred Southern college-bred men and laid before them a plan of systematic investigation into certain problems of Negro city life, as, for instance, family conditions, dwellings, rents, ownership of homes, occupations, earnings, disease and death-rates. Each investigator took one or more small groups to study, and in this way fifty-nine groups, aggregating 5000 people in various parts of the country, were studied, and the results have been published by the United States Bureau of Labor. Such purely scientific work, done with an eye single to ascertaining true conditions, marks an era in our conception of the place of the Negro college, and it is certainly to be desired that Atlanta University may be enabled to continue this work as she proposes to do.

Finally the necessity must again be emphasized of keeping clearly before students the object of all science, amid the turmoil and intense feeling that clouds the discussion of a burning social question. We live in a day when in spite of the brilliant accomplishments of a remarkable century, there is current much flippant criticism of scientific work; when the truth-seeker is too often pictured as devoid of human sympathy, and careless of human ideals. We are still prone in spite of all our culture to sneer at the heroism of the laboratory while we cheer the swagger of the street broil. At such a time true lovers of humanity can only hold higher the pure ideals of science, and continue to insist that if we would solve a problem we must study it, and that there is but one coward on earth, and that is the coward that dare not know.

2. The Promise of Sociology*

C. Wright Mills

Nowadays men often feel that their private lives are a series of traps. They sense that within their everyday worlds, they cannot overcome their troubles, and in this feeling, they are often quite correct: What ordinary men are directly aware of and what they try to do are bounded by the private orbits in which they live; their visions and their powers are limited to the close-up scenes of job, family, neighborhood; in other milieux, they move vicariously and remain spectators. And the more aware they become, however vaguely, of ambitions and of threats which transcend their immediate locales, the more trapped they seem to feel.

Underlying this sense of being trapped are seemingly impersonal changes in the very structure of continent-wide societies. The facts of contemporary history are also facts about the success and the failure of individual men and women. When a society is industrialized, a peasant becomes a worker; a feudal lord is liquidated or becomes a businessman. When classes rise or fall, a man is employed or unemployed; when the rate of investment goes up or down, a man takes new heart or goes broke. When wars happen, an insurance salesman becomes a rocket launcher; a store clerk, a radar man; a wife lives alone; a child grows up without a father. Neither the life of an individual nor the history of a society can be understood without understanding both.

Yet men do not usually define the troubles they endure in terms of historical change and institutional contradiction. The well-being they enjoy, they do not usually impute to the big ups and downs of the societies in which they live. Seldom aware of the intricate connection between the patterns of their own lives and the course of world history, ordinary men do not usually know what this connection means for the kinds of men they are becoming and for the kinds of history-making in which they might take part. They do not possess the quality of mind essential to grasp the interplay of man and society, of biography and history, of self and world. They cannot cope with their personal troubles in such ways as to control the structural transformations that usually lie behind them.

Surely it is no wonder. In what period have so many men been so totally exposed at so fast a pace to such earthquakes of change? That Americans have not known such catastrophic changes as have the men and women of other societies is due to historical facts that are now quickly becoming 'merely history.' The history that now affects every man is world history. Within this scene and this period, in the course of a single generation, one sixth of mankind is transformed from all that is feudal and backward into all that is modern, advanced, and fearful. Political colonies are freed; new and less visible forms of imperialism installed. Revolutions occur; men feel the intimate grip of new kinds of authority. Totalitarian societies rise, and are smashed to bits—or succeed fabulously. After two centuries of hope, even formal democracy is restricted to a quite small portion of mankind. Everywhere in

* From Wright Mills, C. (2000 [1959]) *The Sociological Imagination* (Oxford: Oxford University Press). Extracts from pp. 3–7, 8–11.

the underdeveloped world, ancient ways of life are broken up and vague expectations become urgent demands. Everywhere in the overdeveloped world, the means of authority and of violence become total in scope and bureaucratic in form. Humanity itself now lies before us, the super-nation at either pole concentrating its most co-ordinated and massive efforts upon the preparation of World War Three.

The very shaping of history now outpaces the ability of men to orient themselves in accordance with cherished values. And which values? Even when they do not panic, men often sense that older ways of feeling and thinking have collapsed and that newer beginnings are ambiguous to the point of moral stasis. Is it any wonder that ordinary men feel they cannot cope with the larger worlds with which they are so suddenly confronted? That they cannot understand the meaning of their epoch for their own lives? That—in defense of selfhood—they become morally insensible, trying to remain altogether private men? Is it any wonder that they come to be possessed by a sense of the trap?

It is not only information that they need—in this Age of Fact, information often dominates their attention and overwhelms their capacities to assimilate it. It is not only the skills of reason that they need—although their struggles to acquire these often exhaust their limited moral energy.

What they need, and what they feel they need, is a quality of mind that will help them to use information and to develop reason in order to achieve lucid summations of what is going on in the world and of what may be happening within themselves. It is this quality, I am going to contend, that journalists and scholars, artists and publics, scientists and editors are coming to expect of what may be called the sociological imagination.

1

The sociological imagination enables its possessor to understand the larger historical scene in terms of its meaning for the inner life and the external career of a variety of individuals. It enables him to take into account how individuals, in the welter of their daily experience, often become falsely conscious of their social positions. Within that welter, the framework of modern society is sought, and within that framework the psychologies of a variety of men and women are formulated. By such means the personal uneasiness of individuals is focused upon explicit troubles and the indifference of publics is transformed into involvement with public issues.

The first fruit of this imagination—and the first lesson of the social science that embodies it—is the idea that the individual can understand his own experience and gauge his own fate only by locating himself within his period, that he can know his own chances in life only by becoming aware of those of all individuals in his circumstances. In many ways it is a terrible lesson; in many ways a magnificent one. We do not know the limits of man's capacities for supreme effort or willing degradation, for agony or glee, for pleasurable brutality or the sweetness of reason. But in our time we have come to know that the limits of 'human nature' are frighteningly broad. We have come to know that every individual lives, from one generation to the next, in some society; that he lives out a biography, and that he lives it out within some historical sequence. By the fact of his living he contributes, however minutely, to the shaping of this society and to the course of its history, even as he is made by society and by its historical push and shove.

The sociological imagination enables us to grasp history and biography and the relations between the two within society. That is its task and its promise. [. . .]

No social study that does not come back to the problems of biography, of history and of their intersections within a society has completed its intellectual journey. Whatever the specific problems of the classic social analysts, however limited or however broad the features of social reality they have examined, those who have been imaginatively aware of the promise of their work have consistently asked three sorts of questions:

(1) What is the structure of this particular society as a whole? What are its essential components, and how are they related to one another? How does it differ from other varieties of social order? Within it, what is the meaning of any particular feature for its continuance and for its change?

(2) Where does this society stand in human history? What are the mechanics by which it is changing? What is its place within and its meaning for the development of humanity as a whole? How does any particular feature we are examining affect, and how is it affected by, the historical period in which it moves? And this period—what are its essential features? How does it differ from other periods? What are its characteristic ways of history-making?

(3) What varieties of men and women now prevail in this society and in this period? And what varieties are coming to prevail? In what ways are they selected and formed, liberated and repressed, made sensitive and blunted? What kinds of 'human nature' are revealed in the conduct and character we observe in this society in this period? And what is the meaning for 'human nature' of each and every feature of the society we are examining?

[. . .]

2

Perhaps the most fruitful distinction with which the sociological imagination works is between 'the personal troubles of milieu' and 'the public issues of social structure.' This distinction is an essential tool of the sociological imagination and a feature of all classic work in social science.

Troubles occur within the character of the individual and within the range of his immediate relations with others; they have to do with his self and with those limited areas of social life of which he is directly and personally aware. Accordingly, the statement and the resolution of troubles properly lie within the individual as a biographical entity and within the scope of his immediate milieu—the social setting that is directly open to his personal experience and to some extent his willful activity. A trouble is a private matter: values cherished by an individual are felt by him to be threatened.

Issues have to do with matters that transcend these local environments of the individual and the range of his inner life. They have to do with the organization of many such milieux into the institutions of an historical society as a whole, with the ways in which various milieux overlap and interpenetrate to form the larger structure of social and historical life. An issue is a public matter: some value cherished by publics is felt to be threatened. Often there is a debate about what that value really is and about what it is that really threatens it. This debate is often without focus if only because it is the very nature of an issue, unlike even widespread trouble, that it cannot very well be defined in terms of the immediate and everyday environments of ordinary men. An issue, in fact, often involves a crisis in institutional arrangements, and often too it involves what Marxists call 'contradictions' or 'antagonisms.'

In these terms, consider unemployment. When, in a city of 100,000, only one man is unemployed, that is his personal trouble, and for its relief we properly look to the character of the man, his skills, and his immediate opportunities. But when in a nation of 50 million employees, 15 million men are unemployed, that is an issue, and we may not hope to find its solution within the range of opportunities open to any one individual. The very structure of opportunities has collapsed. Both the correct statement of the problem and the range of possible solutions require us to consider the economic and political institutions of the society, and not merely the personal situation and character of a scatter of individuals.

Consider war. The personal problem of war, when it occurs, may be how to survive it or how to die in it with honor; how to make money out of it; how to climb into the higher safety of the military apparatus; or how to contribute to the war's termination. In short, according to one's values, to find a set of milieux and within it to survive the war or make one's death in it meaningful. But the structural issues of war have to do with its causes; with what types of men it throws up into command; with its effects upon economic and political, family and religious institutions, with the unorganized irresponsibility of a world of nation-states.

Consider marriage. Inside a marriage a man and a woman may experience personal troubles, but when the divorce rate during the first four years of marriage is 250 out of every 1,000 attempts, this is an indication of a structural issue having to do with the institutions of marriage and the family and other institutions that bear upon them.

Or consider the metropolis—the horrible, beautiful, ugly, magnificent sprawl of the great city. For many upper-class people, the personal solution to 'the problem of the city' is to have an apartment with private garage under it in the heart of the city, and forty miles out, a house by Henry Hill, garden by Garrett Eckbo, on a hundred acres of private land. In these two controlled environments—with a small staff at each end and a private helicopter connection—most people could solve many of the problems of personal milieux caused by the facts of the city. But all this, however splendid, does not solve the public issues that the structural fact of the city poses. What should be done with this wonderful monstrosity? Break it all up into scattered units, combining residence and work? Refurbish it as it stands? Or, after evacuation, dynamite it and build new cities according to new plans in new

places? What should those plans be? And who is to decide and to accomplish whatever choice is made? These are structural issues; to confront them and to solve them requires us to consider political and economic issues that affect innumerable milieux.

In so far as an economy is so arranged that slumps occur, the problem of unemployment becomes incapable of personal solution. In so far as war is inherent in the nation-state system and in the uneven industrialization of the world, the ordinary individual in his restricted milieu will be powerless—with or without psychiatric aid—to solve the troubles this system or lack of system imposes upon him. In so far as the family as an institution turns women into darling little slaves and men into their chief providers and unweaned dependents, the problem of a satisfactory marriage remains incapable of purely private solution. In so far as the overdeveloped megalopolis and the overdeveloped automobile are built-in features of the overdeveloped society, the issues of urban living will not be solved by personal ingenuity and private wealth.

What we experience in various and specific milieux, I have noted, is often caused by structural changes. Accordingly, to understand the changes of many personal milieux we are required to look beyond them. And the number and variety of such structural changes increase as the institutions within which we live become more embracing and more intricately connected with one another. To be aware of the idea of social structure and to use it with sensibility is to be capable of tracing such linkages among a great variety of milieux. To be able to do that is to possess the sociological imagination.

3. Sociology as the Study of Figurations: Beyond Individual and Society?*

Norbert Elias

The emancipation of sociological theories from the hegemony of contemporary political ideologies was, to be sure, no simple undertaking – to start with because this task was not understood. It may take a series of generations before the confusing preponderance of social and political ideologies can be overcome and sociology can safely move forward on the twin tracks of empirical and theoretical research. A single person can only take a few steps along this path; but I hope I have shown that the breakthrough is possible – an escape from the trap set by present-day political beliefs and social doctrines.

The theory of civilization and state formation, the symbol theory of knowledge and the sciences and, more broadly, the theory of processes and figurations that I have tried to elaborate are neither Marxian nor liberal, neither socialist nor conservative. The hidden party doctrines, the veiled social ideals dressed up in scholarly garb seem to me not only fake but sterile. That was – and is – undoubtedly one of the reasons for the difficult reception this theory, and the books in which it is contained, have had. A sociological theory is expected to put forward arguments for or against this or that side in the great conflicts of social beliefs and interests of modern times. It is disorientating to find that that expectation is not fulfilled – although there has certainly been no lack of attempts to interpret my work in that way. For example, it is quite easy to overlook the fact that the concept of the figuration is expressly coined to bypass the ingrained polarization of sociological theories, by which they are divided into those which place the 'individual' above 'society', and those which place 'society' above the 'individual' – a polarization which used to correspond to the main axis of the conflicts of beliefs and interests in the wider world. But as a sociologist one should, of course, resist the pressure coming from these conflicts, especially as in reality that axis has long been overshadowed by others.

I think I can say today that thinking in terms of the figurations that people (including oneself) form with each other has proved its worth in my further work. I do not lack understanding of the fact that the conceptual tool I have tried to elaborate in the form of the concept of figuration has been mainly tested to see what it has in common with earlier theories which placed the collective level of human integration above the individual level, as in Durkheim's and Simmel's proposals, or those of the 'system theorists'. I cannot teach the blind to see, cannot make them understand the difference, however unambiguously I say it. For in the end that depends on a further act of self-detachment, on rising to the next level on the winding stair of self-consciousness, and if people are unable to perform this act of self-detachment, my explanation falls on deaf ears.

The beginnings of such a rise to a higher level were to be found in the preceding sociological

* From Elias, N. (1994) *Reflections on a Life* (Cambridge: Polity). Extracts from pp. 134–138, 139–141.

theories. Some of the theories of Marx and Weber give evidence of a high degree of detachment, embedded in evidence of their involvement. But they do not yet make detachment and involvement into a sociological problem. They do not take a further step upwards to raise self-detachment as such into consciousness. Until that happens, one cannot help seeing oneself as an individual looking out at society, and thus all other people as 'individuals' outside and beyond society – or, conversely, society as something existing beyond and outside single individuals.

Until one has taken this further step of self-detachment, and is able to come to terms with it conceptually, it is, in brief, difficult to steer the ship of sociology, as of the human sciences in general, between the ideologies of individualism and collectivism. What distinguishes the concept of figuration from previous concepts with which it may be compared is precisely this perspective on human beings that it represents. It helps us to escape the traditional trap – the trap of polarities like that of 'individual' and 'society', sociological atomism and sociological collectivism. The very words 'individual' and 'society' often block perception. If one is able to perform the further act of self-detachment, one is in a position, in climbing the staircase of consciousness, to perceive oneself as if on the previous level, as a human being among others, and society itself as a figuration made up of many fundamentally interdependent human beings; only then is one able intellectually to transcend the ideological polarization of individual and society. The task is as easy as that posed by Columbus's egg and as difficult as the breakthrough of Copernicus.

The resistance to this ascent to a higher level of self-consciousness stems in part from a stratum of experience that is seen most openly in an infant and is never quite submerged: the stratum on the basis of which one sees oneself as the centre of the whole world. It manifests itself, for example, in the selfevident way in which people at earlier stages of development experienced their land and their group on it as the centre of the world. It is manifested again, veiled in a thick curtain of

scholarly words, in the solipsistic and nominalist tendencies of the philosophy of the modem age, from Descartes and Kant to Husserl and Popper.

Undoubtedly, the resistance to perceiving oneself as a person forming specific figurations with other people is, by virtue of this primary egoism in human experience, no less strong than resistance to the idea that the earth has only a rather inconspicuous place in the constellation of planets around the sun, and that there are a great many stars like the sun. But in addition, the prevalent form of the civilizing moulding of human beings reinforces the illusion that each person is inwardly something that cannot make its way 'outward', and that this 'inner' part is the 'genuine' part of one's person, its 'core' and 'essence'. The theory of the civilizing process makes it possible to perceive that this type of experience of oneself and of individualization is itself something that has evolved, is part of a social process. But against this is pitted the whole weight of the personal feeling of existing inwardly quite for oneself, independently of other people, and the corresponding aversion of people formed like this to the knowledge that even their most personal and essential part is itself something that has evolved in this way in the course of the long development of society.

On the basis of these layers of experience there is a very strong inclination to construe human society from the point of view of oneself, of the 'individual' as an isolated, wholly selfcontained being. The resistance to the obvious fact that, from birth, life within figurations of people is one of the basic facts of human existence therefore has its origin partly in a personality structure, a stage in the development of consciousness, which nourishes the illusion that the 'core' of the individual person is, as it were, imprisoned under lock and key in his or her 'inside', and is thus hermetically sealed from the 'outside world', and especially from other people or natural objects.

At the same time, however, a certain political ideology finds expression in this image of humans as *homo clausus*. The notion of the totally independent individual, of the absolutely autonomous but therefore also absolutely free single human being, forms the centrepiece of a bourgeois ideology that has a very definite place in the spectrum of contemporary social and political creeds. Whatever it is called, it is an ideal or a utopia that does not correspond, and cannot correspond, to anything in social reality.

The entrepreneur is often taken as the real social model for this ideal image of the free, self-reliant and independent individual. As the head of a trading, manufacturing or financial organization, independent of bureaucratic state intervention, obeying only his own judgement, as absolute master of his house and in this sense a wholly free individual, in a competitive struggle with other equally free entrepreneurs unhindered by the state, he increases his own wealth and at the same time contributes to the creation of jobs and to the welfare of his country by leading a flourishing enterprise. [. . .]

[. . .]

[. . .] The entrepreneur who sees himself as a freely competing individual, because the mechanism of free competition is not strangled or restricted by state intervention, does not include in the scope of his conceptual interpretation of himself the social compulsions to which himself and his decisions are subject because of the immanent dynamic operating in a field of freely competing units. The answer I was given by an entrepreneur in whose factory I worked for a time, when I asked him why he, a very wealthy man, risked his health in the enormous exertions of his daily work, was very revealing. 'You know', he said, 'it's a hunt. It's a pleasure to snatch the contracts from the competitors, and if you don't do it you soon fall behind.' That was in the 1920s and it was a family firm which, to all appearances, a single man was able to direct with a free hand. But he had enough insight to understand that the representative of a firm which is part of a field of freely competing units cannot decide, for example, whether or not he wants to take part in the competition. He is – by the peculiarity of

the competitive figuration – forced to compete, if he does not want to lapse into dependence or to go under, that is, go bankrupt. For that is the regularity of every field of freely competing units, which are interdependent precisely as competitors: in a field of freely competing units, within which some units grow larger than the others, a single competitor automatically grows smaller if and because he does not grow larger. As the card player depends on his cards and on the skill of the other players, the entrepreneur is dependent on the market and the skill of his competitors.

Here, at the same time, we have an example of the act of self-detachment that is needed if one is to climb from the stage of consciousness on which one experiences the world from the standpoint of oneself as the centre, to the stage above from which once can see oneself as an individual among others, with whom one forms figurations of a specific kind. From the perspective of the earlier step, one may well regard oneself as the absolutely free master of one's own decisions. From the perspective of the next step up one does not see oneself – as it sometimes appears in keeping with the present political polarities – as a passive object of anonymous social forces existing as it were outside the single human being and driving human beings before them entirely regardless of their actions. One sees oneself rather as someone whose scope for decision is limited because he or she lives together with many other people who also have needs, set themselves goals and take decisions.

Fundamentally, then, it is a simple step that has to be taken in order to orientate oneself better than is now possible in the world that people form with each other. Instead of thinking from the standpoint of the single individual or of social data beyond individuals, it is necessary to think from the standpoint of the multiplicity of people. What we refer to as social constraints are the compulsions that many people impose on each other in accordance with their mutual dependence. But this simple conceptual step seems to be hardly less difficult for many people today than it once was to think of the Earth as merely one solar planet among others. Perhaps the self-detachment involved in seeing one's own person as a person among others is still rather too difficult at present; perhaps it is difficult to entertain the thought that the many individual people never live together in a totally fortuitous and arbitrary manner. The very fact that the others, like oneself, have wills of their own places boundaries on the wilfulness of each of them and gives their communal life a structure and dynamic of its own that cannot be understood or explained if each human being is considered in isolation. They can only be understood and explained if one starts out from the multiplicity of people, from the diverse degrees and kinds of their mutual dependence.

4. Decolonizing Sociology*

Raewyn Connell

The idea of decolonizing the curriculum is now under discussion in universities in many parts of the world. Behind this lies the question of decolonizing the knowledge economy as a whole, and the disciplines and domains within it.

In this paper I outline what is involved in decolonizing the discipline of sociology. This is not actually a new issue: there is a whole backstory of social critiques of empire. We need to access this history as well as understand how contemporary sociology is shaped by the global economy of knowledge.

Dealing with those matters raises conceptual problems about power and agency, the agenda of change, and epistemological structure. But this work also leads to practical questions: how to redesign curricula, reshape sociology's workforce, and redistribute resources. There is no single blueprint for change; but there is enormous scope for invention and experiment, on the small scale and the large.

The Question of Empire

It is now five hundred years since the overseas connections of Europe with other parts of the world took the shape of armed conquest, permanent colonies, and colonial states—in other words, the structures of empire. Perhaps the decisive moment was not 1492 but 1505, when the Portuguese sent their seventh armed fleet (*armada*) into the Indian Ocean and appointed Francisco de Almeida the first Viceroy of the Indies. He was given the job of setting up permanent bases, grabbing control of the intercontinental spice trade, and fighting off local rulers. All this he did. The Indians didn't get rid of the Portuguese until 1961.

The dividends of empire were not only spices and gold. They also included knowledge, on an increasing scale. Reports flowed back to imperial centers from sailors, soldiers, governors, missionaries, explorers, surveyors, doctors, translators, and more. In time this became professionalized, with specific data-collecting expeditions, some of them including great names in the history of science: Joseph Banks, Alexander von Humboldt, Charles Darwin. The great botanist Linnaeus didn't go himself but sent out his apostles: one of them was aboard Lieutenant Cook's *Endeavour*, sent to make astronomical observations from Tahiti, when the ship arrived at "Botany Bay."

Information from the colonized world was crucial for the growth of—among other fields—botany, linguistics, geography, geology, evolutionary biology, astronomy, atmospheric science, oceanography, and of course sociology (Connell 1997; Steinmetz 2013). The hegemonic modern knowledge system is not so much western science as imperial science.

Empire was challenged from the start by the physical resistance of the colonized. Soon intellectual contestation was added. One of the most remarkable documents in the history of empire is the *Nueva Corónica* of Guamán Poma, a

* From Connell, R. (2018) 'Decolonizing Sociology', *Contemporary Sociology*, 47(4): 399–407. Extracts from pp. 399–402, 404, 405.

descendant of the Andean nobility. It is an illustrated description of the social and political order under the Incas, a narrative of conquest, and an extended critique of the violence and inequality of colonial society under Spanish rule—and it was written about 1615. The author was a contemporary of Shakespeare.[1]

Critique from the perspective of the colonized continued throughout the history of empire. Striking examples include the Islamic anti-imperialism of Sayyid Jamal ad-Din al-Afghani in the nineteenth century (translations in al-Afghani 1968); Chinese perspectives on western empire in the early twentieth century, such as the nationalism of Sun Zhongshan (Yat-sen) (1927) and the socialist feminism of He-Yin Zhen (translations in Liu et al. 2013); and the powerful analysis of settler colonialism in southern Africa by Solomon Tshekisho Plaatje, published as *Native Life in South Africa* in 1916.

We are today more familiar with the post-1950 texts known as "postcolonial" theory or critique in the humanities. One of its best-known documents, Frantz Fanon's *The Wretched of the Earth*, grew immediately out of the military struggle for independence in Algeria. Edward Said's cultural critique in *Orientalism* was less directly based on anti-colonial struggle, but Said had grown up under British colonial rule in Palestine and Egypt and knew the story.

There was a continuing *social* critique of empire, colonial life, and postcolonial dependence. In the 1930s the young Jomo Kenyatta managed the amazing feat of turning Malinowskian ethnography into a critique of colonization, in *Facing Mount Kenya*; Gilberto Freyre published the first version of his famous account of slave society in colonial Brazil, *Casa-Grande e Senzala*; and C. L. R. James published his dramatic history of slave revolution in colonial Haiti, *The Black Jacobins*.

In the 1950s, the young Samir Amin launched the rethinking of political economy that eventually was published as *Accumulation on a World Scale*; and the not-so-young Raúl Prebisch launched the CEPAL analysis of Latin American economies that transformed development studies

and developing state strategies. In the 1960s, Ali Shariati launched his synthesis of Shiite theology and critical sociology in scathing critiques of neocolonial society, and Syed Hussein Alatas launched his sociological critique of colonialist culture, postcolonial stagnation, and intellectual dependence. These are just some high points.

There is, then, a big back-story to the renewal of interest in postcolonial perspectives among social scientists; we have a legacy. It is only recently, however, that an agenda of transforming the discipline of sociology in a postcolonial direction has gained traction and has begun to look like a collective undertaking.

[. . .]

Reasons for Action

Sociology is part of the global economy of knowledge that grew out of the imperial traffic in knowledge. In a process most clearly formulated by the philosopher Paulin Hountondji (1997), empire generated a structural division of intellectual labor between periphery and metropole. This division is still deeply embedded in modern knowledge formation. The colonized world was, first and foremost, a source of *data*. Here raw material of very diverse kinds was collected, often with the aid of indigenous knowledge workers, for shipment to the metropole.

The metropole, or imperial center, aggregated data from different parts of the colonized world in libraries, scientific societies, universities, museums, botanic gardens, and research institutes—a process now automated in databanks. This milieu in the metropole became the site of the theoretical moment in knowledge production. Research methods were formalized and routinized; and specialized workforces were created for producing and circulating knowledge, forming the modern collective intellectual worker. In northern institutions, research was further transformed into applied sciences such as engineering, agronomy, and medicine. In this applied form, knowledge was returned to the global periphery. Here it was used by colonial powers and, later, postcolonial states, in the mines, in agriculture, and in government.

In our time, this traffic continues. The periphery is as vital a source of raw materials for the knowledge economy as it is for the material economy, yielding data for the new biology, pharmaceuticals, astronomy, social science, linguistics, archaeology, and more. It is, for instance, a key source of data for the giant quantitative models central to climate science, a relationship that can be seen in the famous reports of the Intergovernmental Panel on Climate Change.

In this economy of knowledge, intellectual workers in the global periphery are pushed toward a particular cultural and intellectual stance. Hountondji calls this stance "extraversion": being oriented to authority external to your own society. It is reflected, in the simplest possible way, in citation patterns. Researchers in the global North usually cite other researchers in the global North, often *only* researchers in the global North; researchers in the global South mainly cite researchers, and especially theorists, in the global North. But extraversion is expressed in many other ways, too: in academic travel, in appointments to jobs, in research practices, in publication preferences, and so on.

Sociology is part of this global economy and reproduces its structure. The discipline's main institutional base is a set of elite universities in the United States with PhD programs and equivalent elite universities and institutes in western and northern Europe. All the top-rated journals are edited here, most of the research funding is concentrated here, the hegemonic curriculum is formed and practiced here, overseas scholars travel to study or visit here, and the PhD graduates from these institutions are strategically placed to shape sociology in the next generation.

In mainstream theory (including methodology), there is little sense of being the product of such a specific milieu. Read a modern-classic text like Garfinkel's *Studies in Ethnomethodology*, Coleman's *Foundations of Social Theory*,

Bourdieu's *Logic of Practice*, or Habermas's *Theory of Communicative Action* and you will see, rather, an assumption that the thoughts produced here simply apply universally. "The tasks of a critical theory of society"—to quote the final chapter of Habermas's magisterial work—are the tasks that can be seen from a window in Starnberg, Westwood, or Hyde Park. And in due course, sociologists everywhere in the world start looking at their own societies through those windows in Starnberg, Westwood, and Hyde Park.

This pattern is familiar to every sociologist in the global periphery. I'll give just one example. When sociology was being launched as a new discipline in Australian universities, the most coherent statement of what the name meant was an article in an Australian journal by Harold Fallding, "The Scope and Purpose of Sociology" (1962). Fallding declared that sociology was the study of systems of social action, analyzed functionally in the manner of Talcott Parsons. He was quite clear that there was no other path for sociology. Theoretical fashions change, but extraversion remains. Fifty years later, in 2013, the Australian Sociological Association's journal published a special issue, in fact a double issue, called "Antipodean Fields: Working with Bourdieu."

What's wrong with that? Bourdieu was an impressive theorist; so, for that matter, was Parsons. But to understand them in depth is to realize that their theorizing embeds perspectives on the world that arise from the social formations of the global North, because of their historical position in imperialism and their current core position in the neoliberal world economy. I've made a rough inventory of these effects: the claim of universality; reading from the center; gestures of exclusion; and grand erasure (Connell 2006). I'm sure that list can be improved on.

Extraverted sociology in the periphery, then, is the project of understanding colonial and postcolonial societies through concepts proposed in the metropole for understanding the metropole; using methods developed in the metropole; and, following the demands of corporate-style managers, trying to publish the results in top journals of the metropole after jumping through the hoops of assessment by researchers in the metropole.

Extraverted sociology in the periphery is a viable academic project. It's acceptable organizationally because its practices appear to Rectors, Deans, and Vice-Presidents (Research) quite like the practices of the biomedical and engineering research that they love. It's acceptable educationally because it fits with the bestselling northern textbooks, which need only minor local adaptations. It's acceptable professionally since it speaks a conceptual and methodological language known all over the world. It might get you published in the *American Sociological Review*.

But if you do that, you are reproducing the conventional global division of labor, supplying data from the periphery for theoretical processing in the North. Extraverted sociology is endlessly disappointing as an *intellectual* project, a continuous, cautious remaking of the intellectual dependency that Hussein Alatas (1977) was analyzing forty years ago. Because the discipline in the metropole took almost no interest in the social critics of empire mentioned earlier—they don't fit the story of the Three Founding Fathers, or the old and new testament of Classical Theory and Modern Theory—extraverted sociology in the periphery hasn't taken much interest in these critics either. A gulf arose between the professionalized discipline of sociology and the many projects of critical social thought in the majority world. It's that gulf that the movement for postcolonial sociology is trying to bridge.

That is why a key task for some of the participants has simply been recovering the history of social thought from the colonized world and bringing it into contemporary sociological discussion (see, e.g., Patel 2011; Maia 2008, 2011; Qi 2014). Farid Alatas's *Alternative Discourses in Asian Social Thought* is exemplary here. It is notable that Alatas (2012, 2014) has gone on to make a deeper analysis of a powerful social thinker entirely outside the European canon, showing how ideas from Ibn Khaldun can cast light on states and political-economic changes beyond Ibn Khaldun's own time.

What "decolonizing sociology" means, then, is correcting the distortions and exclusions produced by empire and global inequality and reshaping the discipline in a democratic direction *on a world scale*. It concerns sociology in the global North as much as the global South.

[. . .]

Questions of Practice

Coming down from these heights, what does the project of decolonizing sociology mean for our everyday work as sociologists?

First and foremost, decolonizing the curriculum. There's now a lot of discussion about this, and some sharp controversies, more focused on the humanities than the social sciences. The idea is relevant not only to disciplinary sociology but also to applied sociology teaching in areas like health, education, and counseling. It involves rewriting course plans, textbooks, and online resources to give weight to the social experience of the colonized and postcolonial world.

There is pressure for this kind of change from the increased diversity of student bodies, and from mobilizations like the "Why Is My Curriculum White?" campaign in British universities.[2] Yet deparochializing teaching in the social sciences can be justified whoever the students are. We simply need to ask ourselves what is required for an adequate knowledge of the major social questions facing humanity now.

[. . .]

Decolonizing sociology therefore requires rethinking the composition of sociology's workforce and changing the conditions in which it produces and circulates knowledge. I don't think we currently have a clear picture of sociology's workforce on a world scale. We do have some valuable snapshots, for instance in the short accounts from different countries in the ISA's excellent *Global Dialogue* (http://isa-global-dialogue.

net/), or in the discussion of underfunding and political pressure on social scientists in Thandika Mkandawire's *African Intellectuals* (2005).

What is clear is the existence of massive inequalities in income, research funding, and other resources—within particular countries, but especially important on a world scale. Resource inequalities, as well as language questions, are reflected in very unequal participation in meetings like the ISA World Congresses of Sociology and more generally in publication and citation patterns. These contribute to inequalities of recognition in the global economy of knowledge.

Decolonizing sociology, then, involves questions of redistribution, and that is something we do not normally imagine for an individual discipline. In today's managerial university, individual academics and even departments don't control large funds; most have to campaign to get even a single line for a new appointment. The big questions of overall levels of investment in research and higher education are beyond the power of individual universities.

But perhaps we give up too easily. Sociologists in rich countries seeking grants might take care to include some international collaboration in every project. Resources put into course development can be shared internationally by making curricula and curriculum materials available online. To be really useful this needs organizing through a body such as the ISA, but the inherent costs are low. Resources from the global North can be used to support South/South links and research cooperation. This has been done, for instance, by the Dutch funded SEPHIS program in combination with the Ford Foundation for social research on sexuality (Wieringa and Sívori 2013).

I'd like to finish with a do-it-yourself plea. We do not know the answers to many of the questions touched on in this essay. We will only find them by trying.

Colleagues and students interested in the decolonization project have often asked how I found the materials in *Southern Theory*, so they can find such material themselves. The answer is embarrassingly low-tech: I went and looked. I was confident the material was there to find, so I haunted libraries and bookshops (second-hand bookshops a specialty!), visited universities and institutes, read lots of regional histories, struggled with languages, and annoyed colleagues in every country I could reach with requests for their advice. When I began doing this, the Internet was in a primitive state; I had the advantage of international travel. I'm sure similar things can now be done with a much smaller carbon footprint.

And the beauty of any project for widening our own knowledge is this: nobody can stop us.

NOTES

1. It was not published in Guamán Poma's lifetime but survived in manuscript and can be seen in an excellent online edition today: http://www.kb.dk/permalink/2006/poma/titlepage/en/text/?open=idp23904
2. See https://www.nus.org.uk/en/news/whyis-my-curriculum-white/.

REFERENCES

Al-Afghani, Sayyid Jamal ad-Din. 1968. *An Islamic Response to Imperialism: Political and Religious Writings of Sayyid Jamal ad-Din "al- Afghani."* Translated by Nikki R. Keddie and Hamid Algar. Berkeley: University of California Press.

Alatas, Syed Farid. 2006. *Alternative Discourses in Asian Social Science: Responses to Eurocentrism.* New Delhi: SAGE Publications.

Alatas, Syed Farid. 2012. *Ibn Khaldun.* New Delhi: Oxford University Press.

Alatas, Syed Farid. 2014. *Applying Ibn Khaldun: The Recovery of a Lost Tradition in Sociology.* London: Routledge.

Alatas, Syed Hussein. 1977. *Intellectuals in Developing Societies.* London: Frank Cass.

Amin, Samir. 1969. *Accumulation on a World Scale: A Critique of the Theory of*

Underdevelopment. New York: Monthly Review Press.

Bourdieu, Pierre. 1990. *The Logic of Practice.* Stanford, CA: Stanford University Press.

Coleman, James S. 1990. *Foundations of Social Theory.* Cambridge, MA: Harvard University Press.

Connell, Raewyn. 1997. "Why is Classical Theory Classical?" *American Journal of Sociology* 102(6):1511–57.

Connell, Raewyn. 2006. "Northern Theory: The Political Geography of General Social Theory." *Theory & Society* 35(2):237–64.

Connell, Raewyn. 2007. *Southern Theory: The Global Dynamics of Knowledge in Social Science.* Malden, MA: Polity.

Fallding, Harold. 1962. "The Scope and Purpose of Sociology." *Australian Journal of Politics and History* 8(1):78–92.

Fanon, Frantz. 1968. *The Wretched of the Earth.* Translated by Constance Farrington. New York: Grove.

Freyre, Gilberto. 1956. *The Masters and the Slaves.* Translated by Samuel Putnam. New York: Knopf.

Garfinkel, Harold. 1967. *Studies in Ethnomethodology.* Englewood Cliffs, NJ: Prentice Hall.

Habermas, Jürgen. 1984–1987. *The Theory of Communicative Action.* Translated by Thomas A. McCarthy. Boston: Beacon Press.

Hountondji, Paulin J., ed. 1997. *Endogenous Knowledge: Research Trails.* Dakar: CODESRIA.

James, C. L. R. 1963. *The Black Jacobins: Toussaint L'Ouverture and the San Domingo Revolution.* New York: Vintage Books.

Kenyatta, Jomo. 1938. *Facing Mount Kenya.* London: Secker and Warburg.

Liu, Lydia H., Rebecca E. Karl, and Dorothy Ko, eds. 2013. *The Birth of Chinese Feminism: Essential Texts in Transnational Theory.* New York: Columbia University Press.

Maia, João Marcelo Ehlert. 2008. *A Terra como Invenção: O Espaço no Pensamento Social Brasileiro.* Rio de Janeiro: Jorge Zahar.

Maia, João Marcelo Ehlert. 2011. "Space, Social Theory and Peripheral Imagination: Brazilian Intellectual History and De-Colonial Debates." *International Sociology* 26(3): 392–407.

Mkandawire, Thandika, ed. 2005. *African Intellectuals: Rethinking Politics, Language, Gender and Development.* Dakar: CODESRIA.

Patel, Sujata, ed. 2011. *Doing Sociology in India: Genealogies, Locations, and Practices.* New York: Oxford University Press.

Plaatje, Solomon Tshekisho. 1982. *Native Life in South Africa: Before and Since the European War and the Boer Rebellion.* Johannesburg: Ravan Press.

Qi, Xiaoying. 2014. *Globalized Knowledge Flows and Chinese Social Theory.* New York: Routledge.

Said, Edward. 1978. *Orientalism.* New York: Vintage Books.

Steinmetz, George, ed. 2013. *Sociology and Empire: The Imperial Entanglements of a Discipline.* Durham, NC: Duke University Press.

Sun, Yat-sen. 1975. *San Min Chu I: The Three Principles of the People.* New York: Da Capo Press.

Wieringa, Saskia, and Horacio Sívori, ed. 2013. *The Sexual History of the Global South: Sexual Politics in Africa, Asia, and Latin America.* London: Zed Books.

5. Understanding Ourselves and Others*

Zygmunt Bauman and Tim May

Freedom in Living with Others

We are surrounded by particular ideas of individuals and, from there, their actions, choices, and degrees of responsibility. Adverts of all types are targeted at aspirations linked to what one wants to be in the world linked to the possession of goods. Surrounded by these techniques of persuasion into which are poured enormous resources, can we say our choices are the product of conscious decisions that we formulate in a clear, rational manner, prior to the determination of any action? Many of our actions are *habitual* and not subject to deliberate and open choice. Despite that, we may be reminded that our decisions leave us responsible for their consequences. You can hear it now: "No one forced you to do so, you have only yourself to blame!" If we break rules that are meant to guide people's conduct we may be punished and those punishments can range from informal to formal sanctions: for example, breaking the norms of a group may lead to us being ridiculed or temporarily excluded, to having our liberty removed through incarceration in prison due to law-breaking. The act of punishment is one confirmation that we are held responsible for our actions. Rules, in this sense, orientate not only our actions, but coordinate interactions with

others enabling an anticipation of how we and they are likely to act. Without this orientation in place, communication and understanding in everyday life would seem inconceivable.

If we are the authors of our destinies we have the power to act in controlling our lives. We have both the ability to monitor our actions *and* the capability to determine their outcomes. Nevertheless, is this really how life works for most people? It might be claimed, for example, that being unemployed is entirely the fault of the individual concerned who, if they tried hard enough and acquired suitable knowledge and skills, could earn a living. People might retrain themselves and look for work, but the area in which they live has high unemployment and they cannot afford to move, or have relatives and friends for whom they care and so, despite actively seeking employment, there is none on offer or they have limited mobility due to dependents. There are many circumstances in which our freedom to act is limited by circumstances over which we have little or no control. It is one thing to have the ability to change or modify our skills and quite another to possess the capability to reach our goals. Let us consider this in more detail.

Take conditions of scarcity. These, as well as how we are judged by others, limit our capabilities. People might seek the same goals, but not all reach them because access to what they seek is limited. In this case we might compete with each other and the outcome may be only partially dependent on our efforts. We might seek a

* From Bauman, Z. and May, T. (2019) *Thinking Sociologically* (3rd edn, Chichester: John Wiley & Sons). Extracts from pp. 15–18, 21, 22–23, 24–25.

college place, only to find out that there are 20 candidates for every place available and that most of them have the qualifications required. In addition, the college may tend to favor candidates from certain social backgrounds and those with connections to those who have attended before. Our actions are dependent upon the judgments of others over whom we may exercise limited control, but also related to our social networks and how those enable and constrain our aspirations. Others set the rules of the game and act as the referees. They are *positioned* by their institutions to exercise discretion and, in so doing, draw a boundary around the freedoms of others. Factors such as these heavily influence the outcome of our efforts. In this case we become dependent on others because they evaluate whether our efforts are good enough and consider whether we exhibit the right characteristics and background to justify our admission.

Material factors inform our capability to reach our goals. Whilst self-determination is important, what if we lack the means? We might be able to move to seek work in places where more jobs are available, only to discover that the cost of houses or of rents is far beyond our means. Similarly, we might wish to escape overcrowded and polluted conditions in order to move to a healthier location. However, we find those with more money have already done so and therefore it is not affordable, or they have created enclosures or live in high-rise buildings to secure environments separate from their surroundings. In the process house prices increase, rents go up, and the job does not pay enough to obtain somewhere to live. We can say the same thing about education and health. Some areas have better equipped schools and hospitals, yet are too far away, whilst our society does not have a public, universal health-care system and private health insurance is beyond our income. Thus, freedom of choice does not guarantee freedom to act on those choices, nor does it secure the freedom to attain our desired ends. To be able to act freely, we need more than an idea of *free will*.

[. . .]

How we are positioned in these ways interacts with how we feel about and act in the social situations into which we enter. Let us return to our college example. We may find that a mode of speaking and particular accent is expected during the interview, but it is one with which we are unfamiliar. Coming from a working-class background, we may feel uneasy among middle-class students, or our sexual orientation is not judged to be "normal" and so we experience a sense of isolation and an absence of others seeing our choices as valid. Perhaps, being a Catholic who follows orthodoxy, we cannot accept divorce and abortion as the choices that others have a right to make.

Here we come to a possibility: those groups with whom we feel most at ease may actually limit our freedom by restricting the range of opinions we can hold. Informal and formal groups are often constituted by the expectations that they place upon their members and in so doing exclude those who are presumed not to live up to those requirements or ways of life. When these gaps in understanding occur between groups, they are frequently filled by stereotypical assumptions which are prejudicial and inaccurate, but enable a separation between "us" and "them." The very fact that we may be adjusted to the conditions of action inside our group circumscribes our freedom by preventing us from engaging with experiences beyond the confines of that group. Having been trained in the ways of our groups, we practice a freedom whose price is to limit engagement with other ideas and practices.

We are both enabled and constrained in the everyday practices of freedom. At one level we are taught that there are types of desires that are acceptable and achievable within a group. Appropriate ways to act, talk, dress, and conduct ourselves provide an orientation to get us through life within the groups to which we belong. We judge ourselves according to those expectations and our self-esteem is directly informed in these ways. Groups enable boundaries that orientate us through common interests and/or by proximity and these advantages may become problems as we traverse from one group to another and find ourselves in environments where different ways of being and forms of evaluation are promoted. Alternative ways of conducting ourselves may be seen as appropriate and the connections between other people's conduct and their intentions are not familiar to us and appear alien. The French sociologist Pierre Bourdieu referred to this gap as the "Don Quixote" effect: that is, between our dispositions and the social contexts in which we find ourselves.

[. . .]

The formation of the social self is not a passive process. Activity and initiative mark both sides of the interaction. After all, one of the first skills that a child learns is to discriminate and select, which cannot be acquired unless supported by the ability to resist and withstand pressure; in other words, to take a stand and act against external forces. Because of the contradictory signals from various significant others, the "I" must stand aside, at a distance, looking at the external pressure *internalized* in the "Me." The stronger the "I," the more autonomous becomes the character of the child. The strength of the "I" expresses itself in the person's ability and readiness to put the social pressures internalized in the "Me" to the test, checking their true powers and their limits and so challenging them and bearing the consequences. In the course of this acquisition, we ask questions of ourselves and the first reflexive question of selfhood is, as the French philosopher Paul Ricoeur put it, "Who am I?" Here we experience the contradiction between freedom and dependence as an inner conflict between what we desire and what we feel obliged to do because of the presence of significant others and the expectations placed upon us. Images and meanings of acceptable behavior become part of our "internal" conversations as we reflexively consider our "being" and "doing."

At this point we meet the interactions between

the biological and the social. A great deal of money is being spent on trying to determine the genetic bases of different aspects of human behavior and neuroscience can easily lapse into seeking the basis of the social in the structure and function of the brain. Interpretations among those influenced, for example, by Darwin's theory of evolution differ on whether we are competitive or cooperative by nature. Equally, we know that actions and how they are evaluated differ between cultures. As the geneticist Steve Jones put it, the most problematic word in genetics is "for" – as if finding a gene meant that it then stood *for* a particular form of behavior. Whilst vast sums of money are being poured into genetic research that produce potential gains in the treatment of diseases, the control of that knowledge and for what reasons remains a vital issue for us all.

[. . .]

How our selves are formed and how instincts may or may not be suppressed is often given the name *socialization*. We are socialized to become capable of living in society through the internalization of norms and values from society in general and significant others in particular. Who are those significant people with whom we interact and who socialize us in this way? We have seen that the force that operates in the development of the self is the child's image of the intentions and expectations of significant others. A freedom to select from these expectations is not complete, for some may force their views into the child's perception more effectively than others within their worlds, but there is no avoidance of choice, even if the demands themselves are contradictory. After all, some of them must be paid more attention than others and so assigned greater significance in our lives.

The need to assign differential significance to the expectations of others is not restricted to children. We experience this as a matter of routine in our daily lives from families, friends, and work colleagues. We risk the displeasure of some in order to placate others. Whenever we express political views, there will be those who care about what we say and listen and others who say that issues of politics, religion, or money, for example, should not be subject for discussion. Assigning significance whether through our utterances or actions means, unavoidably, assigning less importance and even irrelevance to other views. The risks of this process grow to the degree that the environments we inhabit are heterogeneous, that is, characterized by different views, values, and interests, or homogeneous, where expectations of conformity via an unquestioning individual allegiance are strictly enforced through group surveillance and pressure.

[...]

Socialization never ends. It brings with it changing and complex forms of interaction between ideas of freedom and dependence. We move across spaces and places and bring with us our histories: for example, those brought up in small rural communities may find themselves lost in a strange city in which the indifference of strangers leads to feelings of helplessness; all of which is exacerbated by the volumes of traffic, rushing crowds, and forms of architecture. Equally, there are those at home in the city whose anonymity may provide for ease of movement across cultures as a source of their cosmopolitan identities. Our feelings of risk and trust then mix in differing degrees. There are also those situations over which we may have no control. Sudden economic depression, the onset of mass unemployment, floods, famine, and the outbreak of war, are just some examples. These changes have the potential to place in doubt our patterns of socialization and require a radical restructuring of what we have taken for granted.

In the absence of such major upheavals, each of us confronts problems on a daily basis that call for reflexive examination and perhaps question our modes of being or expectations: changing schools or jobs, entering and graduating from university, starting a new relationship, acquiring a place to live, becoming parents, and experiencing the death of those close to us. Relations between experiences of freedom and dependence do not then reach a final destination, but are part of processes of change, learning, resistance, and negotiation that start at birth and end only with death. Our freedom is never complete, but a struggle in which we are routinely engaged and which defines us. Present actions are informed by past actions and each has an embryonic sense of the future in our performance.

Freedom for some may be bought at the cost of greater dependence for others. We have spoken of the role that material and symbolic resources play in making choices viable, realistic propositions and that not all people enjoy access to these in order to realize their ends. While people are free and bound to take responsibility for what they do, some have more degrees of freedom than others. A consequence of this can be to restrict the horizon of opportunity for others. We can say that the ratio between freedom and dependence is an indicator of the relative position a person, or a whole category of persons, occupies in a society. What we call privilege appears, under closer scrutiny, to be a higher degree of freedom and a lesser degree of dependence.

Introduction – Further reading

Anyone new to sociology will find the new edition of our own companion volume useful: Giddens, A., and Sutton, P. W. (2021) *Essential Concepts in Sociology* (3rd edn, Cambridge: Polity). Other 'key concepts' texts are, of course, available! A good guide to terminology in sociology is Scott, J. (2014) *Oxford Dictionary of Sociology* (4th edn, Oxford: Oxford University Press). One of the more engaging introductions to sociology remains Bauman, Z., and May, T. (2019) *Thinking Sociologically* (3rd edn, Chichester: Wiley Blackwell). For a rather more brief orientation, try Bruce, S. (2018) *Sociology: A Very Short Introduction* (Oxford: Oxford University Press).

Sociology, 9th edition

Chapter 1 – unsurprisingly – is the place to go for our introduction to the discipline, though chapters 2 and 3, on methods and theories respectively, also contain some helpful material as part of this three-chapter introductory block.

Part 1 Thinking Sociologically

The origins of sociology lie in the eighteenth century with the French and Industrial revolutions, which marked the end of medieval social relations and the onset of the machine age of 'modernity'. This was a revolutionary transformation with immense social consequences, including rapid industrialization, urbanization, the creation of a new industrial working class, erosion of rural community life, large-scale migration and expanding cities. Exploring this new landscape was the primary task for the early sociologists. Yet it was not enough just to collect a mass of data; they also needed theories – logically related statements which interpret and explain the available data and evidence – that provided a deeper understanding of social change. This section focuses on the industrialized societies of the Global North, illustrating, through a mixture of classical and contemporary theories, what sociological thinking means.

Although Karl Marx was not a professional sociologist, his ideas have had an enormous impact in sociology that shows no signs of abating. Perhaps Marx is best known for his theory of capitalist economic development and its seemingly inevitable collapse and replacement by communism. There is no doubt that Marx saw the capitalist economic system as ultimately pernicious, bringing misery and poverty to the working classes. But we should remember that he also saw capitalism as a genuinely revolutionary development in human affairs and

was fulsome in his praise for its productivity. Indeed, there is no better source than Marx for anyone looking to grasp the positive elements of capitalism. Hence, Reading 6 sets out his ideas in *The Communist Manifesto* of 1848, in which he waxes lyrical about the fabulous productive assets and wealth-creating potential of capitalism that are unrivalled across human history. And he is quite clear that, without the capitalist revolution, there can be no communism, which, for Marx, is the necessary endpoint of economic and social development.

Thinking sociologically means moving beyond a simple account of individual choices and actions to explore groups, communities and wider social formations. For example, many sociologists have studied the formation and lifestyles of social classes, looking to understand how class location influences and shapes the opportunities and obstacles for individuals. One of the most systematic studies in this field is that of Pierre Bourdieu, whose work linked class position to cultural needs and preferences. In Reading 7, Bourdieu sets out the basic premise of his argument that cultural tastes are the product of upbringing and level of education and, consequently, that the consumption of culture reflects the hierarchy of class divisions. This then produces a series of taste distinctions such as superior/inferior or refined/vulgar, which mark out individuals and reinforce class divisions. Bourdieu's broader theoretical framework has been enormously influential in a number of socio-logical specialisms.

While social class has long been a key concern in sociology, studies examining inequalities of gender, race and ethnicity, disability and sexuality have added to the complexity of sociological analysis. Reading 8, from Patricia Hill Collins, is among the first to theorize the concept of intersection-ality – in this case, the intertwining of class, race and gender in the production of advantage and disadvantage in society. Here, Collins discusses the 'interlocking' nature of these divisions, arguing that intersectional-ity has long been a feature of 'Black feminist thought' and is one of its key contributions to scholarly debates. Collins also argues that the marginalization of black women in academic circles gives them the status of the 'outsider within'. Yet it is this marginal status that gives black women a unique standpoint from which to view and assess existing sociological perspectives and ena-bles them to make a significant contribution to our understanding.

The concept of 'modernity' was, for a long period, central to much sociological work, but it came under sustained criticism in the 1980s and 1990s as postmodern ideas ques-tioned its validity. As a prominent theorist of modernity, Anthony Giddens has explored what we mean by this concept, what its main consequences are and where it may be lead-ing. Reading 9 lays out some of his answers to these questions. For example, he argues that modern life is characterized by *reflexiv-ity* and *time–space distanciation*. Reflexivity refers to the way that social scientific knowl-edge moves into and out of wider society, changing both knowledge and society in that process. This is quite unlike the position

with the natural sciences, and it means that sociology is both the study of modernity and is constitutive of it; hence we cannot simply use natural science methods in the social sciences. Time–space distanciation draws attention to the way that modern technolo-gies have effectively compressed time and distance via faster transport and digital com-munications, a key concept in understanding the process of globalization.

In the final reading here, Gurminder K. Bhambra argues forcefully that the concept of modernity developed in a Eurocentric way, stripped of any sense of colonialism. This is not simply a failure to discuss and account for colonial regimes and their deleterious impact on colonized societies; it also means that the processes of empire-building were not embedded within sociology's theoretical perspectives and explanatory frameworks. One simple example is the thesis (as stated above) that sociology was a product of the French and Industrial revolutions without reference to colonialism. Bhambra describes the omission of postcolonial arguments and ideas as yet another of sociology's 'missing revolutions'. The latter include feminism and queer theory, both of which are debated and drawn on by sociologists but have not fundamentally altered the character of the discipline. The more recent attempt to study different forms of modernity around the world carried the prospect of saving the concept of modernity by exploring national variations, but Bhambra argues that this move has not removed the reliance on the original Eurocentric formulation. It seems likely that sociology's engagement with post-colonial theorizing will continue to challenge some of the discipline's basic assumptions, but it is less clear what the outcome will be.

6. The Capitalist Revolution*

Karl Marx and Friedrich Engels

The modern bourgeois society that has sprouted from the ruins of feudal society has not done away with class antagonisms. It has but established new classes, new conditions of oppression, new forms of struggle in place of the old ones.

Our epoch, the epoch of the bourgeoisie, possesses, however, this distinctive feature: it has simplified the class antagonisms. Society as a whole is more and more splitting up into two great hostile camps, into two great classes directly facing each other: Bourgeoisie and Proletariat.

From the serfs of the Middle Ages sprang the chartered burghers of the earliest towns. From these burgesses the first elements of the bourgeoisie were developed.

The discovery of America, the rounding of the Cape, opened up fresh ground for the rising bourgeoisie. The East-Indian and Chinese markets, the colonization of America, trade with the colonies, the increase in the means of exchange and in commodities generally, gave to commerce, to navigation, to industry, an impulse never before known, and thereby, to the revolutionary element in the tottering feudal society, a rapid development.

The feudal system of industry, under which industrial production was monopolized by closed guilds, now no longer sufficed for the growing wants of the new markets. The manufacturing system took its place. The guild-masters were pushed on one side by the manufacturing middle class; division of labour between the different corporate guilds vanished in the face of division of labour in each single workshop.

Meantime the markets kept ever growing, the demand ever rising. Even manufacture no longer sufficed. Thereupon, steam and machinery revolutionized industrial production. The place of manufacture was taken by the giant, Modern Industry, the place of the industrial middle class, by industrial millionaires, the leaders of whole industrial armies, the modern bourgeois.

Modern industry has established the world market, for which the discovery of America paved the way. This market has given an immense development to commerce, to navigation, to communication by land. This development has, in its turn, reacted on the extension of industry; and in proportion as industry, commerce, navigation, railways extended, in the same proportion the bourgeoisie developed, increased its capital, and pushed into the background every class handed down from the Middle Ages.

We see, therefore, how the modern bourgeoisie is itself the product of a long course of development, of a series of revolutions in the modes of production and of exchange.

Each step in the development of the bourgeoisie was accompanied by a corresponding political advance of that class. An oppressed class under the sway of the feudal nobility, an armed and self-governing association in the medieval commune;[1] here independent urban republic (as in Italy and Germany), there taxable 'third estate' of the monarchy (as in France), afterwards, in the period of manufacture proper, serving either

* From Marx, K. and Engels, F. (1983 [1848]) *The Communist Manifesto* (Harmondsworth: Penguin). Extracts from pp. 80–83, 84–87.

the semi-feudal or the absolute monarchy as a counterpoise against the nobility, and, in fact, corner-stone of the great monarchies in general, the bourgeoisie has at last, since the establishment of Modern Industry and of the world market, conquered for itself, in the modern representative State, exclusive political sway. The executive of the modern State is but a committee for managing the common affairs of the whole bourgeoisie.

The bourgeoisie, historically, has played a most revolutionary part.

The bourgeoisie, wherever it has got the upper hand, has put an end to all feudal, patriarchal, idyllic relations. It has pitilessly torn asunder the motley feudal ties that bound man to his 'natural superiors', and has left remaining no other nexus between man and man than naked self-interest, than callous 'cash payment'. It has drowned the most heavenly ecstasies of religious fervour, of chivalrous enthusiasm, of philistine sentimentalism, in the icy water of egotistical calculation. It has resolved personal worth into exchange value, and in place of the numberless indefeasible chartered freedoms, has set up that single, unconscionable freedom – Free Trade. In one word, for exploitation, veiled by religious and political illusions, it has substituted naked, shameless, direct, brutal exploitation.

The bourgeoisie has stripped of its halo every occupation hitherto honoured and looked up to with reverent awe. It has converted the physician, the lawyer, the priest, the poet, the man of science, into its paid wage-labourers.

The bourgeoisie has torn away from the family its sentimental veil, and has reduced the family relation to a mere money relation.

The bourgeoisie has disclosed how it came to pass that the brutal display of vigour in the Middle Ages, which Reactionists so much admire, found its fitting complement in the most slothful indolence. It has been the first to show what man's activity can bring about. It has accomplished wonders far surpassing Egyptian pyramids, Roman aqueducts, and Gothic cathedrals; it has conducted expeditions that put in the shade all former Exoduses of nations and crusades.

The bourgeoisie cannot exist without constantly revolutionizing the instruments of production, and thereby the relations of production, and with them the whole relations of society. Conservation of the old modes of production in unaltered form, was, on the contrary, the first condition of existence for all earlier industrial classes. Constant revolutionizing of production, uninterrupted disturbance of all social conditions, everlasting uncertainty and agitation distinguish the bourgeois epoch from all earlier ones. All fixed, fast-frozen relations, with their train of ancient and venerable prejudices and opinions are swept away, all new-formed ones become antiquated before they can ossify. All that is solid melts into air, all that is holy is profaned, and man is at last compelled to face with sober senses, his real conditions of life, and his relations with his kind.

[...]

The bourgeoisie, by the rapid improvement of all instruments of production, by the immensely facilitated means of communication, draws all, even the most barbarian, nations into civilization. The cheap prices of its commodities are the heavy artillery with which it batters down all Chinese walls, with which it forces the barbarians' intensely obstinate hatred of foreigners to capitulate. It compels all nations, on pain of extinction, to adopt the bourgeois mode of production; it compels them to introduce what it calls civilization into their midst, i.e., to become bourgeois themselves. In one word, it creates a world after its own image.

The bourgeoisie has subjected the country to the rule of the towns. It has created enormous cities, has greatly increased the urban population as compared with the rural, and has thus rescued a considerable part of the population from the idiocy of rural life. Just as it has made the country dependent on the towns, so it has made barbarian and semi-barbarian countries dependent on the civilized ones, nations of peasants on nations of bourgeois, the East on the West.

The bourgeoisie keeps more and more doing away with the scattered state of the population, of the means of production, and of property. It has agglomerated population, centralized means of production, and has concentrated property in a few hands. The necessary consequence of this was political centralization. Independent, or but loosely connected, provinces with separate interests, laws, governments and systems of taxation, became lumped together into one nation, with one government, one code of laws, one national class-interest, one frontier and one customs-tariff.

The bourgeoisie, during its rule of scarce one hundred years, has created more massive and more colossal productive forces than have all preceding generations together. Subjection of Nature's forces to man, machinery, application of chemistry to industry and agriculture, steam-navigation, railways, electric telegraphs, clearing of whole continents for cultivation, canalization of rivers, whole populations conjured out of the ground – what earlier century had even a presentiment that such productive forces slumbered in the lap of social labour?

We see then: the means of production and of exchange, on whose foundation the bourgeoisie built itself up, were generated in feudal society. At a certain stage in the development of these means of production and of exchange, the conditions under which feudal society produced and exchanged, the feudal organization of agriculture and manufacturing industry, in one word, the feudal relations of property became no longer compatible with the already developed productive forces; they became so many fetters. They had to be burst asunder; they were burst asunder.

Into their place stepped free competition, accompanied by a social and political constitution adapted to it, and by the economical and political sway of the bourgeois class.

A similar movement is going on before our own eyes. Modern bourgeois society with its relations of production, of exchange and of property, a society that has conjured up such gigantic means of production and of exchange, is like the sorcerer, who is no longer able to control the powers of the nether world whom he has called up by his spells. For many a decade past the history of industry and commerce is but the history of the revolt of modern productive forces against modern conditions of production, against the property relations that are the conditions for the existence of the bourgeoisie and of its rule. It is enough to mention the commercial crises that by their periodical return put on its trial, each time more threateningly, the existence of the entire bourgeois society. In these crises a great part not only of the existing products, but also of the previously created productive forces, are periodically destroyed. In these crises there breaks out an epidemic that, in all earlier epochs, would have seemed an absurdity – the epidemic of overproduction. Society suddenly finds itself put back into a state of momentary barbarism; it appears as if a famine, a universal war of devastation had cut off the supply of every means of subsistence; industry and commerce seem to be destroyed; and why? Because there is too much civilization, too much means of subsistence, too much industry, too much commerce. The productive forces at the disposal of society no longer tend to further the development of the conditions of bourgeois property; on the contrary, they have become too powerful for these conditions, by which they are fettered, and so soon as they overcome these fetters, they bring disorder into the whole of bourgeois society, endanger the existence of bourgeois property. The conditions of bourgeois society are too narrow to comprise the wealth created by them. And how does the bourgeoisie get over these crises? On the one hand by enforced destruction of a mass of productive forces; on the other, by the conquest of new markets, and by the more thorough exploitation of the old ones. That is to say, by paving the way for more extensive and more destructive crises, and by diminishing the means whereby crises are prevented.

The weapons with which the bourgeoisie felled feudalism to the ground are now turned against the bourgeoisie itself.

But not only has the bourgeoisie forged the weapons that bring death to itself; it has also called into existence the men who are to wield those weapons – the modern working class – the proletarians.

NOTE

1. 'Commune' was the name taken, in France, by the nascent towns even before they had conquered from their feudal lords and masters local self-government and political rights as the 'Third Estate'. Generally speaking, for the economical development of the bourgeoisie, England is here taken as the typical country; for its political development, France. [*Note by Engels to the English edition of 1888.*]

This was the name given their urban communities by the townsmen of Italy and France, after they had purchased or wrested their initial rights of self-government from their feudal lords. [*Note by Engels to the German edition of 1890.*]

7. Tastes, Distinctions and Social Structure*

Pierre Bourdieu

There is an economy of cultural goods, but it has a specific logic. Sociology endeavours to establish the conditions in which the consumers of cultural goods, and their taste for them, are produced, and at the same time to describe the different ways of appropriating such of these objects as are regarded at a particular moment as works of art, and the social conditions of the constitution of the mode of appropriation that is considered legitimate. But one cannot fully understand cultural practices unless 'culture', in the restricted, normative sense of ordinary usage, is brought back into 'culture' in the anthropological sense, and the elaborated taste for the most refined objects is reconnected with the elementary taste for the flavours of food.

Whereas the ideology of charisma regards taste in legitimate culture as a gift of nature, scientific observation shows that cultural needs are the product of upbringing and education: surveys establish that all cultural practices (museum visits, concert-going, reading etc.), and preferences in literature, painting or music, are closely linked to educational level (measured by qualifications or length of schooling) and secondarily to social origin.[1] The relative weight of home background and of formal education (the effectiveness and duration of which are closely dependent on social origin) varies according to the extent to which the different cultural practices are recognized and taught by the education system, and the influence of social origin is strongest—other things being equal—in 'extra-curricular' and avant-garde culture. To the socially recognized hierarchy of the arts, and within each of them, of genres, schools or periods, corresponds a social hierarchy of the consumers. This predisposes tastes to function as markers of 'class'. The manner in which culture has been acquired lives on in the manner of using it: the importance attached to manners can be understood once it is seen that it is these imponderables of practice which distinguish the different—and ranked—modes of culture acquisition, early or late, domestic or scholastic, and the classes of individuals which they characterize (such as 'pedants' and *mondains*). Culture also has its titles of nobility—awarded by the educational system—and its pedigrees, measured by seniority in admission to the nobility.

The definition of cultural nobility is the stake in a struggle which has gone on unceasingly, from the seventeenth century to the present day, between groups differing in their ideas of culture and of the legitimate relation to culture and to works of art, and therefore differing in the conditions of acquisition of which these dispositions are the product.[2] Even in the classroom, the dominant definition of the legitimate way of appropriating culture and works of art favours those who have had early access to legitimate culture, in a cultured household, outside of scholastic disciplines, since even within the educational system it devalues scholarly knowledge and interpretation as 'scholastic' or even 'pedantic' in favour of direct experience and simple delight.

* From Bourdieu, P. (1984) *Distinction: A Social Critique of the Judgement of Taste* (New York: Routledge). Extracts from pp. 1–3, 5–7, 11–12, 13.

The logic of what is sometimes called, in typically 'pedantic' language, the 'reading' of a work of art, offers an objective basis for this opposition. Consumption is, in this case, a stage in a process of communication, that is, an act of deciphering, decoding, which presupposes practical or explicit mastery of a cipher or code. In a sense, one can say that the capacity to see (*voir*) is a function of the knowledge (*savoir*), or concepts, that is, the words, that are available to name visible things, and which are, as it were, programmes for perception. A work of art has meaning and interest only for someone who possesses the cultural competence, that is, the code, into which it is encoded. The conscious or unconscious implementation of explicit or implicit schemes of perception and appreciation which constitutes pictorial or musical culture is the hidden condition for recognizing the styles characteristic of a period, a school or an author, and, more generally, for the familiarity with the internal logic of works that aesthetic enjoyment presupposes. A beholder who lacks the specific code feels lost in a chaos of sounds and rhythms, colours and lines, without rhyme or reason. Not having learnt to adopt the adequate disposition, he stops short at what Erwin Panofsky calls the 'sensible properties', perceiving a skin as downy or lace-work as delicate, or at the emotional resonances aroused by these properties, referring to 'austere' colours or a 'joyful' melody. He cannot move from the 'primary stratum of the meaning we can grasp on the basis of our ordinary experience' to the 'stratum of secondary meanings', i.e., the 'level of the meaning of what is signified', unless he possesses the concepts which go beyond the sensible properties and which identify the specifically stylistic properties of the work.[3] Thus the encounter with a work of art is not 'love at first sight' as is generally supposed, and the act of empathy, *Einfühlung,* which is the art-lover's pleasure, presupposes an act of cognition, a decoding operation, which implies the implementation of a cognitive acquirement, a cultural code.[4]

[. . .]

Although art obviously offers the greatest scope to the aesthetic disposition, there is no area of practice in which the aim of purifying, refining and sublimating primary needs and impulses cannot assert itself, no area in which the stylization of life, that is, the primacy of forms over function, of manner over matter, does not produce the same effects. And nothing is more distinctive, more distinguished, than the capacity to confer aesthetic status on objects that are banal or even 'common' (because the 'common' people make them their own, especially for aesthetic purposes), or the ability to apply the principles of a 'pure' aesthetic to the most everyday choices of everyday life, e.g., in cooking, clothing or decoration, completely reversing the popular disposition which annexes aesthetics to ethics.

In fact, through the economic and social conditions which they presuppose, the different ways of relating to realities and fictions, of believing in fictions and the realities they simulate, with more or less distance and detachment, are very closely linked to the different possible positions in social space and, consequently, bound up with the systems of dispositions (habitus) characteristic of the different classes and class fractions. Taste classifies, and it classifies the classifier. Social subjects, classified by their classifications, distinguish themselves by the distinctions they make, between the beautiful and the ugly, the distinguished and the vulgar, in which their position in the objective classifications is expressed or betrayed. And statistical analysis does indeed show that oppositions similar in structure to those found in cultural practices also appear in eating habits. The antithesis between quantity and quality, substance and form, corresponds to the opposition—linked to different distances from necessity—between the taste of necessity, which favours the most 'filling' and most economical foods, and the taste of liberty—or luxury—which shifts the emphasis to the manner (of presenting, serving, eating etc.) and tends to use stylized forms to deny function.

The science of taste and of cultural consumption begins with a transgression that is in no way aesthetic: it has to abolish the sacred frontier which makes legitimate culture a separate universe, in order to discover the intelligible relations which unite apparently incommensurable 'choices', such as preferences in music and food, painting and sport, literature and hairstyle. This barbarous reintegration of aesthetic consumption into the world of ordinary consumption abolishes the opposition, which has been the basis of high aesthetics since Kant, between the 'taste of sense' and the 'taste of reflection', and between facile pleasure, pleasure reduced to a pleasure of the senses, and pure pleasure, pleasure purified of pleasure, which is predisposed to become a symbol of moral excellence and a measure of the capacity for sublimation which defines the truly human man. The culture which results from this magical division is sacred. Cultural consecration does indeed confer on the objects, persons and situations it touches, a sort of ontological promotion akin to a transubstantiation. Proof enough of this is found in the two following quotations, which might almost have been written for the delight of the sociologist:

'What struck me most is this: nothing could be obscene on the stage of our premier theatre, and the ballerinas of the Opera, even as naked dancers, sylphs, sprites or Bacchae, retain an inviolable purity.'[5]

'There are obscene postures: the stimulated intercourse which offends the eye. Clearly, it is impossible to approve, although the interpolation of such gestures in dance routines does give them a symbolic and aesthetic quality which is absent from the intimate scenes the cinema daily flaunts before its spectators' eyes ... As for the nude scene, what can one say, except that it is brief and theatrically not very effective? I will not say it is chaste or innocent, for nothing commercial can be so described. Let us say it is not shocking, and that the chief objection is that it serves as a box-office gimmick.... In *Hair,* the nakedness fails to be symbolic.'[6]

The denial of lower, coarse, vulgar, venal, servile—in a word, natural—enjoyment, which constitutes the sacred sphere of culture, implies an affirmation of the superiority of those who can

be satisfied with the sublimated, refined, disinterested, gratuitous, distinguished pleasures forever closed to the profane. That is why art and cultural consumption are predisposed, consciously and deliberately or not, to fulfil a social function of legitimating social differences.

[...]

Sociology is rarely more akin to social psychoanalysis than when it confronts an object like taste, one of the most vital stakes in the struggles fought in the field of the dominant class and the field of cultural production. This is not only because the judgement of taste is the supreme manifestation of the discernment which, by reconciling reason and sensibility, the pedant who understands without feeling and the *mondain*[7] who enjoys without understanding, defines the accomplished individual. Nor is it solely because every rule of propriety designates in advance the project of defining this indefinable essence as a clear manifestation of philistinism—whether it be the academic propriety which, from Alois Riegl and Heinrich Wölfflin to Elie Faure and Henri Focillon, and from the most scholastic commentators on the classics to the avant-garde semiologist, insists on a formalist reading of the work of art; or the upperclass propriety which treats taste as one of the surest signs of true nobility and cannot conceive of referring taste to anything other than itself.

Here the sociologist finds himself in the area par excellence of the denial of the social. It is not sufficient to overcome the initial self-evident appearances, in other words, to relate taste, the uncreated source of all 'creation', to the social conditions of which it is the product, knowing full well that the very same people who strive to repress the clear relation between taste and education, between culture as the state of that which is cultivated and culture as the process of cultivating, will be amazed that anyone should expend so much effort in scientifically proving that self-evident fact. He must also question that relationship, which only appears to be self-explanatory, and unravel the paradox whereby the relationship with educational capital is just as strong in areas which the educational system does not teach. And he must do this without ever being able to appeal unconditionally to the positivistic arbitration of what are called facts. Hidden behind the statistical relationships between educational capital or social origin and this or that type of knowledge or way of applying it, there are relationships between groups maintaining different, and even antagonistic, relations to culture, depending on the conditions in which they acquired their cultural capital and the markets in which they can derive most profit from it. [. . .]

[. . .] The survey sought to determine how the cultivated disposition and cultural competence that are revealed in the nature of the cultural goods consumed, and in the way they are consumed, vary according to the category of agents and the area to which they applied, from the most legitimate areas such as painting or music to the most 'personal' ones such as clothing, furniture or cookery, and, within the legitimate domains, according to the markets—'academic' and 'non-academic'—in which they may be placed. Two basic facts were thus established: on the one hand, the very close relationship linking cultural practices (or the corresponding opinions) to educational capital (measured by qualifications) and, secondarily, to social origin (measured by father's occupation); and, on the other hand, the fact that, at equivalent levels of educational capital, the weight of social origin in the practice- and preference-explaining system increases as one moves away from the most legitimate areas of culture.

NOTES

1. Bourdieu et al., *Un art moyen: essai sur les usages sociaux de la photographie* (Paris, Éd. de Minuit, 1965); P. Bourdieu and A. Darbel, *L'Amour de l'art: les musées et leur public* (Paris, Éd. de Minuit, 1966).
2. The word *disposition* seems particularly suited to express what is covered by the concept of habitus (defined as a system of dispositions)—used later in this chapter. It expresses first the *result of an organizing action,* with a meaning close to that of words such as structure; it also designates a way of being, a habitual state (especially of the body) and, in particular, a *predisposition, tendency, propensity* or *inclination.* [The semantic cluster of 'disposition' is rather wider in French than in English, but as this note—translated literally—shows, the equivalence is adequate. Translator.] P. Bourdieu, *Outline of a Theory of Practice* (Cambridge, Cambridge University Press, 1977), p. 214. n. 1.
3. E. Panofsky, 'Iconography and Iconology: An Introduction to the Study of Renaissance Art', *Meaning in the Visual Arts* (New York, Doubleday, 1955), p. 28.
4. It will be seen that this internalized code called culture functions as cultural capital owing to the fact that, being unequally distributed, it secures profits of distinction.
5. O. Merlin, 'Mlle. Thibon dans la vision de Marguerite', *Le Monde,* 9 December 1965.
6. F. Chenique, '*Hair* est-il immoral?'*Le Monde,* 28 January 1970.
7. The *mondain,* the 'man of the world', is discussed later in this chapter in the section 'Scholars and Gentlemen' (translator).

8. Learning from the Outsiders Within*

Patricia Hill Collins

Afro-American women have long been privy to some of the most intimate secrets of white society. Countless numbers of Black women have ridden buses to their white "families," where they not only cooked, cleaned, and executed other domestic duties, but where they also nurtured their "other" children, shrewdly offered guidance to their employers, and frequently, became honorary members of their white "families." These women have seen white elites, both actual and aspiring, from perspectives largely obscured from their Black spouses and from these groups themselves.[1]

On one level, this "insider" relationship has been satisfying to all involved. The memoirs of affluent whites often mention their love for their Black "mothers," while accounts of Black domestic workers stress the sense of self-affirmation they experienced at seeing white power demystified—of knowing that it was not the intellect, talent, or humanity of their employers that supported their superior status, but largely just the advantages of racism.[2] But on another level, these same Black women knew they could never belong to their white "families." In spite of their involvement, they remained "outsiders."[3]

This "outsider within" status has provided a special standpoint on self, family, and society for Afro-American women.[4] A careful review of

the emerging Black feminist literature reveals that many Black intellectuals, especially those in touch with their marginality in academic settings, tap this standpoint in producing distinctive analyses of race, class, and gender. For example, Zora Neal Hurston's 1937 novel, *Their Eyes Were Watching God,* most certainly reflects her skill at using the strengths and transcending the limitations both of her academic training and of her background in traditional Afro-American community life.[5] Black feminist historian E. Frances White (1984) suggests that Black women's ideas have been honed at the juncture between movements for racial and sexual equality, and contends that Afro-American women have been pushed by "their marginalization in both arenas" to create Black feminism. Finally, Black feminist critic bell hooks captures the unique standpoint that the outsider within status can generate. In describing her small-town, Kentucky childhood, she notes, "living as we did—on the edge—we developed a particular way of seeing reality. We looked both from the outside and in from the inside out . . . we understood both" (1984: vii).

[. . .]

Sociologists might benefit greatly from serious consideration of the emerging, cross-disciplinary literature that I label Black feminist thought, precisely because, for many Afro-American female intellectuals, "marginality" has been an excitement to creativity. As outsiders within, Black feminist scholars may be one of many distinct groups of marginal intellectuals whose

* From Collins, P. H. (1986) 'Learning from the Outsider Within: The Sociological Significance of Black Feminist Thought', *Social Problems*, 33(6): S14–S32. Extracts from S14–S15, S16–S17, S19–S20, S21–S22, S26–S27.

standpoints promise to enrich contemporary sociological discourse. Bringing this group—as well as others who share an outsider within status vis-a-vis sociology—into the center of analysis may reveal aspects of reality obscured by more orthodox approaches.

[. . .]

Three Key Themes in Black Feminist Thought

Black feminist thought consists of ideas produced by Black women that clarify a standpoint of and for Black women. Several assumptions underlie this working definition. First, the definition suggests that it is impossible to separate the structure and thematic content of thought from the historical and material conditions shaping the lives of its producers (Berger and Luckmann 1966; Mannheim 1936). Therefore, while Black feminist thought may be recorded by others, it is produced by Black women. Second, the definition assumes that Black women possess a unique standpoint on, or perspective of, their experiences and that there will be certain commonalities of perception shared by Black women as a group. Third, while living life as Black women may produce certain commonalities of outlook, the diversity of class, region, age, and sexual orientation shaping individual Black women's lives has resulted in different expressions of these common themes. Thus, universal themes included in the Black women's standpoint may be experienced and expressed differently by distinct groups of Afro-American women. Finally, the definition assumes that, while a Black women's standpoint exists, its contours may not be clear to Black women themselves. Therefore, one role for Black female intellectuals is to produce facts and theories about the Black female experience that will clarify a Black woman's standpoint for Black women. In other words, Black feminist thought contains observations and interpretations about Afro-American womanhood that

describe and explain different expressions of common themes.

[. . .]

An affirmation of the importance of Black women's self-definition and self-valuation is the first key theme that pervades historical and contemporary statements of Black feminist thought. Self-definition involves challenging the political knowledge-validation process that has resulted in externally-defined, stereotypical images of Afro-American womanhood. In contrast, self-valuation stresses the content of Black women's self-definitions—namely, replacing externally derived images with authentic Black female images.

Both Mae King's (1973) and Cheryl Gilkes' (1981) analyses of the importance of stereotypes offer useful insights for grasping the importance of Black women's self-definition. King suggests that stereotypes represent externally-defined, controlling images of Afro-American womanhood that have been central to the dehumanization of Black women and the exploitation of Black women's labor. Gilkes points out that Black women's assertiveness in resisting the multifaceted oppression they experience has been a consistent threat to the status quo. As punishment, Black women have been assaulted with a variety of externally-defined negative images designed to control assertive Black female behavior.

The value of King's and Gilkes' analyses lies in their emphasis on the function of stereotypes in controlling dominated groups. Both point out that replacing negative stereotypes with ostensibly positive ones can be equally problematic if the function of stereotypes as controlling images remains unrecognized. John Gwaltney's (1980) interview with Nancy White, a 73-year-old Black woman, suggests that ordinary Black women may also be aware of the power of these controlling images in their everyday experiences. In the following passage, Ms. White assesses the difference between the controlling images applied to Afro-American and white women as being those of degree, and not of kind:

My mother used to say that the black woman is the white man's mule and the white woman is his dog. Now, she said that to say this: we do the heavy work and get beat whether we do it well or not. But the white woman is closer to the master and he pats them on the head and lets them sleep in the house, but he ain't gon' treat neither one like he was dealing with a person (1980:148).

This passage suggests that while both groups are stereotyped, albeit in different ways, the function of the images is to dehumanize and control both groups. Seen in this light, it makes little sense, in the long run, for Black women to exchange one set of controlling images for another even if, in the short run, positive stereotypes bring better treatment.

[. . .]

Attention to the interlocking nature of race, gender, and class oppression is a second recurring theme in the works of Black feminists (Beale, 1970; Davis, 1981; Dill, 1983; hooks, 1981; Lewis, 1977; Murray, 1970; Steady, 1981).[6] While different socio-historical periods may have increased the saliency of one or another type of oppression, the thesis of the linked nature of oppression has long pervaded Black feminist thought. For example, Ida Wells Barnett and Frances Ellen Watkins Harper, two prominent Black feminists of the late 1800s, both spoke out against the growing violence directed against Black men. They realized that civil rights held little meaning for Black men and women if the right to life itself went unprotected (Loewenberg and Bogin, 1976:26). Black women's absence from organized feminist movements has mistakenly been attributed to a lack of feminist consciousness. In actuality, Black feminists have possessed an ideological commitment to addressing interlocking oppression yet have been excluded from arenas that would have allowed them to do so (Davis, 1981).

[. . .]

The Black feminist attention to the interlocking nature of oppression is significant for two reasons. First, this viewpoint shifts the entire focus of investigation from one aimed at explicating elements of race or gender or class oppression to one whose goal is to determine what the links are among these systems. The first approach typically prioritizes one form of oppression as being primary, then handles remaining types of oppression as variables within what is seen as the most important system. For example, the efforts to insert race and gender into Marxist theory exemplify this effort. In contrast, the more holistic approach implied in Black feminist thought treats the interaction among multiple systems as the object of study. Rather than adding to existing theories by inserting previously excluded variables, Black feminists aim to develop new theoretical interpretations of the interaction itself.

Black male scholars, white female scholars, and more recently, Black feminists like bell hooks, may have identified one critical link among interlocking systems of oppression. These groups have pointed out that certain basic ideas cross-cut multiple systems of domination. One such idea is either/or dualistic thinking, claimed by hooks to be "the central ideological component of all systems of domination in Western society" (1984:29).

While hooks' claim may be somewhat premature, there is growing scholarly support for her viewpoint.[7] Either/or dualistic thinking, or what I will refer to as the construct of dichotomous oppositional difference, may be a philosophical lynchpin in systems of race, class, and gender oppression. One fundamental characteristic of this construct is the categorization of people, things, and ideas in terms of their difference from one another. For example, the terms in dichotomies such as black/white, male/female, reason/emotion, fact/opinion, and subject/object gain their meaning only in *relation* to their difference from their oppositional counterparts. Another fundamental characteristic of this construct is that difference is not complementary in that the halves of the dichotomy do not enhance each other. Rather, the dichotomous halves are different and inherently opposed to one another. A third and more important characteristic is that these oppositional relationships are intrinsically unstable. Since such dualities rarely represent different but equal relationships, the inherently unstable relationship is resolved by subordinating one half of each pair to the other. Thus, whites rule Blacks, males dominate females, reason is touted as superior to emotion in ascertaining truth, facts supersede opinion in evaluating knowledge, and subjects rule objects. Dichotomous oppositional differences invariably imply relationships of superiority and inferiority, hierarchical relationships that mesh with political economies of domination and subordination.

[. . .]

A third key theme characterizing Black feminist thought involves efforts to redefine and explain the importance of Black women's culture. In doing so, Black feminists have not only uncovered previously unexplored areas of the Black female experience, but they have also identified concrete areas of social relations where Afro-American women create and pass on self-definitions and self-valuations essential to coping with the simultaneity of oppression they experience.

In contrast to views of culture stressing the unique, ahistorical values of a particular group, Black feminist approaches have placed greater emphasis on the role of historically-specific political economies in explaining the endurance of certain cultural themes. The following definition of culture typifies the approach taken by many Black feminists. According to Mullings, culture is composed of

the symbols and values that create the ideological frame of reference through which people attempt to deal with the circumstances in which they find themselves. Culture . . . is not composed of static, discrete traits moved from one locale to another. It is constantly changing and transformed, as new forms are created out of old ones. Thus culture . . .

does not arise out of nothing: it is created and modified by material conditions (1986a:13).

Seen in this light, Black women's culture may help provide the ideological frame of reference—namely, the symbols and values of self-definition and self-valuation—that assist Black women in seeing the circumstances shaping race, class, and gender oppression. Moreover, Mullings' definition of culture suggests that the values which accompany self-definition and self-valuation will have concrete, material expression: they will be present in social institutions like church and family, in creative expression of art, music, and dance, and, if unsuppressed, in patterns of economic and political activity. Finally, this approach to culture stresses its historically concrete nature. While common themes may link Black women's lives, these themes will be experienced differently by Black women of different classes, ages, regions, and sexual preferences as well as by Black women in different historical settings. Thus, there is no monolithic Black women's culture—rather, there are socially-constructed Black women's cultures that collectively form Black women's culture.

The interest in redefining Black women's culture has directed attention to several unexplored areas of the Black female experience. One such area concerns the interpersonal relationships that Black women share with each other. It appears that the notion of sisterhood—generally understood to mean a supportive feeling of loyalty and attachment to other women stemming from a shared feeling of oppression—has been an important part of Black women's culture (Dill, 1983: 132). Two representative works in the emerging tradition of Black feminist research illustrate how this concept of sisterhood, while expressed differently in response to different material conditions, has been a significant feature of Black women's culture. For example, Debra Gray White (1985) documents the ways Black slave women assisted each other in childbirth, cared for each other's children, worked together in sex-segregated work units when pregnant or nursing children, and depended on one another when married to males living on distant farms. White paints a convincing portrait of Black female slave communities where sisterhood was necessary and assumed. Similarly, Gilkes' (1985) work on Black women's traditions in the Sanctified Church suggests that the sisterhood Black women found had tangible psychological and political benefits.[8]

[. . .]

Black Women and the Outsider Within Status

Black women may encounter much less of a fit between their personal and cultural experiences and both elements of sociological paradigms than that facing other sociologists. On the one hand, Black women who undergo sociology's lengthy socialization process, who immerse themselves in the cultural pattern of sociology's group life, certainly wish to acquire the insider skills of thinking in and acting according to a sociological worldview. But on the other hand, Black women's experienced realities, both prior to contact and after initiation, may provide them with "special perspectives and insights . . . available to that category of outsiders who have been systematically frustrated by the social system" (Merton, 1972:29). In brief, their outsider allegiances may militate against their choosing full insider status, and they may be more apt to remain outsiders within.[9]

In essence, to become sociological insiders, Black women must assimilate a standpoint that is quite different than their own. White males have long been the dominant group in sociology, and the sociological worldview understandably reflects the concerns of this group of practitioners. As Merton observes, "white male insiderism in American sociology during the past generations has largely been of the tacit or de facto . . . variety. It has simply taken the form of patterned expectations about the appropriate . . . problems for investigation" (1972:12). In contrast, a good deal of the Black female experience

has been spent coping with, avoiding, subverting, and challenging the workings of this same white male insiderism. It should come as no surprise that Black women's efforts in dealing with the effects of interlocking systems of oppression might produce a standpoint quite distinct from, and in many ways opposed to, that of white male insiders. Seen from this perspective, Black women's socialization into sociology represents a more intense case of the normal challenges facing sociology graduate students and junior professionals in the discipline. Black women become, to use Simmel's (1921) and Schutz's terminology, penultimate "strangers."

> The stranger . . . does not share the basic assumptions of the group. He becomes essentially the man who has to place in question nearly everything that seems to be unquestionable to the members of the approached group. . . . To him the cultural patterns of the approached group do not have the authority of a tested system of recipes . . . because he does not partake in the vivid historical tradition by which it has been formed (Schutz, 1944:502).

Like everyone else, Black women may see sociological "thinking as usual" as partially organized, partially clear, and contradictory, and may question these existing recipes. However, for them, this questioning process may be more acute, for the material that they encounter—white male insider-influenced observations and interpretations about human society—places white male subjectivity at the center of analysis and assigns Afro-American womanhood a position on the margins.

In spite of a lengthy socialization process, it may also be more difficult for Afro-American women to experience conversion and begin totally to think in and act according to a sociological worldview. Indeed, since past generations of white male insiderism has shaped a sociological worldview reflecting this group's concerns, it may be self-destructive for Black women to embrace that worldview. For example, Black women would have to accept certain fundamental and self-devaluing assumptions: (1) white males are more worthy of study because they are more fully human than everyone else; and (2) dichotomous oppositional thinking is natural and normal. More importantly, Black women would have to act in accordance with their place in a white male worldview. This involves accepting one's own subordination or regretting the accident of not being born white and male. In short, it may be extremely difficult for Black women to accept a worldview predicated upon Black female inferiority.

NOTES

1. In 1940, almost 60 percent of employed Afro-American women were domestics. The 1970 census was the first time this category of work did not contain the largest segment of the Black female labor force. See Rollins (1985) for a discussion of Black domestic work.

2. For example, in *Of Women Born: Motherhood as Experience and Institution,* Adrienne Rich has fond memories of her Black "mother," a young, unstereotypically slim Black woman she loved. Similarly. Dill's (1980) study of Black domestic workers reveals Black women's sense of affirmation at knowing that they were better mothers than their employers, and that they frequently had to teach their employers the basics about children and interaction in general. Even though the Black domestic workers were officially subordinates, they gained a sense of self-worth at knowing they were good at things that they felt mattered.

3. For example, in spite of Rich's warm memories of her Black "mother," she had all but forgotten her until beginning research for her book. Similarly, the Black domestic workers in both Dill's (1980) and Rollins' (1985) studies discussed the limitations that their subordinate roles placed on them.

4. For a discussion of the notion of a special standpoint or point of view of oppressed groups, see Hartsock (1983). See Merton's (1972) analysis of the potential contributions of insider and outsider perspectives to

sociology. For a related discussion of outsider within status, see his section "Insiders as 'Outsiders'" (1972:29–30).

5. Hurston has been widely discussed in Black feminist literary criticism. For example, see selected essays in Walker's (1979) edited volume on Hurston.

6. Emerging Black feminist research is demonstrating a growing awareness of the importance of including the simultaneity of oppression in studies of Black women. For example, Paula Giddings' (1984) history of Afro-American women emphasizes the role of class in shaping relations between Afro-American and white women, and among Black women themselves. Elizabeth Higginbotham's (1985) study of Black college women examines race and class barriers to Black women's college attendance. Especially noteworthy is the growing attention to Black women's labor market experiences. Studies such as those by Dill (1980), Rollins (1985), Higginbotham (1983), and Mullings (1986b) indicate a new sensitivity to the interactive nature of race, gender, and class. By studying Black women, such studies capture the interaction of race and gender. Moreover, by examining Black women's roles in capitalist development, such work taps the key variable of class.

7. For example, African and Afro-American scholars point to the role dualistic thinking has played in domestic racism (Asante, 1980; Baldwin, 1980; Richards 1980). Feminist scholars note the linkage of duality with conceptualizations of gender in Western cultures (Chodorow, 1978; Keller, 1983; Rosaldo, 1983). Recently, Brittan and Maynard, two British scholars, have suggested that dualistic thinking plays a major role in linking systems of racial oppression with those of sexual oppression. They note that

there is an implicit belief in the duality of culture and nature. Men are the creators and mediators of culture—women are the manifestations of nature.

The implication is that men develop culture in order to understand and control the natural world, while women being the embodiment of forces of nature, must be brought under the civilizing control of men . . . This duality of culture and nature . . . is also used to distinguish between so-called higher nations or civilizations, and those deemed to be culturally backward. . . . Non-European peoples are conceived of as being nearer to nature than Europeans. Hence, the justification . . . for slavery and colonialism . . . (1984:193–94).

8. During a period when Black women were widely devalued by the dominant culture, Sanctified Church members addressed each other as "Saints." During the early 1900s, when basic literacy was an elusive goal for many Blacks, Black women in the Church not only stressed education as a key component of a sanctified life, but supported each other's efforts at educational excellence. In addition to these psychological supports, the Church provided Afro-American women with genuine opportunities for influence, leadership, and political clout. The important thing to remember here is that the Church was not an abstract, bureaucratic structure that ministered to Black women. Rather, the Church was a predominantly female community of individuals in which women had prominent spheres of influence.

9. Jackson (1974) reports that 21 of the 145 Black sociologists receiving doctoral degrees between 1945 and 1972 were women. Kulis et al. (1986) report that Blacks comprised 5.7 percent of all sociology faculties in 1984. These data suggest that historically, Black females have not been sociological insiders, and currently, Black women as a group comprise a small portion of sociologists in the United States.

REFERENCES

Asante, Molefi Kete 1980 "International/intercultural relations." Pp. 43–58 in Molefi Kete Asante and Abdulai S. Vandi (eds.), Contemporary Black Thought. Beverly Hills, CA: Sage.

Baldwin, Joseph A. 1980 "The psychology of oppression." Pp. 95–110 in Molefi Kete Asante and Abdulai S. Vandi (eds.), Contemporary Black Thought. Beverly Hills, CA: Sage.

Beale, Frances 1970 "Double jeopardy: to be Black and female." Pp. 90–110 in Toni Cade (ed.), The Black Woman. New York: Signet.

Berger, Peter L. and Thomas Luckmann 1966 The Social Construction of Reality. New York: Doubleday.

Brittan, Arthur and Mary Maynard 1984 Sexism, Racism and Oppression. New York: Basil Blackwell.

Chodorow, Nancy 1978 The Reproduction of Mothering. Berkeley, CA: University of California Press.

Davis, Angela 1981 Women, Race and Class. New York: Random House.

Dill, Bonnie Thornton 1980 "'The means to put my children through': child-rearing goals and strategies among Black female domestic servants." Pp. 107–23 in LaFrances Rodgers-Rose (ed.), The Black Woman. Beverly Hills, CA: Sage.

Dill, Bonnie Thornton 1983 "Race, class, and gender: prospects for an all-inclusive sisterhood." Feminist Studies 9: 131–50.

Giddings, Paula 1984 When and Where I Enter. The Impact of Black Women on Race and Sex in America. New York: William Morrow.

Gilkes, Cheryl Townsend 1981 "From slavery to social welfare: racism and the control of Black women." Pp. 288–300 in Amy Smerdlow and Helen Lessinger (eds.), Class, Race, and Sex: The Dynamics of Control. Boston: G.K. Hall.

Gilkes, Cheryl Townsend 1985 "'Together and in harness': women's traditions in the sanctified church." Signs 10:678–99.

Gwaltney, John Langston 1980 Drylongso, a Self-portrait of Black America. New York: Vintage.

Hartsock, Nancy M. 1983 "The feminist standpoint: developing the ground for a specifically feminist historical materialism." Pp. 283–310 in Sandra Harding and Merrill Hintikka (eds.), Discovering Reality. Boston: D. Reidel.

Higginbotham, Elizabeth 1983 "Laid bare by the system: work and survival for Black and Hispanic women." Pp. 200–15 in Amy Smerdlow and Helen Lessinger (eds.), Class, Race, and Sex: The Dynamics of Control. Boston: G.K. Hall.

Higginbotham, Elizabeth 1985 "Race and class barriers to Black women's college attendance." Journal of Ethnic Studies 13:89–107.

hooks, bell 1981 Aint' I a Woman: Black Women and Feminism. Boston: South End Press.

hooks, bell 1984 From Margin to Center. Boston: South End Press.

Jackson, Jacquelyn 1974 "Black female sociologists." Pp. 267–98 in James E. Blackwell and Morris Janowitz (eds.), Black Sociologists. Chicago: University of Chicago Press.

Keller, Evelyn Fox 1983 "Gender and science." Pp. 187–206 in Sandra Harding and Merrill Hintikka (eds.), Discovering Reality. Boston: D. Reidel.

King, Mae 1973 "The politics of sexual stereotypes." Black Scholar 4: 12–23.

Kulis, Stephen, Karen A. Miller, Morris Axelrod, and Leonard Gordon 1986 "Minority representation of U.S. departments." ASA Footnotes 14:3.

Lewis, Diane 1977 "A response to inequality: Black women, racism and sexism." Signs 3:339–61.

Loewenberg, Bert James and Ruth Bogin (eds.) 1976 Black Women in Nineteenth-century Life. University Park, PA: Pennsylvania State University.

Mannheim, Karl 1954 [1936] Ideology and Utopia: An Introduction to the Sociology of Knowledge. New York: Harcourt, Brace & Co.

Merton, Robert K. 1972 "Insiders and outsiders: a chapter in the sociology of knowledge." American Journal of Sociology 78:9–47.

Mullings, Leith 1986a "Anthropological perspectives on the Afro-American family." American Journal of Social Psychiatry 6:11–16.

Mullings, Leith 1986b "Uneven development: class, race and gender in the United States before 1900." Pp. 41–57 in Eleanor Leacock and Helen Safa (eds.), Women's Work, Development and the Division of Labor by Gender. South Hadley, MA: Bergin & Garvey.

Murray, Pauli 1970 "The liberation of Black women." Pp. 87–102 in Mary Lou Thompson (ed.), Voices of the New Feminism. Boston: Beacon Press.

Rich, Adrienne 1976 Of Woman Born: Motherhood as Experience and Institution. New York: Norton.

Richards, Dona 1980 "European mythology; the ideology of 'progress'." Pp. 59–79 in Molefi Kete Asante and Abdulai S. Vandi (eds.), Contemporary Black Thought. Beverly Hills, CA: Sage.

Rollins, Judith 1985 Between Women, Domestics and Their Employers. Philadelphia: Temple University Press.

Rosaldo, Michelle Z. 1983 "Moral/analytic dilemmas posed by the intersection of feminism and social science." Pp. 76–96 in Norma Hann, Robert N. Bellah, Paul Rabinow, and William Sullivan (eds.), Social Science as Moral Inquiry. New York: Columbia University Press.

Schutz, Alfred 1944 "The stranger: an essay in social psychology." American Journal of Sociology 49:499–507.

Simmel, Georg 1921 "The sociological significance of the 'stranger.'" Pp. 322–27 in Robert E. Park and Ernest W. Burgess (eds.), Introduction to the Science of Sociology. Chicago: University of Chicago Press.

Walker, Alice (ed.) 1979 I Love Myself When I Am Laughing . . . A Zora Neal Hurston Reader. Westbury, NY: Feminist Press.

White, Deborah Gray 1985 Art'n't I a Woman? Female Slaves in the Plantation South. New York: W.W. Norton.

White, E. Frances 1984 "Listening to the voices of Black feminism." Radical America 18:7–25.

9. The Consequences of Modernity*

Anthony Giddens

Sociology and Modernity

Sociology is a very broad and diverse subject, and any simple generalisations about it as a whole are questionable. But we can point to three widely held conceptions, deriving in some part from the continuing impact of classical social theory in sociology, which inhibit a satisfactory analysis of modern institutions. The first concerns the institutional diagnosis of modernity; the second has to do with the prime focus of sociological analysis, "society"; the third relates to the connections between sociological knowledge and the characteristics of modernity to which such knowledge refers.

1. The most prominent theoretical traditions in sociology, including those stemming from the writings of Marx, Durkheim, and Weber, have tended to look to a single overriding dynamic of transformation in interpreting the nature of modernity. For authors influenced by Marx, the major transformative force shaping the modern world is capitalism. With the decline of feudalism, agrarian production based in the local manor is replaced by production for markets of national and international scope, in terms of which not only an indefinite variety of material goods but also human labour power become commodified. The emergent social order of modernity is *capitalistic* in both its economic system and its other institutions. The restless, mobile character

* From Giddens, A. (1991) *The Consequences of Modernity* (Cambridge: Polity). Extracts from pp. 10–11, 12–13, 13–16, 40–41, 43–45.

of modernity is explained as an outcome of the investment-profit-investment cycle which, combined with the overall tendency of the rate of profit to decline, brings about a constant disposition for the system to expand.

[. . .]

Do we now live in a capitalist order? Is industrialism the dominant force shaping the institutions of modernity? Should we rather look to the rationalised control of information as the chief underlying characteristic? I shall argue that these questions cannot be answered in this form—that is to say, we should not regard these as mutually exclusive characterisations. Modernity, I propose, is *multidimensional on the level of institutions*, and each of the elements specified by these various traditions plays some part.

2. The concept of "society" occupies a focal position in much sociological discourse. "Society" is of course an ambiguous notion, referring both to "social association" in a generic way and to a distinct system of social relations. I am concerned here only with the second of these usages, which certainly figures in a basic fashion in each of the dominant sociological perspectives. While Marxist authors may sometimes favour the term "social formation" over that of "society," the connotation of "bounded system" is similar.

[. . .]

Why should we have reservations about the notion of society as ordinarily utilised in sociological thought? There are two reasons. Even where they do not explicitly say so, authors who regard sociology as the study of "societies" have in mind the societies associated with modernity. In conceptualising them, they think of quite clearly delimited systems, which have their own inner unity. Now, understood in this way, "societies" are plainly *nation-states*. Yet although a sociologist speaking of a particular society might casually employ instead the term "nation," or "country," the character of the nation-state is rarely directly theorised. In explicating the nature of modern societies, we have to capture the specific characteristics of the nation-state—a type of social community which contrasts in a radical way with pre-modern states.

A second reason concerns certain theoretical interpretations that have been closely connected with the notion of society. One of the most influential of these is that given by Talcott Parsons.[1] According to Parsons, the preeminent objective of sociology is to resolve the "problem of order." The problem of order is central to the interpretation of the boundedness of social systems, because it is defined as a question of integration—what holds the system together in the face of divisions of interest which would "set all against all."

I do not think it is useful to think of social systems in such a way.[2] We should reformulate the question of order as a problem of how it comes about that social systems "bind" time and space. The problem of order is here seen as one of *time-space distanciation*—the conditions under which time and space are organised so as to connect presence and absence. This issue has to be conceptually distinguished from that of the "boundedness" of social systems. Modern societies (nation-states), in some respects at any rate, have a clearly defined boundedness. But all such societies are also interwoven with ties and connections which crosscut the sociopolitical system of the state and the cultural order of the "nation." Virtually no premodern societies were as clearly bounded as modern nation-states. Agrarian civilisations had "frontiers," in the sense attributed to that term by geographers, while smaller agricultural communities and hunting and gathering societies normally shaded off into other groups around them and were not territorial in the same sense as state-based societies.

In conditions of modernity, the level of time-space distanciation is much greater than in even the most developed of agrarian civilisations. But there is more than a simple expansion in the capability of social systems to span time and space. We must look in some depth at how modern institutions become "situated" in time and space to identify some of the distinctive traits of modernity as a whole.

3. In various otherwise divergent forms of thought, sociology has been understood as generating knowledge about modern social life which can be used in the interests of prediction and control. Two versions of this theme are prominent. One is the view that sociology supplies information about social life which can give us a kind of control over social institutions similar to that which the physical sciences provide in the realm of nature. Sociological knowledge is believed to stand in an instrumental relation to the social world to which it relates; such knowledge can be applied in a technological fashion to intervene in social life. Other authors, including Marx (or, at least, Marx according to certain interpretations) have taken a different standpoint. For them, the idea of "using history to make history" is the key: the findings of social science cannot just be applied to an inert subject matter, but have to be filtered through the self-understandings of social agents.

This latter view is undeniably more sophisticated than the other, but it is still inadequate, since its conception of reflexivity is too simple. The relation between sociology and its subject matter—the actions of human beings in conditions of modernity—has to be understood instead in terms of the "double hermeneutic."[3] The development of sociological knowledge is parasitical upon lay agents' concepts; on the other hand, notions coined in the metalanguages of the social sciences routinely reenter the universe of actions they were initially formulated to describe or account for. But it does not lead in a direct way to a transparent social world. *Sociological knowledge spirals in and out of the universe of social life, reconstructing both itself and that universe as an integral part of that process.*

This is a model of reflexivity, but not one in which there is a parallel track between the accumulation of sociological knowledge on the one side and the steadily more extensive control of social development on the other. Sociology (and the other social sciences which deal with extant human beings) does not develop cumulative knowledge in the same way as the natural sciences might be said to do. Per contra, the "feed-in" of sociological notions or knowledge claims into the social world is not a process that can be readily channeled, either by those who propose them or even by powerful groups or governmental agencies. Yet the practical impact of social science and sociological theories is enormous, and sociological concepts and findings are constitutively involved in what modernity *is*. [. . .]

[. . .]

No knowledge under conditions of modernity *is* knowledge in the "old" sense, where "to know" is to be certain. This applies equally to the natural and the social sciences. In the case of social science, however, there are further considerations involved. We should recall at this point the observations made earlier about the reflexive components of sociology.

In the social sciences, to the unsettled character of all empirically based knowledge we have to add the "subversion" which comes from the reentry of social scientific discourse into the contexts it analyses. The reflection of which the social sciences are the formalised version (a specific genre of expert knowledge) is quite fundamental to the reflexivity of modernity as a whole.

Because of the close relation between the Enlightenment and advocacy of the claims of reason, natural science has usually been taken as the preeminent endeavour distinguishing the modern outlook from what went before. Even

those who favour interpretative rather than naturalistic sociology have normally seen social science as the poor relation of the natural sciences, particularly given the scale of technological development consequent upon scientific discoveries. But the social sciences are actually more deeply implicated in modernity than is natural science, since the chronic revision of social practices in the light of knowledge about those practices is part of the very tissue of modern institutions.[4]

All the social sciences participate in this reflexive relation, although sociology has an especially central place. Take as an example the discourse of economics. Concepts like "capital," "investment," "markets," "industry," and many others, in their modern senses, were elaborated as part of the early development of economics as a distinct discipline in the eighteenth and early nineteenth centuries.

These concepts, and empirical conclusions linked to them, were formulated in order to analyse changes involved in the emergence of modern institutions. But they could not, and did not, remain separated from the activities and events to which they related. They have become integral to what "modern economic life" actually is and inseparable from it. Modern economic activity would not be as it is were it not for the fact that all members of the population have mastered these concepts and an indefinite variety of others.

The lay individual cannot necessarily provide formal definitions of terms like "capital" or "investment," but everyone who, say, uses a savings account in a bank demonstrates an implicit and practical mastery of those notions. Concepts such as these, and the theories and empirical information linked to them, are not merely handy devices whereby agents are somehow more clearly able to understand their behaviour than they could do otherwise. They actively constitute what that behaviour is and inform the reasons for which it is undertaken. There cannot be a clear insulation between literature available to economists and that which is either read or filters through in other ways to interested parties in the

population: business leaders, government officials, and members of the public. The economic
environment is constantly being altered in the
light of these inputs, thus creating a situation of
continual mutual involvement between economic
discourse and the activities to which it refers.

[...]

The discourse of sociology and the concepts,
theories, and findings of the other social sciences
continually "circulate in and out" of what it is
that they are about. In so doing they reflexively
restructure their subject matter, which itself has
learned to think sociologically. *Modernity is itself
deeply and intrinsically sociological.* Much that is
problematic in the position of the professional
sociologist, as the purveyor of expert knowledge
about social life, derives from the fact that she or
he is at most one step ahead of enlightened lay
practitioners of the discipline.

Hence the thesis that more knowledge about
social life (even if that knowledge is as well but-
tressed empirically as it could possibly be) equals
greater control over our fate is false. It is (arguably) true about the physical world, but not about
the universe of social events. Expanding our
understanding of the social world might produce
a progressively more illuminating grasp of human
institutions and, hence, increasing "technological" control over them, if it were the case either
that social life were entirely separate from human
knowledge about it or that knowledge could be
filtered continuously into the reasons for social
action, producing step-by-step increases in the
"rationality" of behaviour in relation to specific
needs.

Both conditions do in fact apply to many circumstances and contexts of social activity. But
each falls well short of that totalising impact
which the inheritance of Enlightenment thought
holds out as a goal. This is so because of the
influence of four sets of factors.

One—factually very important but logically the
least interesting, or at any rate the least difficult

to handle analytically—is differential power. The
appropriation of knowledge does not happen in a
homogeneous fashion, but is often differentially
available to those in power positions, who are
able to place it in the service of sectional interests.

A second influence concerns the role of values.
Changes in value orders are not independent of
innovations in cognitive orientation created by
shifting perspectives on the social world. If new
knowledge could be brought to bear upon a tran-
scendental rational basis of values, this situation
would not apply. But there is no such rational
basis of values, and shifts in outlook deriving
from inputs of knowledge have a mobile relation
to changes in value orientations.

The third factor is the impact of unintended
consequences. No amount of accumulated
knowledge about social life could encompass all
circumstances of its implementation, even if such
knowledge were wholly distinct from the environment to which it applied. If our knowledge about
the social world simply got better and better, the
scope of unintended consequences might become
more and more confined and unwanted consequences rare. However, the reflexivity of modern
social life blocks off this possibility and is itself
the fourth influence involved. Although least discussed in relation to the limits of Enlightenment
reason, it is certainly as significant as any of the
others. The point is not that there is no stable
social world to know, but that knowledge of
that world contributes to its unstable or mutable
character.

The reflexivity of modernity, which is directly
involved with the continual generating of systematic self-knowledge, does not stabilise the
relation between expert knowledge and knowledge applied in lay actions. Knowledge claimed
by expert observers (in some part, and in many
varying ways) rejoins its subject matter, thus (in
principle, but also normally in practice) altering
it. There is no parallel to this process in the natural sciences; it is not at all the same as where, in
the field of microphysics, the intervention of an
observer changes what is being studied.

NOTES

1. Talcott Parsons, *The Social System* (Glencoe, Ill.: Free Press, 1951).
2. I have elaborated the reasons for this in *Constitution of Society* (Cambridge, Eng.: Polity, 1984).
3. Anthony Giddens, *New Rules of Sociological Method* (London: Hutchinson, 1974); *Constitution of Society.*
4. Giddens, *Constitution of Society,* ch. 7.

QUEEN MARGARET UNIVERSITY LRC

10. Sociology after the Postcolonial Turn*

Gurminder K. Bhambra

The neglect of colonial relations is, perhaps, particularly surprising in the case of British sociology, given Britain's past as an imperial power and the fact that the institutionalization of British sociology in the post-war period – indicated by the 40-year anniversary of this journal – occurred in the context of a legacy of decolonization and the dissolution of the British Empire. The limited engagement between sociology and postcolonialism is primarily concerned, on the side of sociology, with 'saving' the universality of sociology's core concepts in the light of a postcolonial (and other) politics of knowledge production (see Delanty, 2006; McLennan, 2006).[1] There is little engagement with what could be learnt, whether from the initial failure to address colonial relationships as integral to modernity, or from the subsequent neglect of decolonization and postcolonialism.

Sociology is also frequently represented as a discipline peculiarly associated with issues of order and integration, and with social movements calling that social order into question (Habermas, 1984). Initially, these were associated with problems of class, but in recent decades new social movements, such as feminism and the lesbian/gay movement, have been particularly significant in sociological debates. However, scholars who have attempted to revise the discipline from the perspective of these new social movements have frequently come to believe that sociology is particularly (unusually, even, when compared to other disciplines) immune to influence.

This, in essence, is the argument made by those proposing revolutions in thought – for example, 'feminist' and 'queer' – which are 'missing' in sociology (Alway, 1995; Seidman, 1994; Stacey, 2000; Stacey and Thorne, 1985, 1996; Stanley, 2000; Stein and Plummer, 1994; Thistle, 2000). If these arguments are correct, then we should now be beginning to see discussions of the 'missing postcolonial revolution', since this is the most recent claim to have purchase in the humanities and other social sciences. That this is not the case, I argue, can be seen to be a consequence of the particular structure of sociology, a structure that explains both the perceived 'missing revolutions' associated with gender and sexuality *and the seemingly paradoxical absence* of a 'missing revolution' of postcolonialism.[2]

While gender, sexuality, and race have come to be regarded as significant aspects of experience that deserve sociological consideration, they are nonetheless organized in terms of pre-existing orderings which render them an adjunct to general sociological understandings. In other words, while there may be recognition of the claims of gender or sexuality or race within standard sociological approaches, there is also an attempt to protect core categories of analysis from any reconstruction that such recognition would entail. Typically, this occurs by positing a distinction between the 'system' and the 'social', where the system refers to that which is general and the social to that which is particular (see Holmwood, 2000).

* From Bhambra, G. K. (2007) 'Sociology and Postcolonialism: Another "Missing" Revolution?', *Sociology*, 41(5): 871–884. Extracts from pp. 872–873, 875–877, 878–880.

[. . .]

Since the remit of sociology has generally been understood to be 'modern societies' – that is, societies engaged in processes of modernization – the 'postcolonial' is necessarily associated with 'pre-modern' societies, societies that have traditionally fallen to anthropology. For their part, feminism and the gay/lesbian movement arose within modern Western societies and, in their critique of sociology, did not fundamentally contest the self-understanding of those societies as modern, just the exclusion of women and gays and lesbians from the dominant narratives of modernization (see Marshall, 1994; Seidman, 1994). The particular identities articulated by these critiques, then, were more readily assimilated to the categories for understanding the modern social. The 'postcolonial', however, is not only missing from sociological understandings, but is also not recognized as present *within* the 'modern social' except as constituting the context of modernization for once colonized societies. Within sociology, then, the 'postcolonial' faces a double displacement – it can be seen as 'missing' from the structural framework and absent from the social framework (insofar as the social is categorized as the 'modern social').

The 'Modern Social' and the Structure of Sociology

To pose the question of the 'modern social' is to return to sociology's perceived origins. Regardless of the different interpretations put forward by sociologists in terms of the nature of modernity, the timing of its emergence, or its continued character today, all agree, as I have argued, on the importance of modernity to the establishment of sociology as a discipline. Further, there is general agreement that in its attempt to understand modernity what was to be understood was a new form of society defined by rupture and difference: a temporal *rupture* that distinguished a traditional, agrarian past from the modern, industrial present; and a cultural *difference* between Europe and the rest of the world. Moreover, in its own self-understanding as a discipline, setting out these parameters was defined as a key task of modern sociology. This is highlighted in the work of the primary theorists of classical sociology – Durkheim, Weber, and Marx – who all express, in differing ways, the challenges faced by modern European society, as well as across the range of contemporary sociological positions from Parsons to Giddens and Habermas (for further discussion, see Bhambra, 2007).

As argued by Habermas (1984), the emergence of sociology also has to be understood in the context of economics and politics establishing themselves as specialized sciences and, as a consequence, leaving sociology with the residue of problems that were no longer of concern to them. This disciplinary construction separates the sphere of the rational (system) – that is, economics, with its object being the market; and politics, with its object being administration and strategic action (or bureaucracy) – from the sphere of the non-rational (social). Where economics and politics became disciplines restricted to questions of economic equilibrium and rational choice, framed within an understanding of system integration, Habermas argues that sociology's focus was framed by the problems of social integration which were seen to have been brought about 'by the rise of the modern system of national states and by the differentiation of a market-regulated economy' (1984: 4).[3] In this perspective, sociology emerges as a particular form of reflection upon the sphere of the 'system', how it impinges on the social and, in turn, how it is impinged upon by the social.

Sociology, then, is integral to the understanding of the structural differentiation of modernity into distinct spheres and their interaction. In distinction from the objects of economics and politics, sociology's specific object of investigation is the social, understood as the particular and 'non-rational' that deviates from the 'rational'. At the same time, however, sociology is also associated with an overarching framework that locates these other disciplines in relation to itself. This is done by putting forward a *general* definition of the 'social' (alongside its meaning as the particular) that encompasses the two dimensions of system integration and social integration (as Habermas puts it).

With these distinctions in mind, questions of difference and identity have traditionally been taken up in terms of the theorization of the social in its more restricted sense. It is their absence from the sphere of the system and the general framework – which locates (or relates) the system and the social – that is highlighted as an area of concern by theorists arguing for the 'missing revolutions' of feminism and sexuality. For example, while gender has been recognized in recent decades as an important social variable, there has been little revision of sociology in terms of any particular identity claim being made. It is the extent to which gender, or any other social variable, is taken simply to *inflect* the structural form of the system (see, for example, Sayer, 2000), as opposed to being understood as constitutive of that system, that has led scholars to put forward arguments for a 'missing feminist/sexual revolution' in sociology.

Understanding the way in which sociology focuses on the social, as distinct from the system, and at the same time creates the general framework within which its relation to the 'system' is located, is of primary importance. It is the argument of this article, that it is this understanding of sociology in terms of a system/social division and its consequent relation to the idea of general theory that poses fundamental limitations for sociological projects (see Holmwood, 1996, 2001). Thus, the failure of feminism and queer theory – the 'missing revolutions' of gender and sexuality – to effect a transformation of the disciplinary categories of sociology rests on their reproduction of the very aspects of sociology that constitute the problem in the first place. Once the space of the social had been opened up by feminists and queer theorists it was easy for their concerns to be absorbed within the 'diffuse complexity' of the social in terms of addressing just another potential (non-rational) identity within it. Ditto race.

Although feminists and queer theorists have frequently sought to question the fundamental parameters of the discipline, the particular identities of gender and sexuality have, in fact, been assimilable to the standard sociological understandings of the social. In this way, the initial address by feminist and queer studies, challenging the absence of women and 'the sexual self' within sociology, could be absorbed by the discipline to the chagrin of those proclaiming a 'missing revolution'. That this initial acknowledgement of particular identities did not have subsequent effect, in terms of reconsidering the very categories of the discipline, can be understood in terms of the failure of these bodies of thought to develop their critique beyond a concern with the particular. In the end, neither feminist nor queer theory has challenged the constitution of sociology in terms of its founding categories of modernity, but instead, has made an accommodation within it: an accommodation, I argue, that has the effect of reducing the social to identity and the challenge of gender and sexuality (and race) to *issues* of identity. The promise of postcolonialism is precisely to bring about a revolution in thought so far missing from other challenges.[4]

[...]

The demise of colonialism as an explicit political formation has given rise to understandings of postcoloniality and, perhaps ironically, an increased recognition of the role of colonialism in the formation of modernity. In this context, then, it is insufficient to regard postcolonialism as simply implying new ways of understanding modernity's future(s), but, also, the contribution of postcolonialism to reconstructing modernity's past(s) needs to be acknowledged. To do the latter, however, requires a reconstruction of the forms of understanding – concepts, categories, and methods – within which past events were rendered insignificant. Pluralizing understandings of the social, to include the experiences and histories of other cultures and societies (in a similar manner to that of gender and sexuality), does no more than lay those experiences and histories in parallel to European ones and within a framework determined by the dominant experiences. What is necessary is to identify and explain the existing partiality with a view to the *reconstruction* of those theories – a reconstruction that, while it could be more adequate, could never be final.

As suggested, then, the simple pluralization of 'other' voices in fields previously dominated by particular voices can never be enough. The emergence of these new voices must call into question the structures of knowledge that had previously occluded such voices and, further, necessitates a reconsideration of previous theoretical categories. One way in which this can be done, I suggest, is by addressing difference in the context of what the historian Sanjay Subrahmanyam (1997) calls *connected histories*. These are histories that do not derive from a singular standpoint, be that a universal standpoint, or the standpoint of any particular identity claimant. Instead, connected histories allow for the deconstruction of dominant narratives at the same time as being open to different perspectives and seeking to reconcile these perspectives systematically, both in the incorporation of new data and evidence and in terms of the reconstruction of theoretical categories.

[. . .]

While feminism and queer studies have opened up interesting and productive avenues of thinking about gender and sexuality, to the extent that they have allowed these concepts to be regarded as constitutive of the social, merely inflecting processes of the system, they have remained, and reproduced, a way of thinking that undermines the force of the challenge posed. The postcolonial critique is not substantially different from that made by feminism and queer studies, but the nature of its location outside of the dominant understanding of the 'modern social' enables

it to resist assimilation into the domain of the socio-cultural (despite the efforts of theorists of multiple modernities to so contain it) and open up discussion of general categories. The postcolonial revolution, then, points to what is missing in sociology: an engagement with difference that makes a difference to what was initially thought. While it may be seen as threatening by some, what postcolonial thought truly threatens is to provide a revolution in thinking that would make sociology genuinely dialogic by making its fundamental categories part of that dialogue.

NOTES

1. Seidman's (1996) review of Edward W. Said's (1978) *Orientalism*, for example, was published almost 20 years after the initial publication and appears to be the only review of this seminal book in a mainstream Western sociology journal.

2. Significantly, the civil rights movement in the USA, which was contemporaneous with feminist and queer movements, has not generated discussion in terms of a 'missing revolution' of race within sociology. The long-standing existence of separate black higher educational institutions in the USA, where sociology was an early part of the curriculum and was inextricably linked with race, occurred alongside a separate consideration of race as a social problem within predominantly white institutions (see Himes, 1949; Singh, 2004). The lack of dialogue between them allowed both a consideration of race that developed into various forms of Race and Ethnic Studies, and the positing of race as a problem within mainstream white sociology, but it did not lead to race being analyzed as constitutive of sociology. Although one can find some contributions making the latter claim (see the edited volume by Ladner, 1973) it was not one that was taken up systematically within sociology as a whole. As such, the relationship of sociology to race can be seen to be

one of an 'unfinished' revolution and is one that requires further address by sociologists. While I am unable to do this here, I am grateful to one of the anonymous reviewers for highlighting this issue.

3. Giddens, for his part, argues that 'sociology involves a disciplinary concentration upon those institutions and modes of life brought into being by "modernity" – that massive set of social changes emanating first of all from Europe (and which today have become global in scope) creating modern social institutions' (1987: 25). This also echoes Parsons's earlier claim for sociology to be seen as emerging as a distinct discipline in terms of its association 'with factors which emerge in "economics" . . . but lie outside its central categories' (Parsons, 1937; for discussion, see Holmwood, 1996: 33).

4. This is not to suggest that feminists, queer theorists, and race scholars have not contributed substantially to sociology, but rather to make the argument that these contributions, to the extent that they do not challenge the accepted structure of sociology, are liable to assimilation within its dominant categories thereby diminishing the force of any critique. As such, the missing revolution that is being referred to, is that relating to the structure of the discipline itself and not the engagement of scholars seeking to make a difference to it.

REFERENCES

Alway, J. (1995) 'The Trouble with Gender: Tales of the Still-Missing Feminist Revolution in Sociological Theory', *Sociological Theory* 13(3): 209–28.

Bhambra, G.K. (2007) *Rethinking Modernity: Postcolonialism and the Sociological Imagination*. Basingstoke: Palgrave MacMillan.

Delanty, G. (2006) 'Modernity and the Escape from Eurocentrism', in Gerard Delanty (ed.) *Handbook of Contemporary European Social Theory*, pp. 266–78. London: Routledge.

Giddens, A. (1987) *Social Theory and Modern Sociology*. Cambridge: Polity Press.

Habermas, J. (1984) *The Theory of Communicative Action, Volume I: Reason and the Rationalization of Society*. London: Heinemann.

Himes Jr., J.S. (1949) 'Development and Status of Sociology in Negro Colleges', *Journal of Educational Sociology* 23(1): 17–32.

Holmwood, J. (1996) *Founding Sociology? Talcott Parsons and the Idea of General Theory*. Harlow: Longman.

Holmwood, J. (2000) 'Sociology and its Audience(s): Changing Perceptions of Sociological Argument', in J. Eldridge et al. (eds) *For Sociology: Legacies and Prospects*, pp. 33–55. Durham: Sociologypress.

Holmwood, J. (2001) 'Gender and Critical Realism: A Critique of Sayer', *Sociology* 35(4): 947–65.

Ladner, J.A. (ed.) (1973) *The Death of White Sociology*. New York: Random House.

McLennan, G. (2006) *Sociological Cultural Studies: Reflexivity and Positivity in the Human Sciences*. Basingstoke: Palgrave MacMillan.

Marshall, B.L. (1994) *Engendering Modernity: Feminism, Social Theory and Social Change*. Cambridge: Polity.

Parsons, T. (1937) *The Structure of Social Action: A Study in Social Theory with Special Reference to a Group of Recent European Writers*. New York: The Free Press of Glencoe.

Said, E.W. (1978) *Orientalism: Western Conceptions of the Orient*. London: Routledge and Kegan Paul.

Sayer, A. (2000) 'System, Lifeworld and Gender: Associational versus Counterfactual Thinking', *Sociology* 34(4): 707–25.

Seidman, S. (1994) 'Queer-ing Sociology, Sociologizing Queer Theory: An Introduction', *Sociological Theory* 12(2):166–77.

Seidman, S. (1996) 'Empire and Knowledge: More Troubles, New Opportunities for Sociology', *Contemporary Sociology* 25(3): 313–16.

Singh, N.P. (2004) *Black is a Country: Race*

and the Unfinished Struggle for Democracy. Cambridge, MA: Harvard University Press.

Stacey, J. (2000) 'Is Academic Feminism an Oxymoron?', *Signs* 25(4): 1189–94.

Stacey, J. and B. Thorne (1985) 'The Missing Feminist Revolution in Sociology', *Social Problems* 32(4): 301–16.

Stacey, J. and B. Thorne (1996) 'Is Sociology Still Missing its Feminist Revolution?', *Perspectives: The ASA Theory Section Newsletter* 18(3): 1–3.

Stanley, L. (2000) 'For Sociology, Gouldner's and Ours', in John Eldridge et al. (eds) *For Sociology: Legacies and Prospects*, pp. 56–82. Durham: Sociologypress.

Stein, A. and K. Plummer (1994) '"I Can't Even Think Straight": "Queer Theory" and the Missing Sexual Revolution in Sociology', *Sociological Theory* 12(2): 178–87.

Subrahmanyam, S. (1997) 'Connected Histories: Notes towards a Reconfiguration of Early Modern Eurasia', *Modern Asian Studies* 31(3): 735–62.

Thistle, S. (2000) 'The Trouble with Modernity: Gender and the Remaking of Social Theory', *Sociological Theory* 18(2): 275–88.

Part 1 – Further reading

There are many 'key thinkers' books and even more introductions to sociology, so if our selections here are not to your taste it is worth dipping into others. An excellent introduction to sociology and its contribution to knowledge is Kilminster, R. (2001) *The Sociological Revolution: From the Enlightenment to the Global Age* (London: Routledge), while Morrison, K. (2006) *Marx, Durkheim, Weber: Formations of Modern Social Thought* (London: Sage) is very reliable on the classical theorists. The postcolonial critique and reconstruction of sociology is discussed in Go, J. (2016) *Postcolonial Thought and Social Theory* (Oxford: Oxford University Press). Then, for contemporary theorists, Dillon, M. (2019) *Introduction to Sociological Theory: Theorists, Concepts and Their Applicability to the Twenty-First Century* (3rd edn, Chichester: Wiley Blackwell).

Sociology, 9th edition

Chapter 3 covers sociological theories and brings the story up to date with postcolonialism, cosmopolitanism and risk theory. The theoretical sections in chapter 4, 'Globalization and Social Change', chapter 12, 'Social Interaction and Daily Life', and chapter 6, 'Global Inequality', can all be consulted for useful discussions of theories.

Part 2   Doing Sociology

Research in sociology ranges from the study of small-scale interactions to long-term social development, changes to the structure of societies, as well as everything in between. The methods adopted by sociologists are also diverse, and any suggestion of a uniform or single way of 'doing sociology' is unrealistic. However, we should see this as a strength, because good sociology always begins from a problem or an issue in the real world. From there, sociologists can explore the most appropriate methods or techniques that allow them to carry out the study and reach their conclusions. This rosy picture is something of an ideal situation, though, as it is clear that the sociologist's initial view of the nature of the social world (its ontology) shapes their decision of how it can best be studied. Of course, many sociologists have their personal preferences in the selection of research methods, and these tend to reflect the kinds of issues and subjects they deal with.

Reading 11 is from one of the classic statements of sociological method from Émile Durkheim's 1895 book, which laid out some of the basic 'rules' that would help to establish sociology among the other sciences. One of Durkheim's aims was to persuade a sceptical community that there was a need for a new science – sociology – that studies 'social facts', not the individual psyche or the human brain. Social facts are all of those phenomena that exert or are capable of exerting constraints on people and which

individuals often perceive as a coercive and 'external' power. Social facts may be norms of behaviour or ways of acting and thinking that individuals experience as exerting influence over them, shaping their actions. Language and symbols, the financial system and currency, the legal framework and community values may all be social facts. Of course we may decide not to speak the common language or use the currency, but, if so, their power becomes more evident as we would have to struggle against their reality. Hence Durkheim's maxim 'Treat social facts as things'. We should remember that the constraints exerted by social facts are not simply obstacles; they also *enable* people to interact and engage with others to achieve their goals. Most sociologists today would probably reject Durkheim's limitations on their research, and many do study individuals and relationships.

The study of social development and change is fundamental to the sociological enterprise and is a common theme in the work of the early sociologists. When did Western economies become capitalistic? How are the French, Russian and Chinese revolutions similar and how are they different? Today, where is globalization heading? Questions such as these demand that sociologists look to historical sources to construct their explanations. In Reading 12, Philip Abrams argues that sociology and history are closely related and can learn from each other. Historians can better understand the patterns that emerge in long-term social change, while sociologists can begin to appreciate the value of interpreting a wider variety of sources of information. Abrams contends that 'historical sociology' is not a specific form of sociology reserved for the study of long-term change but should be at the centre of all sociological research. Focusing on the concept of 'process' and the continuous creation and reproduction of social structures is an approach that is shared by numerous sociologists, including Anthony Giddens, Norbert Elias and Charles Wright Mills.

In the past, sociology seemed irrevocably split between those who favoured quantitative methods and others who preferred qualitative research. Qualitative researchers objected to the very principle of trying to measure meaningful human action, while quantitative researchers viewed qualitative methods as too subjective to provide the basis for social *science*. To some extent this basic division still exists. However, there are now many research projects that mix the qualitative and the quantitative, a process which, it is argued, may strengthen the validity of sociologists' findings. Pullen, Jackson and Silk's study, extracted here, explores the sentiments and consumption patterns of Paralympic Games audiences in the UK, which they argue is the first mixed-method, integrated empirical analysis of this phenomenon. Bringing together a large-scale survey and findings from a series of focus groups, the authors discuss some of the connections between sport, broadcasting, diverse audience reception and social change.

The digital revolution in communications has impacted most aspects of social life, and young people are the digital natives whose always-on digital devices rarely leave their side. As digitization infuses every sphere of life, it becomes ever clearer that sociologists need both to understand this process and its consequences and to make use of digital data and tools in their projects. Digital infrastructures and data provide new opportunities for the analysis of, for example, social interactions, behavioural patterns and social movement activism. In Reading 14, Noortje Marres sets out to understand better the relationships between digital technologies and social life and between knowledge, society and technology. Issues of privacy, confidentiality, data collection and data storage also take on a renewed importance given the enormous amount of personal data that our information age makes available and accessible. It seems likely that the current interest in 'digital sociology' as a specialist field of enquiry will be temporary. As societies and communications are increasingly digitized, sociologists in every specialism will have to be digitally aware and able to handle digital data.

Since the 1970s, feminist research and theorizing have had a major impact in sociology. Our final reading in Part 2, by Patricia Leavy and Anne Harris, discusses some of the important elements of specifically feminist research. These include new questions about the nature of knowledge about the social world, what should count as valid knowledge, and which research methods are most effective and appropriate for the purpose of gaining knowledge about gender and women's lives. However, in addition, they argue that feminist research is inevitably critical, and not just in the sense that it 'criticizes' existing social arrangements that are rooted in discrimination and inequality. It is critical because it lays bare these arrangements and seeks to change them. And, yet, Leavy and Harris note that some of the questions asked in early feminist research are still with us, alongside new ones. For example, are there specifically 'feminist' research methods? Are qualitative methods more appropriate in feminist research? How is feminist research responding to the postcolonial challenge and digitization? The extract asks some of these questions and highlights some of the ways in which contemporary feminist researchers are tackling them.

11. Treat Social Facts as Things*

Émile Durkheim

When this book appeared for the first time, it aroused lively controversy. Current thought, shaken out of itself, resisted at first so loudly that for a time it was almost impossible for us to make ourselves heard. On the very points on which we had expressed ourselves most explicitly, views were freely attributed to us which had nothing in common with our own; and our opponents held that they were refuting us in refuting these mistaken ideas. Whereas we had declared repeatedly that the individual consciousness was for us not material, but only a more or less systematized aggregate of phenomena, we were charged with realism and with ontologism. Whereas we had expressly stated and reiterated that social life is constituted wholly of collective "representations,"[1] we were accused of eliminating the mental element from sociology. Our critics even went so far as to resurrect old controversies which we had supposed long settled. They imputed to us certain opinions that we had never upheld, under the plea of their being "in conformity with our principles." Fortunately, experience has demonstrated the weakness of such attacks, since the arbitrary methods by which these critics have supposedly reconstructed our system permits an easy refutation.

[. . .]

---

* From Durkheim, É. (1966 [1895]) *The Rules of Sociological Method* (New York: The Free Press). Extracts from pp. xli, xliii, 1–4, 10, 13, 141, 144–145.

I

The proposition which states that social facts are to be treated as things—the proposition at the very basis of our method—is one of those which have provoked most contradiction. It has been considered not only paradoxical but ridiculous for us to compare the realities of the social world with those of the external world. But our critics have curiously misinterpreted the meaning and import of this analogy, for it was not our intention to reduce the higher to the lower forms of being, but merely to claim for the higher forms a degree of reality at least equal to that which is readily granted to the lower. We assert not that social facts are material things but that they are things by the same right as material things, although they differ from them in type.

What, precisely, is a "thing"? A thing differs from an idea in the same way as that which we know from without differs from that which we know from within. Things include all objects of knowledge that cannot be conceived by purely mental activity, those that require for their conception data from outside the mind, from observations and experiments, those which are built up from the more external and immediately accessible characteristics to the less visible and more profound. To treat the facts of a certain order as things is not, then, to place them in a certain category of reality but to assume a certain mental attitude toward them on the principle that when approaching their study we are absolutely ignorant of their nature, and that their characteristic properties, like the unknown causes on which they depend, cannot be discovered by even the most careful introspection.

[. . .]

Before inquiring into the method suited to the study of social facts, it is important to know which facts are commonly called "social." This information is all the more necessary since the designation "social" is used with little precision. It is currently employed for practically all phenomena generally diffused within society, however small their social interest. But on that basis, there are, as it were, no human events that may not be called social. Each individual drinks, sleeps, eats, reasons; and it is to society's interest that these functions be exercised in an orderly manner. If, then, all these facts are counted as "social" facts, sociology would have no subject matter exclusively its own, and its domain would be confused with that of biology and psychology.

But in reality there is in every society a certain group of phenomena which may be differentiated from those studied by the other natural sciences. When I fulfil my obligations as brother, husband, or citizen, when I execute my contracts, I perform duties which are defined, externally to myself and my acts, in law and in custom. Even if they conform to my own sentiments and I feel their reality subjectively, such reality is still objective, for I did not create them; I merely inherited them through my education. How many times it happens, moreover, that we are ignorant of the details of the obligations incumbent upon us, and that in order to acquaint ourselves with them we must consult the law and its authorized interpreters! Similarly, the church-member finds the beliefs and practices of his religious life ready-made at birth; their existence prior to his own implies their existence outside of himself. The system of signs I use to express my thought, the system of currency I employ to pay my debts, the instruments of credit I utilize in my commercial relations, the practices followed in my profession, etc., function independently of my own use of them. And these statements can be repeated for each member of society. Here, then, are ways of acting, thinking, and feeling that present the noteworthy property of existing outside the individual consciousness.

These types of conduct or thought are not only external to the individual but are, moreover, endowed with coercive power, by virtue of which they impose themselves upon him, independent of his individual will. Of course, when I fully consent and conform to them, this constraint is felt only slightly, if at all, and is therefore unnecessary. But it is, nonetheless, an intrinsic characteristic of these facts, the proof thereof being that it asserts itself as soon as I attempt to resist it. If I attempt to violate the law, it reacts against me so as to prevent my act before its accomplishment, or to nullify my violation by restoring the damage, if it is accomplished and reparable, or to make me expiate it if it cannot be compensated for otherwise.

In the case of purely moral maxims; the public conscience exercises a check on every act which offends it by means of the surveillance it exercises over the conduct of citizens, and the appropriate penalties at its disposal. In many cases the constraint is less violent, but nevertheless it always exists. If I do not submit to the conventions of society, if in my dress I do not conform to the customs observed in my country and in my class, the ridicule I provoke, the social isolation in which I am kept, produce, although in an attenuated form, the same effects as a punishment in the strict sense of the word. The constraint is nonetheless efficacious for being indirect. I am not obliged to speak French with my fellow-countrymen nor to use the legal currency, but I cannot possibly do otherwise. If I tried to escape this necessity, my attempt would fail miserably. As an industrialist, I am free to apply the technical methods of former centuries; but by doing so, I should invite certain ruin. Even when I free myself from these rules and violate them successfully, I am always compelled to struggle with them. When finally overcome, they make their constraining power sufficiently felt by the resistance they offer. The enterprises of all innovators, including successful ones, come up against resistance of this kind.

Here, then, is a category of facts with very distinctive characteristics: it consists of ways of acting, thinking, and feeling, external to the individual, and endowed with a power of coercion, by reason of which they control him. These ways of thinking could not be confused with biological phenomena, since they consist of representations and of actions; nor with psychological phenomena, which exist only in the individual consciousness and through it. They constitute, thus, a new variety of phenomena; and it is to them exclusively that the term "social" ought to be applied. And this term fits them quite well, for it is clear that, since their source is not in the individual, their substratum can be no other than society, either the political society as a whole or some one of the partial groups it includes, such as religious denominations, political, literary, and occupational associations, etc. On the other hand, this term "social" applies to them exclusively, for it has a distinct meaning only if it designates exclusively the phenomena which are not included in any of the categories of facts that have already been established and classified. These ways of thinking and acting therefore constitute the proper domain of sociology. [. . .]

[. . .]

We thus arrive at the point where we can formulate and delimit in a precise way the domain of sociology. It comprises only a limited group of phenomena. A social fact is to be recognized by the power of external coercion which it exercises or is capable of exercising over individuals, and the presence of this power may be recognized in its turn either by the existence of some specific sanction or by the resistance offered against every individual effort that tends to violate it. One can, however, define it also by its diffusion within the group, provided that, in conformity with our previous remarks, one takes care to add as a second and essential characteristic that its own existence is independent of the individual forms it assumes

in its diffusion. This last criterion is perhaps, in certain cases, easier to apply than the preceding one. In fact, the constraint is easy to ascertain when it expresses itself externally by some direct reaction of society, as is the case in law, morals, beliefs, customs, and even fashions. But when it is only indirect, like the constraint which an economic organization exercises, it cannot always be so easily detected. [. . .]

[. . .]

[. . .] Our definition will then include the whole relevant range of facts if we say: *A social fact is every way of acting, fixed or not, capable of exercising on the individual an external constraint;* or again, *every way of acting which is general throughout a given society, while at the same time existing in its own right independent of its individual manifestations.*[2]

[. . .]

To sum up, the distinctive characteristics of our method are as follows: First, it is entirely independent of philosophy. Because sociology had its birth in the great philosophical doctrines, it has retained the habit of relying on some philosophical system and thus has been continuously overburdened with it. It has been successively positivistic, evolutionary, idealistic, when it should have been content to be simply sociology. We should even hesitate to describe it as naturalistic, unless the term indicates merely that the sociologist considers social facts as capable of being explained naturally, or that he is a scientist and not a mystic. We reject the term if it is given a doctrinal meaning concerning the essence of social objects—if, e.g., by it is meant that social objects are reducible to the other cosmic forces.

Sociology does not need to choose between the great hypotheses which divide metaphysicians. It needs to embrace free will no more than determinism. All that it asks is that the principle of causality be applied to social phenomena. Again, this principle is enunciated for sociology not as a rational necessity but only as an empirical postulate, produced by legitimate induction. Since the law of causality has been verified in the other realms of nature, and since it has progressively extended its authority from the physicochemical world to the biological, and from the latter to the psychological, we are justified in claiming that it is equally true of the social world; and it is possible to add today that the researches undertaken on the basis of this postulate tend to confirm it. [...]

[...]

If we consider social facts as things, we consider them as *social things*. The third trait that characterizes our method is that it is exclusively sociological. It has often appeared that these phenomena, because of their extreme complexity, were either inhospitable to science or could be subject to it only when reduced to their elemental conditions, either psychic or organic, that is, only when stripped of their proper nature. We have, on the contrary, undertaken to establish that it is possible to treat them scientifically without removing any of their distinctive characteristics. We have even refused to identify the immateriality which characterizes them with the complex immateriality of psychological phenomena; we have, furthermore, refused to reabsorb it, with the Italian school, into the general properties of organized matter.[3] We have shown that a social fact can be explained only by another social fact; and, at the same time, we have shown how this

sort of explanation is possible by pointing out, in the internal social milieu, the principal factor in collective evolution. Sociology is, then, not an auxiliary of any other science; it is itself a distinct and autonomous science, and the feeling of the specificity of social reality is indeed so necessary to the sociologist that only distinctly sociological training can prepare him to grasp social facts intelligently.

NOTES

1. [This word, *représentations*, which might be translated "ideas" (cf. the German *Vorstellungen*), is used by M. Durkheim in a technical sense, essential to his sociological theory. See C. E. Gehlke, *Émile Durkheim's Contributions to Sociological Theory* (1915), p. 17.—Editor.]

2. This close connection between life and structure, organ and function, may be easily proved in sociology because between these two extreme terms there exists a whole series of immediately observable intermediate stages which show the bond between them. Biology is not in the same favorable position. But we may well believe that the inductions on this subject made by sociology are applicable to biology and that, in organisms as well as in societies, only differences in degree exist between these two orders of facts.

3. Our method has, therefore, been quite wrongly described as "materialistic."

12. Sociology's Historical Imagination*

Philip Abrams

Try asking serious questions about the contemporary world and see if you can do without historical answers. Whether it is a matter of conflict in the Middle East or in Northern Ireland, or racism in urban ghettoes, of poverty and social problems on the Clyde or the Tyne, or of the fall of governments in Italy or Chile, we tend to assume that an adequate answer, one that satisfactorily explains whatever it is that puzzles us, will be one that is couched in historical terms. This appeal to history is not a natural human inclination but it has become almost natural to the modern western mind. The idea that 'in my beginning is my end', that the present needs to be understood as a product of the past, is one we have come to take for granted. And in taking it for granted we achieve, perhaps unconsciously, an important sociological insight. For it is indeed not the 'problem families' living in west Newcastle or south Chicago today who explain the concentration of social ills in those areas, but the long-term workings of housing markets and job markets of which those families are the present victims. It is not the intransigence of the present governments of Israel or Syria that explains the persistent risk of war in Palestine, but the meaning and depth of that intransigence in the setting of centuries of cultural and religious struggle, imperialism and mistrust. It is not the incompetence or opportunism of contemporary Italian politicians that accounts

for Italy's endless crisis of government, but the problems resulting from attempts throughout the past century to make a unified nation state but of a deeply divided and fragmented society. Insofar as we reject explanations of the present that deal with the present, insofar as we turn to history for more satisfactory explanations, we are turning towards a deeper and more realistic understanding. And we are also turning towards sociology.

Sociological explanation is necessarily historical. Historical sociology is thus not some special kind of sociology; rather, it is the essence of the discipline. All varieties of sociology stress the so-called 'two-sidedness' of the social world, presenting it as a world of which we are both the creators and the creatures, both makers and prisoners; a world which our actions construct and a world that powerfully constrains us. The distinctive quality of the social world for the sociologist is, accordingly, its *facticity* – the way in which society is experienced by individuals as a fact-like system, external, given, coercive, even while individuals are busy making and re-making it through their own imagination, communication and action. Thus the central issue for sociological analysis can be said, by Berger and Luckmann (1967), to be the resolution of the 'awesome paradox' discovered in turn by each of the founding fathers of sociology: 'how is it possible that human activity should produce a world of things?' And increasingly sociologists have come to affirm the wisdom of their founding fathers in concluding that there is only one way in which that paradox can be resolved: namely,

* From Abrams, P. (1982) *Historical Sociology* (Shepton Mallet: Open Books). Extracts from pp. 1–5, 16–17.

historically. The two-sidedness of society, the fact that social action is both something we choose to do and something we have to do, is inseparably bound up with the further fact that whatever reality society has is an historical reality, a reality in time. When we refer to the two-sidedness of society we are referring to the ways in which, in time, actions become institutions and institutions are in turn changed by action. Taking and selling prisoners becomes the institution of slavery. Offering one's services to a soldier in return for his protection becomes feudalism. Organising the control of an enlarged labour force on the basis of standardised rules becomes bureaucracy. And slavery, feudalism and bureaucracy become the fixed, external settings in which struggles for prosperity or survival or freedom are then pursued. By substituting cash payments for labour services the lord and peasant jointly embark on the dismantling of the feudal order their great-grandparents had constructed.

In both its aspects, then, the social world is essentially historical. Process is the link between action and structure. The idea of process and the study of process are the tools to unlock Berger and Luckmann's 'awesome paradox'. What we choose to do and what we have to do are shaped by the historically given possibilities among which we find ourselves. But history is not a force in its own right any more than society is. Rather, as the French historical sociologist Roland Mousnier puts it (1973: 145): 'History has no direction of its own accord, for it is shaped by the will of men and the choices they make. Yet with every second that passes, men are making their choice by their behaviour.' And how we behave now – whether we throw a bomb or go on a peace march, whether we protest about inequality or thrive on it – is very largely a matter of what previous experience has made possible and meaningful for us. The conscientious exam candidate and the truant are both dominated by the historically established weight of the institutions of education; the meaning of their activity derives from the reality of those institutions. We can construct new worlds but only on the basis

and within the framework of what our predecessors have constructed for us. On that basis and within that framework the content of our activity may re-make or un-make the institutions that surround us. This shaping of action by structure and transforming of structure by action both occur as processes in time. It is by seizing on that idea that history and sociology merge and that sociology becomes capable of answering our urgent questions about why the world is as it is; about why particular men and women make the particular choices they do and why they succeed or fail in their projects.

In this sense historical sociology has always been a core element of sociology as a whole. The idea of process is crucial to the way sociological work is done. But sociology became historical in more specific ways, too. As a distinct way of thought sociology came into being in the face of momentous historical changes and from the first was shaped by the experience of those changes. By the 1840s, when systematic social analysis first became widespread in Europe, it was a common feeling that the pace and range of change associated with the political and industrial revolutions of the previous two generations had left the social world an incomprehensible chaos in which only the fact of change itself was certain. In the words of the poet Lamartine 'the world had jumbled its catalogue' (cited in Burrow, 1966: 94). Faced with the prospect of intellectual and social anarchy the early sociologists sought an ordered understanding of the processes of social change and above all of the changes involved in the transition to industrialism. Marx, Weber and Durkheim, the three founding fathers whose influence is greatest today, all made the nature of the transition to industrialism the basic organising concern of their work and sought through understanding that particular transition to move to a larger understanding of social process, or history, in general. So, too, did their contemporaries Comte, Spencer and Hobhouse. All were sharply aware of living in a world that was changing dramatically from year to year and in which the relationships between the changes people wanted and the changes that actually occurred were mysterious, frustrating and obscure. Why did the pursuit of wealth seem to generate poverty on an unprecedented scale? Why did the triumph of the principles of liberty and equality appear to go hand in hand with monstrous new forms of oppression? Was what was happening to social relationships in the course of industrialisation a matter of chance, of choice or of necessity? How far was industrialism an unavoidable destiny? Which of its characteristics could be altered by human action, and how. Such questions could be answered in many different ways. What the early sociologists agreed about was that these were the important questions to ask. The transition to industrialism compelled the imagination. From the analysis of that transition one could move to a more general but no less historical sociology.

Thus Max Weber emphasised the ever increasing bureaucratisation of the social world which he saw as a dominant tendency of industrialisation. And he sought to relate that tendency to other characteristic tendencies of the same transition: changes in the scale of organisation, in the form of the division of labour and its complexity, in the nature of legitimate authority and in the social bases of power. But his interest went beyond identifying the tendency to bureaucracy and relating it to its causes and correlates. He was also concerned with the strength of the tendency to bureaucracy, with the extent to which it was a necessity of industrial society and with the extent to which and the ways in which it could be resisted or eluded. The study of bureaucratisation was thus at a deeper level a study of the relationship between individuals and institutions, a study of the *possible* ways of living in industrial society. In much the same manner Karl Marx's emphasis on the formation of classes and the structuring of class conflict was also an interest in identifying ways in which men could act within a powerfully given social setting to bring about desired results, a study of the relationship of social action and

social structure in general. And the same can be said of Émile Durkheim's exploration of the relationship between the division of labour and the moral disorder he terms anomie. At the heart of each of these formidable contributions to sociology was the simple question: to what extent does the world have to be the way it is? It was the decision to seek an historical answer to that question that made each of these men sociologists.

[. . .]

Historical sociology is not, then, a matter of imposing grand schemes of evolutionary development on the relationship of the past to the present. Nor is it merely a matter of recognising the historical background to the present. It is the attempt to understand the relationship of personal activity and experience on the one hand and social organisation on the other as something that is continuously constructed in time. It makes the continuous process of construction the focal concern of social analysis. That process may be studied in many different contexts: in personal biographies and careers; in the rise and fall of whole civilisations; in the setting of particular events such as a revolution or an election, or of particular developments such as the making of the welfare state or the formation of the working class. The particular context to which sociologists have chosen to pay most attention is the one I have called the transition to industrialism. But in the end historical sociology is more a matter of how one interprets the world than of what bit of it one chooses to study. And on that basis one can say firstly, that there is no necessary difference between the sociologist and the historian, and secondly that sociology which takes itself seriously must be historical sociology. As C. Wright Mills (1959) put it, the whole 'intellectual promise' of the discipline is 'to enable men . . . to become aware of historical structures and of their own place within them'.

REFERENCES

Berger, P. and Luckmann, T. (1967) *The Social Construction of Reality*. London: Allen Lane.

Burrow, J. (1966) *Evolution and Society*. Cambridge: Cambridge University Press.

Mills, C. W. (1959) *The Sociological Imagination*. New York: Oxford University Press.

Mousnier, R. (1973) *Social Hierarchies*. London: Croom Helm.

13. Mixing Methods in Empirical Research*

Emma Pullen, Daniel Jackson and Michael Silk

Compared to the Olympics, the Paralympics has received relatively limited scholarly attention as a media spectacle (Howe 2008). Whilst across wider media content and broadcasting disability continues to remain significantly underrepresented, the Paralympics provides what we have previously termed a "hyper-visible" space of disability representation on television (Pullen and Silk 2020). Indeed, given its position on primetime schedules in many countries, it is arguably the most dominant mediated space in which non-disabled audiences "see" disability. Unsurprisingly then, Paralympic scholarship has typically been directed toward a critique of disability representation focusing on how para-athletes and disability are portrayed through Paralympic media content. Predicated on a number of dominant disability stereotypes historically seen across wider media, scholars (Beacom et al. 2016; Bruce 2014) have pointed to the marginalization of para-athletes; the reinforcement of medicalized and individualized understandings of disability; and the framing of para-athletes as particularly heroic, inspirational, and having triumphed over adversity. This latter framing, defined as the "supercrip" (Silva and Howe 2012), has been critiqued for its seemingly positive representation of disability, whilst remaining centered on successful technologically enhanced para-athletes given their approximation to normative (able-bodied) expectations of sporting success and corporeality. This modicum of studies has highlighted the extent the "supercrip" attempts to make disability palatable in a commercial media culture that privileges aesthetic labor (Pullen et al. 2019). This is particularly pronounced in the sport media economy framed on the legitimization of media narratives for capital accumulation (advertising, sponsorship revenues), normative production practices, preferred narratives of nation, and a non-disabled sporting corporeality (see, e.g., Jhally 1989).

However, important as these studies are in critiquing Paralympic representation, there continues to remain a scholarly absence of Paralympic research on the wider production context and audience receptions. Here, and excluding our own work in this area (see Pullen et al. 2019), less than a handful of studies have paid attention to Paralympic production, the conditions that impinge of cultural production, and the logics and practices of Paralympic broadcasters. This is a concern given the significant cultural shifts—particularly though not exclusively in the UK—in the production landscape since 2012, marking an important social and cultural shift in Paralympic broadcasting and, subsequently, reception and representation. Moreover, despite a corpus of studies on representation (e.g., Beacom et al. 2016; Silva and Howe 2012) few focus on live sporting coverage and the distinctive organizational and cultural practices of sports broadcasting that shape content.

* From Pullen, E., Jackson, D. and Silk, M. (2021) 'Paralympic Broadcasting and Social Change: An Integrated Mixed Method Approach to Understanding the Paralympic Audience in the UK', *Television & New Media*, March: 1–21. Extracts from pp. 3–4, 7–9, 16–17.

[Channel 4 (C4)]'s practices in Paralympic broadcasting are relatively distinct when compared with other broadcasters and their approach forms an important contextual backdrop to this paper. In the words of their Disability Executive, Alison Walsh, "Our ambition was simple: two years to change attitudes to disability and disability sport. We wanted to create a nation at ease with disability" (Walsh 2015, 27). They pursued this through (a) unprecedented exposure of para sport, including over nine hours a day of live sport, plus extensive build-up programs, (b) a "no-holds-barred approach to portrayal of disabled people" (Walsh 2015, 49) which included incorporating their own extra (multilateral) cameras to supplement the (unilateral) footage provided by the host Olympics Broadcasting Service (OBS) in order to show the disabled body (c) marketing Paralympians to the British public with an emphasis on athlete backstories in order to familiarize audiences with GB para-athletes, and (d) developing disabled talent both on screen and in production. All of these practices formed a significant shift from those of the former Paralympic broadcaster, the BBC (See Pullen et al. 2019).

[. . .]

Method

Drawing on national survey and focus group data from Paralympic audiences across the UK, this study provides the first mixed method and integrated empirical analysis of Paralympic audiences to date. Given no quantitative Paralympic audience research exists, our research design sought to engage audiences in a qualitative setting in the first instance so as to inform the quantitative survey design.

Audience Focus Groups

Eighteen focus groups lasting approximately ninety minutes were conducted with 216 members of the public between June and December 2017. Focus groups were held in sites across England and Wales, including London, Bristol, Cardiff, Liverpool, Bournemouth, and Nottingham and were held in publicly accessible meeting rooms (e.g., university seminar rooms, hotel meeting facilities). Participant numbers were spread relatively equally across each location (ten participants per group at each site) and the demographic spread (age, race, ethnicity, social class, gender) and geographical spread was diverse and captured a range of experiences and voices. At each site multiple focus groups were conducted with groups who self-identified as disabled and non-disabled, with approximately half of our participants self-identifying as disabled. Recruitment involved the use of a recruitment agency through a purposeful sampling technique against an inclusion criteria that required the following: for participants to be aged over eighteen years; able to provide full informed consent; and have watched the Rio 2016 Paralympic Games. The dataset contained self-selection bias that resulted from the inclusion criteria with the most visible being an interest in Paralympic sport.

The focus group guide was structured around three topics which respond to the RQs. This included: (1) audience backgrounds and experience of disability; (2) interest, perceptions and opinions of Paralympic broadcast coverage; (3) the impact of the Paralympics on their perceptions of elite para-sport and their wider attitudes toward disability and disability rights progress. Focus groups were audio recorded and transcribed verbatim by an internal university transcriptions service before being entered into QRS NVivo data management program. Full anonymity has been given to all participants with assigned pseudonyms with only the gender of each participant marked throughout the transcripts. A process of manual interpretive coding was undertaken followed by a closer reading of themes and sub-categorization of dominant themes through a process of meaning condensation (Coffey and Atkinson 1996). Themes were discussed between colleagues as "critical friends" establishing empirical validity in the process of qualitative analysis.

Audience Survey

An online survey with a UK-based commercial research agency (DJS Research) on a UK representative sample of sixteen plus year olds ($N = 2008$) was conducted through a web interface between the 16th and 28th February 2019. The questionnaire was sent out to a sample of those registered on the DJS Research database (over 40,000 individuals), and where stratification (by age, ethnicity, gender, region, and social class) was used to ensure representativeness.

Survey Variables

In lieu of existing measures from previous studies of Paralympic audiences, survey measures were developed from the focus group findings and grounded in the literature. To establish who is interested in following Paralympic broadcasting in the UK (RQ1), we asked (on a four point scale) the extent to which they followed the three Paralympic events since 2012: the Summer Paralympics in Rio 2016 (Brazil) and the Winter Paralympics in Sochi 2014 (Russia) and PyeongChang 2018 (South Korea). To gauge the extent to which Paralympic audiences are just general mega sporting event audiences (see Hodges et al. 2015) we asked (on a five point scale) whether participants "enjoy watching programs featuring disability sport, other than the Paralympic Games themselves, when they are on TV." We also asked various demographic questions (e.g., age, ethnicity, disability, gender) of participants.

To measure interest in Paralympic athletes (RQ2a) we asked participants to rate (on a five point scale) their agreement with two statements: "I am interested in the sporting achievements of Paralympic athletes" and "I am interested in the backgrounds of Paralympic athletes (including

how they deal with their disability)." The latter question responds to an emergent finding from focus groups alongside interviews conducted with C4 and an analysis of their Paralympic broadcasting (as part of the wider project, see Pullen et al. 2019) which established the importance of athlete backstories in engaging audiences with disability.

To explore the impact of Paralympic broadcasting on perceptions of disabled people (RQ2b), we developed four measures (on a five point scale) that ask participants whether they agree that the Paralympics have "had a positive impact on the lives of people with disabilities," "have challenged my attitudes about people with disabilities," "have inspired me to engage with other media content that features disability," and "have given me more confidence in interacting with people with disabilities in everyday life." Finally, emerging from focus group themes and previous research (Hodges et al. 2015), we asked three questions that explored different barriers to engagement with the Paralympics (RQ3): "The Paralympic Games don't really represent elite sport," "I don't like the way the media portray people with disabilities at the Paralympic Games," and "I feel uncomfortable watching people with disabilities at the Paralympic Games."

[. . .]

Discussion and Conclusion

The findings presented here provide the first mixed methods and integrated empirical analysis of Paralympic audiences to date. Building on the findings of extant qualitative studies (see, Hodges et al. 2015), we asked: who is the audience for the Paralympics in the UK (RQ1); how has watching the Paralympics shaped interest in the achievements of disabled athletes? (RQ2(a)); how has watching the Paralympics shaped perceptions toward disabled people in everyday life? (RQ2(b)), and, what barriers exist amongst UK audiences toward engaging with Paralympic broadcasting? (RQ3). Beyond the detail of the audience data presented hitherto, in the following discussion we present four overarching findings that stand out as important for taking our understanding of mediated para-sport forward.

Our findings could be read as highly promising for the Paralympic vision and the role of national [public service broadcasters (PSB)] therein. Before 2012, the Paralympics operated on the margins of UK TV schedules, only receiving daily highlights to relatively small audiences. Audience research conducted prior to 2012 suggested there was little more than a niche audience following, with significant barriers to engaging with disability sport for many (Hodges et al. 2015). After two Paralympic cycles since 2012—and with its elevation to mainstream TV schedules—*our first key finding is that the UK Paralympic audience is both considerable and demographically diverse* largely reflecting Olympic fan demographics (see Tainsky et al. 2014; Tang and Cooper 2012). Indeed, given the considerable audience following, we would suggest there is a para-sport media market beyond the Paralympic Games; an important finding for broadcasters who have yet to fully realize both the commercial and cultural potential of para-sport beyond the dictates of the mega-event marketplace.

Further, our data implies that *spectatorship of the Paralympics has facilitated progressive social change* (RQ2(a,b)); our second key finding. This is important given the philosophy of the Paralympic movement, aims of the [International Paralympics Committee (IPC)], and C4's statutory remit as a PSB. Despite this vision—largely at odds with the logics of the sport media economy—the Paralympics has indeed managed to capture a considerable audience, be commercially successful, and shift attitudes toward disability and disability sport by stimulating many audience members to reflect on their own assumptions and perceptions. Certainly, perceptions of Paralympic athletes and disability sport by non-disabled audiences were positive and tensions concerning representation and obstacles to engagement were far less pronounced than prior

to 2012. This finding has important cultural significance insofar as it demonstrates progressive social change *over time* and the power of public service broadcasting remits in contributing to challenging attitudes and understandings around marginalized sporting groups and identities. With the global retreat of public service broadcasting and rising tide of digital narrowcasting and neoliberal deregulation, this finding is of critical importance in demonstrating the *cultural value* of PSB in sports broadcasting and its role as a crucial platform, beyond sports broadcasting, for challenging the status quo and disability rights.

REFERENCES

Beacom, Aaron, Liam French, and Scott Kendall. 2016. "Reframing Impairment? Continuity and Change in Media Representations of Disability Through the Paralympic Games." *International Journal of Sport Communication* 9: 42–62. doi:10.1123/ijsc.2015-0077.

Bruce, Toni. 2014. "Us and Them: The Influence of Discourses of Nationalism on Media Coverage of the Paralympics." *Disability & Society* 29: 1443–59. doi:10.1080/09687599.2013.816624.

Coffey, Amanda, and Paul Atkinson. 1996. *Making Sense of Qualitative Data*. London, England: Sage.

Hodges, C, Scullion, R, Jackson, D (2015) "From awww to awe factor: UK audience meaning-making of the 2012 Paralympics as mediated spectacle." *Journal of Popular Television* 3(2): 195–212.

Howe, David. 2008. *The Cultural Politics of the Paralympic Movement*. London: Routledge.

Jhally, Sut. 1989. "Cultural Studies and the Sports/Media Complex." In *Media, Sports & Society*, edited by L. Wenner, 70–97. London: SAGE.

Pullen, Emma, Daniel Jackson, Michael Silk and Richard Scullion. 2019. Re-Presenting the Paralympics: (Contested) Philosophies, Production Practices and the Hypervisibility of

Disability." *Media, Culture & Society* 41 (4): 465–81. doi:10.1177/0163443718799399.

Pullen, Emma, and Michael Silk. 2020. "Gender, Technology and the Ablenational Paralympic Body Politic." *Cultural Studies* 34 (3): 466–88. doi:10.1080/09502386.2019.1621917.

Silva, Carla, and David Howe. 2012. "The (In)Validity of Supercrip Representation of Paralympic Athletes." *Journal of Sport and Social Issues* 36: 174–94. doi:10.1177/0193723511433865.

Tainsky, Scott, Shannon Kerwin, Jie Xu and Yilun Zhou. 2014. "Will the Real Fans Please Remain Seated? Gender and Television Ratings for Pre-Game and Game Broadcasts."

Sport Management Review 17 (2): 190–204. doi:10.1016/j.smr.2013.04.002.

Tang, Tang, and Roger Cooper. 2012. "Gender, Sports and New Media: Predictors of Viewing During the 2008 Beijing Olympics." *Journal of Broadcasting & Electronic Media* 56 (1): 27–91. doi:10.1080/08838151.2011.648685.

Walsh, Alison. 2015. "Out of the Shadows, Into the Light? The Broadcasting Legacy of the 2012 Paralympics for Channel 4." In *Reframing Disability?: Media, (Dis)Empowerment, and Voice in the London Paralympics*, edited by D. Jackson, C. Hodges, M. Molesworth, & R. Scullion, 26–36. London: Routledge.

14. Digital Sociology: Opportunities and Dangers*

Noortje Marres

One of the puzzles of 'digital sociology' is that the label has come into usage only relatively recently: it only started appearing in print towards the end of the 2000s.[1] This is strange because sociologists have studied the role of computational technology in social life and society at large for many decades (Athique, 2013). It was in 1976 that the sociologist Daniel Bell (1976) announced the coming of the post-industrial society, a societal transformation in which the computer and its uptake in industry, government and organizations played a central role. In the new society that was announced by Bell, it was no longer the production of material goods, but information- and data processing that would function as 'the engine' of social transformation. Not just grand theories of society, but also empirical studies of social life, have for many decades already insisted that computational technologies play a formative role in social life. It was almost thirty years ago that Lucy Suchman published *Plans and Situated Actions* (1987), a classic fieldwork study of the interactions between people and computational systems, most notably a 'smart' photocopier, in everyday work places. Suchman's book made the case for a more-than-technological, 'socio-technical' understanding of computational practices and arrangements. Her field studies showed how capacities that are often ascribed to digital technology – such as the ability to represent reality, or to coordinate action – in actuality are the outcomes of social and technical interactions *between* people and machines, as well as with everyday environments and objects.

To be sure, the rise to prominence of personal computing and the widespread uptake of Internet technologies from the 1990s onwards meant that the analysis of the computational society, and of computational social practice, had to be updated. But this job was largely done in the late 1990s and early 2000s, with the appearance of Manuel Castells' *Network Society* (1996) and Miller and Slater's *The Internet: An Ethnographic Approach* (2001). These classic studies broadly followed in the footsteps respectively of Bell and Suchman but showed that after PCs, the Web and e-mail, computerization no longer primarily affected the professional spheres of industry, organizational life and state bureaucracy, as earlier accounts of the computerization of society had argued: computing now came to transform social relations, practices and structures, *in everyday, cultural, political, and public life.* [. . .]

[. . .]

In social research, as in other fields, the idea has taken root that the digital makes possible new ways of contributing to society. Actual efforts to realize this promise of the digital have proven the initial optimism to be partly misguided. One sobering example is the Samaritan Radar, a social media application that was launched by the Samaritans, an important UK suicide prevention agency, in October 2014. At its launch, the tool was introduced as a way of identifying users at

* From Marres, N. (2017) *Digital Sociology: The Reinvention of Social Research* (Cambridge: Polity). Extracts from pp. 12, 7–10, 11.

risk of suicide by way of real-time, textual analysis of Twitter data. Once an 'at risk' account has been detected, the Radar would send a message to the followers of the identified account alerting them and 'offering guidance on the best way of reaching out and providing support'.[2] Perhaps unsurprisingly, the Samaritans were forced to close the experimental service after a short time, and it was subjected to harsh criticisms in both news and online media. Many argued that notifying people's social media contacts of their supposed malaise without prior consent amounted to a 'privacy violation', while some flagged the risk of stigmatization of individuals already deemed 'at risk'. Yet others questioned the hubristic presumption that a complex and sensitive phenomenon like suicide risk could be detected and managed using simple methods of data analytics.[3] Indeed, social researchers could no doubt propose different, better methods to understand and communicate with people in trouble using social media, and providing the impulse to do so could be one positive outcome of this episode.[4] However, the Samaritan Radar debacle also sheds light on a wider, rather diffuse phenomenon, namely the remarkably strong expectations, in our societies, that digital technology will make it possible for social research to help solve social problems.

Digital technology presents an important societal phenomenon today, as popular online platforms like Facebook, smart phones and 'intelligent' computational systems have been taken up across the full breadth of society during the last decade or so, from transport to education, from family life to activism, from prison management to wildlife conservation. Whereas the digital used to refer to a fairly special set of practices, those that early adopters, experts, the 'tech savvy' and the young engaged in, today it touches on most aspects of social life. This development has important implications for sociology. But the ongoing digitization of society does not only present an important topic of investigation, it also has the potential to transform the very role that social research itself plays in society. Across society,

digital infrastructures, devices and practices are widely seen to offer important, new opportunities for making social research relevant to social life (Back, 2012), for turning knowledge about society into action.[5] As I will discuss in this chapter, what distinguishes the digital technologies of today – what sets them apart from the 'Web' and 'information and communication technologies' (ICT) that went before – is their extensive capabilities for monitoring, analysing and informing social life. Today's digital infrastructures, devices and practices collect an abundance of data that can be used to analyse people's interactions and movements, from the SMS exchanges captured by phone companies to the location data amassed through smart phone apps. They also make it possible to translate data analysis into targeted feedback in everyday settings and user activities, from the query terms suggested by search engines, to the personalized updates that are offered by transport and weather apps and other digital services. It is these interactive capacities of digital technology, in combination with its ubiquity in society—the fact that digital technology can appear to be everywhere—that today feed the conviction that the digital makes it possible to re-connect social analysis with social intervention, as in the example of the Samaritan Radar app above.

What makes the digital such a relevant phenomenon for sociology then goes beyond its importance as a research topic. Its contemporary significance must also be understood in terms of the transformations of social research, and of its role in society that it makes possible. These transformations have been described in various ways, but they can be summed up in the belief that social research, through its implementation in computational infrastructures, may gain the capacity to intervene in social life and thereby to address or even solve social problems. The Samaritan Radar project was presented as a way of taking advantage of the widespread uptake of a social media platform like Twitter across society for a progressive purpose, and it did this by outlining a new way of using methods of textual analysis to act on the issue of suicide risk. As such, this project offers a clear demonstration of the belief in the power of the digital to confer onto the analysis of social life the capacity to help solve social problems. However, once the project was underway, multiple challenges to this ambition came into view, such as the risks of privacy violation and stigmatization. Furthermore, as a blogger speculated a few months later, the fact that a suicide prevention agency is monitoring social media might even lead users to practise self-censorship, thereby affecting the very fabric of interaction in these settings.[6] As such, the Samaritan Radar episode can also be interpreted as a kind of 'critical' test of progressive hopes invested in the digital. This is partly what makes it such a relevant case from a sociological perspective.

I would like to argue that the digital today does offer fresh opportunities for connecting social analysis and social intervention, but not in the way in which this promise is usually understood. This is because digital societies are marked by far more complex interactions between social life and knowledge – between social research and social action – than tends to be recognized when data analysis is put forward as a way of acting on social problems. The Samaritan Radar episode highlighted some of these more complex dynamics. This tool did not only facilitate interaction – feedback – in the technical sense of sending a notification to an identified user's social media contacts. It also brought into relief more comprehensive forms of interaction between social research and social life. When the monitoring and analysis of everyday activities is used as a basis for intervention into these activities, a complex set of exchanges between knowledge and behaviour is set in motion, as the public debate that followed on the launch of Samaritan Radar also highlighted. When users are identified as a 'suicide risk', this designation may initiate a dynamic in which social concepts – like 'suicide risk' – and social life inter-react: once individuals (as well as others) are 'aware of how they are classified', this produces a situation in which these actors are likely to 'modify their

behavior accordingly', to quote the description that social theorist and philosopher Ian Hacking (2000, p. 32) has provided of what he calls the 'interactivity' between social research and social life. This type of transformative effect, by which the description of a social situation transforms that situation, has long been of special concern to sociologists and philosophers (Thomas and Thomas, 1928; Becker, 1963). As I will discuss in what follows, one of the key questions that arises in digital societies is how computational forms of interaction at work here combine with sociological dynamics of interactivity between knowledge and social life.

[. . .] Interactivity – in the broad sense of exchange and traffic between the analysis of activities and those activities themselves presents a crucial sociological dynamic. Indeed, in the classic view of the early twentieth-century sociologist Max Weber (1905/1968), this is the defining challenge of social science. As Weber famously noted, what distinguishes social enquiry from other forms of research is that it must contend with the fact that the ideas people have about the social world interact with what happens in it. As sociologists have since argued, social research presents a special form of knowledge insofar as it is *inherently interactive*: social research must expect, and indeed anticipate, that knowledge about social life and social life itself mutually influence one another (Cicourel, 1964). This is also to say that social dynamics of interactivity are not at all new in themselves. However, in today's digital societies, technology must increasingly be factored into these complex processes. Remarkably, however, while there has been much interest in the new ways of knowing society that digital technology makes possible, both inside and outside the university, the complex interactions between digital technology, social research and social life have received much less attention. [. . .]

[. . .] I will provide an overview of this emerging work on digital sociology, with a special focus on the claim that the digitization of society makes possible a new way of knowing and intervening in society. The chapter situates this claim in relation to longstanding engagements in sociology with computational technologies, as both an object and instrument of social enquiry. By considering recent interest in digital sociology against this historical backdrop, we are able to move beyond two equally dissatisfying claims: the claim that the digital ways of knowing society emerging today present a radically innovative form of knowledge, as some advocates of the 'new' computational social science have suggested; but also beyond the claim that there is nothing new about digital sociology, that it is basically 'old sociology' with a few new 'sexy' but superficial and unconvincing technological features built in.

Rather, the research practices that today go by the name of 'digital sociology' contain both old and new elements – old and new techniques, methods, concepts, sources of data, and forms of intervention (Latour et al., 2012; Watts, 2004; Law and Ruppert, 2013; MacKenzie et al., 2015). This insight will allow us to confront a different set of questions from those pushed into the foreground by the opposition between the old and the new. The question for digital sociology is not only whether today's digital societies give rise to new social forms or give us more of the same, or whether digital sociology presents a new or an old way of knowing society. We must equally consider whether and how 'the digital' entails changes in the relations *between* technologies and social life; *between* knowledge, society and technology. Indeed, I want to argue that it may be ultimately more productive to adopt the latter, relational perspective. We will need to come to terms with these changing relations if we are serious about deploying digital technologies for progressive purposes. Today's digital transformations invoke important debates from sociology's past and about the role of ideas and technology in social life. I would like to show how digital transformations render these sociological traditions newly relevant to contemporary problems. And that they do so in ways that challenge us to develop a more 'technology-aware' way of understanding social life.

NOTES

1. One of the first written occurrences is in the title of an article by Wynn (2009) in *Sociological Forum*, which deals with the question of how sociologists can use digital formats like blogging in their teaching.
2. 'Samaritans launches Twitter app to help identify vulnerable people.' Samaritans, 29 October, 2014. At the time of writing, it was announced that Facebook launched a next iteration of this service, developed in collaboration with Samaritans, 19 February 2016. http://www.bbc.co.uk/newsbeat/article/35608276/facebook-adds-new-suicide-prevention-tool-in-the-uk
3. McVeigh, K. (2014) Samaritans Twitter app identifying user's moods criticized as invasive, 4 November, http://www.theguardian.com/society/2014/nov/04/samaritans-twitter-app-mental-health-depression. Thanks to Nissa Ramsay for drawing my attention to the Samaritans Radar controversy.
4. Not coincidentally, one the most famous demonstrations of sociology's capacity to produce distinctive knowledge about social problems – by the early twentieth century French sociologist Émile Durkheim – had suicide risk as its topic. However, here I draw on different sociological traditions, those building on interpretative sociology, pragmatism and symbolic interactionism, to explore what a sociological study of 'suicide risk' in digital societies might involve and would need to consider.
5. 'Turning knowledge into action' was the phrase used in 2008 by the info-activist organization The Tactical Technology Collective to describe their data visualization toolkit for advocacy organizations.
6. Anonymous, 'Goodbye Samaritans Radar. . . . Hello Facebook Report Button', Purple Persuasion blog, 11 March 2015 https://purplepersuasion.wordpress.com/2015/03/11/goodbye-samaritans-radar-hello-facebook-report-button/

REFERENCES

Athique, A. (2013). *Digital Media and Society: An Introduction*. Cambridge: Polity.

Back, L. (2012). Live sociology: social research and its futures. *The Sociological Review, 60*(S1): 18–39.

Bell, D. (1976). The coming of the post-industrial society. *The Educational Forum*, 40 (4): 574–9.

Castells, M. (1996). *The Rise of the Network Society: The Information Age: Economy, Society, and Culture* (Vol. 1). New York: John Wiley and Sons.

Cicourel, A. V. (1964). *Method and Measurement in Sociology*. New York: Free Press.

Hacking, I (2000). *The Social Construction of What?* Cambridge, MA: Harvard University Press.

Latour, B., Jensen, P., Venturini, T., Grauwin, S. and Boullier, D. (2012). 'The whole is always smaller than its parts' – a digital test of Gabriel Tardes' monads. *The British Journal of Sociology, 63*(4): 590–615.

Law, J. and Ruppert, E. (2013). The social life of methods: Devices. *Journal of Cultural Economy, 6*(3): 229–40.

Mackenzie, A., Mills, R., Sharples, S., Fuller, M. and Goffey, A. (2015). Digital sociology in the field of devices. *Routledge International Handbook of the Sociology of Art and Culture*, L. Hanquinet and M Savage (eds). London: Routledge: pp. 367–382.

Miller, D. and D. Slater (2001). *The Internet: An Ethnographic Approach*. Oxford: Berg.

Suchman, L. A. (1987). *Plans and Situated Actions: The Problem of Human-Machine Communication*. Cambridge: Cambridge University Press.

Watts, D. (2004). The 'new' science of networks. *Annual Review of Sociology* (30): 243–270.

Weber, M. (1968 (1905)). *Economy and Society: An Outline of Interpretative Sociology*. Berkeley and Los Angeles: University of California Press.

Wynn, J. R. (2009). Digital sociology: Emergent technologies in the field and the classroom. *Sociological Forum* 24, (2): 448–56.

15. What is Feminist Research?*

Patricia Leavy and Anne Harris

Beginning with the status of girls and women, but not ending there, feminism is an engaged human rights position that seeks to expose and remedy gender inequities. The study of gender, as a starting point for approaching feminist research, cannot be understood without consideration of other aspects of human existence that influence the ways in which human beings interact socially, including race, physical ability, class, geolocations, and sexuality. We are not bodies that are only gendered, but rather, we simultaneously occupy race, ethnicity, social class, sexuality, and other positionalities. Feminist research recognizes the inescapable need to approach the study of gender in a way that recognizes the simultaneous nature of our complex selves, and the ways in which multiple aspects of privilege or oppression are being exercised at once.

[. . .]

As you might imagine, **gender** is central to defining what feminist research does and believes, yet gender is not the only focus of feminist research. These intersectional commitments of feminist research as a field constitute a **feminist research ethics**—the political, methodological, and in some cases spiritual beliefs that underpin this area of scholarly research. But this feminist research ethics is not just an abstract idea—it

points to additional feminist concerns, including ontology (the nature of knowledge itself), epistemology (what counts as knowledge and how that knowledge is represented), and methodology (the theories and tools of doing research). As a critical research approach it also suggests a range of ways in which feminist researchers believe in changing the world. "Critical" in this sense does not imply "to criticize," but rather to *challenge* the status quo. Feminist research is by its nature a critical research approach, because it challenges the gender-based inequities that are still pervasive around the globe. For example, the gender pay gap (unequal pay for equal work, based on gender) is a social justice issue concerning both gender *and* economics. But gender pay inequity is an issue that also intersects with geography, race, religion, and other conditions. [. . .]

[. . .]

Feminist research is no longer a singular field, if ever it was. From the vast and sweeping range of its diverse core concepts, concerns, leading figures, and guiding principle, feminist research praxis is—more than ever—a multiplicity, a bridge across difference and a thread between perspectives. It questions in new ways for this era the very notions of truth and truth claims, multiple perspectives, and the knowledge creation that sits at the heart of research practices. Feminist scholarship is no longer defined only as research that concerns itself with gender, but a component of all scholarship concerned with

* From Leavy, P. and Harris, A. (2019) *Contemporary Feminist Research from Theory to Practice* (New York: Guilford Press). Extracts from pp. 4–5, 12–13, 16–20.

social change and its real-world applications. Indeed, feminist scholar Elizabeth Grosz argues that any contemporary social justice research agenda or project must address how understandings of freedom are now fundamentally linked to "our habitual relations to the material world, [and] may serve feminist and other radical political thought" (2011, p. 5). These kinds of approaches to feminist research highlight the ways in which its disciplinarity and theoretical multiplicity make feminism a most generative and exciting area of contemporary social research today.

Feminist Research Similarities and Differences

There are vast differences across the current feminist research landscape between more established and emergent feminist scholars from every field and methodological approach. One established leader in feminist research, Alison Jaggar, and her pivotal contribution *Just Methods: An Interdisciplinary Feminist Reader* (2014), are significant for the ways in which they advance feminist research, interweaving methods, disciplines, approaches, and their interrelationship with issues of power and research ethics. Jaggar's text (and Halsanger, 2005, among others), like this one, focuses on research methodologies, epistemologies, and dissemination through (and beyond) public and popular cultural channels, yet ours also offers readers a critical discussion of the transformative potential of digital and social media.

Others have moved non-Western feminisms forward over the past 15 years in exciting and expansive ways.[1] Still others continue to expand more traditional approaches to feminist research subdisciplines, including Sprague's [2016] comprehensive attention to positivist and sociological theories and methods. One thing is for sure: feminist research has never been more alive and diverse, in part due to the proliferation of forms of research output and dissemination, but also due to the political and socioeconomic moment in which we find ourselves. [...]

[...]

A Brief History of the Field

The feminist philosopher Megan Boler (1997) noted that

> Radical feminism's challenge to the gendered spheres of "public vs. private" has forever changed Western thought, culture and legislative, judicial and political paradigms.... The radical feminist slogan "the personal is political" symbolized the revolutionary reconceptualization of what counts as personal (women's lives, feelings, experience, and labor) and what counts as political (e.g., men's experience and rationality as the governing structure of political and public spaces). The emphasis on women's experiences, including her feelings, as *political* and not merely personal, was a key feature of the radical feminist agenda. (p. 113)

Some feminist scholars still question whether we have progressed beyond arguing for the political importance of women's experiences, observations, scholarship, and other feminist human capital, which continues to be sidelined or invisibilized in the academy. Today, feminist scholarship still systematically argues the possibilities and problematic of women's feelings (and emotions and feeling more generally) as "valid" research and posits their place in rigorous scholarship.

Contemporary feminist research includes now well-worn questions about the defining of feminist theory, as well as the "doing" of feminist research. Is there a feminist method? it asks. Indeed, feminism in qualitative, quantitative, arts-based, participatory, and other emergent paradigms continues to demand attention to how feminist approaches and lenses might help us think differently about a range of age-old questions. What is the role of feminism in the great range of so-called scientific research? How might feminist and decolonial geographies be changing and promise to accelerate in this change over the next ecologically unstable 20 or 30 years?

Margaret Somerville and other scholars of space, place, and belonging continue to look to nonhuman others for multisensory answers to (or further questions for) these investigations. Feminist new materialism, posthumanism, and new hybrid forms of feminist research are appearing in works like Anna Hickey-Moody's "femifesta" feminist manifesto for arts education in *Posthuman Research Practices in Education* (Taylor & Hughes, 2016) and beyond. But even a cursory glance through scholarship limited to the human world (and not concerned with the posthuman or more-than-human) reveals an ever greater diversity of platforms, approaches, and subjectivities: as just one example, transgender and disgender feminisms are in dynamic conversation as never before.

The Early Years

When feminism as a scholarly field began around the beginning of the 1970s, the emphasis was firmly fixed on "sex differences and the extent to which such differences might be based on the biological properties of individuals" (Sprague, 2016, p. vii). Fifteen years later, however, by feminist research's second stage, "the focus [had] shifted to the individual sex roles and socialization, exposing gender as the product of specific social arrangements, although still conceptualizing it as an individual trait" (Sprague, 2016, p. vii). The so-classed third stage of feminist research is typified by a

> Recognition of the centrality of gender as an organizing principle in all social systems, including work, politics, everyday interaction, families, economic development, law, education, and a host of other social domains. As our understanding of gender has become more social, so has our awareness that gender is experienced and organized in race- and class-specific ways. (Sprague, 2016, p. vii)

If epistemology is the study of theories of knowledge, *feminist* epistemology is the study of knowledge from a feminist perspective; that is, the production of knowledge through a feminist lens. In this volume, we address both epistemology and ontology, interrelated aspects of research knowledge creation that are both pivotal in understanding exactly why feminism in research has been so fundamentally challenging to the academic establishment.

This chapter (and this book) offers researchers an accessible approach to understanding feminist epistemologies and ontologies, or what some feminist researchers refer to as "onto-epistemologies,"[2] and their implications. In what ways is gender "experienced and organized"? – in *all ways*. To that end, the remainder of this chapter is devoted to a brief overview of the ways in which feminism has moved beyond a field of research and proliferated as an epistemological lens through which researchers can both *see* and *do* any and all kinds of research. Throughout this chapter's overview of pivotal moments and key figures are scattered highlights of field-defining epistemologies and conceptual leaps that have moved the field forward and expanded it outward like the circles that emanate from a stone tossed into a pond.

Feminist Research Leaps Forward

One pivotal example of this widening out of feminist lenses into all realms of research is the work of educational, race, feminist, and social justice scholar Cynthia Dillard [. . .]. Dillard's concept of an endarkened feminist epistemology addresses identity, difference, and the politics of representation through the field of education by offering a critical theoretical lens through which readers see how these areas of study are impossible to disentangle.

Patti Lather (2008), a noted feminist scholar in her own right, has paid homage to Cynthia Dillard's work in noting the ways it has crossed educational, racialized, and gendered boundaries, enriching multidisciplinary research as it goes. For example, even though Dillard's primary discipline is education and literacy, her particular way of approaching the study of literacies and education has influenced critical race theory (the study of the impact of race on all walks of life), feminism, and qualitative research[3] more generally. Through Lather's own notion of "getting lost as a methodology" (Lather, 2007), she seeks to clarify from Dillard's work what a "feminist epistemology" actually might look and move like. To do so, she draws on the foundational queer and gender theorist Eve Kosofsky Sedgwick's (1997) notion of "reparative critique." In this example, we purposefully link three pivotal feminist scholars whose works are in conversation with one another in order to begin highlighting the genealogy of a field that some still claim has no discernible scholarly history or trajectory of its own.

Feminist research has rapidly evolved and promises new directions in a 21st-century research landscape that is increasingly concerned with feminist geographies, posthuman others, and gender-expansive borders. In addition to Judith Butler, Donna Haraway (and others, discussed in detail in Chapters 3 and 4), Sedgwick can be counted among the foundational scholars of a 21st-century feminist scholarship, and one whose works have been applied in diverse ways by those like Dillard working cross-disciplinarily.

Lather (2008) values, as we do, the ways in which Dillard's work "examines the 'life notes' of three African American female academics in order to develop a cultural standpoint epistemology out of the intersectionalities of identities 'and the historical and contemporary contexts of oppression and resistance' for such women (Dillard, 2000: 661)" (p. 219). Out her own cultural, racial, and gendered experience and scholarship, Dillard positions her "endarkened feminist epistemology" as a tool for moving toward more ethical, decolonizing methodologies (Tuhiwai Smith, 1999) and away from traditional Western ways of knowing. Decolonizing methodologies refer to the intersections of imperialism and research and make transparent the ways in which imperialism is embedded in scholarly work, and

what is considered scholarly knowledge. Dillard's work is just one example of the layered and multidisciplinary nature of contemporary feminist research.

Like feminist scholars writing from queer, (dis)ability, and religiously minoritarian subjectivities, Dillard (and Lather in discussing her) advocate a more transparent and critically self-reflexive acknowledgment of the intersectionalities of our research selves and projects, which shape our (and all) research agendas; one tool offered by Dillard in practical terms is her "six assumptions to guide culturally relevant inquiry" (in Lather, 2008, p. 219). We highlight this part of Dillard's work to make particular note of the need for both theoretically robust and practically efficient tools in feminist research and scholarship, a goal toward which this book contributes.

Tracking Innovations

Other important feminist scholarship innovations in the late 20th and early 21st centuries include feminist science, physics and its evolution into/ with **new materialist theory** (which looks at the independent agency of nonhuman objects and subjects), **posthumanism** (scholarship focused on the more-than-human), **postfeminism** (evolutions in feminist social codes), **affect theory** (study of emotions and feelings), and **digital feminism** (online and off-line), all of which will be explored in detail throughout the subsequent chapters.

Much feminist scholarship over the past 20 years can be characterized by either a social science approach or a postmodern one (see Chapters 3 and 4 for more on this). This volume, like any comprehensive feminist research text today, includes discussions of feminist standpoints, feminist ethnography, postmodern, poststructural, and critical epistemologies, social movement research, activism, globalization and globalizing feminist research, health and social work, feminist pedagogies and praxis, authority and representation in feminist research, science and feminism, and gender diversity. We note the value of, and need to be in, dialogue with a wide range of research and teaching perspectives, student perspectives, policy makers and activists—as all contemporary research and research texts must be, whether they are methodological or conceptual (Sprague, 2016; Hesse-Biber, 2012).

We also want to highlight that the nature of feminist knowledge production is inherently global, and decentred from traditional White, Western, global North, and often still male producers of "legitimate" academic knowledge.

It's a great time to be a feminist researcher. Just at the time when a notion of "postfeminism" seems to suggest that we have attained our goals and feminism is no longer needed, along comes a proliferation of antifeminist and antiwomen backlash, bringing a rich tide of new feminist research and passion.

NOTES

1. See, for example, Lee-Koo and D'Costa (2008), who use feminist frameworks and research to address feminism and activism to internationl contexts, in an edited volume focused solely on the Asia-Pacific, a most welcome contribution.

2. The term was coined (or at least conjoined) by new materialist scholar Karen Barad, who has theorized a concept of agential realism. She argues that the theoretic is at once an epistemology (theory of knowing), an ontology (theory of being), and an ethics. They are mutually informing, and co-constructive, so she uses "onto-epistemology" to represent their interdependence.

3. Most research today falls into two main "paradigms" or structural ways of doing things: qualitative and quantitative (although scholars including the co-authors have noted that arts-based research offers a new paradigm that goes beyond this simple binarism, while other scholars are developing the notion of post-qualitative research as well). Qualitative research primarily attends to small, in-depth studies at the individual level and gathers information that is not in numerical form, for example, diary accounts, open-ended questionnaires, unstructured interviews, and unstructured observations. Quantitative data is usually numerical (statistical) and more focused on large-scale studies, large data sets, and generalizable claims. As shorthand, many say qualitative research "goes deep," while quantitative research "goes wide."

REFERENCES

Boler, M. (1999). *Feeling power: Emotions and education*. New York: Routledge.

Dillard, C. B. (2000). The substance of things hoped for, the evidence of things not seen: Examining an endarkened feminist epistemology in educational research and leadership. *International Journal of Qualitative Studies in Education*, *13*(6), 661–681.

Grosz, E. (2011). *Becoming undone: Darwinian reflections on life, politics and art*. Durham, NC: Duke University Press.

Halsanger, S. (Ed.). (2005). *Theorizing feminisms: A reader*. Oxford: Oxford University Press.

Hesse-Biber, S. N. (2012). *The handbook of feminist research theory and praxis* (2nd ed.). London: SAGE.

Jaggar, A. M. (Ed.). (2014) *Just methods: An interdisciplinary feminist reader* (2nd ed.). New York: Pluto Press.

Lather, P. (2007). *Getting Lost: Feminist efforts towards a double(d) science*. Albany: State University of New York Press.

Lather, P. (2008). Getting lost: critiquing across difference as methodological practice. In K. Gallagher (Ed.), *The methodological dilemma: Creative, critical and collaborative approaches to qualitative research* (pp. 219–231). Abingdon, VA: Routledge.

Lee-Koo, K., & D'Costa, B. (2008). *Gender and global politics in the Asia Pacific*. New York: Palgrave Macmillan.

Sedgwick, E. K. (1997). Paranoid reading and reparative reading, or, you're so paranoid, you probably think this introduction is about you. In E. K. Sedgwick (ed.)., *Novel gazing: Queer readings in fiction* (pp. 123–151). Durham, NC: Duke University Press.

Sprague, J. (2016) *Feminist methodologies for critical researchers: Bridging differences* (2nd ed.). London: Rowman & Littlefield.

Taylor, C. A., & Hughes, C. (2016) *Posthuman research practices in education*. London: Palgrave Macmillan.

Tuhiwai Smith, L. (1999). *Decolonizing methodologies: Research and indigenous peoples*. Dunedin: University of Otago Press.

Part 2 – Further reading

An engaging 'methods' text based on a narrative approach that intriguingly uses stories is McDonough, B. (2020) *Flying Aeroplanes and Other Sociological Tales: An Introduction to Sociology and Research Methods* (Abingdon: Routledge). Bryman, A. (2016) *Social Research Methods* (5th edn, Oxford: Oxford University Press) is a more conventional text, but none the worse for that, as it is an excellent introduction. An up-to-date account of how research methods have changed in contemporary sociological research is Kara, H. (2016) *Creative Research Methods in the Social Sciences: A Practical Guide* (Bristol: Policy Press).

Sociology, 9th edition

Chapter 2 is the obvious place to go, though chapter 3, 'Theories and Perspectives', should also be useful, as there are clear links between theoretical perspectives and their preferred methodologies. Also, every chapter review section includes research studies, and it is worth working through these on subjects of interest.

Part 3 Environment and Urbanism

The emergence and rapid growth of modern cities and urban environments during the late nineteenth and early twentieth century fascinated many sociologists and divided opinion. Some saw urbanization as destroying longstanding communities and ways of life, but others focused on the liberating new opportunities that were opening up. This combination of extremes – more freedom and independence, but with the constant threat of this tipping over into isolation and loneliness – is still with us today. Yet we are now much more aware of environmental issues and the human impact on the natural world, and more sociologists are interested in society–environment interactions. Our readings in this section cover established work on urban life and more recent interest in the natural environment.

How does life in large cities differ from that in towns and villages? How do people cope with the stresses and strains of life in the most densely populated areas? One of the first sociologists to explore these questions was Georg Simmel, whose brief account of life in the modern metropolis has become a classic. Writing at the start of the twentieth century, Simmel brings out some of the ways that city dwellers adapt and cope. City living overloads the senses with stimuli from all directions – shops and window displays, dense populations, bright lights, signals and signs, vehicles, a cacophony of noise and a multitude of smells – all of which combine to make the city an exciting place. Yet it

is also an environment that can drain our energy and force us to 'switch off' just to get through the day. Simmel argues that the way to survive all this is effectively to block out some of it to preserve our psychic health and energy. Simmel drew on his experience of Berlin, an expanding city that by twenty-first-century standards was relatively small, and the extent to which his analysis could be extended to cities in the Global South must be questioned. However, the social-psychological insights he provided still capture something of the quality of urban living in many of the world's large cities.

Since the 1970s, environmentalists and 'green' campaigners have voiced strong criticisms of cities because of their destruction of the natural environment. Since the 1980s, interest in the natural environment has hesitantly entered sociology. It took sociologists some time to appreciate just how significant environmental issues might be. Today there is little doubt that environmental issues are both caused (in part) by and have deleterious consequences for societies and can no longer be ignored. The most obvious sign of this is in the subject of global warming. In Reading 17, John Urry examines the various ways that sociology can contribute to our understanding of the causes of climate change and in the assessment of various schemes to tackle it. One under-researched area he highlights is that of energy generation and resource use, which has long been the province of economics. Urry argues that the urgent need to deal with global warming means that sociologists need to take a much stronger interest in the energy-base of societies and its social and environmental consequences.

Sociological work on the quality of life in cities has produced some insightful general findings, but the urban experience clearly differs in significant ways across a range of social divisions, such as class position, gender, race and ethnicity. For example, studies in the USA have found that some neighbourhoods are segregated along racial lines, with distinct 'white' and 'black' spaces, though there are also mixed 'cosmopolitan' areas. Elijah Anderson's study, Reading 18, explores the way that the growth of a large black middle class has highlighted racialized city spaces and their consequences. Anderson argues that US society has many overwhelmingly white neighbourhoods, in which black people are just not expected and are marginalized when they are present. Conversely, black people often consider these places as 'the white space', an environment to be approached with care and one that leads to feelings of unease. Perceptions of the urban black ghetto have taken on an iconic status in the USA, and its negative connotations continue to inform and reinforce stereotypical assumptions about black people. Hence, many middle-class black people still find themselves rendered invisible or treated with suspicion, especially when navigating the white space. Anderson sees this as the basis of a new form of symbolic racism, long after the physical ghetto has been eliminated, which still carries the potential to stigmatize black people.

Urban sociology and studies of the character of urban life have long been dominated by research in the industrialized societies of the Global North, such as London, New York, Paris and Berlin. Indeed, generations of sociologists have been schooled in the classic works of Simmel, the Chicago School, Richard Sennett and others working out of the high-income group of advanced economies. More recently attention has shifted to the developing cities and urban regions in the Global South and the extent to which these can or should be studied with the same set of concepts, theories and methodologies that were previously adopted. Our reading from Simone and Pieterse is a social scientific and polemical piece that examines both the experience of urban life for the diverse range of social groups in African and Asian cities and the structural relationships that shape urbanization processes. In doing so, the authors highlight some of the misleading assumptions about cities in the South and suggest ways in which academics can engage with multiple research methods to reach a better understanding.

We end the section with a paper that considers whether we are entering, or have already entered, a new era for the planet. In recent years, prompted by growing evidence of human-induced global warming, there have been several attempts to theorize a new geophysical era known as the Anthropocene. This is said to be a new age in which global humanity has become *the* defining force acting to shape the planetary system. Rolf Lidskog and Claire Waterton note that the concept envisages a shift from an era we know pretty well – the Holocene – to a much more uncertain age that will require interdisciplinary research to reach a better understanding. Such a move has long been a fundamental tenet of environmental sociology, though, in practice, the amount of inter- or multi-disciplinary work has been limited. While welcoming discussions about the Anthropocene, the authors suggest that a 'cautious welcome' would be prudent. This is because there is a risk that its basis in the earth sciences may lead in the direction of 'naturalizing' social and political life, a form of reductionism long resisted in the social sciences. Nonetheless, given the recognition of the power of global humanity to shape natural systems, environmental sociology ought to be at the centre of scholarly attempts to understand the Anthropocene era.

16. The Metropolis and Mental Life*

Georg Simmel

The deepest problems of modern life flow from the attempt of the individual to maintain the independence and individuality of his existence against the sovereign powers of society, against the weight of the historical heritage and the external culture and technique of life. This antagonism represents the most modern form of the conflict which primitive man must carry on with nature for his own bodily existence. The eighteenth century may have called for liberation from all the ties which grew up historically in politics, in religion, in morality and in economics in order to permit the original natural virtue of man, which is equal in everyone, to develop without inhibition; the nineteenth century may have sought to promote, in addition to man's freedom, his individuality (which is connected with the division of labour) and his achievements which make him unique and indispensable but which at the same time make him so much the more dependent on the complementary activity of others; Nietzsche may have seen the relentless struggle of the individual as the prerequisite for his full development, while socialism found the same thing in the suppression of all competition – but in each of these the same fundamental motive was at work, namely the resistance of the individual to being levelled, swallowed up in the social-technological mechanism. [. . .]

* From Simmel, G. (1903) 'The Metropolis and Mental Life' in G. Bridge and S. Watson (Eds) *The Blackwell City Reader* (Malden, MA: Blackwell Publishing): 11–19. Extracts from pp. 11–15.

The psychological foundation, upon which the metropolitan individuality is erected, is the intensification of emotional life due to the swift and continuous shift of external and internal stimuli. Man is a creature whose existence is dependent on differences, i.e. his mind is stimulated by the difference between present impressions and those which have preceded. Lasting impressions, the slightness in their differences, the habituated regularity of their course and contrasts between them, consume, so to speak, less mental energy than the rapid telescoping of changing images, pronounced differences within what is grasped at a single glance, and the unexpectedness of violent stimuli. To the extent that the metropolis creates these psychological conditions – with every crossing of the street, with the tempo and multiplicity of economic, occupational and social life – it creates in the sensory foundations of mental life, and in the degree of awareness necessitated by our organization as creatures dependent on differences, a deep contrast with the slower, more habitual, more smoothly flowing rhythm of the sensory-mental phase of small town and rural existence. Thereby the essentially intellectualistic character of the mental life of the metropolis becomes intelligible as over against that of the small town which rests more on feelings and emotional relationships. These latter are rooted in the unconscious levels of the mind and develop most readily in the steady equilibrium of unbroken customs. The locus of reason, on the other hand, is in the lucid, conscious upper strata of the mind and it is the most adaptable of our inner forces. In order to adjust itself to the shifts and contradictions in events, it does not require the disturbances and inner upheavals which are the only means whereby more conservative personalities are able to adapt themselves to the same rhythm of events. Thus the metropolitan type – which naturally takes on a thousand individual modifications – creates a protective organ for itself against the profound disruption with which the fluctuations and discontinuities of the external milieu threaten it. Instead of reacting emotionally, the metropolitan type reacts primarily in a rational manner, thus creating a mental predominance through the intensification of consciousness, which in turn is caused by it. Thus the reaction of the metropolitan person to those events is moved to a sphere of mental activity which is least sensitive and which is furthest removed from the depths of the personality.

This intellectualistic quality which is thus recognized as a protection of the inner life against the domination of the metropolis, becomes ramified into numerous specific phenomena. The metropolis has always been the seat of money economy because the many-sidedness and concentration of commercial activity have given the medium of exchange an importance which it could not have acquired in the commercial aspects of rural life. But money economy and the domination of the intellect stand in the closest relationship to one another. They have in common a purely matter-of-fact attitude in the treatment of persons and things in which a formal justice is often combined with an unrelenting hardness. The purely intellectualistic person is indifferent to all things personal because, out of them, relationships and reactions develop which are not to be completely understood by purely rational methods – just as the unique element in events never enters into the principle of money. Money is concerned only with what is common to all, i.e. with the exchange value which reduces all quality and individuality to a purely quantitative level. All emotional relationships between persons rest on their individuality, whereas intellectual relationships deal with persons as with numbers, that is, as with elements which, in themselves, are indifferent, but

which are of interest only insofar as they offer something objectively perceivable. It is in this very manner that the inhabitant of the metropolis reckons with his merchant, his customer and with his servant, and frequently with the persons with whom he is thrown into obligatory association. These relationships stand in distinct contrast with the nature of the smaller circle in which the inevitable knowledge of individual characteristics produces, with an equal inevitability, an emotional tone in conduct, a sphere which is beyond the mere objective weighting of tasks performed and payments made. What is essential here as regards the economic-psychological aspect of the problem is that in less advanced cultures production was for the customer who ordered the product so that the producer and the purchaser knew one another. The modern city, however, is supplied almost exclusively by production for the market, that is, for entirely unknown purchasers who never appear in the actual field of vision of the producers themselves. Thereby, the interests of each party acquire a relentless matter-of-factness, and its rationally calculated economic egoism need not fear any divergence from its set path because of the imponderability of personal relationships. This is all the more the case in the money economy which dominates the metropolis in which the last remnants of domestic production and direct barter of goods have been eradicated and in which the amount of production on direct personal order is reduced daily. Furthermore, this psychological intellectualistic attitude and the money economy are in such close integration that no one is able to say whether it was the former that effected the latter or vice versa. [. . .]

[. . .] The modern mind has become more and more a calculating one. The calculating exactness of practical life which has resulted from a money economy corresponds to the ideal of natural science, namely that of transforming the world into an arithmetical problem and of fixing every one of its parts in a mathematical formula. It has been money economy which has thus filled the daily life of so many people with weighing, calculating, enumerating and the reduction of qualitative values to quantitative terms. Because of the character of calculability which money has there has come into the relationships of the elements of life a precision and a degree of certainty in the definition of the equalities and inequalities and an unambiguousness in agreements and arrangements, just as externally this precision has been brought about through the general diffusion of pocket watches. It is, however, the conditions of the metropolis which are cause as well as effect for this essential characteristic. The relationships and concerns of the typical metropolitan resident are so manifold and complex that, especially as a result of the agglomeration of so many persons with such differentiated interests, their relationships and activities intertwine with one another into a many-membered organism. In view of this fact, the lack of the most exact punctuality in promises and performances would cause the whole to breakdown into an inextricable chaos. If all the watches in Berlin suddenly went wrong in different ways even only as much as an hour, its entire economic and commercial life would be derailed for some time. Even though this may seem more superficial in its significance, it transpires that the magnitude of distances results in making all waiting and the breaking of appointments an ill-afforded waste of time. For this reason the technique of metropolitan life in general is not conceivable without all of its activities and reciprocal relationships being organized and coordinated in the most punctual way into a firmly fixed framework of time which transcends all subjective elements. But here too there emerge those conclusions which are in general the whole task of this discussion, namely, that every event, however restricted to this superficial level it may appear, comes immediately into contact with the depths of the soul, and that the most banal externalities are, in the last analysis, bound up with the final decisions concerning the meaning and the style of life. Punctuality, calculability and exactness, which are required by the complications and extensiveness of metropolitan life, are not only most intimately connected with

its capitalistic and intellectualistic character but also colour the content of life and are conductive to the exclusion of those irrational, instinctive, sovereign human traits and impulses which originally seek to determine the form of life from within instead of receiving it from the outside in a general, schematically precise form. [. . .]

The same factors which, in the exactness and the minute precision of the form of life, have coalesced into a structure of the highest impersonality, have on the other hand, an influence in a highly personal direction. There is perhaps no psychic phenomenon which is so unconditionally reserved to the city as the blasé outlook. It is at first the consequence of those rapidly shifting stimulations of the nerves which are thrown together in all their contrasts and from which it seems to us the intensification of metropolitan intellectuality seems to be derived. On that account it is not likely that stupid persons who have been hitherto intellectually dead will be blasé. Just as an immoderately sensuous life makes one blasé because it stimulates the nerves to their utmost reactivity until they finally can no longer produce any reaction at all, so, less harmful stimuli, through the rapidity and the contradictoriness of their shifts, force the nerves to make such violent responses, tear them about so brutally that they exhaust their last reserves of strength and, remaining in the same milieu, do not have time for new reserves to form. This incapacity to react to new stimulations with the required amount of energy constitutes in fact that blasé attitude which every child of a large city evinces when compared with the products of the more peaceful and more stable milieu.

Combined with this physiological source of the blasé metropolitan attitude there is another, which derives from a money economy. The essence of the blasé attitude is an indifference toward the distinctions between things. Not in the sense that they are not perceived, as is the case of mental dullness, but rather that the meaning and the value of the distinctions between things, and therewith of the things themselves, are experienced as meaningless. They appear to the blasé person in a homogeneous, flat and grey colour with no one of them worthy of being preferred to another. This psychic mood is the correct subjective reflection of a complete money economy to the extent that money takes the place of all the manifoldness of things and expresses all qualitative distinctions between them in the distinction of how much. To the extent that money, with its colourlessness and its indifferent quality, can become a common denominator of all values, it becomes the frightful leveller – it hollows out the core of things, their peculiarities, their specific values and their uniqueness and incomparability in a way which is beyond repair. They all float with the same specific gravity in the constantly moving stream of money. They all rest on the same level and are distinguished only by their amounts. In individual cases this colouring, or rather this de-colouring of things, through their equation with money, may be imperceptibly small. In the relationship, however, which the wealthy person has to objects which can be bought for money, perhaps indeed in the total character which, for this reason, public opinion now recognizes in these objects, it takes on very considerable proportions. This is why the metropolis is the seat of commerce and it is in it that the purchasability of things appears in quite a different aspect than in simpler economies. It is also the peculiar seat of the blasé attitude. In it is brought to a peak, in a certain way, that achievement in the concentration of purchasable things which stimulates the individual to the highest degree of nervous energy. Through the mere quantitative intensification of the same conditions this achievement is transformed into its opposite, into this peculiar adaptive phenomenon – the blasé attitude – in which the nerves reveal their final possibility of adjusting themselves to the content and the form of metropolitan life by renouncing the response to them. We see that the self-preservation of certain types of personalities is obtained at the cost of devaluing the entire objective world, ending inevitably in dragging the personality downward into a feeling of its own valuelessness.

Whereas the subject of this form of existence must come to terms with it for himself, his self-preservation in the face of the great city requires of him a no less negative type of social conduct. The mental attitude of the people of the metropolis to one another may be designated formally as one of reserve. If the unceasing external contact of numbers of persons in the city should be met by the same number of inner reactions as in the small town, in which one knows almost every person he meets and to each of whom he has a positive relationship, one would be completely atomized internally and would fall into an unthinkable mental condition. Partly this psychological circumstance and partly the privilege of suspicion which we have in the face of the elements of metropolitan life (which are constantly touching one another in fleeting contact) necessitates in us that reserve, in consequence of which we do not know by sight neighbours of years standing and which permits us to appear to small-town folk so often as cold and uncongenial. Indeed, if I am not mistaken, the inner side of this external reserve is not only indifference but more frequently than we believe, it is a slight aversion, a mutual strangeness and repulsion which, in a close contact which has arisen any way whatever, can break out into hatred and conflict. The entire inner organization of such a type of extended commercial life rests on an extremely varied structure of sympathies, indifferences and aversions of the briefest as well as of the most enduring sort. This sphere of indifference is, for this reason, not as great as it seems superficially. Our minds respond, with some definite feeling, to almost every impression emanating from another person. The unconsciousness, the transitoriness and the shift of these feelings seem to raise them only into indifference. Actually this latter would be unnatural to us as immersion into a chaos of unwished-for suggestions would be unbearable. From these two typical dangers of metropolitan life we are saved by antipathy which is the latent adumbration of actual antagonism since it brings about the sort of distantiation and deflection without which this type of life could not be carried on at all. Its extent and its mixture, the rhythm of its emergence and disappearance, the forms in which it is adequate – these constitute, with the simplified motives (in the narrower sense) an inseparable totality of the form of metropolitan life. What appears here directly as dissociation is in reality only one of the elementary forms of socialization.

17. A Sociology of Climate Change*

John Urry

A major item on a 2009 BBC news programme showed how by 2030 the world may be confronted by a catastrophic 'perfect storm'.[1] This perfect storm would comprise runaway climate change; huge water, food and energy shortages; and enormous population growth. It was striking to have the analysis of such a potential perfect storm as a mainstream news item. It was illustrated by various reports on developments occurring worldwide that showed how such a possible perfect storm was already being formed. The storm, we might say, was already out at sea.

This BBC report went on to suggest that, without the reversal of various systems, the world is racing headlong into multiple interlocking catastrophes. In other words, the storm will soon come onshore. And these interlocking catastrophes would leave much of the world's population poorer, less mobile, hungrier and more likely to be fighting for increasingly scarce resources. It is this bleak future that provides the context for this current book which examines how to analyse the most significant issues confronting human societies in this new and possibly catastrophic twenty-first century.

The understanding of these processes has been mainly dominated by two groups of analysts. First, there are thousands of climate change scientists working in and across various scientific disciplines. Much of their work comes to be synthesized every few years in the authoritative and extensive Reports of the IPCC, reports endorsed by most governments around the world. The IPCC first documented the scale and impact of global climate change in 1990 and its fourth Report appeared in 2007.[2] Drawing upon this science are many scientific journalists and popularizers who play a key role in interpreting and disseminating the sciences of climate change for a much wider public, as well as others disputing key aspects of the science.[3] The sciences of climate change are preeminent here, a 'science first' model with relatively little understanding of how 'societies' are organized and, indeed, might be reorganized so as to change the likely causes and consequences of climate change.

The second group of analysts are economists. It is clear that in many ways climate change is not a purely 'scientific' problem and human actions are complicit within the apparent warming of the planet. Also such warming will only be slowed down or reduced if 'humans' around the world behave differently. There are thus human causes and responses to climate change as well as to various other resource shortages. It is, moreover, economists who are typically viewed as being able to examine these 'human' dimensions of such global climate change, both in terms of the causes and in terms of what are known as adaptations to, and mitigations of, climate change. This central role of economics is reflected in the very influential *Stern Review* that appeared in 2006 and was then published as the 700-page *The Economics of Climate Change*.[4] Economics dominates. Stern states that: 'reversing the trend to higher global temperatures requires an urgent shift towards a

* From Urry, J. (2011) *Climate Change and Society* (Cambridge: Polity). Extracts from pp. 1–5, 7–8.

low-carbon economy … Economics has much to say about assessing and managing the risks of climate change.'[5]

So, in terms of disciplines, the physical sciences and economics have got there first and dominate climate change analyses, and much of the literature on resource shortages – such as those of oil, gas, water and food – which all interconnect with changing climates. This book though argues against this division of academic labour, and in particular the neglect of 'society' in analysing current and future climate and resource processes. This book brings society centrally into the analysis of climate change and especially into examining the history, functioning and consequences of a high carbon society. Also, in terms of the politics of climate change, millions of 'environmentalists' around the world perfectly well know how climate change and resource scarcity are the result of societal processes. Moreover, the possibilities of reducing the chances of a perfect storm depend upon transforming the patterns of social life, especially as they developed in the 'rich North' of the world. [. . .]

Although the scale of future temperature increase is much contested, as Mark Lynas' book on *Six Degrees* shows, the science of climate change has come to be reasonably stabilized (this is examined in detail in chapter 2).[6] But the social science is not at all well established. This is because of the dominance of economic models of human behaviour in much of the academic and especially the environmental policy world. There is, as just noted, an 'economic imperialism', the colonization of the other social sciences by economics.[7] Much analysis 'reduces' humans and their pattern of life to 'economic calculation' and to the workings of predominantly 'economic' markets. There are three major limitations of this imperialism of 'economics' which this book contests.

First, while economic institutions are of course very important, this is often because of their social and indeed political consequences and not just their economic effects. Large global corporations exert social and political power controlling the lives of both workers and consumers and not just the workings of 'markets', which is what the discipline of economics mostly examines. Economic institutions have many consequences, apart from being entities responding to signals that markets provide to households and corporations. Such powerful institutions make, transform and remake markets through their effects upon social life and upon local, national and international politics. One clear example of this concerns the vested interests of those companies that find, drill and pump oil and then refine it into petroleum, kerosene and most plastic products (which are oil-made and not man-made). Such carbon interests are explored in various chapters.

The second point is that society matters, that very many different social processes are central to high carbon lives and also to potential low carbon lives. Most of the time, most people do not behave as individually rational separate economic consumers maximizing their individual utility from the basket of goods and services they purchase and use given fixed and unchanging preferences. People are rather creatures of social routine and habit, but also of fashion and fad. These patterns of routine and fashion stem from how people are, much of the time, locked into and reproduce different social practices and institutions, including families, households, social classes, genders, work groups, schools, ethnicities, generations, nations and so on. The purchase of goods and services helps to constitute these forms of social life, and it is such forms or practices that are the stuff of life. Goods and services are embedded and embodied within these social worlds; and hence transforming the worlds of producing and consuming goods and services so as to bring about, say, a lower-energy economy requires changing such embedded and embodied social worlds. But changes do take place and they may take place very rapidly, such as the astonishing development of mobile technology that came from nowhere and which has transformed mobile lives through new social fashions and fads.

Society also matters because there are many

different ways in which people organize, often now in and through the old and new media. People seek to preserve, extend or develop relations with others as they fight for or against many different aspects of their often changing environment. Sometimes this can involve organizing for the local, sometimes organizing to generate national actions and policies, and sometimes connecting with others across the globe in an imagined community. Often these actions are intertwined with the perceived arguments of science and of people's own understandings and interpretations of the physical world. Thus, there are many sets of relations of civil society and their significance brings out how economics needs to be put into its place. It is important, but not really relevant to examining many social practices of life, some involving resistance and organization in and through civil society, locally, nationally and globally.

Third, this book seeks to show how resources matter and that there needs to be developed an appropriate social science of the 'resources' that underlie each 'economy-and-society'. Especially, the energy-base of different kinds of society is not analysed within most social science. Economists typically regard energy as being responsible for producing about 5 per cent of the Gross Domestic Product (GDP) of an economy because this is roughly what energy costs as a proportion of the national income of most societies.[8] Some economists treat energy as a free good, partly because the sun is in a way 'free'. Overall, economists assume that what the market decides is the cost of energy is what its contribution is to each economy. Some economists presume that, if there are shortages, this is only a temporary blip that the 'market' will in turn rectify – in part because energy is, after all, a commodity just like any other.

However, this 'neo-classical' economics underestimates the significance of energy, and more generally of resources, to the functioning of economies and societies. Strahan argues that, if 'energy really is between ten and fourteen times more productive than the neoclassical model

allowed, then the "real" price of oil may also be ten to fourteen times higher'.[9] Such a revised price of oil and other resources would, of course, transform societies around the world and usher in totally different forms of economic, social and political life. This is especially so given that an astonishing 8 billion tons of oil, gas and coal are consumed or used up each year in order to sustain high carbon systems of producing and consuming goods and services.[10]

Overall, therefore, 'economics' needs to be displaced from its preeminent or imperialist role in examining and explaining the 'human' causes and consequences of climate change. [. . .]

[. . .]

The 'social'

Various aspects of changing climates are examined in this book, including the nature of the physical sciences which lead most scientists to conclude that human activities are significantly responsible for such changes. I especially seek to establish how 'society' is implicated within the processes and practices that generate this warming of the earth and to various dire consequences. In asserting the importance of 'society' to climate change, I am making a rather unfamiliar argument. The social sciences mostly operate on the clear separation between nature and society, between what is natural and what is social and hence studied by the social sciences. This divide between the two reached its high point during the later nineteenth century.

But this was paradoxically the very moment when nature was being irreversibly transformed across western Europe and north America. Nature was viewed as a realm of unfreedom and hostility that was to be subdued and controlled. 'Modernity' indeed involved the belief that human progress should be measured and evaluated in terms of society's domination and exploitation of nature, rather than through transforming the very relations between 'humans' and 'nature'. The realization of the collective powers of societies over 'nature' resulted in remarkable increases in the rates of extraction, organization and exploitation of energy that made possible the very notion of a modern society based upon machinizing both energy and movement.

Sociology as a specific academic practice was the product of this historical moment, of an emergent industrial movement-based capitalism in western Europe and north America. It took for granted the success of modern societies in their overcoming of nature. Sociology specialized in describing and explaining the institutions of these modern societies based upon industries that enabled and utilized dramatic new forms of energy, movement and patterns of social life. These modern societies were presumed to be qualitatively different from the past. This dichotomy of tradition and modernity was formulated in various ways: Maine's status to contract, Marx's feudalism to capitalism, Tönnies' *Gemeinschaft* to *Gesellschaft*, Durkheim's mechanical to organic forms of the division of labour and, much later, Foucault's classical to bourgeois ages.[11]

But, overall, sociology was based upon the acceptance and enhancement of the presumed division of academic labour stemming from Durkheim's identification of the region of the social that was to be investigated and explained autonomously.[12] In a way sociology employed the strategy of modelling itself on biology and arguing for its specific and autonomous realm of facts, which Durkheim famously termed 'social facts', separate from their material underpinnings.

Until recently this academic division between a world of natural facts and one of social facts was uncontentious. It made good sense as a professionalization strategy for sociology since social facts provided a clear sphere of investigation. This sphere was parallel to, but did not challenge or confront, those physical sciences that dealt with an apparently distinct and analysable nature, and which had an enormous head-start in the race for academic respectability and funding. There was presumed to be a chasm between nature and society, a chasm sometimes conceived

of as methodological, sometimes ontological. It was assumed that the natural sciences were just that – 'natural' – and their scientific method had been largely resolved.

This book seeks to undermine these chasms. I embed society, and hence sociology, as a subject within the analyses of climate change, and more generally within a world of objects, technologies, machines and environments. A strong claim is made here that the social and the physical/material worlds are utterly intertwined and the dichotomy between the two is an ideological construct to be overcome (as much writing in the sociology of science and technology has long maintained). [. . .]

NOTES

1. *BBC News*, 10 p.m., 24 August 2009. The UK Government Chief Scientist, John Beddington, was the source of this material.
2. IPCC, www.ipcc.ch/ (2007) (accessed 2 June 2008).
3. See Fred Pearce, *With Speed and Violence: Why Scientists Fear Tipping Points in Climate Change* (Boston: Beacon Press, 2007).
4. Nicholas Stern, *The Economics of Climate Change: The Stern Review* (Cambridge: Cambridge University Press, 2007).
5. Nicholas Stern, *The Economics of Climate Change: The Stern Review* (Cambridge: Cambridge University Press, 2007), p. xiii.
6. Mark Lynas, *Six Degrees: Our Future on a Hotter Planet* (London: Fourth Estate, 2007).
7. See Ben Fine, *The World of Consumption* (London: Routledge, 2002), p. xi.
8. See David Strahan, *The Last Oil Shock* (London: John Murray, 2007), ch. 5; Richard Heinberg, *The Party's Over: Oil, War and the Fate of Industrial Society* (New York: Clearview Books, 2005), pp. 3–5.
9. David Strahan, *The Last Oil Shock* (London: John Murray, 2007), p. 123.

10. Jeremy Leggett, *Half Gone: Oil, Gas, Hot Air and Global Energy Crisis* (London: Portobello Books, 2005), p. 11.

11. As discussed in the classic text on the *modern* mobile world, Marshall Berman, *All That Is Solid Melts into Air* (New York: Simon and Schuster, 1982).

12. Émile Durkheim, *The Rules of Sociological Method* (New York: Free Press, 1964).

18. Navigating the 'White Space'*

Elijah Anderson

Over the past half century, American society has undergone a major racial incorporation process, during which large numbers of black people have made their way from urban ghettos into many settings previously occupied only by whites. Toward the end of the Civil Rights Movement, massive riots occurred in cities across the country, as blacks grew increasingly insistent and militant (see Wicker 1968). It was in this context that the federal government passed far-reaching legislation that made black people full citizens while targeting for reform racially segregated workplaces, neighborhoods, schools, and universities. These reforms, coupled with a prolonged period of economic expansion, set the stage for the historic period of racial integration and incorporation, including the subsequent growth of the black middle class, which is now the largest in American history. White society's reception of upwardly and outwardly mobile black people, however, was decidedly mixed. To be sure, many whites encouraged and supported racial equality and progress, but many others, consumed by deeply held prejudices, powerfully resisted these changes, which they feared abrogated their own rights and assumed privileges.

The Civil Rights Movement is long past, yet segregation persists. The wider society is still replete with overwhelmingly white neighborhoods, restaurants, schools, universities, workplaces, churches and other associations, courthouses, and cemeteries, a situation that reinforces a normative sensibility in settings in which black people are typically absent, not expected, or marginalized when present. In turn, blacks often refer to such settings colloquially as "the white space"—a perceptual category—and they typically approach that space with care.

When present in the white space, blacks reflexively note the proportion of whites to blacks, or may look around for other blacks with whom to commune if not bond, and then may adjust their comfort level accordingly; when judging a setting as too white, they can feel uneasy and consider it to be informally "off limits." For whites, however, the same settings are generally regarded as unremarkable, or as normal, taken-for-granted reflections of civil society.

The city's public spaces, workplaces, and neighborhoods may now be conceptualized essentially as a mosaic of white spaces, black spaces, and cosmopolitan spaces (racially diverse islands of civility) that may be in various stages of flux, from white to black or from black to white (Anderson 2011). As demographics change, public spaces are subject to change as well, impacting not only how a space is occupied and by whom but also the way in which it is perceived.

What whites see as "diverse," blacks may perceive as homogeneously white and relatively privileged (see Jackson 1999). While the respective white and black spaces may appear to be racially homogeneous, typically they can be subclassified in terms of ethnicity and social class. "White spaces," for instance, often include not only traditional Americans of European descent

* From Anderson, E. (2015) '"The White Space"', *Sociology of Race and Ethnicity*, 1(1): 10–21. Extracts from pp. 10–11, 12, 13–15, 19–20.

but also recently arrived European immigrants and visitors as well as others who may be perceived as phenotypically "white." Similarly, those inhabiting "black space" are not always simply traditional African Americans but may be subclassified as African, Latino, Haitian, Caribbean, Cape Verdean, and so on. Accordingly, the racially mixed urban space, a version of which I have referred to elsewhere as "the cosmopolitan canopy," exists as a diverse island of civility located in a virtual sea of racial segregation. While white people usually avoid black space, black people are required to navigate the white space as a condition of their existence.

[. . .]

Although increasingly present in the consciousness of the larger society, members of the black middle class can be rendered almost invisible by the iconic ghetto. Police officers, taxi drivers, small business owners, and other members of the general public often treat blackness in a person as a "master status" that supersedes their identities as ordinary law-abiding citizens. Depending on the immediate situation, this treatment may be temporary or persistent while powerfully indicating the inherent ambiguity in the anonymous black person's public status (see Anderson 1990; Becker 1973; Hughes 1944). In popular parlance, whether hailing from the ghetto or the middle-class suburbs, most critically, they exist "while black." And for many, their black skin designates them as being "from the ghetto." While operating in the white space, they can be subject to social, if not physical, jeopardy. Thus, while navigating the white space, they risk a special penalty—their putative transgression is to conduct themselves in ordinary ways in public while being black at the same time.

[. . .]

For the larger society, from the nightly news and media reports of rampant black-on-black crime and at times from close observation of black people in public, images of the black ghetto loom large. Here, the ghetto becomes intensely more iconic, symbolized as a distressed place to which blacks have been relegated to live apart from the larger society, thereby encouraging a universally low opinion of blacks as a racial category (see Feagin 2006; Massey and Denton 1998). Thus, not only does the physical ghetto persist, but it also has become a highly negative icon in American society and culture, serving increasingly as a touchstone for prejudice, a profound source of stereotypes, and a rationalization for discrimination against black people in general.

The White Space

For black people in particular, white spaces vary in kind, but their most visible and distinctive feature is their overwhelming presence of white people and their absence of black people. When the anonymous black person enters the white space, others there immediately try to make sense of him or her—to figure out "who that is," or to gain a sense of the nature of the person's business and whether they need to be concerned. In the absence of routine social contact between blacks and whites, stereotypes can rule perceptions, creating a situation that estranges blacks. In these circumstances, almost any unknown black person can experience social distance, especially a young black male— not because of his merit as a person but because of the color of his skin and what black skin has come to mean as others in the white space associate it with the iconic ghetto (see Anderson 2011, 2012).

In other words, whites and others often stigmatize anonymous black persons by associating them with the putative danger, crime, and poverty of the iconic ghetto, typically leaving blacks with much to prove before being able to establish trusting relations with them. Accordingly, the most easily tolerated black person in the white space is often one who is "in his place"—that is, one who is working as a janitor or a service person or one who has been vouched for by white people in good standing. Such a person may be believed to be less likely to disturb the implicit racial order—whites as dominant and blacks as subordinate.

Strikingly, a black person's deficit of credibility may be minimized or tentatively overcome by a performance, a negotiation, or what some blacks derisively refer to as a "dance," through which individual blacks are required to show that the ghetto stereotypes do not apply to them; in effect, they perform to be accepted. This performance can be as deliberate as dressing well and speaking in an educated way or as simple as producing an ID or a driver's license in situations in which this would never be demanded of whites.

Depending on how well the black person performs or negotiates, he or she may "pass inspection," gaining provisional acceptance from the immediate audience. But others there may require additional proof on demand. In public white spaces, like upscale shops or restaurants, many blacks take this sort of racial profiling in stride; they expect it, treat it as a fact of life, and try to go on about their business, hoping to move through the world uneventfully. And most often, with the help of social gloss to ease their passage, they do (E. Goffman 1959); however, on occasion they experience blatant discrimination, which may leave them deflated and offended. White salesmen, security guards, and bouncers repeatedly approach black persons with a disingenuous question, "Can I help you?" The tone of voice and the circumstances belie a true offer of help and define the situation as slightly ominous. A young black male hears the question as "What is your business here?" Most defenders of such spaces prefer to be more indirect in their challenges and queries to avoid offending the black person or incurring lawsuits.

When the anonymous black person can demonstrate that he or she has business in the white space, by producing an ID card, or simply passing an initial inspection, the defending "agents" may relax their guard, at least for the time being. They may then advance from concern with the person's deficit of credibility to his or her provisional status, suggesting a conditional "pass." But as the iconic ghetto hovers overhead, this social plateau simply foreshadows further evaluations that typically have little to do with the black person's essential merit as a person. When venturing into or navigating the white space, black people endure such challenges repeatedly.

[. . .]

Several years ago, I vacationed in Wellfleet, Massachusetts, a pleasant Cape Cod town full of upper-middle-class white vacationers, tourists, and working-class white residents. During the two weeks that my family and I spent there, I encountered very few other black people. We had rented a beautiful cottage about a mile from the town center, which consisted of a library and a few restaurants and stores catering to tourists. Early one weekday morning, I jogged down the road from our cottage through the town center and made my way to Route 6, which runs the length of the Cape from the Sagamore Bridge to Provincetown. It was a beautiful morning, about 75 degrees, with low humidity and clear blue skies. I had jogged here many times before. At 6 a.m., the road was deserted, with only an occasional passing car. I was enjoying my run that morning, listening to the nature sounds and feeling a sense of serenity. It seemed I had this world all to myself. Suddenly a red pickup truck appeared and stopped dead in the middle of the road. I looked over at the driver, a middle-aged white man, who was obviously trying to communicate something to me. He was waving his hands and gesticulating, and I immediately thought he might be in distress or in need of help, but I could not make out what he was saying. I stopped, cupped my hand to my ear to hear him better, and yelled back, "What did you say?" It was then that he made himself very clear. "Go home! Go home!" he yelled, dragging out the words to make sure I understood. I felt provoked, but I waved him off and continued on my way (see Anderson 2012).

In the white space, the anonymous black

person's status is uncertain, and he or she can be subject to the most pejorative regard. For their part, in the interest of civility, most whites who harbor them know to keep such negative thoughts to themselves. When a racial epithet, or the attitude underlying it, is expressed, it tells the black person directly that he or she does not belong. As one black informant observed,

> "Once it happens to you, all bets are off, and you do not know what to expect, no matter what you thought of yourself; for the moment, you don't know just where you stand. You feel like a stranger in a strange land."

Almost any white person present in the white space can possess and wield this enormous power. And those who feel especially exercised and threatened by the rise of blacks may feel most compelled to wield that power (see Blumer 1958; Bobo 1999; Feagin 2006). For many of them, blacks in the white space may be viewed as a spectacle of black advancement at the expense of whites. Black presence thus becomes a profound and threatening racial symbol that for many whites can personify their own travail, their own insecurity, and their own sense of inequality. While certainly not all are guilty of such acts, many can be mobilized in complicity to "protect" the white space, which blacks must navigate as a condition of their existence, and where whites belong and black people can so easily be reminded that they do not.

Moral Authority

The negative images others take from the iconic ghetto conspire to negate or undermine the moral authority of the black person in the larger society, and this is at no time more consequential than when he or she navigates the white space. When present there, the black person typically has limited standing relative to his white counterparts and is made aware of this situation by the way others treat him. With a wealth of moral authority, one can experience acceptance, as well as an aura of protection against ritual offenses, including random acts of disrespect; without such authority, the black person is uniquely vulnerable. When respected, a black person exerts a degree of moral sway that constrains, or checks, those inclined to show him disrespect, to offend him, or to mistreat him or her, for the possession of moral authority by the putative victim places the offender on morally dubious ground. This can cause the person so inclined to pause, possibly constrained by what his offenses might mean for what others would think of him, or what he might think of himself if he follows his inclination. With his own esteem or self-concept in the balance, he might anticipate shame for himself. But for the black person, moral authority is actualized only when he is well integrated into the white space, and most often he is not.

When black persons lack moral authority, those who are inclined to offend them on the basis of their color may know no shame and face few sanctions. Thus, without such authority, the black person moves through the larger society in a vulnerable state, which is particularly so when navigating the white space—a world in which he typically has limited social standing, and thus limited respect. Indeed, it is in such settings that the black person meets on occasion acute, racially based disrespect— or, as many black people call it, the "nigger moment" (see Anderson 2011). In navigating the white space, many blacks regard such aggressions as inevitable and have learned to think of them as small and large (see Pierce 1970). Usually, they ignore the small incidents, considering them not worthy of the mental work and trouble that confronting them would require. But the large ones cannot be ignored, for typically they are highly disturbing, volatile, occasionally even violent, and capable of fundamentally changing one's outlook on life—not to mention the glossy exterior many blacks display while negotiating the white space as part of their daily lives; when such a moment occurs, the person can feel that he or she has been "put in his or her place."

[...]

The black ghetto has become a major icon in American society and culture, and as such it has also become an important source of stereotype, prejudice, and discrimination. Despite the progressive changes wrought by the racial incorporation process of the 1960s and 1970s, the color line persists—albeit in a new, emergent form—particularly in those circumstances in which the black body faces acute challenges to its everyday life and existence, most commonly in what many blacks have come to perceive categorically as the white space. Moreover, the racially black and white homogeneous spaces on either side of that line promote a basic confusion between race and class; black skin is typically equated with lower-class status and white skin with privilege. In this way, the negative image of the iconic ghetto and the notion that all blacks come from the ghetto serve to justify the normative sensibility of the white space that excludes or marginalizes blacks, and in which blacks are unexpected, and when present require explanation.

White urbanites often have material and symbolic interests in making the implications of this racial hierarchy unavoidable. In fact, they tend to reify this principle, regardless of the actual socioeconomic position of the black persons to whom it is applied. That makes it real in the sense of W. I. Thomas's (1969) famous theorem: "If men define situations as real, they are real in their consequences." Today, the iconic ghetto and its relation to the white space form the basis of a potent and provocative new form of racism. The old racism created the ghetto. The Civil Rights Movement opened its gates, and a new black middle class emerged. But the new form of symbolic racism emanating from the iconic ghetto hovers, stigmatizing by degrees black people as they navigate the white space.

REFERENCES

Anderson, Elijah. 1990. *Streetwise: Race, Class, and Change in an Urban Community.* Chicago: University of Chicago Press.

Anderson, Elijah. 2011. *The Cosmopolitan Canopy: Race and Civility in Everyday Life.* New York: W.W. Norton.

Anderson, Elijah. 2012. "The Iconic Ghetto." *Annals of the American Academy of Political and Social Sciences* 642:8–24.

Becker, Howard S. 1973. *Outsiders: Studies in the Sociology of Deviance.* New York: Free Press.

Blumer, Herbert. 1958. "Race Prejudice as a Sense of Group Position." *Pacific Sociological Review* 1:3–7.

Bobo, L. 1999. "Prejudice as Group Position: Microfoundations of a Sociological Approach to Racism and Race Relations." *Journal of Social Issues* 55:445–72.

Feagin, Joe. 2006. *Systemic Racism: A Theory of Oppression.* New York: Routledge, Taylor and Francis Group.

Goffman, Erving. 1959. *The Presentation of Self in Everyday Life.* New York: Anchor Books.

Hughes, Everett C. 1944. "Dilemmas and Contradictions of Status." *American Journal of Sociology* 50:353–59.

Jackson, Ronald L. 1999. "White Space, White Privilege: Mapping Discursive Inquiry into the Self." *Quarterly Journal of Speech* 85:38–54.

Massey, Douglas A. and Nancy A. Denton. 1998. *American Apartheid: Segregation and the Making of the Underclass.* Cambridge, MA: Harvard University Press.

Thomas, William I. 1969. *The Definition of the Situation. In Symbolic Interaction: A Reader in Social Psychology.* New York: Allyn & Bacon.

Wicker, Tom. 1968. *U.S. Riot Commission Report: Report of the National Advisory Commission on Civil Disorders.* New York: Bantam Books.

19. Urban Transitions in the Global South*

AbdouMaliq Simone and Edgar Pieterse

If you are one of the scores of millions of residents across much of the urban "South" who cannot depend upon one specific job to earn your keep, who lacks sufficient documentation to secure a place to live over the long term, or who can't afford to get sick or into any kind of trouble, what is it that you pay attention to in order to know something about what to do? What happens if the people you rely upon for support or information are no longer available or suddenly turn against you? What happens when the skills you have to apply are also those of an increasing number of residents, and competition becomes increasingly fierce for opportunities? The question here is how can you best know what is going on and try to situate yourself in a position where opportunities might "come your way"? In other words, how can you be at the right place at the right time when there is no clear map available? We are convinced that these kinds of considerations dominate the minds and spiritual practices of most urban dwellers, yet much of what appears in both urban scholarship and policy prescripts seems oblivious.

In a not dissimilar way, researchers of urban life face difficulties when it comes to engaging with the largely makeshift complexion of many cities in Africa and Asia. The enormous transformations of the built environment and the enhanced possibilities of consumption that have marked even some of the most marginal of the world's cities should not detract from acknowledging just how dependent the majority of the urban residents of these regions are upon constantly putting together some workable form of income and inhabitation. The makeshift character of much of what this majority does is quite literally "make + shift," as pointed out by Vasudevan (2015).

Whatever they come up with is rarely institutionalized into a fixed set of practices, locales or organizational forms. This doesn't mean that relationships and economic activities do not endure, that people do not find themselves rooted in the same place and set of affiliations over a long period of time. Rather, these stabilities come from constant efforts on the part of inhabitants to redefine the boundaries and interfaces between work, leisure, home, neighborhood and elsewhere. It entails constantly addressing the questions "What spaces are relevant to me?," "What do I pay attention to and where?," "Who do I talk to and do things with?," "Who can I depend on and show things to?" In neighborhoods across the urban South, whatever is made, in terms of economic activities, buildings and social solidarities, then shifts in terms of its availability to specific uses and users, as well as its exposure to new potentials and vulnerability.

Drawing upon decades of work in poor, working- and lower-middle-class districts in urban regions across Africa and South-East Asia, this book attempts to weave interconnections among different ways of engaging and thinking about the complexity of how different urban

* From Simone, A. and Pieterse, E. (2017) *New Urban Worlds: Inhabiting Dissonant Times* (Cambridge: Polity). Extracts from pp. x–xiv, 50–54.

actors decide and act within highly circumscribed and often uncertain contexts.

[. . .]

[. . .] While massive and long-term transformations are of course necessary, this book attempts to make use of what exists now but is sometimes not seen, not read, and thus does not become a resource for deciding and acting. While we offer strategic visions for how to face the enormous challenges of impoverishment, urban growth during climate change, and the exigency of justice, we concentrate on mapping out the potentials of the immediate – the lived realms of the "make + shift" city.

Just like the processes through which urban actors decide and act, this task of reworking the immediate is full of twists and turns. This is in part because the urban is full of paradoxes. Clear differentiations between urban and rural, local and global, self and other, time and space, human and nonhuman, North and South, public and private – long critical vehicles of orientation – are simultaneously intensifying and waning, becoming more sharply drawn as they are also being folded into each other. In a world where there is so much to pay attention to, where each decision seems more urgent, imbued with greater significance, it is harder to make distinctions between what is and what is not important to pay attention to, what is salient or irrelevant. This means that decision-making gets simultaneously more complicated and frustrating. The constitutive nature and generative potential of paradox is foregrounded throughout the book.

The capacities of the poor to get by with little, and thus to be rendered either targets of development or manipulated pawns in a game of continuous displacement, may ironically suggest a conceivable future for everyone in light of carbonated dystopias that become more apparent every year that CO_2 emission reduction targets are spectacularly missed. How is it possible to live through these seeming paradoxes? How is it possible to maintain the productive boundaries among places, between spatial exteriors and interiors, and among distinctive ways of life without being disabled by their paradoxical encounters? How to think the doubleness of things, of ways in which differences can move toward and draw from each other as a movement of justice and equanimity?

[. . .]

A powerful prejudicial undertow characterizes outside opinions about the inability of most cities in Asia and Africa to deal decisively with slum urbanism and what is perceived as non-existent planning. This perspective shines through most clearly in reportage accounts about the teeming slums in the megacities of the third world, held in place by a blend of corruption and authoritarianism (Iweala 2016). The unspoken question is this: If London and Paris could solve the problems of slums one hundred years ago, why is it so hard for the developing world to get this right, especially in view of accumulated knowledge and much greater economic resources? Of course, this perspective fails to consider long-term historical impacts of colonial plunder and the deliberate underdevelopment of countries and cities that have to be kept in an economically subservient and supplier relationship with former colonies (Davis 2006).

There is also little regard for the fact that the rate of urban growth and the overall numbers of people considered to be urban dwellers are fundamentally different during the second wave of urbanization as compared to the first, as explicated in great detail by Satterthwaite (2007). Most importantly, there is a fundamental disregard for the relationship between urbanization, technological change and modes of economic development. The technology historian Carlota Perez (2009, 2013, 2014a, 2014b) provides a useful schematic account of the changing patterns of economy, technology and governmental policy from the onset of industrialization in the mid-eighteenth century up to the contemporary moment, marked as it is with uncertainty, incalculable risk and promise (Appadurai 2015). [. . .E]ach technological era is linked to a surge in speculative investments that invariably balloon into a speculative bubble that bursts. Once the crash happens, the state intervenes and an era of widespread dissemination and growth follows within which the new technologies become the new mainstream, embedded in profound cultural and institutional changes, until the pattern gets disrupted by a new cycle of innovative entrepreneurs pushing at the gates.

It is relevant to set Perez's argument alongside the demographic transition defined as the first wave of urbanization: in 1750 the North was 10 percent urban (15 million people), but two hundred years later, in 1950, this figure had risen to 52 percent (423 million people) (Satterthwaite 2007). The harsh impacts of urbanization were unevenly felt, as the painstaking sociological insights of Friedrich Engels (1845)[1] remind us. But, as political opposition grew, there were considerable resources in these metropolitan economies to undertake the necessary infrastructural investments which, in turn, provided the mainstay of a working-class movement seeking political power in the first half of the twentieth century (Mikkelsen 2005). It was on the back of these mobilizations that the welfare state ideology and investments achieved spectacular material effect in the post-World War II era (Mason 2015), when the majority world started to emerge from the iron fist of colonial rule (Nederveen Pieterse 2010). Of course, the decolonial period hardly translated into economic freedom or autonomy, nor did we see the dilution of Western influence in the routine political and economic governance of these territories – to disastrous effect in most African and a large number of Asian countries (Slater 2004).

As the Cold War dynamics set in with full force through the 1950s to the 1970s, the autonomous capacities of so-called post-colonies were thoroughly undermined. This unloosened over time but took on a much more pernicious form in the 1980s with financial conditionalities premised on fundamentalist neoliberal dogmas.

This situation slowly thawed toward the end of the 1990s, when Asian counterpoints started to gain serious political, economic and ideological traction. The collapse of the official communist world provided spectacular impetus to the dilution of Western hegemony and opened up a radically multipolar and conflictual reconfiguration of development agendas and pathways. Materially, however, it has proved much harder to disentangle economic interdependencies and strangleholds, especially as the power of multinational corporations has grown disproportionately since the 1980s (Mitchell 2008).

To put the dynamic of urbanization in Africa and Asia into perspective, it is important to contrast this dynamic with the first wave of urbanization. In 1950, as Europe went beyond the 50 percent urban tipping point to reach 51.5 percent (283 million people), Africa was 14 percent urbanized (32 million), compared with 17.5 percent (245 million) in Asia and 63.9 percent (110 million) in North America (UN-DESA 2015: 40). It is of course striking that, already at this point, Asia had three times more urban dwellers than North America and only slightly fewer than Europe. Fast forward to 2020, when Asia will reach its 50 percent urbanization mark (2.5 billion people), and 2035, when Africa is projected to be half urbanized (900 million people). Clearly, Africa and Asia have to manage a complex demographic transition from rural to predominantly urban in one-third of the time that it took Europe, and on an unprecedented scale. Furthermore, Africa and Asia have to achieve this without the benefit of blood subsidies that slavery and colonialism afforded the imperial powers to extract value and achieve economic dominance.

The point of these statistical juxtapositions is simply to underscore that it is a historical absurdity to expect African or Asian countries simply to replicate the "knowledge" and institutions of the global North to "solve" pernicious problems associated with slum urbanism. The same structural dynamics that made it possible for Europe then to garner the resources, knowledge and technology to make public health advancements are still at play in the contemporary world, fuelling a political ideology that renders universal access to basic services, welfare and a universal basic income as lunacy. The ideological edifice of this power dynamic is neoliberal capitalism (Douzinas 2014). This conclusion is obviously a blatant oversimplification and flattening of vast historical specificities and conjunctures. However, in a polemical vein, it is crucial to shine a light on the long-term effects of ideological assumptions that operate on the basis of historical amnesia and Eurocentrism (Howe et al. 2015). That said, we are interested in fashioning an approach that is historically alert, spatially informed and anticipatory of new possibilities on the horizon.

NOTE

1. The book is available online: www.marx ists.org/archive/marx/works/1845/conditi ons-working-class/index.htm.

REFERENCES

Appadurai, Arjun (2015) Mediants, materiality, normativity, *Public Culture*, 27: 22–37.

Davis, Mike (2006) *Planet of the Slums*. London: Verso.

Douzinas, Costas (2014) Notes towards an analytics of resistance, *New Formations*, 83: 79–98.

Howe, Cymene, Lockrem, Jessica, Appel, Hannah, Hackett, Edward, Boyer, Dominic, Hall, Randal, Schneider-Mayerson, Matthew, Pope, Albert, Gupta, Ahkil, Rodwell, Elizabeth, Ballestero, Andrea, Durbin, Trevor, el-Dahdah, Farès, Long, Elizabeth and Mody, Cyrus (2015) Paradoxical infrastructures: ruins, retrofit, and risk, *Science, Technology, & Human Values*, 41: 547–65.

Iweala, Uzodinma (2016) I dream of a utopian Lagos – but here's what African cities really need to prosper, *The Guardian*, October 13.

Mason, Paul (2015) *Postcapitalism: A Guide to our Future*. London: Penguin.

Mikkelsen, Flemming (2005) Working-class formation in Europe and forms of integration: history and theory, *Labor History*, 46: 277–306.

Mitchell, Timothy (2008) Rethinking economy, *Geoforum*, 39: 1116–21.

Nederveen Pieterse, Jan (2010) *Development Theory*. 2nd edn, London: Sage.

Perez, Carlota (2009) *Technological Revolutions and Techno-Economic Paradigms*, Working Papers in Technology Governance and Economic Dynamics no. 20. Tallinn: University of Technology.

____ (2013) Unleashing a golden age after the financial collapse: drawing lessons from history, *Environmental Innovation and Societal Transitions*, 6: 9–23.

____ (2014a) *A Green and Socially Equitable Direction for the ICT Paradigm*, Globelics Working Paper series, www.globelics.org/wp-content/uploads/2016/05/GWP2014-01.pdf.

____ (2014b) A new age of technological progress, in Chuka Umunna (ed.) *Owning the Future: How Britain Can Make it in a Fast-Changing World*. London: Rowman & Littlefield International.

Satterthwaite, David (2007) *The Transition to a Predominantly Urban World and its Underpinnings*. London: International Institute for Environment and Development; http://pubs.iied.org/pdfs/10550IIED.pdf.

Slater, David (2004) *Geopolitics and the Post-Colonial: Rethinking North–South Relations*. Oxford: Wiley-Blackwell.

UN-DESA (United Nations, Department of Economic and Social Affairs) (2015) *World Urbanization Prospects: The 2014 Revision* (ST/ESA/SER.A/366). New York: United Nations.

Vasudevan, Alexander (2015) The makeshift city: toward a global geography of squatting, *Progress in Human Geography*, 39: 338–59.

20. Entering an Anthropocene Era?*

Rolf Lidskog and Claire Waterton

The origin of the Anthropocene concept can be traced back to a conference that took place in the year 2000 by the International Geosphere-Biosphere Programme (IGBP). The session organizer focussed his contribution on the Holocene (the current geological epoch that began 12,000 years ago, replacing the Pleistocene). Finally one of the participants, the chemist and Nobel laureate Paul Crutzen lost his patience, effectively announcing the end of this current era. As he later recalled: 'I said we no longer live in the Holocene, but in the Anthropocene. After that, it suddenly went very quiet in the hall. In the coffee break the only issue discussed was the Anthropocene' (Crutzen 2013, our translation). Since then, the concept has made a remarkable journey, and is now widely adopted by many environmental scientists. Crutzen and colleagues have since asked themselves why the concept was not discarded as footnote in the history of geological ideas: they believe that the reason for its wide adoption is due to a broader cultural trend – the growing consciousness of humanly induced global environmental change (Zalasiewicz et al. 2010, 2228).

The Anthropocene is, however, still very much a concept in the making, and there is a vibrant debate about its different aspects. [. . .]

Despite the broadness and flexible use of the Anthropocene concept, however, we find it possible to pin down some key elements shared by those who relate positively to it: (i) that earth itself is a single system within which the biosphere is an essential component; (ii) that human impact is global and accelerating, now threatening the fundamental life process of earth; (iii) that this change is traceable geologically, possibly implying a new geological epoch, 'the Anthropocene'; (iv) that there is a need to radically change current human activities in order avoid this threat. These elements stabilize the debate; they also enable movement within the debate whereby different perspectives, tensions and standpoints are communicated, as well as renegotiated. We explore these elements through the metaphor of 'layers' below which helps avoid a unidirectional, overly coherent narrative trajectory – e.g. from an exclusive Earth system view to a more inclusive view that also includes social aspects. Metaphorical layers suggest the possibility (as in geological formations) of ongoing folding, mixing, and even inverting, giving insight into the dynamic tensions and movements between different strata.

Layers of the Anthropocene

We can decipher at least four layers in the discussion of Anthropocene; a geological layer, a biosphere layer, a socio-economic layer and an ethical layer. These layers, it should be noted, can be present and 'mixed up' in any one presentation of what the Anthropocene is, or why it

* From Lidskog, R. and Waterton, C. (2016) 'Anthropocene: A Cautious Welcome from Environmental Sociology?', *Environmental Sociology*, 2(4): 395–406. Extracts from pp. 396, 397, 399–400, 402–403.

matters. Observing them empirically, so to speak, they occur as folded arguments that are part of the emerging knowledge production associated with the Anthropocene concept. We characterise them here as distinct layers only for heuristic reasons. Whereas the first two layers, then, concern the environmental state of the earth, the third addresses the societal causes of this state, and the fourth considers how to evaluate and act upon this diagnosis.

[. . .]

Contributions to environmental sociology

The Anthropocene narrative conceptualises environmental challenges in a way that chimes well with some aspects of sociological thought regarding environment and society. In particular, we find four aspects to be of major relevance for environmental sociology.

First, the Anthropocene narrative is (implicitly) based on a relational ontology where society and nature are co-constructed. It is no longer earth system processes alone that determine or restrict human life – humans have become co-producers of the conditions of possibility for life on earth (Dearing et al. 2015; Knight 2015; Zalasiewicz et al. 2010). This understanding may provide opportunities for sociology to transcend the old debate (or 'dead-lock') about whether environmental sociology should include biophysical realities, or not, in its analyses (for an overview, see Lidskog, Mol, and Oosterveer 2015; White, Rudy, and Gareau 2015). It transcends this debate by not only stating that environmental sociology needs to include an understanding of social life as dependent on ecosystem processes but also that environmental sciences need to include an understanding of how ecosystem processes are heavily influenced by social processes. Not only environmental issues, but also the environment itself is co-constituted by ecological and social processes. The implication is a re-conceptualisation of

environmental–human relationships – something that environmental sociology (especially environmental sociology inflected by STS) has argued for since its inception. The narrative of the Anthropocene, however, deepens our sense of the inter-relations involved (Palsson et al. 2013).

Second, the Anthropocene narrative stresses the need for system change. In a world where political solutions to environmental problems are often seen in terms of a technical quick-fix and where 'post-political' solutions flourish (Swyngedouw 2010) the Anthropocene narrative makes clear that these will not suffice: rather, there is a need for fundamental change. Thereby, it provides the opportunity for a re-politicisation of environmental challenges. It also provides opportunities for a political re-contextualisation where political action is not solely attached to nation-states and international negotiations but implies new forms and arrangements of environmental citizenship and subjectivity (Beck 2009, 2015). By creating a human awareness of, and responsibility for, a vulnerable earth, the Anthropocene provides an opportunity to create a new cosmopolitan public around 'matters' (Beck 2009; Latour 2004, 2010; Stengers 1997). Thus the Anthropocene narrative implicitly opens up not just one, but many futures – imaginaries about worlds that would be good to live in and ways of reaching them (Berkhout 2014; Latour 2010; Lövbrand et al. 2015; Urry 2013). Such arguments reach out to the exciting and demanding strands of social theory, often deriving from within Sociology and STS, that have informed many aspects of environmental sociology over recent years.

Third, as we have suggested, the Anthropocene narrative stresses the need for disciplinary collaboration. Anthropocene stories continuously highlight the multiple, interdependent relations within nature, within different forms of materiality, within technologies and within social systems, but they also stress the interconnections between these domains. As such, the Anthropocene narrative is a generous and inclusive one, inviting all disciplines – from engineering and environmental science to the social sciences and humanities – to work with and through it (Ellis and Trachtenberg 2014; Oldfield et al. 2014). Anthropocene narratives also stress the importance of recognising much closer relations and also configuring much better relations between science and society in order to find agreements on solutions to specific environmental challenges (Barnosky et al. 2014). Thus, the Anthropocene narrative raises a call similar to that of public sociology (Burawoy 2009), which encourages academic engagement between different disciplines and non-academic constituencies without abandoning sociology's reflexive and disciplinary character.

Fourth, the Anthropocene narrative contains a dynamic view not only of nature and society, but also of cause and effect whereby it is acknowledged to be virtually impossible to establish simple, linear links between them (Oldfield et al. 2014). Here the idea of the Anthropocene aligns closely with recent work in post-humanist social theory and feminist STS that acknowledges the indeterminacy and emergence of entities that we usually take for granted as independently existing entities pre-existing their acting upon one another (Barad 2007, 33; Law 2004). 'Realness' in the research of Karen Barad, for example, is understood to be continually emerging within the relations of already entangled agencies. Such work, closely mapping some of the more constructivist and STS-inclined elements of environmental sociology (Hannigan 2014; Irwin 2001), is highly relevant to the way we understand living entities and their inter-relations. It has inspired a rethinking not only of causality, effect, linearity, and the ongoing shaping of things, but also turns questions about responsibility into questions about 'response-ability' (Barad 2007) – i.e. how do humans encounter entities that are constantly 'coming into being'. How do, or might, human societies develop an appropriate responsiveness to such an emergent view of the world? And what are the implications for ideas of management and control (Schrader 2010)?

In sum, then, the Anthropocene narrative evokes recognition of the value of some of the key elements of knowledge production within environmental sociology. Not least, it seems to establish a basis for building and developing a relational, political, collaborative and dynamic environmental sociology – an environmental sociology that draws deeply upon its own diverse theoretical contributions, that acknowledges global complexity, and that can analyse a world characterised by increasing interrelatedness, interconnectedness and shifting boundaries and borders (Gross and Heinrichs 2010; Lidskog, Mol, and Oosterveer 2015; White, Rudy, and Gareau 2015). Simultaneously, the Anthropocene narrative has a number of ambiguities which offer significant challenges for the discipline of environmental sociology and provide a sense of some frictions that need to be faced. [. . .]

[. . .]

Twenty-five years ago the sociologist Ted Benton extended a 'cautious welcome' to biology (and biological analyses) from the perspective of a sociology that had 'gone too far', in its fear of biological determinism. Biology, he suggested, needed to be let back into the domain of social analyses, but cautiously so. Interestingly, Benton's model for letting biology 'back in' came not from within the academy, but from homegrown social movements such as the environmental and peace movements. Benton was impressed, seemingly, by the intuitive grasp that such movements seemed to have on the relations and traffic (rather than opposition) between nature and society (Benton 1991, 7). Of course what Benton identified as the intensely relational understandings and practices of social movements pointed precisely to the kind of conceptual terrain that environmental sociologists have been arguing for since Catton and Dunlap (in the United States) and Arthur Mol and others (in European circles) first started thinking of themselves as environmental sociologists. Looking back, it could be said that environmental sociology, in most of its variants, has responded to Benton's suggestion with appropriate care: attempting to include the biological/natural/causal but in such a way as to avoid 'reification' and the return of simplistic deterministic analyses (Castree 2014; Hannigan 2014; Irwin 2001; Lidskog, Mol, and Oosterveer 2015).

The context of our own cautious welcome is somewhat different, however. Today, as sociologists, we are witnessing a surge of interest in a particular rendition of the natural. We suggest that the narrative of the Anthropocene has scaled up a sense of the contemporary socionatural crisis and the place of humans within this and that environmental sociology, in particular, has much to contribute to such debates. When Steffen and colleagues, for example, write that, 'Humankind, our own species, has become so large and active that it now rivals some of the great forces of Nature in its impact on the functioning of Earth system' (Steffen et al. 2011a, 843), there is a need to respond from the sub-discipline that has continually addressed the challenges of thinking in natural and social terms simultaneously. In the face of such claims, on the other hand, many authors in both social and natural sciences have registered a kind of excitement at the idea of the emergent geological agency of the human. The Anthropocene represents a new phase in the history of both humankind and of the Earth, when natural forces and human forces became intertwined, so that the fate of one inflects the fate of the other.

But although we appreciate and are stimulated by developments in the geosciences that have made the tracing of Anthropocene possible (Dalby 2013), we also take the point that the advent of the Anthropocene presents a conjuncture: a moment pregnant with risks as well as generative opportunities (Johnson et al. 2014). In scaling up its narrative to Earth System dimensions, the concept of the Anthropocene has created a new universal 'earth system' and a new universal 'we' loaded with knowledge, responsibility and agency. Not only the limits and thresholds of the earth, but also 'the human' and human socialities and politics are now naturalised.

It will be evident from the above that we are imagining environmental sociology to be able to articulate with the Anthropocene in ways that re-set the narrative, allowing for a much more differentiated sense of this earth and this 'we', including a much more differentiated sense of the responsibilities to be carried, and a more variable accounting of the sense of agency implied by the various calls for new forms of planetary stewardship and action. As we have pointed out, environmental sociology has much to draw upon here from neighbouring disciplines (STS, public sociology, post-humanism, anthropology, political ecology and the environmental humanities, etc.) that have long contributed to its own delta of ideas. What is exciting is that the concept of the Anthropocene reinforces the value of several strands of scholarship and debate within environmental sociology – its understanding of a relational socio-environmental ontology; its acknowledgement of the need for political and institutional system change; its embrace of inter- or post-disciplinary collaborations; its critical appraisal of cause-effect relations. But what is also clear is that environmental sociology also has a delicate role to balance between being critical and being productive. The Anthropocene hitherto has been a fear-based narrative that can lead to a social landscape of surveillance and hierarchical control (Buck 2015; Cook and Balayannis 2015). By stressing alternative, but sociologically realistic, futures, the Anthropocene can be retold, identifying alternative pathways – some of them already in use – that might re-direct socionatural development. These kinds of narrative should, we suggest, include both opportunities and tensions, gains and losses, power and powerlessness in order to stimulate proactive debate.

It has been suggested that what is at stake in the concept of 'the Anthropocene' is the identification and articulation of a world whose social, political, and physical parameters are changing faster than our capacity to process and analyse them (Johnson et al. 2014). However, the real test seems to be to respond calmly and carefully to this pressure and to contribute appropriately according to the core strengths of the discipline. As the challenges to adapt ways of knowing intensify, there is still room for environmental sociology to draw on its own diverse intellectual history, and its critical but constructive disciplinary culture, in order to help build a much more socially robust and reflexive narrative of the times we are in.

REFERENCES

Barad, K. 2007. *Meeting the Universe Halfway.* Durham, UC: Duke University Press.

Barnosky, A. D., M., R. Holmes, E. Kirchholtes, K. C. Lindsey, A. W. Maguire, M. A. Poust, J. Stegner et al. 2014. "Prelude to the Anthropocene: Two New North American Land Mammal Ages (NALMAs)." *The Anthropocene Review* 1 (3): 225–242. doi:10.1177/2053019614547433.

Beck, U. 2009. *World at Risk.* Cambridge: Polity.

Beck, U. 2015. "Emancipatory Catastrophism: What Does it Mean to Climate Change and Risk Society?" *Current Sociology* 63 (1): 75–88. doi:10.1177/0011392114559951.

Benton, T. 1991. "Biology and Social Science: Why the Return of the Repressed Should be Given a (Cautious) Welcome." *Sociology* 25 (1): 1–29. doi:10.1177/0038038591025001002.

Berkhout, F. 2014. "Anthropocene Futures." *The Anthropocene Review* 1 (2): 154–159. doi:10.1177/2053019614531217.

Buck, H. J. 2015. "On the Possibilities of a Charming Anthropocene." *Annals of the Association of American Geographers* 105 (2): 369–377. doi:10.1080/00045608.2014.973005.

Burawoy, M. 2009. "Challenges for a Global Sociology." *Contexts* 8 (4): 36–41. doi:10.1525/ctx.2009.8.4.36.

Castree, N. 2014. "The Anthropocene and Geography III: Future Directions." *Geography Compass* 8 (7): 464–476. doi:10.1111/gec3.v8.7.

Cook, B. R., and A. Balayannis. 2015. "Co-Producing (A Fearful) Anthropocene." *Geographical Research* 53 (3): 270–279. doi:10.1111/geor.2015.53.issue-3.

Crutzen, P. 2013. "Es Macht Mir Angst, Wie Verletzlich Die Atmosphäre Ist. Ein Gespräcnt Mit Dem Nobelpreisträger Paul J. Crutzen zum Anthropozän und den Chancen der Klimapolitik." *Frankfurter Allgemeine* No. 270, 20 November 2013, p. 2.

Dalby, S. 2013. "Biopolitics and Climate Security in the Anthropocene." *Geoforum* 49: 184–192. doi:10.1016/j.geoforum.2013.06.013.

Dearing, J. A., B. Acma, S. Bub, F. M. Chambers, X. Chen, J. Cooper, D. Crook, et al. 2015. "Social-Ecological Systems in the Anthropocene: The Need for Integrating Social and Biophysical Records at Regional Scales." *The Anthropocene Review* 2 (3): 220–246. doi:10.1177/2053019615579128.

Ellis, M. A., and Z. Trachtenberg. 2014. "Which Anthropocene is it to be? Beyond Geology to a Moral and Public Discourse." *Earth's Future* 2 (2): 122–125. doi:10.1002/eft2.2014.2.issue-2.

Gross, M., and H. Heinrichs, eds. 2010. *Environmental Sociology. European Perspectives and Interdisciplinary Challenges.* Dordrecht: Springer.

Hannigan, J. 2014. *Environmental Sociology.* 3th ed. London: Routledge.

Irwin, A. 2001. *Sociology and the Environment. A Critical Introduction to Society, Nature and Knowledge.* Cambridge: Polity.

Johnson, E., H. Morehouse, S. Dalby, J. Lehman, S. Nelson, R. Rowan, S. Wakefield, and K. Yusuff. 2014. "After the Anthropocene: Politics and Geographic Inquiry for a New Epoque." *Progress in Human Geography* 38 (3): 439–456. doi:10.1177/0309132513517065.

Knight, J. 2015. "Anthropocene Futures: People, Resources and Sustainability." *The Anthropocene Review* 2 (2): 152–158. doi:10.1177/2053019615569318.

Latour, B. 2004. *Politics of Nature. How to Bring Science into Democracy.* Cambridge MA: Harvard University Press.

Latour, B. 2010. "An Attempt at a 'Compositionist Manifesto'." *New Literary History* 41 (3): 471–490.

Law, J. 2004. *After Method: Mess in Social Science Research.* London: Routledge.

Lidskog, R., A. Mol, and P. Oosterveer. 2015. "Towards a Global Environmental Sociology? Legacies, Trend and Future Directions." *Current Sociology* 63 (3): 339–368. doi:10.1177/0011392114543537.

Lövbrand, E., S. Beck, J. Chilvers, T. Forsyth, J. Hedrén, M. Hulme, R. Lidskog, and E. Vasileidou. 2015. "Who Speaks for the Future of Earth? How Critical Social Science can Extend the Conversation on the Anthropocene." *Global Environmental Change* 32: 211–218. doi:10.1016/j.gloenvcha.2015.03.012.

Oldfield, F., T. Barnosky, J. Dearing, M. Fischer-Kowalski, J. McNeill, W. Steffen, and J. Zalasiewicz. 2014. "The Anthropocene Review: Its Significance, Implications and the Rationale for a New Transdisciplinary Journal." *The Anthropocene Review* 1 (1): 1–5. doi:10.1177/2053019613500445.

Palsson, G., B. Szerszynski, S. Sörlin, J. Marks, B. Avril, C. Crumley, H. Hackmann, et al. 2013. "Reconceptualizing the 'Anthropos' in the Anthropocene: Integrating the Social Sciences and Humanities in Global Environmental Change Research." *Environmental Science & Policy* 28: 3–13. doi:10.1016/j.envsci.2012.11.004.

Schrader, A. 2010. "Responding to Pfiesteria piscicida (the Fish Killer) Phantomatic Ontologies, Indeterminacy, and Responsibility in Toxic Microbiology." *Social Studies of Science* 40 (2): 275–306. doi:10.1177/0306312709344902.

Steffen, W., J. Grinevald, P. Crutzen, and J. McNeill. 2011. "The Anthropocene: Conceptual and Historical Perspectives." *Philosophical Transactions of the Royal Society A* 369 (1938): 842–867. doi:10.1098/rsta.2010.0327.

Stengers, I. 1997. *Power and Invention: Situating Science.* Minneapolis: University of Minnesota Press.

Swyngedouw, E. 2010. "Apocalypse Forever?: Post-political Populism and the Spectre of Climate Change." *Theory, Culture & Society* 27 (2–3): 213–232. doi:10.1177/0263276409358728.

Urry, J. 2013. *Societies beyond Oil: Oil Dregs and Social Futures.* London: Zed Books.

White, D. F., A. P. Rudy, and B. J. Gareau. 2015. *Environments, Natures and Social Theory: Towards a Critical Hybridity.* London: Palgrave.

Zalasiewicz, J., M. Williams, W. Steffen, and P. Crutzen. 2010. "The New World of the Anthropocene." *Environment, Science & Technology* 44 (7): 2228–2231. doi:10.1021/es903118j.

Part 3 – Further reading

A reliable, engaging and contemporary introduction to sociology and the environment is Bell, M. M., and Ashwood, L. L. (2021) *An Invitation to Environmental Sociology* (6th edn, London: Sage). Another well-respected textbook that uses real-world examples is Hannigan, J. (2014) *Environmental Sociology: A Social Constructionist Perspective* (3rd edn, London: Routledge). On cities and urban life, Abrahamson, M. (2014) *Urban Sociology: A Global Introduction* (New York: Cambridge University Press) is a good place to start, and, as it says, the book adopts a global perspective on urbanism. LeGates, R. T., and Stout, F. (eds) (2020) *The City Reader* (7th edn, London: Routledge) is an excellent collection of readings covering this field.

Sociology, 9th edition

The dedicated chapters here are chapter 5, 'The Environment', and chapter 13, 'Cities and Urban Life'. Chapter 4, 'Globalization and Social Change', also contains a useful discussion on environmental and urban issues, and it is worth using the index to find other sections on urban life, such as those in chapters 8, 9 and 11.

Part 4 Structures of Society

Some sociologists focus primarily on social structures while others concentrate on individual action, but one way of thinking with both is to study the social structures and institutions that not only mould people's lives but are also changed by them over time. These structures and institutions include families, religion, education, work and the economy, and there are readings on all of these subjects across the book. Studying social structures can often be the key to understanding cultural differences and, in a period of rapid globalization, may also help us to appreciate so-called cultural universals – aspects of social life that are common to most societies.

It is well established that capitalism, as Marx predicted, has expanded across the globe, though the specific form it takes differs according to national and regional context. But what exactly is capitalism and when and where did it originate? Is it based on simple human greed, for example? For Max Weber, the origins of capitalism are far removed from sheer greed, and he set out to explain why a rational form of profit-seeking originated in the West. Reading 21 provides the bones of Weber's classic argument, that there was an intimate connection between the 'spirit' of capitalism and the ethical dimension of puritan Protestantism. For Weber, the roots of modern capitalism stem from religious adherents' response to certain tenets of their Protestant belief system. The capitalists' relentless quest for material goods and money actually lies in the rational and systematic pursuit of business success via ever increasing profit.

Work and the making of a living take up a large part of all our lives. The Industrial Revolution altered work for ever, moving people away from agrarian lifestyles and into urban centres with factories, workshops and offices. Since the late 1960s, sociologists have theorized a shift away from manufacturing towards services, and in most advanced industrial economies a majority of people now make their living in education, social care, healthcare, finance, and other service occupations. This broad shift is arguably one key factor in the rapid increase in women's employment. However, our reading focuses instead on the *global* feminization of manufacturing, particularly as it has developed in the Global South. Teri L. Caraway argues that, although feminization is real, it has been selective, with women moving into relatively few low-paid sectors. Better-paid work remains male-dominated, and men work across the whole range of manufacturing sectors. Hence, women have made their way into formal employment in large numbers, but this does not seem to have seriously challenged gender inequality in the workplace. Understanding why this is so forms the basis of Caraway's survey.

The institution of the family can be found in all societies, albeit in widely differing forms, and the sociology of the family is a well-established field of study. However, the development of multicultural societies and a recognition that, even within a single national society, there exist a variety of familial living arrangements have led to serious questioning of family sociology. One significant development has been a growing interest in familial relationships and the wider sphere of personal life more generally. The reading from Deborah Chambers and Pablo Gracia traces the development of family sociology as it has moved beyond a strict focus on the family as a social institution to families as diverse sets of relationships and connections. The authors outline some of the more recent research on individualization, LGBTQ+ 'families of choice' and 'family practices'. They also discuss the increasing interest in the study of 'personal life', a subject that is discussed in Part 6, Relationships and the Life Course, with a reading from Carol Smart.

The sociology of education is one of the discipline's founding subjects, a key element in Durkheim's early sociological ideas. A significant distinction can be made between education as social institution and schooling as the most widely used delivery vehicle for education. Sociological studies have repeatedly shown that education systems are important in social reproduction, and, despite their overt meritocratic ethos, this also involves the reproduction of social inequalities. Much of the work undertaken on this subject has been empirical research in real-world school settings. Christy Kulz's 2014 paper continues this tradition, reporting on her empirical study of one UK secondary academy school, 'Beaumont', examining whether this ostensibly successful school lives up to its headteacher's promotional material. Academy status was introduced in the 1990s to give school heads more freedom over their curricula and budgets and was seen as a way to raise the performance of children in deprived areas. Kulz observed how Beaumont's overriding focus on discipline and structuring the school

day produced both positive and negative outcomes. Overall exam results improved, but this came at the expense of any serious attempt to tackle educational inequality.

Since Marx's theory of capitalist development and collapse, sociology has been in a continuous debate with Marxian ideas and neo-Marxist social scientists, from Gramsci and the Frankfurt School of critical theory to the work of Jürgen Habermas and Slavoj Žižek. However, capitalism has changed considerably since Marx's time, and, today, serious scholarly effort has been made to link the digital revolution with a shifting form of capitalism. The emergence and growth of powerful online platforms such as Facebook and Google, and the creation of a new 'gig economy' sector driven by online profitability, have been described as 'platform capitalism' by some (Srnicek 2016). However, one of the most systematic accounts of this new, 'rogue' form of capitalism is Shoshana Zuboff's (2019) *The Age of Surveillance Capitalism*. Our reading focuses on the development of Google and its operational methods. Zuboff argues that surveillance capitalism 'feeds on every aspect of human experience', using artificial intelligence and algorithms in the collecting and collating of data from a variety of digital devices in the home and at work that can be commercialized. There is a lament here for what the digital revolution *could* have been – a genuine communications revolution that should have led to a strengthening of social networks, communities and democratic norms. But this optimistic vision has been definitively lost to the astonishing assimilative capacity of capitalism, which turns all progressive technological and socio-economic developments into yet more avenues for profit-making. In this way, and in a very short time period, surveillance of all human behaviour and interaction has become the defining feature of the new capitalism.

21. Religion and the Origins of Capitalism*

Max Weber

[. . .] The impulse to acquisition, pursuit of gain, of money, of the greatest possible amount of money, has in itself nothing to do with capitalism. This impulse exists and has existed among waiters, physicians, coachmen, artists, prostitutes, dishonest officials, soldiers, nobles, crusaders, gamblers, and beggars. One may say that it has been common to all sorts and conditions of men at all times and in all countries of the earth, wherever the objective possibility of it is or has been given. It should be taught in the kindergarten of cultural history that this naïve idea of capitalism must be given up once and for all. Unlimited greed for gain is not in the least identical with capitalism, and is still less its spirit. Capitalism *may* even be identical with the restraint, or at least a rational tempering, of this irrational impulse. But capitalism is identical with the pursuit of profit, and forever *renewed* profit, by means of continuous, rational, capitalistic enterprise. For it must be so: in a wholly capitalistic order of society, an individual capitalistic enterprise which did not take advantage of its opportunities for profit-making would be doomed to extinction.

[. . .]

For the purpose of this conception all that matters is that an actual adaptation of economic action to a comparison of money income with money expenses takes place, no matter how primitive the form. Now in this sense capitalism and capitalistic enterprises, even with a considerable rationalization of capitalistic calculation, have existed in all civilized countries of the earth, so far as economic documents permit us to judge. In China, India, Babylon, Egypt, Mediterranean antiquity, and the Middle Ages, as well as in modern times. These were not merely isolated ventures, but economic enterprises which were entirely dependent on the continual renewal of capitalistic undertakings, and even continuous operations. However, trade especially was for a long time not continuous like our own, but consisted essentially in a series of individual undertakings. Only gradually did the activities of even the large merchants acquire an inner cohesion (with branch organizations, etc.). In any case, the capitalistic enterprise and the capitalistic entrepreneur, not only as occasional but as regular entrepreneurs, are very old and were very widespread.

[. . .]

But in modern times the Occident has developed, in addition to this, a very different form of capitalism which has appeared nowhere else: the rational capitalistic organization of (formally) free labour. Only suggestions of it are found elsewhere. Even the organization of unfree labour reached a considerable degree of rationality only on plantations and to a very limited extent in the **Ergasteria** of antiquity. In the manors, manorial workshops, and domestic industries on estates with serf labour it was probably somewhat less

* From Weber, M. (1967 [1904–5]) *The Protestant Ethic and the Spirit of Capitalism* (London: Unwin University Books). Extracts from pp. 17, 19–20, 21–22, 35–36, 48–49, 50–51, 180–183.

developed. Even real domestic industries with free labour have definitely been proved to have existed in only a few isolated cases outside the Occident. The frequent use of day labourers led in a very few cases—especially State monopolies, which are, however, very different from modern industrial organization—to manufacturing organizations, but never to a rational organization of apprenticeship in the handicrafts like that of our Middle Ages.

Rational industrial organization, attuned to a regular market, and neither to political nor irrationally speculative opportunities for profit, is not, however, the only peculiarity of Western capitalism. The modern rational organization of the capitalistic enterprise would not have been possible without two other important factors in its development: the separation of business from the household, which completely dominates modern economic life, and closely connected with it, rational book-keeping. [. . .]

[. . .]

A glance at the occupational statistics of any country of mixed religious composition brings to light with remarkable frequency[1] a situation which has several times provoked discussion in the Catholic press and literature,[2] and in Catholic congresses in Germany, namely, the fact that business leaders and owners of capital, as well as the higher grades of skilled labour, and even more the higher technically and commercially trained personnel of modern enterprises, are over-whelmingly Protestant.[3] This is true not only in cases where the difference in religion coincides with one of nationality, and thus of cultural development, as in Eastern Germany between Germans and Poles. The same thing is shown in the figures of religious affiliation almost wherever capitalism, at the time of its great expansion, has had a free hand to alter the social distribution of the population in accordance with its needs, and to determine its occupational structure. The more freedom it has had, the more clearly is the effect shown. It is true that the greater relative participation of

Protestants in the ownership of capital,[4] in management, and the upper ranks of labour in great modern industrial and commercial enterprises,[5] may in part be explained in terms of historical circumstances[6] which extend far back into the past, and in which religious affiliation is not a cause of the economic conditions, but to a certain extent appears to be a result of them. Participation in the above economic functions usually involves some previous ownership of capital, and generally an expensive education; often both. These are to-day largely dependent on the possession of inherited wealth, or at least on a certain degree of material well-being. A number of those sections of the old Empire which were most highly developed economically and most favoured by natural resources and situation, in particular a majority of the wealthy towns, went over to Protestantism in the sixteenth century. The results of that circumstance favour the Protestants even to-day in their struggle for economic existence. There arises thus the historical question: why were the districts of highest economic development at the same time particularly favourable to a revolution in the Church? The answer is by no means so simple as one might think.

[. . .]

Thus, if we try to determine the object, the analysis and historical explanation of which we are attempting, it cannot be in the form of a conceptual definition, but at least in the beginning only a provisional description of what is here meant by the spirit of capitalism. Such a description is, however, indispensable in order clearly to understand the object of the investigation. For this purpose we turn to a document of that spirit which contains what we are looking for in almost classical purity, and at the same time has the advantage of being free from all direct relationship to religion, being thus, for our purposes, free of preconceptions.

"Remember, that *time* is money. He that can earn ten shillings a day by his labour, and goes abroad, or sits idle, one half of that day, though he spends but sixpence during his diversion or idleness, ought not to reckon *that* the only expense; he has really spent, or rather thrown away, five shillings besides.

"Remember, that *credit* is money. If a man lets his money lie in my hands after it is due, he gives me the interest, or so much as I can make of it during that time. This amounts to a considerable sum where a man has good and large credit, and makes good use of it.["]

[...]

It is Benjamin Ferdinand who preaches to us in these sentences, the same which Ferdinand Kürnberger satirizes in his clever and malicious *Picture of American Culture*[7] as the supposed confession of faith of the Yankee. That it is the spirit of capitalism which here speaks in characteristic fashion, no one will doubt, however little we may wish to claim that everything which could be understood as pertaining to that spirit is contained in it. Let us pause a moment to consider this passage, the philosophy of which Kürnberger sums up in the words, "They make tallow out of cattle and money out of men". The peculiarity of this philosophy of avarice appears to be the ideal of the honest man of recognized credit, and above all the idea of a duty of the individual toward the increase of his capital, which is assumed as an end in itself. Truly what is here preached is not simply a means of making one's way in the world, but a peculiar ethic. The infraction of its rules is treated not as foolishness but as forgetfulness of duty. That is the essence of the matter. It is not mere business astuteness, that sort of thing is common enough, it is an ethos. *This* is the quality which interests us.

[...]

One of the fundamental elements of the spirit of modern capitalism, and not only of that but of all modern culture: rational conduct on the basis of the idea of the calling, was born—that is what this discussion has sought to demonstrate—from the spirit of Christian asceticism. One has only to re-read the passage from Franklin, quoted at the beginning of this essay, in order to see that the essential elements of the attitude which was there called the spirit of capitalism are the same as what we have just shown to be the content of the Puritan worldly asceticism,[8] only without the religious basis, which by Franklin's time had died away. The idea that modern labour has an ascetic character is of course not new. Limitation to specialized work, with a renunciation of the Faustian universality of man which it involves, is a condition of any valuable work in the modern world; hence deeds and renunciation inevitably condition each other to-day. This fundamentally ascetic trait of middle-class life, if it attempts to be a way of life at all, and not simply the absence of any, was what Goethe wanted to teach, at the height of his wisdom, in the *Wanderjahren*, and in the end which he gave to the life of his *Faust*.[9] For him the realization meant a renunciation, a departure from an age of full and beautiful humanity, which can no more be repeated in the course of our cultural development than can the flower of the Athenian culture of antiquity.

The Puritan wanted to work in a calling; we are forced to do so. For when asceticism was carried out of monastic cells into everyday life, and began to dominate worldly morality, it did its part in building the tremendous cosmos of the modern economic order. This order is now bound to the technical and economic conditions of machine production which to-day determine the lives of all the individuals who are born into this mechanism, not only those directly concerned with economic acquisition, with irresistible force. Perhaps it will so determine them until the last ton of fossilized coal is burnt. In Baxter's view the care for external goods should only lie on the shoulders of the "saint like a light cloak, which can be thrown aside at any moment".[10] But fate decreed that the cloak should become an iron cage.

Since asceticism undertook to remodel the world and to work out its ideals in the world, material goods have gained an increasing and finally an inexorable power over the lives of men as at no previous period in history. To-day the spirit of religious asceticism—whether finally, who knows?—has escaped from the cage. But victorious capitalism, since it rests on mechanical foundations, needs its support no longer. The rosy blush of its laughing heir, the Enlightenment, seems also to be irretrievably fading, and the idea of duty in one's calling prowls about in our lives like the ghost of dead religious beliefs. Where the fulfilment of the calling cannot directly be related to the highest spiritual and cultural values, or when, on the other hand, it need not be felt simply as economic compulsion, the individual generally abandons the attempt to justify it at all. In the field of its highest development, in the United States, the pursuit of wealth, stripped of its religious and ethical meaning, tends to become associated with purely mundane passions, which often actually give it the character of sport.[11]

No one knows who will live in this cage in the future, or whether at the end of this tremendous development entirely new prophets will arise, or there will be a great rebirth of old ideas and ideals, or, if neither, mechanized petrification, embellished with a sort of convulsive self-importance. For of the last stage of this cultural development, it might well be truly said: "Specialists without spirit, sensualists without heart; this nullity imagines that it has attained a level of civilization never before achieved."

But this brings us to the world of judgments of value and of faith, with which this purely historical discussion need not be burdened. The next task would be rather to show the significance of ascetic rationalism, which has only been touched in the foregoing sketch, for the content of practical social ethics, thus for the types of organization and the functions of social groups from the conventicle to the State. Then its relations to humanistic rationalism,[12] its ideals of life and cultural influence; further to the development of philosophical and scientific empiricism, to technical development and to spiritual ideals would have to be analysed. Then its historical development from the mediæval beginnings of worldly asceticism to its dissolution into pure utilitarianism would have to be traced out through all the areas of ascetic religion. Only then could the quantitative cultural significance of ascetic Protestantism in its relation to the other plastic elements of modern culture be estimated.

Here we have only attempted to trace the fact and the direction of its influence to their motives in one, though a very important point. But it would also further be necessary to investigate how Protestant Asceticism was in turn influenced in its development and its character by the totality of social conditions, especially economic.[13] The modern man is in general, even with the best will, unable to give religious ideas a significance for culture and national character which they deserve. But it is, of course, not my aim to substitute for a one-sided materialistic an equally one-sided spiritualistic causal interpretation of culture and of history. Each is equally possible,[14] but each, if it does not serve as the preparation, but as the conclusion of an investigation, accomplishes equally little in the interest of historical truth.[15]

NOTES

1. The exceptions are explained, not always, but frequently, by the fact that the religious leanings of the labouring force of an industry are naturally, in the first instance, determined by those of the locality in which the industry is situated, or from which its labour is drawn. This circumstance often alters the impression given at first glance by some statistics of religious adherence, for instance in the Rhine provinces. Furthermore, figures can naturally only be conclusive if individual specialized occupations are carefully distinguished in them. Otherwise very large employers may sometimes be grouped together with master craftsmen who work alone, under the category of "proprietors of enterprises". Above all, the fully developed capitalism

of the present day, especially so far as the great unskilled lower strata of labour are concerned, has become independent of any influence which religion may have had in the past. I shall return to this point.

2. Compare, for instance, Schell, *Der Katholizismus als Prinzip des Fortschrittes* (Würzburg, 1897), p. 31, and V. Hertling, *Das Prinzip des Katholizismus und die Wissenschaft* (Freiburg, 1899), p. 58.

3. One of my pupils has gone through what is at this time the most complete statistical material we possess on this subject: the religious statistics of Baden. See Martin Offenbacher, "Konfession und soziale Schichtung", *Eine Studie über die wirtschaftliche Lage der Katholiken und Protestanten in Baden* (Tübingen und Leipzig, 1901), Vol. IV, part v, of the *Volkswirtschaftliche Abhandlungen der badischen Hochschulen*. The facts and figures which are used for illustration below are all drawn from this study.

4. For instance, in 1895 in Baden there was taxable capital available for the tax on returns from capital:
Per 1,000 Protestants .. 954,000 marks
Per 1,000 Catholics .. 589,000 marks
It is true that the Jews, with over four millions per 1,000, were far ahead of the rest. (For details see Offenbacher, *op. cit.*, p. 21.)

5. On this point compare the whole discussion in Offenbacher's study.

6. On this point also Offenbacher brings forward more detailed evidence for Baden in his first two chapters.

7. *Der Amerikamüde* (Frankfurt, 1855), well known to be an imaginative paraphrase of Lenau's impressions of America. As a work of art the book would to-day be somewhat difficult to enjoy, but it is incomparable as a document of the (now long since blurred-over) differences between the German and the American outlook, one may even say of the type of spiritual life which, in spite of everything, has remained common to

all Germans, Catholic and Protestant alike, since the German mysticism of the Middle Ages, as against the Puritan capitalistic valuation of action.

8. That those other elements, which have here not yet been traced to their religious roots, especially the idea that honesty is the best policy (Franklin's discussion of credit), are also of Puritan origin, must be proved in a somewhat different connection (see the following essay [not translated here]). Here I shall limit myself to repeating the following remark of J. A. Rowntree (*Quakerism, Past and Present*, pp. 95–6), to which E. Bernstein has called my attention: "Is it merely a coincidence, or is it a consequence, that the lofty profession of spirituality made by the Friends has gone hand in hand with shrewdness and tact in the transaction of mundane affairs? Real piety favours the success of a trader by insuring his integrity and fostering habits of prudence and forethought, important items in obtaining that standing and credit in the commercial world, which are requisites for the steady accumulation of wealth" (see the following essay). "Honest as a Huguenot" was as proverbial in the seventeenth century as the respect for law of the Dutch which Sir W. Temple admired, and, a century later, that of the English as compared with those Continental peoples that had not been through this ethical schooling.

9. Well analysed in Bielschowsky's *Goethe*, II, chap. xviii. For the development of the scientific cosmos Windelband, at the end of his *Blütezeit der deutschen Philosophie* (Vol. II of the *Gesch. d. Neueren Philosophie*), has expressed a similar idea.

10. *Saints' Everlasting Rest*, chap. xii.

11. "Couldn't the old man be satisfied with his $75,000 a year and rest? No! The frontage of the store must be widened to 400 feet. Why? That beats everything, he says. In the evening when his wife and daughter read

together, he wants to go to bed. Sundays he looks at the clock every five minutes to see when the day will be over—what a futile life!" In these terms the son-in-law (who had emigrated from Germany) of the leading dry-goods man of an Ohio city expressed his judgment of the latter, a judgment which would undoubtedly have seemed simply incomprehensible to the old man. A symptom of German lack of energy.

12. This remark alone (unchanged since his criticism) might have shown Brentano (*op. cit.*) that I have never doubted its independent significance. That humanism was also not pure rationalism has lately again been strongly emphasized by Borinski in the *Abhandl. der Münchener Akad. der Wiss.*, 1919.

13. The academic oration of v. Below, *Die Ursachen der Reformation* (Freiburg, 1916), is not concerned with this problem, but with that of the Reformation in general, especially Luther. For the question dealt with here, especially the controversies which have grown out of this study, I may refer finally to the work of Hermelink, *Reformation und Gegenreformation*, which, however, is also primarily concerned with other problems.

14. For the above sketch has deliberately taken up only the relations in which an influence of religious ideas on the material culture is really beyond doubt. It would have been easy to proceed beyond that to a regular construction which logically deduced everything characteristic of modern culture from Protestant rationalism.

22. The Feminization of Work[*]

Teri L. Caraway

Introduction

One of the greatest social and economic transformations in industrializing parts of the world has been the dramatic entry of women into paid work in the formal sector. The influx of women into manufacturing work has been especially notable (Economic and Social Commission for Asia and the Pacific 1987; Heyzer 1988; Joekes 1987; Lim 1985; Nash and Fernandez-Kelly 1983; Tomoda 1995; Ward 1990). During the last decades of the twentieth century, industrialization generated millions of new factory jobs in developing countries. Although men historically outnumbered women in formal-sector work in manufacturing, women reached near parity or beyond in many countries in the short space of just one to two decades. Women now constitute a significant share of the working class in much of the developing world, especially in countries that have experienced dramatic industrial expansion. Yet despite this impressive wave of feminization in manufacturing, employers in numerous countries have eschewed female labor and continue to employ primarily men. Moreover, even in countries that did feminize, although some employers hired women with alacrity, others resisted. Their aversion to hiring women is puzzling, as scholars have enumerated an array of attributes that make women the ideal workforce in today's global capitalist economy; women are cheaper to employ than men, docile, and willing to work long hours in dead-end jobs. Most employers, not just those in traditionally female sectors of employment, should find these attributes exceedingly attractive. Explaining the varied topography and timing of women's entry into formal-sector employment in manufacturing is the empirical puzzle at the heart of this book.

The feminization of factory labor has consequences not only for women's access to work but also for gender inequality. Women's incorporation into manufacturing work has been highly selective, with women flowing primarily into low-paid jobs in a few industries. Even in countries that have undergone massive feminization, work in the highest-paying sectors of manufacturing continues to elude women. Men still work across a wider range of industries and hold the most remunerative jobs. Consequently, feminization has had only a modest impact on reducing gender inequalities in labor markets. Indeed, gender has proved to be a particularly resilient dividing line between workers. Massive inflows of women into the workforce result rarely in a seamless integration of women into men's jobs but rather in a redrawing or reconfiguration of the gender divisions of labor that separate men's work from women's work.

My fundamental contention is that understanding either feminization or the persistent gender inequalities in labor markets requires scholars to grapple with the tenacity of gender divisions in labor markets. Why do employers segregate men and women into distinct realms of

[*] From Caraway, T. (2007) *Assembling Women: The Feminization of Global Manufacturing* (Ithaca: Cornell University Press). Extracts from pp. 1–5, 7–8, 9–10.

work, and how are divisions between men and women perpetuated, redrawn, and reconfigured rather than overturned? And how do shop-floor practices of gender segregation cascade through economies and interact with the wider political economy to produce distinctly gendered patterns of manufacturing employment?

The answers to these questions are of vital importance. A necessary condition for improving women's social status is undoubtedly greater access to work, and feminization opens the door of job opportunity to women. A greater understanding of what prompts feminization thus helps to identify the constellation of forces that combine to kick open the door of opportunity. Yet if women flow into feminized ghettos of the workforce, new opportunities may not succeed in undermining gender inequalities in the labor market. Escaping this quandary requires a better understanding of the processes that collectively conspire to reproduce or reconfigure—rather than obliterate—gender divisions at work. Once we comprehend these processes, it becomes possible to change them.

The Argument in Brief

First, how are the doors of opportunity kicked open? How do women gain access to manufacturing work? I show that employment growth in labor-intensive industries is the primary stimulus for feminization. Employment growth has two effects. First, it creates higher demand for labor, including female labor; second, it gives employers the opportunity to dismantle established gender divisions of labor without firing male workers. In contrast to scholars who have argued that export-oriented industrialization (EOI) compels employers to seek out the cheapest labor possible—women—in order to compete in international markets (Chapkis and Enloe 1983; Elson and Pearson 1981; Fernandez-Kelly 1983; Fox 1993; Fuentes and Ehrenreich 1983; Joekes 1987; Lim 1983; Safa 1986: Tiano 1994), I argue that EOI is important only insofar as it

generates employment growth in labor-intensive industries, which it does only during its initial stages. Moreover, as shown in the analysis that follows, the shift of work from men to women which takes place during the early stages of EOI is far more contingent than is portrayed by most scholars, with some employers eagerly feminizing and others sticking with men. As EOI matures, moreover, manufacturing becomes more capital intensive; employment growth slows; and masculinization usually ensues; EOI's positive impact on women's integration into manufacturing work is thus temporary; as countries shift to the production of highly value-added goods, women are expelled from industrial jobs.

In addition to employment growth in labor-intensive industries, two additional factors, the supply characteristics of female labor and mediating institutions, help to explain the differences between countries in women's share of manufacturing employment. Most existing analyses of feminization assume that women are available to work in factories, that women are attractive potential employees, and that employers can hire them. But an ensemble of political factors both determines women's availability for employment and facilitates or obstructs their entry into the workforce. Government policy, through its effects on women's fertility, education levels, and labor force participation rates, affects the availability of women to work in factories and their attractiveness as potential employees. Likewise, institutions such as unions and protective legislation affect the capacity and willingness of employers to hire women. Perhaps the most controversial finding of this book is that strong unions negatively affect women's share of employment in manufacturing. Strong unions allow male workers to oppose employer efforts to replace them with women, and centralized bargaining institutions that set wages throughout the economy prevent employers from cutting wages by hiring women. The repression of labor in Asia is therefore an inseparable part of the explanation for women's impressive presence in manufacturing work in the region. Docile unions, not supposedly docile

THE FEMINIZATION OF WORK   129

women, have been key determinants of the gendered contours of industrialization.

Finally, why does feminization have such a limited impact on gender inequalities in labor markets? Both Marxist and neoclassical political economists would expect feminization, which represents an increase in demand for female labor, to erode gender inequalities (Blau and Ferber 1992; Lim 1983; Marx 1977). Initially, feminists believed that it was women's exclusion from formal-sector work that prevented them from enjoying the fruits of development (Boserup 1970). After feminization began to sweep across the globe and women's presence in manufacturing work expanded, however, feminists began to argue that access to work had disappointing results because women flowed into feminized ghettos in the labor market (Elson and Pearson 1981; Joekes 1987). Continued segregation is an important piece of the puzzle in explaining the limited impact of feminization on reducing gender inequality, but the dynamics of segregation and how it is reconfigured during the course of feminization is still poorly understood. The book contributes to this debate by highlighting a range of unexplored processes that produce this outcome.

A crucial component of the explanations lies in the resistance of high-paying employers in capital-intensive sectors to the siren call of "cheap female labor." Some scholars have insinuated that this defiance is part of a patriarchal conspiracy to perpetuate women's subordination to men (Hartmann 1979), while others have simply noted that since wages are a smaller share of costs in less-competitive, capital-intensive sectors, these employers do not need to cut wages by hiring women (Cohn 2000; Joekes 1982). Dual labor market theorists have emphasized women's instability as workers, noting that capital-intensive firms that invest in training are loath to hire women because they have short work tenures (Doeringer and Piore 1971). I argue that patriarchal conspiracies, indifferences to reducing wage costs and the alleged instability of women workers are insufficient

to explain the resistance of employers to hiring women. The continued closure of many lines of work to women is intimately related to gendered discourses of work—ideas that managers hold about the qualities of male and female labor. Feminization involves both the definition of new jobs as realms of women's activity and the *re*definition as women's work of jobs previously held by men. Employers feminize their workforces only if they imagine that women will be more productive workers than men. Gendered discourses of work and the gendered logic of production in capital-intensive sectors have combined in a toxic mix that provides work opportunities for women but closes off most of the high-paying jobs to them. This outcome is not inevitable, but the workings of capitalism reproduce rather than undermine the processes that create it. Only political intervention in markets will undo it. Illuminating the forces that generate gendered outcomes relies on two crucial components that distinguish this book from other analyses of feminization: a gendered and multilevel methodology, and the use of gender as a category of political economic analysis.

[. . .]

A Gendered Theoretical Apparatus

Just as a gendered and comparative methodology is required to develop an explanation of feminization, so is moving beyond the dominant view of markets as gender-neutral institutions. Scholars agree that gender segregation is a pervasive phenomenon in labor markets (Anker 1998; Charles and Grusky 2004), but most scholars explain the existence and the persistence of these gender divisions through reference to nonmarket forces, in particular to women's role in reproduction and its consequences for their investment in education and their commitment to work. The prevailing view is that labor markets are in principle gender neutral, and premarket differences between men and women determine gender disparities in labor market outcomes (Humphrey 1987; Scott 1986).

The assumed gender neutrality of markets is perhaps most evident in the categories of analysis deployed to study them. On the surface, these categories are gender neutral, but since power relations based on gender are such a salient aspect of lived social relations, allegedly gender-neutral categories generally contain gender bias. In neoclassical political economy, for example, the individual acting in a world of scarcity is the bedrock of all analysis. This sexless individual appears to be free of gender bias, but theorists have shown that the individual in liberal theory, and hence in neoclassical economics theory, is not an abstract individual but conforms to characteristics of (white) men (Fraser 1989; Hanchard 1999; Mehta 1997; Pateman 1988). One of the crowning glories of neoclassical economics, human capital theory, therefore best explains labor market outcomes for white men and performs relatively poorly in accounting for the situations of African American men and of women, regardless of race (Tomaskovic-Devey 1993). Marxist political economy similarly treats the category of labor as a genderless entity that is "free" to sell its labor on the market, even though men and women are rarely equally free to sell their labor, since women bear the burdens of reproduction in most societies.

The theoretical consequence of the male bias in the categories that structure most political economic analysis is that features associated with women are treated as different from the norm. This difference then becomes the explanation for women's fate in labor markets. The labor market thus remains gender neutral and simply reacts to the different qualities that men and women bring to the labor market (e.g., commitment to the workforce; education; role in childbearing). Although women's greater role in reproduction and its effects on women's labor force participation are certainly important in understanding gender segregation and gender inequality in labor markets, attributing segregation to nonmarket factors does not grapple with the ways that gender is embedded in the market mechanism and thus structures the work opportunities of both men and women. Moreover, such a conceptualization does not explain the tenacity of such gender divisions in the face of dramatic declines in fertility, increases in women's education, and women's higher rates of labor force participation.

[. . .]

[. . .] A capitalism unfettered by gender has thus never existed except in the minds of scholars. A gendered analysis of labor markets must bring gender into the heart of production and introduce gender as a category of analysis that affects all spheres of life.

The first step in developing a gendered political economy is to incorporate gender as a category of analysis. I adopt Joan Scott's definition of gender as "the social organization of sexual difference." It is not a synonym for women, so gender can be at work even when women are not present. Gender is a signifier of relationships of power, and gendered "meanings vary across cultures, social groups, and time" (Scott 1988, 2). Gender positions women and men differently in society, structures their lived experiences in distinct ways, and refers not only to social positions and social relations but also to ideas (Rose 1992).

The second step is to integrate gender directly into the study of labor markets. Feminist labor historians have shown persuasively that gendered discourses of work shape the way that employers define their economic interests; in other words, employers' beliefs about gender partially constitute their ideas about rational economic practice (Downs 1995; Rose 1992). Employers have historically considered men and women to be qualitatively different types of labor and have therefore viewed productivity and labor control through a gendered lens. Consequently, they define jobs in gendered terms. On the basis of their assessments of the gendered character of work on the shop floor, employers use gender as a criterion for recruitment. Gendered hiring practices, in turn, produce the gender division of labor on the shop floor and perpetuate the deep occupational and sectoral segregation that exists all over the world. Once embedded in labor markets, gendered discourses of work shape gendered outcomes in labor markets independently of the nonmarket factors so often highlighted by scholars. Integrating gendered discourses of work into political economy brings gender into the heart of the market and allows for a truly gendered analysis of labor markets.

REFERENCES

Anker, Richard. 1998. *Gender and Jobs: Sex Segregation of Occupations in the World*. Geneva: International Labour Office.

Blau, Francine D., and Marianne A. Ferber. 1992. *The Economics of Women, Men, and Work*. Englewood Cliffs, N.J.: Prentice-Hall.

Boserup, Esther. 1970. *Woman's Role in Economic Development*. New York: St. Martin's Press.

Chapkis, Wendy, and Cynthia Enloe. 1983. *Of Common Cloth: Women in the Global Textile Industry*. Washington, D.C.: Institute for Policy Studies.

Charles, Maria, and David B. Grusky. 2004. *Occupational Ghettos: The Worldwide Segregation of Women and Men*. Stanford: Stanford University Press.

Cohn, Samuel. 2000. *Race and Gender Discrimination at Work*. Boulder, Colo.: Westview.

Doeringer, Peter B., and Michael J. Piore. 1971. *Internal Labor Markets and Manpower Analysis*. Lexington, Mass.: Heath Lexington Books.

Downs, Laura Lee. 1995. *Manufacturing Inequality: Gender Division in the French and British Metalworking Industries, 1914–1939*. Ithaca: Cornell University Press.

Economic and Social Commission for Asia and the Pacific. 1987. *Young Women Workers in Manufacturing: A Case Study of Rapidly Industrializing Economies of the ESCAP Region*. Bangkok: United Nations.

Elson, Diane, and Ruth Pearson. 1981. "'Nimble Fingers Make Cheap Workers': An Analysis of Women's Employment in Third World Export Manufacturing." *Feminist Review* 7 (Spring): 87–107.

Fernandez-Kelly, Maria Patricia. 1983. For *We Are Sold, I and My People: Women and Industry in Mexico's Frontier*. Albany: State University of New York Press.

Fox, Julia D. 1993. "Transformations in the Labor Process on a World Scale: Women in the New International Division of Labor." In *The Labor Process and Control of Labor*, ed. Berch Berberoglu, 137–151. Westport, Conn.: Praeger.

Fraser, Nancy. 1989. "What's Critical about Critical Theory? The Case of Habermas and Gender." In *Unruly Practices: Power, Discourse, and Gender in Contemporary Social Theory*, ed. Nancy Fraser, 113–143. Minneapolis: University of Minnesota Press.

Fuentes, Annette, and Barbara Ehrenreich. 1983. *Women in the Global Factory*. Boston: South End Press.

Hanchard, Michael. 1999. "Black Cinderella? Race and the Public Sphere in Brazil." In *Racial Politics in Contemporary Brazil*, ed. Michael Hanchard, 59–81. Durham, N.C.: Duke University Press.

Hartmann, Heidi. 1979. "Capitalism, Patriarchy, and Job Segregation by Sex." In *Capitalist Patriarchy and the Case for Socialist Feminism*, ed. Zillah R. Eisenstein, 206–247. New York: Monthly Review Press.

Heyzer, Noeleen, ed. 1988. *Daughters in Industry: Work, Skills, and Consciousness of Women Workers in Asia*. Kuala Lumpur: Asian and Pacific Development Center.

Humphrey, John. 1987. *Gender and Work in the Third World: Sexual Divisions in Brazilian Industry*. London: Tavistock.

Joekes, Susan P. 1982. *Female-Led Industrialization: Women's Jobs in Third World Export Manufacturing: The Case of the*

Moroccan Clothing Industry. Brighton, Sussex: Institute of Development Studies.

Joekes, Susan P. 1987. *Women in the World Economy: An INSTRAW Study*. New York: Oxford University Press.

Lim, Linda Y. C. 1983. "Capitalism, Imperialism, and Patriarchy: The Dilemma of Third-World Women Workers in Multinational Factories." In *Women, Men, and the International Division of Labor*, ed. June Nash and Maria Patricia Fernandez-Kelly, 70–91. Albany: State University of New York Press.

Lim, Linda Y. C. 1985. *Women Workers in Multinational Enterprises*. Geneva: ILO.

Marx, Karl. 1977. *Capital: Volume One*. New York: Vintage.

Mehta, Uday S. 1997. "Liberal Strategies of Exclusion." In *Tensions of Empire: Colonial Cultures in a Bourgeois World*, ed. Ann Laura Stoler and Frederick Cooper, 59–86. Berkeley: University of California Press.

Nash, June, and Maria Patricia Fernandez-Kelly, eds. 1983. *Women, Men, and the International Division of Labor*. Albany: State University of New York Press.

Pateman, Carole. 1988. *The Sexual Contract*. Stanford: Stanford University Press.

Rose, Sonya O. 1992. *Limited Livelihoods: Gender and Class in Nineteenth-Century England*. Berkeley: University of California Press.

Safa, Helen I. 1986. "Runaway Shops and Female Employment: The Search for Cheap Labor." In *Women's Work: Development and the Division of Labor by Gender*, ed. Eleanor Leacock and Helen Safa, 58–71. New York: Bergin & Garvey.

Scott, Alison MacEwen. 1986. "Industrialization, Gender Segregation, and Stratification Theory." In *Gender and Stratification*, ed Rosemary Crompton and Michael Man, 154–189. New York: Blackwell.

Scott, Joan Wallach. 1988. *Gender and the Politics of History*. New York: Columbia University Press.

Tiano, Susan. 1994. *Patriarchy on the Line: Labor, Gender, and Ideology in the Mexican Maquila Industry*. Philadelphia: Temple University Press.

Tomaskovic-Devey, Donald. 1993. *Gender and Racial Inequality at Work: The Sources and Consequences of Job Segregation*. Ithaca: Cornell University Press.

Tomoda, Shizue. 1995. *Women Workers in Manufacturing, 1971–91*. Geneva: ILO.

Ward, Kathryn. 1990. "Introduction and Overview." In *Women Workers and Global Restructuring*, ed. Kathryn Ward, 1–22. Ithaca: Cornell University Press.

23. Families and Personal Life*

Deborah Chambers and Pablo Gracia

[. . .L]ate nineteenth-century and early twentieth-century sociological theories about the family contributed to or sustained biological and social discourses, often drawing on quite contradictory frameworks of thinking. On the one hand, the family was assumed to be a universal biological unit. On the other hand, sociologists were pre-occupied with the effects of social and economic change on family structures. Although the family was mainly viewed through a biological lens, it was a lens used selectively to authenticate and legitimate an approved, monogamous, patriarchal and nuclear version sanctioned by a companion-ate partnership.

A second area of concern among sociologists was the effects of industrialization and urbaniza-tion on family structures and the desire to elevate a recent, nuclear model as the norm. A major and continuing fear among both academics and governments was the nuclear family's state of decline caused by encroaching individualism and privatization. The ideal companionate marriage was promoted to strengthen modern conjugal relationships in response to this fear of a decline in both the family and traditional communities. Based on positive intimate relationships between partners, this new kind of marriage was viewed as proof that the 'modern marriage' was becoming more egalitarian. By narrowly defining a small, mobile nuclear family as universal, functionalism

treated all other family types as deviations from this family form.

Dramatic changes in family structures across the twentieth century revealed that the nuclear family was neither universal nor permanent. Parsons did not predict the dramatic rise in divorce rates by the end of the twentieth century. In the USA, the number of households with two parents and children declined by 20 per cent between the 1960s and 1990s (Casper and Bianchi 2002:11 and 99). And in 1950, 93 per cent of children in the US lived in a nuclear family, while only 6 per cent lived with their mother and 1 per cent with their father. By 1998, 73 per cent lived in a nuclear family, 22 per cent with their mother and 5 per cent with their father (Casper and Bianchi 2002:99). Similar changes occurred in Europe. More recently, for example, 66 per cent of chil-dren in Denmark aged 11-15 were not living with two parents by 2006 while in France it was 73 per cent, in Hungary it was 74 per cent, in Ireland it was 81 per cent and in Spain 84 per cent (Lappegard, 2017). Similar demographic trans-formations occurred transnationally (for example in Europe, Latin America, North America and South-East Asia), with higher births outside mar-riage, increasing rates of cohabitation, and rising divorce rates occurring until the first decade of the twenty-first century (Lesthaeghe, 2010). This demographic trend diverges from the mid-twentieth-century vision of the family promoted by structural functionalism.

These trends indicate that social attitudes and behaviour changed dramatically during the twentieth century and beyond. However, certain

* From Chambers, D. and Gracia, P. (2022) *A Sociology of Family Life* (2nd edn, Cambridge: Polity). Extracts from pp. 38–39, 41, 42, 205–208.

traditional family values and norms endure. This is illustrated in the next chapter which engages with recent research which demonstrates the importance of continuity and connectedness among family members. One of the major distinctions between traditional and more recent approaches to families, households and individuals is the shift away from the idea of 'the family' as a social institution governed by rigid moral conventions towards an idea of family and wider personal life as a diverse and fluid sets of social customs and practices. The following chapters indicate that the focus today, in sociological debates, is on interactive processes and the agency of individuals and family members in relation to the social constraints of gender, sexuality, generation, social class, race, ethnicity and migration.

[. . .]

Scholars have claimed that, in recent decades, late modern societies have entered a 'new' more democratic phase of family life. New versions of 'family' are said to have been generated by key changes in ideas about love and commitment. However, this chapter also shows that many of the concerns about family decline expressed in the nineteenth and twentieth centuries are still present today. The increasing diversity of contemporary family forms – including same-sex couples, single-parent families, and post-divorce families – has prompted public anxieties about the wider social trends and underlying social conditions that correspond with new kinds of personal relationships. These transformations in family life are said to be part of an ongoing erosion of traditional forms of collective solidarity and community networks.

[. . .]

The concept of individualization has been used by social theorists from the 1990s to explain major changes in the family from the mid twentieth century onwards. The individualization thesis, also referred to as 'de-traditionalization', explains a revision of the boundaries between femininity and masculinity, including changes in the roles of motherhood, fatherhood and childhood. Until the late twentieth century, family life was shaped by relations of gender with husbands typically working outside the home and wives taking responsibility for childcare and domestic work. Women were expected to give up paid work when they married. The individualization thesis draws attention to the weakening of these traditional customs that once defined 'the family'. This thesis foregrounds a corresponding rise in individual agency and personal choice which characterizes a new stage of family life described by Giddens as the 'democratic' family (Giddens 1992).

Individualization refers to the erosion of traditional values and the rise of individual agency (Giddens 1992, 1998; Beck 1992, 1994). Contemporary changes in family life coincide with social and geographical mobility and shifts in employment and class identities. The individualization thesis claims that new kinds of lifestyles that accent the agency and autonomy of the individual have emerged in late modernity by offering a wider range of choices about how to live one's life. One of the general outcomes of these changes is that social categories such as 'gender' and 'sexuality', which were once regarded as biologically determined, are being contested and transformed. Intimacy is being transformed from a set of social obligations and conventions to a new kind of equality between couples. Although inequality may continue to exist in personal relationships, late modern theory suggests that this is more effectively explained at the individual level – guided by active choices and negotiation– rather than resulting from people's gender or class position.

[. . .]

The diverse range of intimacies and household arrangements that characterize present-day societies has prompted new sociological ways of thinking about 'family'. However, the search for new concepts to explain the multiple changes in intimacies and family and personal relations involves challenges. Power relations and inequalities of class, gender, race, age and ethnic identity can often be neglected within attempts to accent the strengths of both 'family' and more fluid personal commitments and reciprocities. As mentioned, many scholars now challenge the very concept of 'family' for being too hierarchical, patriarchal, homophobic and exclusionary (Berlant and Warner 2000; Roseneil and Budgeon 2004; Budgeon 2006). To counter a 'decline thesis' on family values with strong racist and heterosexist inferences, sociologists have made efforts to understand family life in new ways. Researchers who are reluctant to discard the term 'family' have broadened the concept to embrace and address new intimacies and new household arrangements that transcend the centrality of the conjugal bond, heteronormative frameworks, conventional divisions of labour and ethnocentric notions of family structures.

The conventional use of the term 'family' can reify or idealize certain preferred models of family life by favouring or applying a distorted permanency and fixity to certain types of living arrangements. The orthodox notion of 'family' denies the change that families constantly undergo. As Morgan (2011:3) states, "there is no such thing as 'The Family'". We need, then, to shed the 1950s 'cornflake packet' image of the family to avoid the temptation of giving the term 'family' some normative status. 'Family' is not only a vital and energizing term recurrently drawn on to reflect peoples' personal lives. It is also a term instilled with profound symbolic significance and affective meaning, as family values rhetoric reveals. The term 'family' is not a set of values to be confined to 'proper' or 'good' families. To be an effective analytical concept. it must be flexible enough to reflect and embrace multiple intimacies and modes of caregiving.

Intimacy and familial diversity have been addressed by Carol Smart (2007) who developed the concept of *personal life*. The idea of the 'personal' is valuable because it not only avoids the privileging of biological kin or marriage but also focuses on social change in the patterning of intimate relationships and caregiving. The term 'personal life' challenges the potentially static nature of the term 'family' by embracing not only newer family forms and relationships. It also embraces friendships and reconfigured kinship networks beyond conventionally understood families. For Smart, personal life is both socially constructed and relational, with an emphasis on connectivity and the varied meanings associated with being related and intimate. It also connects with Morgan's (2018) notion of personal practices by accenting the 'doing' or performing of relationships over blood relations.

The concept of personal life is flexible enough, then, to concede that household arrangements are no longer dominated by or confined to the nuclear family form. It highlights the significance of friendship in the patterning of intimacies and caregiving and therefore opens up a direct research focus on diverse intimate and caregiving arrangements. Personal life centres attention on both traditional family ties and wider kinship and contemporary arrangements such as same-sex partnerships and relationships created through reproductive technologies, LATS (those living apart together) and friendships. Using the term 'personal' over the term 'individual' enables researchers to address trends such as individualization but also avoids simplistic notions of atomized individualism. As such, Smart's approach entails a critique of the abstract nature of earlier theories about families.

Importantly, both Smart's concept 'personal life' and Morgan's notion of 'family practices' have been developed to be inclusive: to emphasize the wide-ranging nature of relationships that are family-like, including friendships. Smart states:

The 'personal' designates an area of life which impacts closely on people and means much to them, but which does not presume that there is an autonomous individual who makes choices and exercises unfettered agency. This means that the term 'personal life' can invoke the social, indeed it is conceptualized as always already part of the social (Smart 2007:28).

There is nothing intrinsically ethnocentric about the concepts of 'personal life', 'family practices', 'personal communities', 'friends as family' or 'families of choice'. However, given that these terms foreground the personal agency in contemporary western societies, we need to ensure that they are not used so narrowly that they are only pertinent to dominant white, middle class ideas of experimenting identity and agency. Experimentation with personal identity, embedded in the idea of the self as project, should not be abstracted from class, gender and racial inequalities. For example, as mentioned in Chapter 2, research on working-class lesbian couples with children demonstrates the class related difficulties of overcoming the stigma of being lesbian parents (Taylor 2007).

For Smart, 'personal life' blurs the distinctions between private and public spheres - the 'private' space of the home and public spaces and their significance for personal life - since both orbits influence traditional and changing ideas about intimacy, caregiving, and work commitments that encompass everyday life: "For example, personal life includes not only family life at home but also going to school or to work, taking part in financial transactions in shops, and engaging with public policy - for example by filling in official forms or by voting in elections" (May and Nordqvist 2018:2). Families are not necessarily distinct households or institutions detached from other locations and structures, especially in post-divorce families and transnational migrant families - where parents are hundreds of miles apart from their children. And Smart reminds us that personal life need not be regarded as parochial since it is clearly affected by globalization, migration, colonialism and other wider or global processes. It is embedded in and overlaps with public/formal/impersonal life.

REFERENCES

Beck, U. (1992) *Risk Society: Towards a New Modernity*. London: Sage.

Beck, U. (1994) The reinvention of politics: towards a theory of reflexive modernization. In U. Beck and S. Lash (eds), *Reflexive Modernization: Politics, Tradition and Aesthetics in the Modern Social Order*. Cambridge: Polity Press, pp.1–55.

Berlant, L. and Warner, M. (2000) Sex in public. In L. Berlant (ed.), *Intimacy*. Chicago: University of Chicago Press, pp. 311–30.

Budgeon, S. (2006) Friendship and formations of sociality in late modernity: the challenge of 'post-traditional intimacy'. *Sociological Research Online*, 11 (3). Available online at www.socresonline.org.uk/11/3/budgeon.html (accessed 11 December 2011).

Casper, L.M. and Bianchi, S.M. (2002) *Continuity and Change in the American Family*. Thousand Oaks, CA: Sage.

Giddens, A. (1992) *The Transformation of Intimacy: Sexuality, Love and Eroticism in Modern Societies*. Cambridge: Polity Press.

Giddens, A. (1998) *The Third Way: The Renewal of Social Democracy*. Cambridge: Polity Press.

Lappegard, T. (2017). Changing European families. In J. Treas, J. Scott, and M. Richards (eds), *The Wiley-Blackwell Companion to the Sociology of Families*, Chichester: Wiley-Blackwell, pp. 20–42.

Lesthaeghe, R. (2010). The unfolding story of the second demographic transition. *Population and Development Review*, 36(2), 211–251.

May, V. and Nordqvist, P. (2018) Introducing a sociology of personal life. In May, V. and Nordqvist, P. (eds), *Sociology of Personal Life*, London: Macmillan, pp. 1–15.

Morgan, D. (2011) *Rethinking Family Practices*. London: Palgrave Macmillan.

Morgan, D. (2018) Conceptualising the personal, In May, V. and Nordqvist, P. (eds), *Sociology of Personal Life*, London: Macmillan, pp. 16–29.

Roseneil, S. and Budgeon, S. (2004) Cultures of intimacy and care beyond 'the Family': personal life and social change in the early 21st century. *Current Sociology*, 52 (2), 135–59.

Smart, C. (2007) *Personal Life*. Cambridge: Polity Press.

Taylor, Y. (2007) *Working-class Lesbian Life: Classed Outsiders*. Basingstoke: Palgrave Macmillan.

24. Schools: Challenging or Reproducing Social Inequalities?*

Christy Kulz

Academies were established primarily in poor urban areas, often with large ethnic minority populations, to break cyclical underachievement through 'establishing a culture of ambition' (Adonis 2008). My ethnographic research and interviews with students, parents and teachers was conducted at the celebrated Beaumont Academy[1] in Redwood, a fictitious borough in East London over a two-year period. During this time I routinely met one-on-one with twenty-five children from years nine and eleven. I draw on this research to examine how intensively capitalist schools do not eradicate inequality, but re-entrench and reorganize hierarchies of value between students. I show this by exploring how social mixing and mobility is embodied by students and the alterations or eliminations necessary to achieve it, as these adjustments bring raced and classed positions into focus, highlighting who needs to 'do' work on themselves to accrue value. In the context of Beaumont, student (and staff) movements occur under the vigilant eye of a disciplinary regime that asserts its values by passing moral judgements and producing hierarchies that students navigate between, around and through.

Beaumont is continually evidenced to prove the academy programme's effectiveness and has served as a blueprint for numerous schools. Its influence over policy has grown as former head teacher Sir Stanton is now a key actor at a national level, celebrated by both Labour and Conservative politicians. [. . .]

[. . .]

Beaumont Academy opened in 2004 in the East London borough of Redwood where unemployment is twice the national average, half of housing is socially rented, and 40 per cent of Beaumont students receive free school meals. Statistics attesting to poverty and ethnic diversity are frequently juxtaposed with the school's outstanding test scores: in 2011, over 80 per cent of Beaumont's students received five A* to C grades at GCSE level, including maths and English, compared to just 54 per cent of students nationally. Eighty-two A-level students were offered places at elite universities, including seven at Cambridge. Beaumont produces excellent results, yet uncritical celebrations of the space's mixed-ness conceal issues of structural inequality lingering beneath the structures of its 'no excuses' culture.

During our interview, Sir Stanton reclined in his leather executive chair and described how the 'structure liberates' ethos rests on a philosophy that altruistically seeks to provide poor children with the opportunities that wealthier children enjoy 'to show that poor kids, working-class kids can do as well as middle-class kids do'. Stanton describes his second vision as:

* From Kulz, C. (2014) '"Structure Liberates?":
Mixing for Mobility and the Cultural
Transformation of Urban Children in a London
Academy', *Ethnic and Racial Studies*, 37(4):
685–701. Extracts from pp. 687–688, 689–690,
691–692, 694–696, 698, 699.

... the belief that children who come from unstructured backgrounds, as many of our children do, and often very unhappy ones, should be given more structure in their lives ... if they come from unstructured backgrounds where anything goes and rules and boundaries are not clear in their home, we need to ensure that they're clear here.

Stanton places the desire for working-class kids to have the educational advantages automatically afforded to the wealthy alongside assertions that these students come from unstructured, unhappy families. This corrective approach self-consciously applies rituals and routines that provide the structure that Stanton claims is absent from their homes. Yet not all children require this intervention. Stanton clearly differentiates between those who need structure and those who have it built in:

... you need more structure rather than less through experience in dealing with urban children ... you can be a lot more relaxed and free and easy in a nice, leafy middle-class area where the ground rules are clear before they come in, where children go home to lots of books and stuff like that.

The term 'urban children' or 'Redwood children' is used by several teachers to describe a largely ethnic minority and working-class student body. A raced and classed urban child is produced and contrasted with the leafy suburb's middle-class and predominantly white child. Stanton feels that routines are not necessary when dealing with these children because they come from disciplined homes with 'lots of books'. Stanton ties unstructured backgrounds to unhappiness and makes this unstructured unhappiness synonymous with the working-class, ethnic minority 'urban child'. Beaumont's structures are seen to aid the urban child by instigating academic success, which also creates happiness. Sara Ahmed's (2010, pp. 124–5) re-description of empire's civilizing mission as a happiness mission where 'human happiness is increased through the courts (law/justice), knowledge (reason), and manners (culture, habits)' and 'Empire becomes a gift

that cannot be refused, a forced gift' illuminates Stanton's assumptions linking urban children to unhappiness. Ahmed (2010, p. 125) outlines how the unhappy other provides the premise of action, where 'colonial knowledges constitute the other as ... being unhappy, as lacking the qualities or attributes required for a happier state of existence.' Similarly, Stanton's mission functions as a gift to unstructured unhappy students, forcing them to become less ethnic and more middle class so that they can move towards happier futures.

While poverty is briefly mentioned, Stanton's concern centres on creating opportunity and parenting practices. He singles out class, not ethnicity, as the single biggest hurdle to student achievement: 'I think class would be the biggest issue. A child going home to a home which doesn't value education, doesn't support their child, where there are no books, where there is no experience of higher education ... that's the bigger problem.'

Class, or more specifically, working-class parents, are the 'problem', with their detrimental parenting skills and misplaced values. Stanton describes how Beaumont 'becomes a sort of surrogate parent to the child and the child will only succeed if the philosophy of the school is that we will in many ways substitute and take over when necessary.' Class becomes a malleable position that can be changed by the individual's adoption of aspirational attitudes.

[...]

Although class is named as the 'biggest problem', with two-thirds of students coming from ethnic minority backgrounds, there is an implicit, inevitable overlap between the working-class children whose families are portrayed as inadequate and children from ethnic minority backgrounds. Race becomes an embedded, yet unspoken element underpinning the term 'urban children'. The easy amalgamation and unspoken fusion of race and class is apparent through the comments of teachers like Ms Smith:

Ms Smith: We are potentially more classist, if you like, than racist, to be honest.

CK: Hmm. How so?

Ms Smith: I think that sometimes when I look at the white middle-class children I wonder if they are getting away with things that other children wouldn't.

The idealized middle-class child carries implications of whiteness; ethnic minority children fall into the problematic working-class category outlined previously, as race is encapsulated in the term 'urban children'. It becomes a way to 'talk' race through class, sidestepping the need to address racism. Beaumont makes 'a commitment to "colour-blindness" rather than equality', as anti-racism is seen as outdated in our supposedly post-racial era (Lentin 2008, p. 313).

Scrutinizing who is included (and excluded) from the terms 'urban children' and who functions as the 'surrogate parent' demonstrates that 'interpretations of what children are and need patently reflect a white, middle-class cultural hegemony' (Gillies 2007, p. 145). Teachers find it easier to discuss class as a problem, which is unsurprising given the widely acceptable denigration of the working class through use of terms like 'chav' [. . .] describes how abject class disgust is performed through various media outlets and creates a borderline whiteness 'contaminated' by poverty-ridden estates (public housing) and racialized via sexual relations with ethnic minorities. The sluttish, loud, illiterate 'chav mum' with her gaggle of multicoloured illegitimate children is replaced by the (predominantly) white, respectable middle-class 'surrogate parent'; the respectable middle classes claim moral superiority through the working class's 'filthy whiteness' (Tyler 2008, pp. 25–6).

This acceptable class denigration becomes the back door by which race can be brought into the room without needing to announce its arrival. Gilroy's (2004, p. 40) call for 'liberation from white supremacy' and 'from all racialising and raciological thought, from racialised seeing, thinking and thinking about thinking' goes unrealised. Via the construction of the 'urban child', we can see how the production of 'race, class and gender are not distinct realms of experience, existing in splendid isolation from each other . . . rather they come into existence in and through relation to each other – if in contradictory and conflictual ways' (McClintock 1995, p. 5).

[. . .]

Institutional and social structures are [. . .] manipulated or contested by students in pursuit of their own needs or goals, yet their navigation of these structures is made in relation to their position within it. Several students felt circulating between groupings was a positive practice. Joshua, a sixteen-year-old, high-achieving Nigerian student, says he moves from the Afro-Caribbean to the Asian to the 'Caucasian' group, 'having a laugh with each'. He describes how mixing 'opens you up' and prevents narrow-mindedness; you have to interact with and understand a range of people to discover the 'true beauty of life'. The capacity to move between ethnic groups was part of becoming a 'diverse' and 'dynamic person' because 'being British had changed'. Language features heavily once again, as Joshua describes Britain as a diverse country where you need to know how to talk to different people. He describes how some of his black friends do not feel comfortable with his white friends because there were expressions that the white kids would not understand. Yet Joshua says he has 'achieved' an ethnically varied social group and can go anywhere with relative ease.

Isaac, a humorous Afro-Caribbean sixteen year old, relates social mobility to his interest in other people and how they 'get on'. Like Joshua, he feels one should embrace different groups rather than 'try to separate yourself off from others and be afraid of people who are different from you.' He thinks mixing around makes things better and it is what you need to do to get along in life. Mobility has personal benefits, for Isaac adds that he is 'lucky' to circulate, 'zipping in and out' with ease. By the end of year eleven, Isaac had decided to attend the sixth form, proclaiming that his days of 'messing about' were over because he had realized that this was a competition and he was going to turn it on 'full blast next year . . . to be on top'. Part of getting on top involved Isaac shifting his friendship group to hang out with high achievers and thus gain entrance to the sixth form head Ms Gable's 'special club' that visited Oxbridge. Isaac felt being seen to be friends with the set one group would get him in her 'good graces', as the Oxbridge candidates were a 'private sly little club' comprised of 'more serious students'. This shift involves Isaac deliberately moving from a more ethnically mixed social group to a more white middle-class one in order to accrue benefits; future social relations become tied to the acquisition of educational advantages and this shift of self is visually displayed through physical placement.

These boys' narratives highlight a combination of altruistic and self-serving motivations for social mixing. While pointing to the importance of understanding others, circulating also aids the development of a dynamic self, free to move across social space. Mixing is related to social mobility, both spatially and culturally. A key element of this mobility is the capacity to modulate speech styles. Mixing becomes a way of resourcing the self; mobility becomes an achievement, un-fixing students from ethnicity or class so that they can accrue value. Ethnicity becomes a positive asset, provided that they can effectively perform white middle-class norms as promoted by Beaumont's training. Reay et al. (2007) highlight how white middle-class parents depicted their children's proximity to students like Joshua and Isaac as desirable as they accrued 'multicultural capital'. Aspirational ethnic minority children also functioned as symbolic barriers demarcating the white middle classes from their undesirable white working-class 'other'.

These students arguably function as what Ahmed (2010) calls 'conversion points'. Their positive social integration promises happiness as social mixing turns bad feelings into good. These young black men, two of whom have been institutionally honoured by being made prefects, are actively converting themselves and acquiring capital that can be deployed in the future through taking up the idea of integration and happy multiculturalism. They have converted the threat of the pathological black body found in Beaumont's urban chaos discourse into an exemplary black body.

[. . .]

Beaumont promotes a neocolonial civilizing mission through its 'structure liberates' ethos, which pathologizes the urban area of Beaumont while attempting to graft dominant value systems onto students. These institutional structures are shaped by a competitive education market propagated by successive UK governments committed to a neoliberal doctrine of aspirational individualism. Students' social groupings are structured by these institutional norms that they navigate and circumvent from various positions within the hierarchy. Possessing mobility means possessing value, but mixing for mobility is only a necessary strategy for those who do not inhabit the classed and raced position of the ideal student. [. . .]

[. . .] The academy structures the ideal subject through creating distinctions that attribute judgements and values through bodily and social orientations. These orientations form the basis of a moral economy, as Beaumont's moral distinctions of worth become social distinctions of value that are negotiated out in the playground (Skeggs 2004). Stanton demands a 'no excuses culture', claiming that mentioning social factors only 'entrenches mediocrity'. Yet this 'no excuses' mantra enacts a blinkered ignore-and-overcome logic. Divorcing students from their social positioning trivializes continued hardship, institutionalized racism and moral value judgements. Beaumont's 'structures' seek to 'liberate' children from pathological raced, classed identities, but in ignoring the power of inequitable structures they simultaneously reify them.

NOTE

1. The school, borough and all participants have been given pseudonyms so they may remain anonymous.

REFERENCES

ADONIS, ANDREW 2008 'Academies and social mobility', Speech to the National Academies Conference. Available from: http://www.standards.dfes.gov.uk/.../Andrew_Adonis_Speech_feb08.doc [Accessed XX June 2013].

AHMED, SARA 2010 *The Promise of Happiness*, London: Duke University Press.

GILLIES, VAL 2007 *Marginalised Mothers: Exploring Working-Class Experiences of Parenting*, London: Routledge.

LENTIN, ANNA 2008 'After anti-racism?', *European Journal of Cultural Studies*, vol. 11, no. 3, pp. 311–31.

MCCLINTOCK, ANNE 1995 *Imperial Leather: Race, Gender and Sexuality in the Colonial Contest*, New York: Routledge.

REAY, DIANE et al. 2007 'A darker shade of pale?' Whiteness, the middle classes and multi-ethnic inner city schooling', *Sociology*, vol. 41, no. 6, pp. 1041–60.

SKEGGS, BEVERLEY 2004 *Class, Self, Culture*, London: Routledge.

TYLER, IMOGEN 2008 '"Chav mum, chav scum": class disgust in contemporary Britain', *Feminist Media Studies*, vol. 8, no. 1, pp. 17–34.

25. Capitalism and the Digital Revolution*

Shoshana Zuboff

Surveillance capitalism unilaterally claims human experience as free raw material for translation into behavioral data. Although some of these data are applied to product or service improvement, the rest are declared as a proprietary *behavioral surplus*, fed into advanced manufacturing processes known as "machine intelligence," and fabricated into *prediction products* that anticipate what you will do now, soon, and later. Finally, these prediction products are traded in a new kind of marketplace for behavioral predictions that I call *behavioral futures markets*. Surveillance capitalists have grown immensely wealthy from these trading operations, for many companies are eager to lay bets on our future behavior.

As we shall see in the coming chapters, the competitive dynamics of these new markets drive surveillance capitalists to acquire ever-more-predictive sources of behavioral surplus: our voices, personalities, and emotions. Eventually, surveillance capitalists discovered that the most-predictive behavioral data come from intervening in the state of play in order to nudge, coax, tune, and herd behavior toward profitable outcomes. Competitive pressures produced this shift, in which automated machine processes not only *know* our behavior but also *shape* our behavior at scale. With this reorientation from knowledge to power, it is no longer enough to automate information flows *about us*; the goal now is to *automate us*. In this phase of surveillance capitalism's evolution, the means of production are subordinated to an increasingly complex and comprehensive "means of behavioral modification." In this way, surveillance capitalism births a new species of power that I call *instrumentarianism*. Instrumentarian power knows and shapes human behavior toward others' ends. Instead of armaments and armies, it works its will through the automated medium of an increasingly ubiquitous computational architecture of "smart" networked devices, things, and spaces.

In the coming chapters we will follow the growth and dissemination of these operations and the instrumentarian power that sustains them. Indeed, it has become difficult to escape this bold market project, whose tentacles reach from the gentle herding of innocent Pokémon Go players to eat, drink, and purchase in the restaurants, bars, fast-food joints, and shops that pay to play in its behavioral futures markets to the ruthless expropriation of surplus from Facebook profiles for the purposes of shaping individual behavior, whether it's buying pimple cream at 5:45 p.m. on Friday, clicking "yes" on an offer of new running shoes as the endorphins race through your brain after your long Sunday morning run, or voting next week. Just as industrial capitalism was driven to the continuous intensification of the means of production, so surveillance capitalists and their market players are now locked into the continuous intensification of the means of behavioral modification and the gathering might of instrumentarian power.

* From Zuboff, S. (2019) *The Age of Surveillance Capitalism: The Fight for a Human Future at the New Frontier of Power* (London: Profile Books). Extracts from pp. 8–11, 93–94, 95, 96.

Surveillance capitalism runs contrary to the early digital dream, consigning the Aware Home to ancient history. Instead, it strips away the illusion that the networked form has some kind of indigenous moral content, that being "connected" is somehow intrinsically pro-social, innately inclusive, or naturally tending toward the democratization of knowledge. Digital connection is now a means to others' commercial ends. At its core, surveillance capitalism is parasitic and self-referential. It revives Karl Marx's old image of capitalism as a vampire that feeds on labor, but with an unexpected turn. Instead of labor, surveillance capitalism feeds on every aspect of every human's experience.

Google invented and perfected surveillance capitalism in much the same way that a century ago General Motors invented and perfected managerial capitalism. Google was the pioneer of surveillance capitalism in thought and practice, the deep pocket for research and development, and the trailblazer in experimentation and implementation, but it is no longer the only actor on this path. Surveillance capitalism quickly spread to Facebook and later to Microsoft. Evidence suggests that Amazon has veered in this direction, and it is a constant challenge to Apple, both as an external threat and as a source of internal debate and conflict.

As the pioneer of surveillance capitalism, Google launched an unprecedented market operation into the unmapped spaces of the internet, where it faced few impediments from law or competitors, like an invasive species in a landscape free of natural predators. Its leaders drove the systemic coherence of their businesses at a breakneck pace that neither public institutions nor individuals could follow. Google also benefited from historical events when a national security apparatus galvanized by the attacks of 9/11 was inclined to nurture, mimic, shelter, and appropriate surveillance capitalism's emergent capabilities for the sake of total knowledge and its promise of certainty.

Surveillance capitalists quickly realized that they could do anything they wanted, and they did. They dressed in the fashions of advocacy and emancipation, appealing to and exploiting contemporary anxieties, while the real action was hidden offstage. Theirs was an invisibility cloak woven in equal measure to the rhetoric of the empowering web, the ability to move swiftly, the confidence of vast revenue streams, and the wild, undefended nature of the territory they would conquer and claim. They were protected by the inherent illegibility of the automated processes that they rule, the ignorance that these processes breed, and the sense of inevitability that they foster.

Surveillance capitalism is no longer confined to the competitive dramas of the large internet companies, where behavioral futures markets were first aimed at online advertising. Its mechanisms and economic imperatives have become the default model for most internet-based businesses. Eventually, competitive pressure drove expansion into the offline world, where the same foundational mechanisms that expropriate your online browsing, likes, and clicks are trained on your run in the park, breakfast conversation, or hunt for a parking space. Today's prediction products are traded in behavioral futures markets that extend beyond targeted online ads to many other sectors, including insurance, retail, finance, and an ever-widening range of goods and services companies determined to participate in these new and profitable markets. Whether it's a "smart" home device, what the insurance companies call "behavioral underwriting," or any one of thousands of other transactions, we now pay for our own domination.

Surveillance capitalism's products and services are not the objects of a value exchange. They do not establish constructive producer-consumer reciprocities. Instead, they are the "hooks" that lure users into their extractive operations in which our personal experiences are scraped and packaged as the means to others' ends. We are not surveillance capitalism's "customers." Although the saying tells us "If it's free, then you are the product," that is also incorrect. We are the sources of surveillance capitalism's crucial surplus: the objects of a technologically advanced and increasingly inescapable raw-material-extraction operation. Surveillance capitalism's actual customers are the enterprises that trade in its markets for future behavior.

This logic turns ordinary life into the daily renewal of a twenty-first-century Faustian compact. "Faustian" because it is nearly impossible to tear ourselves away, despite the fact that what we must give in return will destroy life as we have known it. Consider that the internet has become essential for social participation, that the internet is now saturated with commerce, and that commerce is now subordinated to surveillance capitalism. Our dependency is at the heart of the commercial surveillance project, in which our felt needs for effective life vie against the inclination to resist its bold incursions. This conflict produces a psychic numbing that inures us to the realities of being tracked, parsed, mined, and modified. It disposes us to rationalize the situation in resigned cynicism, create excuses that operate like defense mechanisms ("I have nothing to hide"), or find other ways to stick our heads in the sand, choosing ignorance out of frustration and helplessness.[1] In this way, surveillance capitalism imposes a fundamentally illegitimate choice that twenty-first-century individuals should not have to make, and its normalization leaves us singing in our chains.[2]

Surveillance capitalism operates through unprecedented asymmetries in knowledge and the power that accrues to knowledge. Surveillance capitalists know everything *about us*, whereas their operations are designed to be unknowable *to us*. They accumulate vast domains of new knowledge *from us*, but not *for us*. They predict our futures for the sake of others' gain, not ours. As long as surveillance capitalism and its behavioral futures markets are allowed to thrive, ownership of the new means of behavioral modification eclipses ownership of the means of production as the fountainhead of capitalist wealth and power in the twenty-first century.

[. . .]

With Google in the lead, surveillance capitalism rapidly became the default model of information capitalism on the web and, as we shall see in coming chapters, gradually drew competitors from every sector. This new market form declares that serving the genuine needs of people is less lucrative, and therefore less important, than selling predictions of their behavior. Google discovered that *we are less valuable than others' bets on our future behavior*. This changed everything.

Behavioral surplus defines Google's earnings success. In 2016, 89 percent of the revenues of its parent company, Alphabet, derived from Google's targeted advertising programs.[3] The scale of raw-material flows is reflected in Google's domination of the internet, processing over 40,000 search queries every second on average: more than 3.5 billion searches per day and 1.2 trillion searches per year worldwide in 2017.[4]

On the strength of its unprecedented inventions, Google's $400 billion market value edged out ExxonMobil for the number-two spot in market capitalization in 2014, only sixteen years after its founding, making it the second-richest company in the world behind Apple.[5] By 2016, Alphabet/Google occasionally wrested the number-one position from Apple and was ranked number two globally as of September 20, 2017.[6]

It is useful to stand back from this complexity to grasp the overall pattern and how the puzzle pieces fit together:

1. *The logic*: Google and other surveillance platforms are sometimes described as "two-sided" or "multi-sided" markets, but the mechanisms of surveillance capitalism suggest something different.[7] Google had discovered a way to translate its nonmarket interactions with users into surplus raw material for the fabrication of products aimed at genuine market transactions with its real customers: advertisers.[8] The translation of behavioral surplus from outside to inside the market finally enabled Google to convert investment into revenue. The corporation thus created out of thin air and at zero marginal cost an asset class of vital raw materials derived from users' non-market online behavior. At first those raw materials were

simply "found," a by-product of users' search actions. Later those assets were hunted aggressively and procured largely through surveillance. The corporation simultaneously created a new kind of marketplace in which its proprietary "prediction products" manufactured from these raw materials could be bought and sold.

The summary of these developments is that the behavioral surplus upon which Google's fortune rests can be considered as *surveillance assets*. These assets are critical raw materials in the pursuit of *surveillance revenues* and their translation into *surveillance capital*. The entire logic of this capital accumulation is most accurately understood as *surveillance capitalism*, which is the foundational framework for a surveillance-based economic order: a *surveillance economy*. The big pattern here is one of subordination and hierarchy, in which earlier reciprocities between the firm and its users are subordinated to the derivative project of our behavioral surplus captured for others' aims. We are no longer the *subjects* of value realization. Nor are we, as some have insisted, the "product" of Google's sales. Instead, we are the *objects* from which raw materials are extracted and expropriated for Google's prediction factories. Predictions about our behavior are Google's products, and they are sold to its actual customers but not to us. *We are the means to others' ends.*

[. . .]

2. *The means of production*: Google's internet-age manufacturing process is a critical component of the unprecedented. Its specific technologies and techniques, which I summarize as "machine intelligence," are constantly evolving, and it is easy to be intimidated by their complexity. The same term may mean one thing today and something very different in one year or in five years. For example, Google has been described as developing and deploying "artificial intelligence" since at least 2003, but the term itself is a moving target, as capabilities have evolved from primitive programs that can play tic-tac-toe to

systems that can operate whole fleets of driverless cars.

Google's machine intelligence capabilities feed on behavioral surplus, and the more surplus they consume, the more accurate the prediction products that result. *Wired* magazine's founding editor, Kevin Kelly, once suggested that although it seems like Google is committed to developing its artificial intelligence capabilities to improve Search, it's more likely that Google develops Search as a means of continuously training its evolving AI capabilities.[9] This is the essence of the machine intelligence project. As the ultimate tapeworm, the machine's intelligence depends upon how much data it eats. In this important respect the new means of production differs fundamentally from the industrial model, in which there is a tension between quantity and quality. Machine intelligence is the synthesis of this tension, for it reaches its full potential for quality only as it approximates totality.

[. . .]

3. *The products*: Machine intelligence processes behavioral surplus into *prediction products* designed to forecast what we will feel, think, and do: now, soon, and later. These methodologies are among Google's most closely guarded secrets. The nature of its products explains why Google repeatedly claims that it does not sell personal data. What? Never! Google executives like to claim their privacy purity because they do not sell their raw material. Instead, the company sells the predictions that only it can fabricate from its world-historic private hoard of behavioral surplus.

Prediction products reduce risks for customers, advising them where and when to place their bets. The quality and competitiveness of the product are a function of its approximation to certainty: the more predictive the product, the lower the risks for buyers and the greater the volume of sales. Google has learned to be a data-based fortune-teller that replaces intuition with science at scale in order to tell and sell our fortunes for profit to its customers, but not to us. Early on, Google's prediction products were largely aimed at sales of targeted advertising, but as we shall see, advertising was the beginning of the surveillance project, not the end.

4. *The marketplace*: Prediction products are sold into a new kind of market that trades exclusively in future behavior. Surveillance capitalism's profits derive primarily from these *behavioral futures* markets. Although advertisers were the dominant players in the early history of this new kind of marketplace, there is no reason why such markets are limited to this group. The new prediction systems are only incidentally about ads, in the same way that Ford's new system of mass production was only incidentally about automobiles. In both cases the systems can be applied to many other domains. The already visible trend, as we shall see in the coming chapters, is that any actor with an interest in purchasing probabilistic information about our behavior and/or influencing future behavior can pay to play in markets where the behavioral fortunes of individuals, groups, bodies, and things are told and sold[.]

NOTES

1. For a prescient early treatment of these issues, see Langdon Winner, "A Victory for Computer Populism," *Technology Review* 94, no. 4 (1991): 66. See also Chris Jay Hoofnagle, Jennifer M. Urban, and Su Li, "Privacy and Modern Advertising: Most US Internet Users Want 'Do Not Track' to Stop Collection of Data About Their Online Activities" (BCLT Research Paper, Rochester, NY: Social Science Research Network, October 8, 2012), https://papers.ssrn.com/abstract=2152135; Joseph Turow et al., "Americans Reject Tailored Advertising and Three Activities That Enable It," Annenberg School for Communication, September 29, 2009, http://papers.ssrn.com/abstract=1478214; Chris Jay Hoofnagle and Jan Whittington, "Free: Accounting for the Costs of the Internet's Most Popular Price," *UCLA Law Review* 61 (February 28, 2014): 606; Jan Whittington and Chris Hoofnagle, "Unpacking Privacy's Price," *North Carolina Law Review* 90 (January 1, 2011): 1327; Chris Jay Hoofnagle, Jennifer King, Su Li, and Joseph Turow, "How Different Are Young Adults from Older Adults When It Comes to Information Privacy Attitudes & Policies?" April 14, 2010, http://repository.upenn.edu/asc_papers/399.

2. The phrase is from Roberto Mangabeira Unger, "The Dictatorship of No Alternatives," in *What Should the Left Propose?* (London: Verso, 2006), 1–11.

3. https://www.scc.gov/Archives/edgar/data/1652044/000165204417000008/goog10-kq42016.htm#s58C60B74D56A630AD6EA2B64F53BD90C. According to Alphabet's account in 2016, its revenues were $90,272,000,000. This included "Google segment revenues of $89.5 billion with revenue growth of 20% year over year and Other Bets revenues of $0.8 billion with revenue growth of 82% year over year." Google Segment advertising revenues were $79,383,000,000, or 88.73 percent of Google Segment revenues.

4. "Google Search Statistics—Internet Live Stats," Internet Live State, September 20, 2017, http://www.internetlivestats.com/google-search-statistics; Greg Sterling, "Data: Google Monthly Search Volume Dwarfs Rivals Because of Mobile Advantage," *Search Engine Land,* February 9, 2017, http://searchengineland.com/data-google-monthly-search-volume-dwarfs-rivals-mobile-advantage-269120. This translated into 76 percent of all desktop searches and 96 percent of mobile searches in the US and corresponding shares of 87 percent and 95 percent worldwide.

5. Roben Farzad, "Google at $400 Billion: A New No. 2 in Market Cap," *BusinessWeek,* February 12, 2014, http://www.business week.com/articles/2014-02-12/google-at-400-billion-a-new-no-dot-2-in-market-cap.

6. "Largest Companies by Market Cap Today," *Dogs of the Dow,* 2017, https://web.archive.org/web/20180701094340/http://dogsof thedow.com/largest-companies-by-market-cap.htm.

7. Jean-Charles Rochet and Jean Tirole, "Two-Sided Markets: A Progress Report," *RAND Journal of Economics* 37, no. 3 (2006): 645–67.

8. For a discussion on this point and its relation to online target advertising, see Katherine J. Strandburg, "Free Fall: The Online Market's Consumer Preference Disconnect" (working paper, New York University Law and Economics, October 1, 2013).

9. Kevin Kelly, "The Three Breakthroughs That Have Finally Unleashed AI on the World," *Wired,* October 27, 2014, https://www.wired.com/2014/10/future-of-artificial-intelligence.

Part 4 – Further reading

Given the variety of social structures, we can only scratch the surface here, and readers will have to search for similar books. On families and the developing field of personal life, a very good entry point is Chambers, D. and Gracia P. (2022) *A Sociology of Family Life: Change and Diversity in Intimate Relations* (2nd edn, Cambridge: Polity). For issues of education and schooling, try Boronski, T., and Hassan, N. (2015) *Sociology of Education* (London: Sage), which is a well-written introduction. Edgell, S., and Granter, E. (2020) *The Sociology of Work: Continuity and Change in Paid and Unpaid Work* (3rd edn, London: Sage) provides an up to the minute account of shifting forms of work. Finally, everybody should know the basics of what is meant by capitalism, and Fulcher, J. (2015) *Capitalism: A Very Short Introduction* (2nd edn, Oxford: Oxford University Press) does exactly what you would expect. The impact of digital technology on capitalism is discussed in Srnicek, N. (2016) *Platform Capitalism* (Cambridge: Polity).

Sociology, 9th edition

Each theme in this section is covered in a distinct chapter in the textbook, so you will need to consult chapter 16, 'Education', chapter 15, 'Families and Intimate Relationships', and chapter 17, 'Work and Employment'. Material on capitalism is scattered across the book, but start with chapter 3, 'Theories and Perspectives'.

Part 5 Unequal Life Chances

For many outsiders, sociology simply *is* the study of social inequality and unequal life chances. It is easy to see why this perception exists, as much sociological work across a varied range of subjects involves issues of inequality. We can legitimately say that sociologists took philosophical thinking about the prospects for equality and turned it into empirical research studies that generated clear evidence of unequal life chances on a series of dimensions. Sociologists have also examined inequalities alongside the evaluation of social policies aimed at mitigating or eliminating their negative effects. Although sociology began with class inequality and urban poverty, over time more forms of inequality were uncovered, including gender, race and ethnicity, disability and sexuality, that have occupied many sociologists over the twentieth century and beyond. At the same time, the terminology used has changed considerably, and we may find discussions of *social inequality*, *social stratification*, *social divisions* and *social exclusion*. However, *social inequality* continues to be the central concept in empirical research, and the readings in this section reflect something of the diverse interests of sociologists today.

In Reading 26, Kimberlé Crenshaw discusses the concept of intersectionality, which has become increasingly widely adopted in studies of social inequality. At its most basic, intersectionality refers to the varied ways in which inequalities of race, ethnicity, gender and social class intertwine in processes of identity formation and structures of inequality. For example, while sociologists have long studied inequalities of gender, black feminists contend that there is no common experience of inequality across women from different social class groups, races and ethnicities. In particular, black feminists have been at the forefront of the scholarly attempt to examine the ways in which class, race and gender intersect to produce different experiences of inequality and advantage. Crenshaw uses the concept of intersectionality in relation to 'violence against women of color' in the USA. She argues that many women of colour who seek refuge in women's shelters to escape domestic violence are poor, unemployed or underemployed. Their structural position in society means they often have childcare responsibilities and lack the skills needed to gain decent employment in what is already a racially discriminatory job market. Hence, interventions based on gender identity are unlikely to be successful, and an intersectional approach that is sensitive to the convergence of race, class and gender is needed. Crenshaw also discusses the political consequences of adopting an intersectional perspective to combat discrimination and oppression.

One form of inequality that has risen to prominence is that of disability, the study of which is today a thriving field of sociological study. Early studies uncovered many discriminatory ideas, assumptions and practices against disabled people and proposed many practical policy mitigation strategies. They also raised awareness of the medicalization of disability as a series of health problems which depended on the medical profession for solutions. A major turning point was the development of an alternative social model of disability, which insisted that social arrangements and beliefs effectively 'disabled' people with impairments, discriminating against them and restricting their lives unnecessarily. Political campaigns for equality and the removal of disabling barriers have, in many ways, been successful, especially in bringing about legislative change. In the twenty-first century, there is a growing interest in the underlying 'ableist' assumptions that present a significant obstacle to further progress for disabled people. Our reading here is from Fiona Kumari Campbell, who explores ableism as a network of 'beliefs, processes and practices' that produce the specific standard for self and body of which disability is understood as a diminished form. Shifting the focus from disability and disabled people to the analysis of ableism and its continual reproduction in everyday life may offer a better understanding of the contours of 'compulsory ableness'.

Studies of class-based stratification are often rooted in the readily available evidence of economic inequality across populations. There is much evidence of a growing gap between rich and poor; in particular, it appears that a small number of super-rich individuals and families have managed not just to hold on to their wealth but to increase it massively, a process that continued even through the COVID-19 pandemic. How has this come about? Easily the most influential explanation for this phenomenon lies in the work of Thomas Piketty, who set out to understand the shifting distribution of wealth. Is it inevitable that capitalism leads to the concentration of wealth in fewer hands, or are there countervailing tendencies

pushing in the opposite direction that might become dominant? Drawing on a wealth of data, Piketty weighs the possibilities. One of his most significant arguments concentrates on the shifting rate of return on capital. He argues that, when the rate of return on capital exceeds the rate of growth of economic output and income, an unsustainable level of inequality is generated. It is unsustainable because it threatens to undermine the capitalist work ethic and the meritocratic principles of democratic societies. The reading covers Piketty's general argument in a brief and, hopefully, digestible form.

The concept of race fell into disrepute in sociology because of the unevidenced claim of fixed races with clear behavioural characteristics, which has no basis in biological science. Ethnicity is now generally used to refer to the different and unequal experience of social groups with specific cultural attributes, such as language, religion and dress codes. At the same time, many sociologists argue that, as long as race remains common currency in the wider society, it has consequences for social relations, and sociologists must not ignore this. This somewhat paradoxical situation has led to a number of difficult theoretical and practical issues, which are discussed in Reading 29, from Michael Banton. He looks at the way the issue played out in 2002, when the American Sociological Association (ASA) was asked to comment on a proposal to stop the California state government from collecting data on race and ethnicity. The proposal's reasoning was that not only does race not refer to anything 'real', but continuing to use the term as if it did risked worsening 'racial divisions'. The ASA advised that data on race *should* be collected as it was an important part of the evidence base for a range of social policies, but, at the same time, the association maintained that the concept of race had no validity in scholarly circles. Banton carefully unpicks these apparently contradictory intellectual and political positions.

As more women have moved into higher education and paid work, there has been a growing interest in how heterosexual couples in particular manage their relationships. When both partners now work full-time, are the necessary household tasks shared more equally than previously? How do couples manage their household finances? Is childcare equally shared? These questions lend themselves to empirical research, which can then inform our understanding of shifting gender relations and the impact of the feminization of work. Although there have been many changes in gender relations, one area that has proved stubbornly resistant to major change is the gendered division of domestic labour. Some sociologists theorized that, as women moved into paid work, and especially in situations where they earned more than male partners, there would be a move towards more equality in the performance of domestic labour and childcare responsibilities. The evidence to date suggests that this has not happened. Reading 30 is based on a piece of qualitative research conducted by Clare Lyonette and Rosemary Crompton into some of the reasons for this continuing gender inequality. The research compared women who earned more than, about the same as, and less than their male partners, seeking to test several theories. The subject is an important one because, as long as they continue to take on the bulk of time-consuming domestic tasks, working women will remain at a disadvantage in the labour market.

26. Intersectionality: Structural and Political*

Kimberlé Crenshaw

Over the last two decades, women have organized against the almost routine violence that shapes their lives.[1] Drawing from the strength of shared experience, women have recognized that the political demands of millions speak more powerfully than the pleas of a few isolated voices. This politicization in turn has transformed the way we understand violence against women. For example, battering and rape, once seen as private (family matters) and aberrational (errant sexual aggression), are now largely recognized as part of a broad-scale system of domination that affects women as a class.[2] This process of recognizing as social and systemic what was formerly perceived as isolated and individual has also characterized the identity politics of African Americans, other people of color, and gays and lesbians, among others. For all these groups, identity-based politics has been a source of strength, community, and intellectual development.

The embrace of identity politics, however, has been in tension with dominant conceptions of social justice. Race, gender, and other identity categories are most often treated in mainstream liberal discourse as vestiges of bias or domination – that is, as intrinsically negative frameworks in which social power works to exclude or marginalize those who are different. According to this understanding, our liberatory objective should be to empty such categories of any social significance. Yet implicit in certain strands of feminist and racial liberation movements, for example is the view that the social power in delineating difference need not be the power of domination; it can instead be the source of social empowerment and reconstruction.

The problem with identity politics is not that it fails to transcend difference, as some critics charge, but rather the opposite – that it frequently conflates or ignores intragroup differences. In the context of violence against women, this elision of difference in identity politics is problematic, fundamentally because the violence that many women experience is often shaped by other dimensions of their identities, such as race and class. Moreover, ignoring difference within groups contributes to tension among groups, another problem of identity politics that bears on efforts to politicize violence against women. Feminist efforts to politicize experiences of women and antiracist efforts to politicize experiences of people of color have frequently proceeded as though the issues and experiences they each detail occur on mutually exclusive terrains. Although racism and sexism readily intersect in the lives of real people, they seldom do in feminist and antiracist practices. And so, when the practices expound identity as woman or person of color as an either/or proposition, they relegate the identity of women of color to a location that resists telling.

[. . .]

* From Crenshaw, K. (1991) 'Mapping the Margins: Intersectionality, Identity Politics, and Violence against Women of Color', *Stanford Law Review*, 43(6): 1241–1299. Extracts from pp. 1241–1242, 1244–1245, 1296–1299.

In an earlier article, I used the concept of intersectionality to denote the various ways in which race and gender interact to shape the multiple dimensions of Black[3] women's employment experiences.[4] My objective there was to illustrate that many of the experiences Black women face are not subsumed within the traditional boundaries of race or gender discrimination as these boundaries are currently understood, and that the intersection of racism and sexism factors into Black women's lives in ways that cannot be captured wholly by looking at the race or gender dimensions of those experiences separately. I build on those observations here by exploring the various ways in which race and gender intersect in shaping structural, political, and representational aspects of violence against women of color.[5]

I should say at the outset that intersectionality is not being offered here as some new, totalizing theory of identity. Nor do I mean to suggest that violence against women of color can be explained only through the specific frameworks of race and gender considered here.[6] Indeed, factors I address only in part or not at all, such as class or sexuality, are often as critical in shaping the experiences of women of color. My focus on the intersections of race and gender only highlights the need to account for multiple grounds of identity when considering how the social world is constructed.[7]

[. . .]

This article has presented intersectionality as a way of framing the various interactions of race and gender in the context of violence against women of color. Yet intersectionality might be more broadly useful as a way of mediating the tension between assertions of multiple identity and the ongoing necessity of group politics. It is helpful in this regard to distinguish intersectionality from the closely related perspective of antiessentialism, from which women of color have critically engaged white feminism for the absence of women of color on the one hand, and for speaking for women of color on the other. One rendition of this antiessentialist critique

– that feminism essentializes the category woman – owes a great deal to the postmodernist idea that categories we consider natural or merely representational are actually socially constructed in a linguistic economy of difference.[8] While the descriptive project of postmodernism of questioning the ways in which meaning is socially constructed is generally sound, this critique sometimes misreads the meaning of social construction and distorts its political relevance.

One version of antiessentialism, embodying what might be called the vulgarized social construction thesis, is that since all categories are socially constructed, there is no such thing as, say, Blacks or women, and thus it makes no sense to continue reproducing those categories by organizing around them.[9] Even the Supreme Court has gotten into this act. In *Metro Broadcasting, Inc. v. FCC*,[10] the Court conservatives, in rhetoric that oozes vulgar constructionist smugness, proclaimed that any set-aside designed to increase the voices of minorities on the air waves was itself based on a racist assumption that skin color is in some way connected to the likely content of one's broadcast.[11]

But to say that a category such as race or gender is socially constructed is not to say that that category has no significance in our world. On the contrary, a large and continuing project for subordinated people – and indeed, one of the projects for which postmodern theories have been very helpful – is thinking about the way power has clustered around certain categories and is exercised against others. This project attempts to unveil the processes of subordination and the various ways those processes are experienced by people who are subordinated and people who are privileged by them. It is, then, a project that presumes that categories have meaning and consequences. And this project's most pressing problem, in many if not most cases, is not the existence of the categories, but rather the particular values attached to them and the way those values foster and create social hierarchies.

This is not to deny that the process of categorization is itself an exercise of power, but the story is much more complicated and nuanced than that. First, the process of categorizing – or, in identity terms, naming – is not unilateral. Subordinated people can and do participate, sometimes even subverting the naming process in empowering ways. One need only think about the historical subversion of the category "Black" or the current transformation of "queer" to understand that categorization is not a one-way street. Clearly, there is unequal power, but there is nonetheless some degree of agency that people can and do exert in the politics of naming. And it is important to note that identity continues to be a site of resistance for members of different subordinated groups. We all can recognize the distinction between the claims "I am Black" and the claim "I am a person who happens to be Black." "I am Black" takes the socially imposed identity and empowers it as an anchor of subjectivity. "I am Black" becomes not simply a statement of resistance but also a positive discourse of self-identification, intimately linked to celebratory statements like the Black nationalist "Black is beautiful." "I am a person who happens to be Black," on the other hand, achieves self-identification by straining for a certain universality (in effect, "I am first a person") and for a concomitant dismissal of the imposed category ("Black") as contingent, circumstantial, nondeterminant. There is truth in both characterizations, of course, but they function quite differently depending on the political context. At this point in history, a strong case can be made that the most critical resistance strategy for disempowered groups is to occupy and defend a politics of social location rather than to vacate and destroy it.

Vulgar constructionism thus distorts the possibilities for meaningful identity politics by conflating at least two separate but closely linked manifestations of power. One is the power exercised simply through the process of categorization; the other, the power to cause that categorization to have social and material consequences. While the former power facilitates the latter, the political implications of challenging one over the other matter greatly. We can look at debates over racial subordination throughout history and see that in each instance, there was a possibility of challenging either the construction of identity or the system of subordination based on that identity. Consider, for example, the segregation system in *Plessy v. Ferguson*.[12] At issue were multiple dimensions of domination, including categorization, the sign of race, and the subordination of those so labeled. There were at least two targets for Plessy to challenge: the construction of identity ("What is a Black?"), and the system of subordination based on that identity ("Can Blacks and whites sit together on a train?"). Plessy actually made both arguments, one against the coherence of race as a category, the other against the subordination of those deemed to be Black. In his attack on the former, Plessy argued that the segregation statute's application to him, given his mixed race status, was inappropriate. The Court refused to see this as an attack on the coherence of the race system and instead responded in a way that simply reproduced the Black/white dichotomy that Plessy was challenging. As we know, Plessy's challenge to the segregation system was not successful either. In evaluating various resistance strategies today, it is useful to ask which of Plessy's challenges would have been best for him to have won—the challenge against the coherence of the racial categorization system or the challenge to the practice of segregation?

The same question can be posed for *Brown v. Board of Education*.[13] Which of two possible arguments was politically more empowering – that segregation was unconstitutional because the racial categorization system on which it was based was incoherent, or that segregation was unconstitutional because it was injurious to Black children and oppressive to their communities? While it might strike some as a difficult question, for the most part, the dimension of racial domination that has been most vexing to African Americans has not been the social categorization as such, but the myriad ways in which those of us so defined have been systematically subordinated. With particular regard to problems confronting women of color, when identity politics fail us, as they frequently do, it is not primarily because those politics take as natural certain categories that are socially constructed but rather because the descriptive content of those categories and the narratives on which they are based have privileged some experiences and excluded others.

Along these lines, consider the Clarence Thomas/Anita Hill controversy. During the Senate hearings for the confirmation of Clarence Thomas to the Supreme Court, Anita Hill, in bringing allegations of sexual harassment against Thomas, was rhetorically disempowered in part because she fell between the dominant interpretations of feminism and antiracism. Caught between the competing narrative tropes of rape (advanced by feminists) on the one hand and lynching (advanced by Thomas and his antiracist supporters) on the other, the race and gender dimensions of her position could not be told. This dilemma could be described as the consequence of antiracism's essentializing Blackness and feminism's essentializing womanhood. But recognizing as much does not take us far enough, for the problem is not simply linguistic or philosophical in nature. It is specifically political: the narratives of gender are based on the experience of white, middle-class women, and the narratives of race are based on the experience of Black men. The solution does not merely entail arguing for the multiplicity of identities or challenging essentialism generally. Instead, in Hill's case, for example, it would have been necessary to assert those crucial aspects of her location that were erased, even by many of her advocates – that is, to state what difference her difference made.

If, as this analysis asserts, history and context determine the utility of identity politics, how then do we understand identity politics today, especially in light of our recognition of multiple dimensions of identity? More specifically, what does it mean to argue that gender identities have been obscured in antiracist discourses, just as race identities have been obscured in feminist discourses? Does that mean we cannot talk about identity? Or instead, that any discourse about

identity has to acknowledge how our identities are constructed through the intersection of multiple dimensions? A beginning response to these questions requires that we first recognize that the organized identity groups in which we find ourselves in are in fact coalitions, or at least potential coalitions waiting to be formed.

In the context of antiracism, recognizing the ways in which the intersectional experiences of women of color are marginalized in prevailing conceptions of identity politics does not require that we give up attempts to organize as communities of color. Rather, intersectionality provides a basis for reconceptualizing race as a coalition between men and women of color. For example, in the area of rape, intersectionality provides a way of explaining why women of color have to abandon the general argument that the interests of the community require the suppression of any confrontation around intraracial rape. Intersectionality may provide the means for dealing with other marginalizations as well. For example, race can also be a coalition of straight and gay people of color, and thus serve as a basis for critique of churches and other cultural institutions that reproduce heterosexism.

With identity thus reconceptualized, it may be easier to understand the need for and to summon the courage to challenge groups that are after all, in one sense, "home" to us, in the name of the parts of us that are not made at home. This takes a great deal of energy and arouses intense anxiety. The most one could expect is that we will dare to speak against internal exclusions and marginalizations, that we might call attention to how the identity of "the group" has been centered on the intersectional identities of a few. Recognizing that identity politics takes place at the site where categories intersect thus seems more fruitful than challenging the possibility of talking about categories at all. Through an awareness of intersectionality, we can better acknowledge and ground the differences among us and negotiate the means by which these differences will find expression in constructing group politics.

NOTES

1. Feminist academics and activists have played a central role in forwarding an ideological and institutional challenge to the practices that condone and perpetuate violence against women. *See generally* SUSAN BROWNMILLER, AGAINST OUR WILL: MEN, WOMEN AND RAPE (1975); LORENNE M. G. CLARK & DEBRA J. LEWIS, RAPE: THE PRICE OF COERCIVE SEXUALITY (1977); R. EMERSON DOBASH & RUSSELL DOBASH, VIOLENCE AGAINST WIVES: A CASE AGAINST THE PATRIARCHY (1979); NANCY GAGER & CATHLEEN SCHURR, SEXUAL ASSAULT: CONFRONTING RAPE IN AMERICA (1976); DIANA E.H. RUSSELL, THE POLITICS OF RAPE: THE VICTIM'S PERSPECTIVE (1974); ELIZABETH ANNE STANKO, INTIMATE INTRUSIONS: WOMEN'S EXPERIENCE OF MALE VIOLENCE (1985); LENORE E. WALKER, TERRIFYING LOVE: WHY BATTERED WOMEN KILL AND HOW SOCIETY RESPONDS (1989); LENORE E. WALKER, THE BATTERED WOMAN SYNDROME (1984); LENORE E. WALKER, THE BATTERED WOMAN (1979).

2. *See, e.g.,* SUSAN SCHECHTER, WOMEN AND MALE VIOLENCE: THE VISIONS AND STRUGGLES OF THE BATTERED WOMEN'S MOVEMENT (1982) (arguing that battering is a means of maintaining women's subordinate position); S. BROWNMILLER, *supra* note 1 (arguing that rape is a patriarchal practice that subordinates women to men); Elizabeth Schneider, *The Violence of Privacy*, 23 CONN. L. REV. 973, 974 (1991) (discussing how "concepts of privacy permit, encourage and reinforce violence against women"); Susan Estrich, *Rape*, 95 YALE L.J. 1087 (1986) (analyzing rape law as one illustration of sexism in criminal law); see also CATHARINE A. MACKINNON, SEXUAL HARASSMENT OF WORKING WOMEN: A CASE OF SEX DISCRIMINATION 143–213 (1979) (arguing that sexual harassment should be redefined as sexual discrimination actionable under Title VII, rather than viewed as misplaced sexuality in the workplace).

3. I use "Black" and "African American" interchangeably throughout this article. I capitalize "Black" because "Blacks, like Asians, Latinos, and other 'minorities,' constitute a specific cultural group and, as such, require denotation as a proper noun." Kimberle Williams Crenshaw, *Race, Reform and Retrenchment: Transformation and Legitimation in Antidiscrimination Law,* 101 HARV. L. REV. 1332 (1998), n.2 (citing Catharine MacKinnon, *Feminism, Marxism, Method, and the State: An Agenda for Theory,* 7 SIGNS 515, 516 (1982)). By the same token, I do not capitalize "white," which is not a proper noun, since whites do not constitute a specific cultural group. For the same reason I do not capitalize "women of color."

4. Kimberle Crenshaw, *Demarginalizing the Intersection of Race and Sex,* 1989 U. CHI. LEGAL F. 139.

5. I explicitly adopt a Black feminist stance in this survey of violence against women of color. I do this cognizant of several tensions that such a position entails. The most significant one stems from the criticism that while feminism purports to speak for women of color through its invocation of the term "woman," the feminist perspective excludes women of color because it is based upon the experiences and interests of a certain subset of women. On the other hand, when white feminists attempt to include other women, they often add our experiences into an otherwise unaltered framework. It is important to name the perspective from

which one constructs her analysis; and for me, that is as a Black feminist. Moreover, it is important to acknowledge that the materials that I incorporate in my analysis are drawn heavily from research on Black women. On the other hand, I see my own work as part of a broader collective effort among feminists of color to expand feminism to include analyses of race and other factors such as class, sexuality, and age. I have attempted therefore to offer my sense of the tentative connections between my analysis of the intersectional experiences of Black women and the intersectional experiences of other women of color. I stress that this analysis is not intended to include falsely nor to exclude unnecessarily other women of color.

6. I consider intersectionality a provisional concept linking contemporary politics with postmodern theory. In mapping the intersections of race and gender, the concept does engage dominant assumptions that race and gender are essentially separate categories. By tracing the categories to their intersections, I hope to suggest a methodology that will ultimately disrupt the tendencies to see race and gender as exclusive or separable. While the primary intersections that I explore here are between race and gender, the concept can and should be expanded by factoring in issues such as class, sexual orientation, age, and color.

7. Professor Mari Matsuda calls this inquiry "asking the other question." Mari J. Matsuda, *Beside My Sister, Facing the Enemy: Legal Theory Out of Coalition*, 43 STAN. L. REV. 1183 (1991). For example,

we should look at an issue or condition traditionally regarded as a gender issue and ask, "Where's the racism in this?"

8. I follow the practice of others in linking antiessentialism to postmodernism. See generally LINDA NICHOLSON, FEMINISM/POSTMODERNISM (1990).

9. I do not mean to imply that all theorists who have made antiessentialist critiques have lapsed into vulgar constructionism. Indeed, antiessentialists avoid making these troubling moves and would no doubt be receptive to much of the critique set forth herein. I use the term vulgar constructionism to distinguish between those antiessentialist critiques that leave room for identity politics and those that do not.

10. 110 S. Ct. 2997 (1990).

11. The FCC's choice to employ a racial criterion embodies the related notions that a particular and distinct viewpoint inheres in certain racial groups and that a particular applicant, by virtue of race or ethnicity alone, is more valued than other applicants because the applicant is "likely to provide [that] distinct perspective." The policies directly equate race with belief and behavior, for they establish race as a necessary and sufficient condition of securing the preference. . . . The policies impermissibly value individuals because they presume that persons think in a manner associated with their race.

Id. at 3037 (O'Connor, J., joined by Rehnquist, C.J., and Scalia and Kennedy, J.J., dissenting) (internal citations omitted).

12. 163 U.S. 537 (1896).

13. 397 U.S. 483 (1954).

27. Producing Disability and Abledness*

Fiona Kumari Campbell

Typically literature within disability and cultural studies has concentrated on the practices and production of disablism, specifically by examining those attitudes and barriers that contribute to the subordination of people with disabilities in liberal society. *Disablism* is a set of assumptions (conscious or unconscious) and practices that promote the differential or unequal treatment of people because of actual or presumed disabilities. On this basis, the strategic positions adopted to facilitate emancipatory social change whilst diverse, essentially relate to reforming those negative attitudes, assimilating people with disabilities into normative civil society and providing compensatory initiatives and safety nets in cases of enduring vulnerability. In other words, the site of reformation has been at the intermediate level of function, structure and institution in civil society and shifting values in the cultural arena. Such an emphasis produces scholarship that contains serious distortions, gaps and omissions regarding the production of disability and re-inscribes an able-bodied voice/lens towards disability. Disability, often quite unconsciously, continues to be examined and taught from the perspective of the Other (Marks, 1996; Solis, 2006). The challenge then is to reverse, to invert this traditional approach, to shift our gaze and concentrate on what the study of disability tells us about the production, operation and maintenance of ableism.

The earlier work of Tom Shakespeare concludes, 'perhaps the maintenance of a non-disabled identity . . . is a more useful problem with which to be concerned; rather than interrogating the other, let us deconstruct the normality-which-is-to-be-assumed' (1999, p. 28). Hughes captures this project forcefully by calling for a study of 'the pathologies of non-disablement' (2007, p. 683). An Abled imaginary relies upon the existence of a hitherto unacknowledged imagined shared community of able-bodied/minded people held together by a common ableist homosocial world view that asserts the preferability and compulsoriness of the norms of ableism. Least [sic] we believe that people who fail to meet the ableist imaginary might think otherwise about human ontology and corporealities. Overboe (1999, 2007) and Campbell (2007, 2008) point to the compulsion to emulate the norm through the internalisation of ableism. Ableist normativity results in compulsive passing, wherein there is a failure to ask about difference, to imagine human beingness differently.

Compulsory ableness and its conviction to and seduction of sameness as the basis to equality claims results in a resistance to consider ontologically peripheral lives as distinct ways of being human least [sic] they produce a heightened devaluation. Ontological reframing poses different preoccupations: what does the study of the politics of 'deafness' tell us about what it means to be 'hearing'? Indeed how is the very conceptualization of 'hearing' framed in the light of discourses of 'deafness'? By decentring abledness, it is possible 'to look at the world from

---

** From Campbell, F. K. (2009) *Contours of Ableism: The Production of Disability and Abledness* (Basingstoke: Palgrave Macmillan). Extracts from pp. 3–6, 11–14.*

the inside out' (Linton, 1998, p. 13) and unveil the 'non-disabled/ableist' stance. In a different context Haraway (1989, p. 152) exclaims, '. . . [this] cannot be said quite out loud, or it loses its crucial position as a pre-condition of vision and becomes the object of scrutiny'.

So what is meant by the concept of 'ableism'? A survey of the literature suggests that the term is often referred to in a fleeting way with limited definitional or conceptual specificity (Clear, 1999; Iwasaki & Mactavish, 2005; Watts & Erevelles, 2004). When there is commentary, ableism is described as denoting an attitude that devalues or differentiates disability through the valuation of able-bodiedness equated to normalcy (Ho, 2008). For some, the term *ableism* is used interchangeably with the term *disablism*. I argue however that these two words render quite radically different understandings of the status of disability to the norm. Furthermore, as a conceptual tool, ableism transcends the procedures, structures, for governing civil society, and locates itself clearly in the arena of genealogies of knowledge. There is little consensus as to what practices and behaviours constitute ableism. We can, nevertheless, say that a chief feature of an ableist viewpoint is a belief that impairment or disability (irrespective or 'type') is inherently negative and should the opportunity present itself, be ameliorated, cured or indeed eliminated. Ableism refers to:

A network of beliefs, processes and practices that produces a particular kind of self and body (the corporeal standard) that is projected as the perfect, species-typical and therefore essential and fully human. Disability then is cast as a diminished state of being human.

(Campbell, 2001, p. 44)

In a similar vein, Veronica Chouniard defines ableism as 'ideas, practices, institutions and social relations that presume ablebodiedness, and by so doing, construct persons with disabilities as marginalized . . . and largely invisible "others"' (1997, p. 380). In contrast, Amundson and Taira attribute a doctrinal posture to ableism in their suggestion that 'ableism is a doctrine that falsely treats impairments as inherently and naturally horrible and blames the impairments themselves for the problems experienced by the people who have them' (2005, p. 54). Whilst there is little argument with this presupposition, what is absent from the definition is any mention of ableism's function in inaugurating the norm. The Campbell (2001; Chouinard, 1997) approach is less about the coherency and intentionalities of ableism; rather their emphasis is on a conception of ableism as a hub network functioning around shifting interest convergences. Linton defines ableism as 'includ[ing] the idea that a person's abilities or characteristics are determined by disability or that people with disabilities as a group are inferior to non-disabled people' (1998, p. 9). There are problems with simply endorsing a schema that posits a particular worldview that either favours or disfavours disabled/able-bodied people as if each category is discrete, self-evident and fixed. As I will argue later, ableism sets up a binary dynamic that is not simply comparative but rather co-relationally constitutive. Campbell's (2001) formulaion of ableism not only problematises the signifier disability but points to the fact that the essential core of ableism is the formation of a naturalized understanding of being fully human and this, as Chouinard (1997) notes, is articulated on a basis of an enforced presumption that erases difference.

Whether it be the 'species typical body' (in science), the 'normative citizen' (in political theory), the 'reasonable man' (in law), all these signifiers point to a fabrication that reaches into the very soul that sweeps us into life and as such is the outcome and instrument of a political constitution: a hostage of the body. The creation of such regimes of ontological separation appears disassociated from power. Bodies in this way become elements that may be moved, used, transformed, demarcated, improved and articulated with others. Daily the identities of *disabled* and *abled* are performed repeatedly. An ethos of compulsory abled-bodiedness as McRuer (2002, p. 93) puts it 'showcase[d] for able-bodied performance' pursuant to the incessant consuming of objects of health, beauty, strength and capability.

[. . .]

Inscribing certain bodies in terms of deficiency and essential inadequacy privileges a particular understanding of normalcy that is commensurate with the interests of dominant groups (and the assumed interests of subordinated groups). Indeed, the formation of ableist relations requires the normate individual to depend upon the self of 'disabled' bodies being rendered beyond the realm of civility, thus becoming an unthinkable object of apprehension. The unruly, uncivil, disabled body is necessary for the reiteration, of the 'truth' of the 'real/essential' human self who is endowed with masculinist attributes of certainty, mastery and autonomy. The discursive practices that mark out bodies of preferability are vindicated by abject life forms that populate the constitutive outside of the thinkable (that which can be imagined and re-presented) and those forms of existence that are unimaginable, and therefore unspeakable. The emptying (*kenosis*) of normalcy occurs through the purging of those beings that confuse, are misrecognisable or as Mitchell (2002, p. 17) describes as 'recalcitrant corporeal matter' into a *bare life* (see Agamben, 1998) residing in the/a zone of exceptionality. This foreclosure depends on necessary unspeakability to maintain the continued operation of hegemonic power. For every outside there is an inside that demands differentiation and consolidation as a unity. To borrow from Heidegger (1977) – in every *aletheia* (unveiling or revealedness) of representation there lies a concealedness. The visibility of the ableist project is therefore only possible through the interrogation of the revealedness of disability/not-health and abled(ness), Marcel Detienne (1979) summarises this system of thought aptly:

[Such a] . . . system is founded on a series of acts of partition whose ambiguity, here as elsewhere, is to open up the terrain of their transgression at the very moment when they mark off a limit. To discover the complete horizon of a society's symbolic values, it is also necessary to map out its transgressions, its deviants (p. ix).

Viewing the disabled body as simply *matter out of place* that needs to be dispensed with or at least cleaned up is erroneous. The disabled body *has* a place, a place in liminality to secure the performative enactment of the normal. Detienne's summation points to what we may call the double bind of ableism when performed within Western neo-liberal polities. The double bind folds in on itself – for whilst claiming 'inclusion', ableism simultaneously always restates and enshrines itself. On the one hand, discourses of equality promote 'inclusion' by way of promoting positive attitudes (sometimes legislated in mission statements, marketing campaigns, equal opportunity protections) and yet on the other hand, ableist discourses proclaim quite emphatically that disability is inherently negative, ontologically intolerable and in the end, a dispensable remnant. This casting results in an ontological foreclosure wherein positive signification of disability becomes unspeakable.

> I've always believed that within tragedy, there is incredible life and emotion. So my condition is not something I think of as sad; I think it's something so beautifully human. It doesn't make me less of a human being. It makes me so rich . . . I see my life as an active experiment; to grasp at greatness I must risk failure. I put instinct before caution, ideals before reality and possibility before negativity. As a result, my life is not easy but it's not boring either.
> (Byrnes, 2000)

Disability cannot be thought of/spoken about on any other basis than the negative, to do so, to invoke oppositional discourses, is to run the risk of further pathologisation. An example of this is the attempt at desiring, or celebrating, disability that is reduced to a fetish or facticity disorder. So to explicate ourselves out of this double bind we need to persistently and continually return to the matter of disability as negative ontology, as a malignancy, that is, as the property of a body constituted by what Michael Oliver (1996, p. 32) refers to as, 'the personal tragedy theory of disability.'

Returning to the matter of definitional clarity around abled(ness), Robert McRuer (2002) is one of the few scholars to journey into ableism's non-axiomatic life. He argues that ableism (McRuer refers to compulsory abled-bodiedness) emanates from everywhere and nowhere, and can only be deduced by crafty reductionisms. Contra the assertions about the uncontainability of disabled bodies which are [re]contained by the hyper-prescription and enumeration, the abled body mediated through its assumption of compulsion is absent in its presence – it just is – but resists being fully deducible. Drawing on Butler's work, McRuer (2002) writes,

> Everyone is virtually disabled, both in the sense that able-bodied norms are 'intrinsically impossible to embody' fully and in the sense that able-bodied status is always temporary, disability being the one identity category that all people will embody if they live long enough. What we might call a critical disability position, however, would differ from such a virtually disabled positions [to engagements that have] resisted the demands of compulsory able-bodiedness (pp. 95–96).

My argument is that insofar as this conception of disability is assumed within discourses of ableism, the presence of disability upsets the modernist craving for ontological security.

The conundrum, disability, is not a mere fear of the unknown, or an apprehensiveness towards that which is foreign or strange. Rather, disability and disabled bodies are effectively positioned in the nether regions of 'unthought'. For the ongoing stability of ableism, a diffuse network of thought depends upon the capacity of that network to 'shut away', to exteriorise, and unthink disability and its resemblance to the essential (ableist) human self. This unthought has been given much consideration through the systematisation and classification of knowledges about pathology, aberration and deviance. That which is

thought about (the Abled norm) rather ironically in its delimitation becomes vacuous and elusive. In order for the notion of ableness to exist and to transmogrify into the sovereign subject, the normate individual of liberalism, it must have a constitutive outside – that is, it must participate in a logic of supplementarity. When looking at relations of disability and ableism we can expand on this idea of symbiosis, an 'unavoidable duality' by putting forward another metaphor, that of the mirror. Here I argue that people deemed disabled take on the performative act of mirroring in the lives of normative subjects:

> . . . To be a Mirror is different from being a Face that looks back . . . with a range of expression and responsiveness that are responses of a Subject-in-Its-Own-Right. To be positioned as a Mirror is to be Put Out of Countenance, to Lose Face.
> (Narayan, 1997, p. 141)

In this respect, we can speak in ontological terms of the history of disability as a history of that which is unthought, to be put out of countenance; this figuring should not be confused with erasure that occurs due to mere absence or exclusion. On the contrary, disability is always present (despite its seeming absence) in the ableist talk of normalcy, normalisation and humanness (cf. Overboe, 2007, on the idea of *normative shadows*). Disability's truth-claims are dependent upon discourses of ableism for their very legitimisation.

REFERENCES

Agamben, G. 1998. *Homo Sacer: Sovereign Power and Bare Life*. Stanford: Stanford University Press.

Amundson, R. & Taira, G. 2005. Our lives and ideologies: The effects of life experience on the perceived morality of the policy of physician-assisted suicide. *Journal of Policy Studies*. 16(1), 53–57.

Byrnes, T. 2000. *Frontispiece*, Online at http://www.theresbyrne.com [Accessed March 2006].

Campbell, F. Kumari. 2001. Inciting legal fictions: Disability's date with ontology and the ableist body of the law. *Griffith Law Review.* 10, 42–62.

Campbell, F. Kumari. 2007. States of exceptionality: Provisional disability, its mitigation and citizenship. *Sociol-Legal Review.* 3, 28–50.

Campbell, F. Kumari. 2008. Exploring internalised ableism using critical race theory. *Disability & Society.* 23(2), 151–162.

Chouniard, V. 1997. Making space for disabling difference: Challenging ableist geographies. Environment and Planning D: Society and Space. 15, 379–387.

Clear, M. 1999. The 'normal' and the monstrous in disability research. *Disability & Society.* 14(4), 435–448.

Detienne, M. 1979. *Dionysos Slain.* Baltimore: Johns Hopkins University Press.

Haraway, D. 1989. *Primate Visions: Gender, Race, and Nature in the World of Modern Science.* New York: Routledge.

Ho, A. 2008. The individual's model of autonomy and the challenge of disability. *Journal of Bioethic Inquiry.* 5, 193–207.

Hughes, B. 2007. Being disabled: Toward a critical social ontology for disability studies. *Disability & Society.* 22(7), 673–684.

Iwasaki, Y. & Mactavish, J. 2005. Ubiquitous yet unique: Perspectives of people with disabilities on stress. *Rehabilitation Counselling Bulletin.* 48(4), 194–208.

Linton, S. 1998. *Claiming Disability: Knowledge and Identity.* New York: New York University Press.

Marks, D. 1996. Abled-bodied dilemmas in teaching disability studies. *Feminism & Psychology.* 6, 69–73.

McRuer, R. 2002. Compulsory able-bodiedness and queer/disabled existence. In S. Snyder, B. Brueggemann & R. Garland-Thomson, eds. *Disability Studies: Enabling the Humanities.* New York: Modern Language Association, pp. 88–90.

Mitchell, D. 2002. Narrative prosthesis and the materiality of metaphor. In S. Snyder, B. Brueggemann & R. Garland-Thomson, eds. *Disability Studies: Enabling the Humanities.* New York: Modern Language Association, pp. 15–30.

Narayan, U. 1997. *Dislocating Cultures: Identities, Traditions and Third World Feminism.* London: Routledge.

Oliver, M. 1996. *Understanding Disability: From Theory to Practice.* Basingstoke: Macmillan.

Overboe, J. 1999. Difference in itself: Validating disabled people's lived experience. *Body and Society.* 5, 17–29.

Overboe, J. 2007. Vitalism: Subjectivity exceeding racism, sexism and (psychiatric) ableism. *Wagadu: A Journal of Transnational Women's & Gender Studies.* 4, 23–34.

Shakespeare, T. 1999. Losing the plot? Medical and activist discourses of contemporary genetics and disability. *Sociology of Health & Illness.* 21(5), 669–688.

Solis, S. 2006. I'm coming out as disabled but I'm staying in to rest: Reflecting on elected and imposed segregation. *Equity & Excellence in Education.* 39, 146–153.

Watts, I & Erevelles, N. 2004. These deadly times: Reconceptualizing school violence by using critical race theory and disability studies. *American Educational Research Journal.* 41(2), 271–299.

28. Wealth Concentration and Inequality*

Thomas Piketty

What are the major conclusions to which these novel historical sources have led me? The first is that one should be wary of any economic determinism in regard to inequalities of wealth and income. The history of the distribution of wealth has always been deeply political, and it cannot be reduced to purely economic mechanisms. In particular, the reduction of inequality that took place in most developed countries between 1910 and 1950 was above all a consequence of war and of policies adopted to cope with the shocks of war. Similarly, the resurgence of inequality after 1980 is due largely to the political shifts of the past several decades, especially in regard to taxation and finance. The history of inequality is shaped by the way economic, social, and political actors view what is just and what is not, as well as by the relative power of those actors and the collective choices that result. It is the joint product of all relevant actors combined.

The second conclusion, which is the heart of the book, is that the dynamics of wealth distribution reveal powerful mechanisms pushing alternately toward convergence and divergence. Furthermore, there is no natural, spontaneous process to prevent destabilizing, inegalitarian forces from prevailing permanently.

Consider first the mechanisms pushing toward convergence, that is, toward reduction and compression of inequalities. The main forces for convergence are the diffusion of knowledge

and investment in training and skills. The law of supply and demand, as well as the mobility of capital and labor, which is a variant of that law, may always tend toward convergence as well, but the influence of this economic law is less powerful than the diffusion of knowledge and skill and is frequently ambiguous or contradictory in its implications. Knowledge and skill diffusion is the key to overall productivity growth as well as the reduction of inequality both within and between countries. We see this at present in the advances made by a number of previously poor countries, led by China. These emergent economies are now in the process of catching up with the advanced ones. By adopting the modes of production of the rich countries and acquiring skills comparable to those found elsewhere, the less developed countries have leapt forward in productivity and increased their national incomes. The technological convergence process may be abetted by open borders for trade, but it is fundamentally a process of the diffusion and sharing of knowledge—the public good par excellence—rather than a market mechanism.

From a strictly theoretical standpoint, other forces pushing toward greater equality might exist. One might, for example, assume that production technologies tend over time to require greater skills on the part of workers, so that labor's share of income will rise as capital's share falls: one might call this the "rising human capital hypothesis." In other words, the progress of technological rationality is supposed to lead automatically to the triumph of human capital over financial capital and real estate, capable

* From Piketty, T. (2014) *Capital in the Twenty-First Century* (Cambridge, MA: Harvard University Press). Extract from pp. 20–27.

managers over fat cat stockholders, and skill over nepotism. Inequalities would thus become more meritocratic and less static (though not necessarily smaller): economic rationality would then in some sense automatically give rise to democratic rationality.

Another optimistic belief, which is current at the moment, is the idea that "class warfare" will automatically give way, owing to the recent increase in life expectancy, to "generational warfare" (which is less divisive because everyone is first young and then old). Put differently, this inescapable biological fact is supposed to imply that the accumulation and distribution of wealth no longer presage an inevitable clash between dynasties of rentiers and dynasties owning nothing but their labor power. The governing logic is rather one of saving over the life cycle: people accumulate wealth when young in order to provide for their old age. Progress in medicine together with improved living conditions has therefore, it is argued, totally transformed the very essence of capital.

Unfortunately, these two optimistic beliefs (the human capital hypothesis and the substitution of generational conflict for class warfare) are largely illusory. Transformations of this sort are both logically possible and to some extent real, but their influence is far less consequential than one might imagine. There is little evidence that labor's share in national income has increased significantly in a very long time: "nonhuman" capital seems almost as indispensable in the twenty-first century as it was in the eighteenth or nineteenth, and there is no reason why it may not become even more so. Now as in the past, moreover, inequalities of wealth exist primarily within age cohorts, and inherited wealth comes close to being as decisive at the beginning of the twenty-first century as it was in the age of Balzac's *Père Goriot*. Over a long period of time, the main force in favor of greater equality has been the diffusion of knowledge and skills.

Forces of Convergence, Forces of Divergence

The crucial fact is that no matter how potent a force the diffusion of knowledge and skills may be, especially in promoting convergence between countries, it can nevertheless be thwarted and overwhelmed by powerful forces pushing in the opposite direction, toward greater inequality. It is obvious that lack of adequate investment in training can exclude entire social groups from the benefits of economic growth. Growth can harm some groups while benefiting others (witness the recent displacement of workers in the more advanced economies by workers in China). In short, the principal force for convergence—the diffusion of knowledge—is only partly natural and spontaneous. It also depends in large part on educational policies, access to training and to the acquisition of appropriate skills, and associated institutions.

I will pay particular attention in this study to certain worrisome forces of divergence—particularly worrisome in that they can exist even in a world where there is adequate investment in skills and where all the conditions of "market efficiency" (as economists understand that term) appear to be satisfied. What are these forces of divergence? First, top earners can quickly separate themselves from the rest by a wide margin (although the problem to date remains relatively localized). More important, there is a set of forces of divergence associated with the process of accumulation and concentration of wealth when growth is weak and the return on capital is high. This second process is potentially more destabilizing than the first, and it no doubt represents the principal threat to an equal distribution of wealth over the long run.

To cut straight to the heart of the matter: in Figures 1.1 and 1.2 I show two basic patterns that I will try to explain in what follows. Each graph represents the importance of one of these divergent processes. Both graphs depict "U-shaped curves," that is, a period of decreasing inequality followed by one of increasing inequality. One might assume that the realities the two graphs represent are similar. In fact they are not. The phenomena underlying the various curves are quite different and involve distinct economic, social, and political processes. Furthermore, the curve in Figure 1.1 represents income inequality in the United States, while the curves in Figure 1.2 depict the capital/income ratio in several European countries (Japan, though not shown, is similar). It is not out of the question that the two forces of divergence will ultimately come together in the twenty-first century. This has already happened to some extent and may yet become a global phenomenon, which could lead to levels of inequality never before seen, as well as to a radically new structure of inequality. Thus far, however, these striking patterns reflect two distinct underlying phenomena.

The US curve, shown in Figure 1.1, indicates the share of the upper decile of the income hierarchy in US national income from 1910 to 2010. It is nothing more than an extension of the historical series Kuznets established for the period 1913–1948. The top decile claimed as much as 45–50 percent of national income in the 1910s–1920s before dropping to 30–35 percent by the end of the 1940s. Inequality then stabilized at that level from 1950 to 1970. We subsequently see a rapid rise in inequality in the 1980s, until by 2000 we have returned to a level on the order of 45–50 percent of national income. The magnitude of the change

is impressive. It is natural to ask how far such a trend might continue.

I will show that this spectacular increase in inequality largely reflects an unprecedented explosion of very elevated incomes from labor, a veritable separation of the top managers of large firms from the rest of the population. One possible explanation of this is that the skills and productivity of these top managers rose suddenly in relation to those of other workers. Another explanation, which to me seems more plausible and turns out to be much more consistent with the evidence, is that these top managers by and large have the power to set their own remuneration, in some cases without limit and in many cases without any clear relation to their individual productivity, which in any case is very difficult to estimate in a large organization. This phenomenon is seen mainly in the United States and to a lesser degree in Britain, and it may be possible to explain it in terms of the history of social and fiscal norms in those two countries over the past century. The tendency is less marked in other wealthy countries (such as Japan, Germany, France, and other continental European states), but the trend is in the same direction. To expect that the phenomenon will attain the same proportions elsewhere as it has done in the United States would be risky until we have subjected it to a full analysis—which unfortunately is not that simple, given the limits of the available data.

Figure 1.1 Income inequality in the United States, 1910–2010
The top decile share in US national income dropped from 45–50 percent in the 1910s–1920s to less tan 35 per cent in the 1950s (this is the fall documented by Kuznets); it then rose from less than 35 percent in the 1970s to 45–50 percent in the 2000s–2010s.

Sources and series: see piketty/pse.ens.fr/capital21c.

The Fundamental Force for Divergence: $r > g$

The second pattern, represented in Figure 1.2, reflects a divergence mechanism that is in some ways simpler and more transparent and no doubt exerts greater influence on the long-run evolution of the wealth distribution. Figure 1.2 shows the total value of private wealth (in real estate, financial assets, and professional capital, net of debt) in Britain, France and Germany, expressed in years of national income, for the period 1870–2010. Note, first of all, the very high level of private wealth in Europe in the late nineteenth century: the total amount of private wealth hovered around six or seven years of national income, which is a lot. It then fell sharply in response to the shocks of the period 1914–1945: the capital/income ratio decreased to just 2 or 3. We then observe a steady rise from 1950 on, a rise so sharp that private fortunes in the early twenty-first century seem to be on the verge of returning to five or six years of national income in both Britain and France. (Private wealth in Germany, which started at a lower level, remains lower, but the upward trend is just as clear.)

This "U-shaped curve" reflects an absolutely crucial transformation, which will figure largely in this study. In particular, I will show that the return of high capital/income ratios over the past few decades can be explained in large part by the return to a regime of relatively slow growth. In slowly growing economies, past wealth naturally takes on disproportionate importance, because it takes only a small flow of new savings to increase the stock of wealth steadily and substantially.

If, moreover, the rate of return on capital remains significantly above the growth rate for an extended period of time (which is more likely when the growth rate is low, though not automatic), then the risk of divergence in the distribution of wealth is very high.

This fundamental inequality, which I will write as $r > g$ (where r stands for the average annual rate of return on capital, including profits, dividends, interest, rents, and other income from capital, expressed as a percentage of its total value, and g stands for the rate of growth of the economy, that is, the annual increase in income or output), will play a crucial role in this book. In a sense, it sums up the overall logic of my conclusions.

When the rate of return on capital significantly exceeds the growth rate of the economy (as it did through much of history until the nineteenth century and as is likely to be the case again in the twenty-first century), then it logically follows that inherited wealth grows faster than output and income. People with inherited wealth need save only a portion of their income from capital to see that capital grow more quickly than the economy as a whole. Under such conditions, it is almost inevitable that inherited wealth will dominate wealth amassed from a lifetime's labor by a wide margin, and the concentration of capital will attain extremely high levels—levels potentially incompatible with the meritocratic values

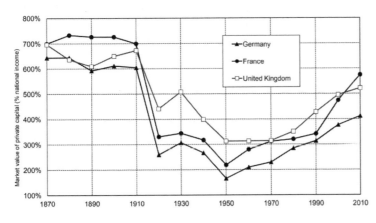

Figure 1.2 The capital/income ratio in Europe, 1870–2010
Aggregate private wealth was worth about six to seven years of national income in Europe in 1910, between two and three years in 1950, and between four and six years in 2010.

Sources and series: see piketty/pse.ens.fr/ capital21c.

and principles of social justice fundamental to modern democratic societies.

What is more, this basic force for divergence can be reinforced by other mechanisms. For instance, the savings rate may increase sharply with wealth.[1] Or, even more important, the average effective rate of return on capital may be higher when the individual's initial capital endowment is higher (as appears to be increasingly common). The fact that the return on capital is unpredictable and arbitrary, so that wealth can be enhanced in a variety of ways, also poses a challenge to the meritocratic model. Finally, all of these factors can be aggravated by the Ricardian scarcity principle: the high price of real estate or petroleum may contribute to structural divergence.

To sum up what has been said thus far: the process by which wealth is accumulated and distributed contains powerful forces pushing toward divergence, or at any rate toward an extremely high level of inequality. Forces of convergence also exist, and in certain countries at certain times, these may prevail, but the forces of divergence can at any point regain the upper hand, as seems to be happening now, at the beginning of the twenty-first century. The likely decrease in the rate of growth of both the population and the economy in coming decades makes this trend all the more worrisome.

My conclusions are less apocalyptic than those implied by Marx's principle of infinite accumulation and perpetual divergence (since Marx's theory implicitly relies on a strict assumption of zero productivity growth over the long run). In the model I propose, divergence is not perpetual and is only one of several possible future directions for the distribution of wealth. But the possibilities are not heartening. Specifically, it is important to note that the fundamental $r > g$ inequality, the main force of divergence in my theory, has nothing to do with any market imperfection. Quite the contrary: the more perfect the capital market (in the economist's sense), the more likely r is to be greater than g. It is possible to imagine public institutions and policies that would counter the effects of this implacable logic: for instance, a progressive global tax on capital. But establishing such institutions and policies would require a considerable degree of international coordination. It is unfortunately likely that actual responses to the problem—including various nationalist responses—will in practice be far more modest and less effective.

NOTE

1. This destabilizing mechanism (the richer one is, the wealthier one gets) worried Kuznets a great deal, and this worry accounts for the title of his 1953 book *Shares of Upper Income Groups in Income and Savings*. But he lacked the historical distance to analyze it fully. This force for divergence was also central to James Meade's classic *Efficiency, Equality, and the Ownership of Property* (London: Allen and Unwin, 1964), and to Atkinson and Harrison, *Distribution of Personal Wealth in Britain*, which in a way was the continuation of Meade's work. Our work follows in the footsteps of these authors.

29. Racial Distinctions and Social Structures*

Michael Banton

In 2002 the American Sociological Association (ASA) formally noted:

> Some scholarly and civic leaders believe that the very idea of 'race' has the effect of promoting social division and they have proposed that the government stop collecting these data altogether. Respected voices from the fields of human molecular biology and physical anthropology (supported by research from the Human Genome Project) assert that the concept of race has no validity in their respective fields.[1]

This may have been a reference to the statement issued by the American Association of Physical Anthropologists that declared, among other things, that 'there is no national, religious, linguistic or cultural group or economic class that constitutes a race'.[2]

The ASA statement continued: 'Growing numbers of humanist scholars, social anthropologists, and political commentators have joined the chorus in urging the nation to rid itself of the concept of race'. One scholar was quoted saying that 'identifying people by race only deepens the racial divide'. The ASA thereby recognized an intellectual challenge. Scholars in several different fields were asking the ASA to help supersede an obsolete expression earlier advanced for the identification of certain kinds of biological difference.

The Association was in a fix. There was an intellectual issue and a political issue, for it was urged to respond to a proposal to forbid the California state government from collecting information on race and ethnicity.[3] Understandably, the political issue was given priority because a professional association can take a vote on a proposal of this kind, whereas an intellectual issue is better addressed by debate in academic books, journal articles and seminars.

So the Association issued an official statement on the 'Importance of Collecting Data on Race'. It maintained that such data should be collected because they were needed for the monitoring of social policies in the United States. There was no reference to ethnicity or to any 'racial divide' other than that between blacks and whites. The Association did not seize the opportunity to remind interested persons that, as a party to the International Convention on the Elimination of Racial Discrimination (ICERD), the United States had, since 1994, been under a treaty obligation to monitor and report to the Secretary-General of the United Nations about any inequalities affecting racial and ethnic groups within its population.

The position adopted by the ASA was paradoxical in that it combined two contradictory elements: a recognition that race no longer had any validity in the academic field within which it originated together with a defence of procedures which implied the opposite.

Its response was reactive, neglecting the opportunity to comment on the basis on which population data are collected. The US census of 2000 had introduced an important change when (in Question 6) it asked, 'What is this person's

* From Banton, M. (2015) *What We Now Know about Race and Ethnicity* (Oxford: Berghahn). Extracts from pp. 1–3, 5–7, 8, 18–19, 27.

race? Mark one or more races to indicate what this person considers himself/herself to be'; this was followed by fifteen tick boxes. This momentous change, however, had come about by accident! A former director of the Census Bureau has reported that it was an 'anomaly' that had been left on the form 'inadvertently'.[4] The same question was then repeated in 2010. The old 'one-drop rule' required that many persons be classed as either black or white, and that a single drop of black 'blood' made that person black. Today, in the United States, there are many persons who value more than one line of descent and do not wish to be identified by one alone. How their wishes are to be respected, and data on the national population to be collected, is a political decision to be taken by the federal government and other authorities (including the Office of Management and Budget). The ASA, as a non-political body, could have offered its advice on the alternative possibilities. Instead, its statement endorsed the existing procedures.

The usage that the ASA defended was one peculiar to the United States. It addressed, not the concept of race, but the practice by which blacks in that country were identified by the one-drop rule; this is a peculiar mode of classification that is not applied to any other social category in the United States and is unknown outside that country. If some other mode of classification was sought, what should it be? In censuses within the United Kingdom of Great Britain and Northern Ireland people have been asked, 'What is your ethnic group?' and offered choices that used words like 'white' and 'mixed'. This last word is questionable, for everyone's ancestry is in some degree mixed. Some persons may not identify with an ethnic group for any purpose other than that of completing the census form. The reality is not one of 'groups', but of social categories. The practical challenge confronting the ASA was the greater because the ordinary English-language vocabulary encourages categorizations like 'mixed' even though they are misleading and can be offensive. Since this particular contrast implies that the unmixed are purer than the mixed, it is morally objectionable as well as scientifically indefensible.

For several reasons the intellectual challenge was, and remains, more difficult than the political challenge. One of them is that states have obligations under international law that require them to use the words 'race' and 'racial'. The perception of a conflict between scientific knowledge and public practice has arisen because scientists and legislators have different objectives and use different vocabularies in order to attain them. The scientists say, in effect, that 'once some of our predecessors thought that race might be a useful concept in biology; now we know that there is no place for such a word in our vocabulary'. The legislators say, in effect, that 'we know that the word race has misleading associations that we hope to dispel by educational measures, but at the present time its use is necessary to the discharge of our international and domestic obligations'.

It is instructive to reflect upon the paradoxical aspect of the ASA statement because it casts light on a general intellectual problem confronting the contemporary social sciences. It will be argued here that the only way to resolve the paradox is to distinguish two kinds of knowledge, practical and theoretical. In them, the most important words are used in different ways because they serve different purposes. For this reason, the argument has to be philosophical as well as sociological. It challenges today's sociologists to reconsider some of their fundamental assumptions. They will not easily be persuaded that there is such a paradox, that it calls for resolution, or that this is the only way to resolve it.

[. . .]

A good research problem is one that can lead to a reliable and interesting result. If the explanation is to have the vital quality of cogency, its terms have to be defined, and no term can be acceptably defined without agreement on the purpose for which a definition is wanted. This is the source of the difference between ordinary (or practical) language and theoretical language. In ordinary language, a definition has to facilitate communication in contexts in which fine distinctions or possible ambiguities may not be important. To ascertain the meaning of an ordinary language word, the inquirer looks it up in a dictionary and selects the most appropriate of the alternatives offered. In the development of theoretical explanations, it is the nature of the explanandum that decides which concepts and which definitions are useful to achieve a result. Concepts have to be fit for purpose, and the explanandum embodies the purpose.[5]

Ordinary language conceptions, being limited to particular times and places, have been called folk concepts; they have been contrasted with analytical concepts that seek to transcend any such limitations. However, a simpler formulation of the same distinction is one drawn by American anthropologists when they contrast emic and etic constructs. An everyday example of the difference is that when a patient goes to a doctor for treatment, he or she reports his or her symptoms in ordinary language using emic constructs. The doctor makes a diagnosis, drawing upon technical knowledge expressed in etic constructs. According to one encyclopaedia, emic constructs are accounts expressed in categories meaningful to members of the community under study, whereas etic constructs are accounts expressed in categories meaningful to the community of scientific observers.[6]

The emic/etic distinction identifies two kinds of vocabulary. In sociology, some expressions are candidates for inclusion as concepts in an etic vocabulary, such as reciprocity, relative deprivation, social mobility, socio-economic status, and so on, for their users strive to make them culture-free.

Much academic writing about race has concentrated on the potentially misleading features of the ordinary language – or emic – conception concerned with practical knowledge, and has neglected the distinction between explanandum and explanans. The chief intellectual problem is to account for human variation, physical and cultural; that is the explanandum. When addressing this problem, the notion of race has to be evaluated as part of an explanans, and its value within the body of theoretical knowledge that attempts to account for human variation has to be assessed.

There are therefore two kinds of answer to the question of what we now know about race and ethnicity. An answer in terms of practical knowledge would set out current knowledge about the meanings of these words and how they can be used for the formulation and implementation of public policy in one or more specific countries at the present time. It would not regard the conceptions of race and ethnicity as problematic. An answer in terms of theoretical knowledge – such as is offered in this book – must maintain that our knowledge of the present-day situation is deepened if we know how we have come by this knowledge, for it teaches lessons about how our knowledge has grown and continues to grow. It also explains why some lines of argument, though popular in their time, have been proven wrong. In particular, it considers whether the expressions 'race' and 'ethnicity' are fit for purpose: do they satisfactorily identify the behaviour that calls for explanation? An answer in these terms offers knowledge in greater depth.

[. . .]

The reaction of many US sociologists in 2002 was to maintain that race, as 'a principal category in the organization of daily social life', was something quite separate from the possibility that it might be a biological category. Maybe it was separate for them, but that was no answer to the charge that its use in the United States promoted social division. Their argument that 'race as a social construct . . . is central to societal organization' reinforced an over-simple belief about the relation between a social and a biological category, and it legitimated administrative practices that some of their members must, on political grounds, have considered in need of reform. The 'social construct' argument does not resolve the paradox. The only way to dismantle it, according to this book, is to build on the distinction between practical and theoretical knowledge.

Does this still matter? While this book was in preparation, a volume appeared from Princeton University Press under the title *Creating a New Racial Order: How Immigration, Multiracialism, Genomics, and the Young can Remake America.*[7] It was hailed by Henry Louis Gates, of Harvard University, as showing that 'racial order remains one of the most reliable ways of organizing our past and present as Americans'. Why should he write 'racial order' rather than 'social order'? Why should the authors, and their respected colleague, assume that 'racial' is the adjective that most correctly identifies the division they deplore? They recycle an obsolete and pernicious mode of thought.

The argument of the pages that follow is that one of the main tasks of social science is to discover better explanations of the social significance attributed to human physical differences, comparing the significance attributed to various phenotypical differences with other kinds of difference, both physical and social. As part of this task, it is necessary to consider how effective prevailing ideas of race and ethnicity are in accounting for those differences, and whether they can be improved upon. If they are in any way defective, how is it that they have they come into general use?

[. . .]

[. . . W]ithin a little less than a hundred years, the ordinary language conception of race as a division, of either the Hominidae or of *Homo sapiens*, could gain such a hold in the minds of Europeans and North Americans that even the specialists had difficulty liberating their work from it. After an interval, it is now possible to trace the course by which knowledge grew. Moreover, hindsight makes it possible to see that the contrast between a social conception of race and a supposed biological concept only confers respectability upon an idea that was never

properly accepted in biological science. The popular impression of race as a biological concept lingered because the eugenics movement captured public attention and because – in a diffuse fashion – it attracted politically motivated support. Most of the anthropologists of this generation could not cope with the reorientation demanded by new biological knowledge. Their disorientation was demonstrated by the failure of the 1934 'Race and Culture' committee of the Royal Anthropological Institute in London to agree on which forms of human variation could be explained as the outcome of biological inheritance.[8]

The second lesson is that, by seeking explanations of puzzling observations, knowledge about human variation never ceases to grow. The sociologist gains little from trying to ascertain the very most up-to-date account of thought in genetics because knowledge in this field is growing so rapidly that any statement may quickly be rendered out of date by the publication of new findings. In no scientific field can knowledge be regarded as static. In the social sciences, the growth of knowledge follows the same rules, though it has to grow within a more contentious political environment, both international and national.

[. . .]

Sociologists can learn lessons from the history summarized in this chapter. Many discussions of the history of racial thought start from the use that has been made of the word, treating all uses as equally legitimate. This chapter has argued that it is more informative to start from a consideration of the purpose for which the word has been employed in order to examine how well it serves a purpose. It has stressed the importance of accurately identifying a problem that calls for explanation.

Sociologists can analyse the process by which the ordinary language conception has become so powerful in the United States, especially since 1865, surviving the challenges from technical language in 1909 (Johannsen), 1930 (Fisher) and 2000 (Venter). While they cannot undertake the sorts of experiments that Mendel conducted, a later chapter will contend that, like social psychologists, sociologists can design studies that will lead to observations of a standardized character, and then look to see what best accounts for their special features. They can concentrate upon the study of problems that are capable of explanation.

NOTES

1. Retrieved 8 November 2012 from http://www.asanet.org/footnotes/septoct02/index two.html.
2. AAPA Statement on Biological Aspects of Race, point 10. Retrieved 13 August 2012 from http://physanth.org/association/position-statemenrs/biological-aspects-of-race?searchterm=race.
3. Proposition 54 in the California ballot of 2003.
4. Kenneth Prewitt. *What is Your Race? The Census and Our Flawed Attempts to Classify Americans* (Princeton: Princeton University Press, 2013), 135.
5. Max Weber also drew a distinction in kind between two vocabularies. He maintained that in contrast to historical writing (which must use constructs with multiple meanings), sociology must seek univocal constructs, each with but one meaning, and be *eindeutig*. See *Wirtschaft und Gesellschaft. Grundriss der Verstehenden Soziologie*, 5th edition (Tübingen: Mohr Siebeck, 1972), 9–10. Insofar as the difference between the two kinds of vocabulary poses a problem, the simple solution is to recognize the two forms of knowledge. Weber offered a more complex solution. It was in order to achieve *Eindeutigkeit* that he advocated the development of 'ideal types'. Many contemporary sociologists would recognize his ideal types as models. The full significance of Weber's distinction is not brought out in the *Economy and Society* translation of Weber's book.
6. James W. Lett, 'Emic/Etic Distinctions', in David Levinson and Melvin Ember (eds.), *Encyclopedia of Cultural Anthropology*, vol. 2 (New York: Holt, 1996), 382–383. Alternatively, see http://faculty.ircc.edu/faculty/jlett/.
7. Jennifer L. Hochschild, Vesla Weaver and Traci Burch, *Creating a New Racial Order: How Immigration, Multiracialism, Genomics, and the Young Can Remake Race in America* (Princeton: Princeton University Press, 2012).
8. Elazar Barkan, *The Retreat of Scientific Racism: Changing concepts of race in Britain and the United States between two world wars* (Cambridge: Cambridge University Press, 1992), pp. 285–296. Barkan's book offers an admirable account of its subject matter, a series of failed explanantia. In contrast, the present book attempts to start from the social significance of phenotypical characteristics as an explanandum.

30. 'Doing Gender' via Domestic Labour*

Clare Lyonette and Rosemary Crompton

Although women have been entering paid work in increasing numbers, contemporary employment continues to be constructed on a full-time 'adult worker' model (Acker, 1990). Women's continued responsibility for the majority of domestic work and childcare makes it difficult to meet 'adult worker' requirements and many women with such responsibilities scale down their employment intensity, working in a less challenging job, often on a part-time basis (e.g. Connolly and Gregory, 2008; Grant et al., 2005), even though such strategies are incompatible with career success (e.g. Thornley, 2007).

Men *have* increased the amount of domestic work they do (Kan et al., 2011) and spend more time with their children than before (Coltrane, 2009). These changes may in part be due to the increased time pressures on working women, but may also reflect substantial changes in attitudes to gender roles. Evidence from the US and the UK suggests, however, that women continue to do more domestic work than men (Bianchi et al., 2000; Kan et al., 2011).

Domestic work is of practical and symbolic significance and, if male partners do more, it may follow that employed women's lives will improve considerably, allowing them to take on additional workplace responsibilities and compete on a more equal footing with men. The interactional level – at which the allocation of domestic tasks is largely worked out between partners – is an important site of potential change to both gender consciousness and practices (Sullivan, 2004). It is also a site of resistance and contestation of the gender order, particularly by women (Gatrell, 2005), but persistent conflict may also lead to a lack of accommodation and negotiation between partners. It has been argued that incremental changes in the division of domestic labour between partners (as opposed to major rapid or revolutionary change) can still effect a radical transformation over time (Sullivan, 2011). The research presented here sets out to examine why women continue to do more housework than men, if and how this is changing, and whether or not male contributions to housework are differentiated by occupational class, as well as by relative and absolute earnings. Daily interactions between men and women in the UK are explored, drawing on qualitative data from women who earn more, women who earn around the same and those who earn less than their male partners.

[. . .]

Methodology

Interview sample

Semi-structured, face-to-face interviews were undertaken with 36 partnered women and 12 partnered men, all of whom had at least one

* From Lyonette, C. and Crompton, R. (2015) 'Sharing the Load? Partners' Relative Earnings and the Division of Domestic Labour', *Work, Employment and Society*, 29(1): 23–40. Extracts from pp. 23–24, 27–29, 33–34.

child under the age of 14 (only one partner per couple was interviewed to minimize the potential for both partners being present at the same time, thereby limiting the 'honesty' of responses, although this means that the information gathered relies on one partner's responses only). Only those households where women worked full-time (defined as 30 hours a week or more), and those with complete data on their own and their partners' incomes, are included (in a small number of cases, male partners did not work or worked very few hours). In this way, arguments related to time availability are minimized (e.g. if the female partner is not working or is working part-time hours, she will have more hours to devote to domestic work). There are, however, differences in what constitutes 'full-time' hours, reflecting the existing differences in hours worked by women from different occupational classes within the UK labour market.

Respondents were employed within four different occupational sectors: medicine, accountancy, finance and retail, and came from a variety of occupational levels. The female sample included 21 professional/managerial respondents, 11 intermediates and four routine/manual respondents, and the male sample included eight professional/managerials, one intermediate and three routine/manuals.[1] The sample, therefore, is biased towards professional and managerial employees, due to the selection of occupational sectors in the early stages of the research and the fact that many of the female respondents or female partners of respondents in lower-level occupations worked part-time. A definition of class based on occupational level is clearly not ideal but allowed us to explore some of the differences in household work between partners in couples from varied backgrounds. The inclusion of only full-time women also allowed for the analysis of a reasonable number of households in which the woman earned more than the man (Woman Earns More, or WEMs, using a relative measure of income) and earned a high salary (absolute income). In the female sample, there were 15 WEMs, 16 SINCs (Same Income Couples, using a relative

measure) and 5 MEMs (Man Earns More, also using the relative measure). In the male sample, there was 1 WEM, 5 SINCs and 6 MEMs. Of the 48 interviewees, only 12 of the female partners earned less than £30,000 per annum, and 15 earned £90,000 per annum or more. All of the professional/managerial male respondents were married to similarly-qualified women, and all the routine/manual men were married to similar women, except one intermediate man who was married to a routine/manual worker.

Interviews were normally conducted at the participant's workplace in a private room, although some were conducted in participants' homes. All interviewees were offered a gift voucher for participating. Interviews lasted around an hour, followed a semi-structured interview guide and were audiotaped and fully transcribed. The qualitative data were entered into NVivo, with both researchers involved in coding and data analysis to minimize bias, and thematic analysis was used to identify key themes emerging from the data. [...]

[...]

Respondents were overwhelmingly supportive of domestic sharing, reflecting the substantial shift in gender role attitudes that has taken place since the 1970s for both men and women (Crompton and Lyonette, 2008). Almost all women stated, irrespective of their relative and absolute income, that domestic chores should be shared, although many qualified their statements with reasoning that also reflected both relative resource and time availability explanations of the domestic division of labour. For example:

> I think it depends on what your paid working arrangements are. We divide them up according to how much time each of us has because of our outside-the-house responsibilities, and I'm very comfortable with what we do. (A1, female WEM, earning £90K; female responsibility for housework)

Some women demonstrated relatively traditional gender role attitudes overall but nevertheless felt that if both partners were working, there should be a more equal distribution of housework:

> It should be a shared thing because if the woman is going out to work I think, you know, you're paying money. I feel it should not be just for a lady to do. I mean if, for example, I'm staying at home, I'm not going to work and my husband is going out to work and he's coming home tired, I'll expect him to come and find a clean house, his dinner is ready and stuff like that for him. So I wouldn't expect him to do that much, really.
> (Interviewer): But if you're working, it should be shared?
> Equally shared, yes. (R11, female SINC, earning £23K; shared responsibility for housework)

Men, too, reported almost unanimously that housework should be shared, with similar qualifications regarding time availability. Despite the widespread support for sharing, respondents' behaviour tended to comply with more traditional patterns of domestic labour, however. Very few couples had discussed housework and childcare before having children, but many reported a more traditional division of labour after having children, partly as a result of women taking some time out of the labour market. Only one woman reported that her partner was mainly responsible for housework and none of the men said that they were mainly responsible.

We deliberately set out to minimize 'time availability' explanations by focusing only on couples in which the woman works full-time. However, there were large differences in the hours worked, both between partners in couples, and also between the women in the study. Seventeen women worked 50 per cent or more of the total paid hours within their households: of these, 10 reported that the male partner shared the housework and one woman reported that her partner took the main responsibility (65 per cent of the women working more than 50 per cent of total paid hours). For those 29 women working less than 50 per cent of the total hours, only seven (24 per cent of the group) reported equal sharing [. . .]. These differences reflect some support for time availability explanations, although in 35 out

of 46 couples with complete data (76 per cent of these couples), partners worked similar hours.[2] In only seven cases, the woman worked 60 per cent or more of the total hours of paid employment and of these, five said that housework was shared or done mainly by the man.

[. . .]

Gender deviance neutralization theory suggests that gender differences should reduce as women earn a similar income to their partners and then re-emerge, with greater differences apparent between the women in the 'SINC' and the 'WEM' groups, as women begin to 'display' their gender. There is little to support this argument, however, as WEMs who earned substantially more than their partners (between 70 and 100 per cent of the couple's total income) were in fact *more* likely to report that they shared housework with their partners and one woman, earning 72 per cent of the total income, reported that her partner took the main responsibility.

The interviews also gave no indication that WEMs were assuming the major responsibility for housework in an effort to neutralize gender deviance. On the contrary, many were aware of gender issues around housework, and presented a heightened 'gender consciousness' (Sullivan, 2004: 208), sharpened by their enhanced material contribution to their households:

> I watched my mum . . . was a stay-at-home mum. She did all the housework. I was brought up, little girls run around with feather dusters, don't they? . . . if I had a husband who refused to do housework or thought it was beneath him or had an attitude problem because I was earning too much money, I wouldn't be married to him anymore, let's put it that way. (F22, female WEM, earning £100K; female responsibility for housework)

Indeed, among this group of interviewees, housework often represented a bone of contention, signifying the importance of challenges made at the interactional level, as highlighted by Sullivan (2004, 2011). In many cases efforts were being made to achieve a more gender-neutral division of domestic work, although some demonstrated greater success than others:

> I've made it known to my husband that, listen, I know you don't like ironing but ... it would help to just shove a wash load on so that at least I can come home and whatever ... but I have hinted it would be nice to come home and not have to think about dinner every night, so we share, but I mean if you ask me who does the ironing, the hoovering, the majority, then I still do it ... when my husband cleans he surface cleans, when I clean, I clean. (R1 female WEM, earning £45K; female responsibility for housework)

A woman in a SINC household was making similar efforts:

> ... (housework) should definitely be shared. I'm a definite advocate of it not being a woman's job. My husband might be bad at it but I make him do it. I don't have time to do everything. He'll do the washing; he's very good at getting the washing in the machine, getting it out, dry. I'll do the dusting, the cleaning and the hoovering, because he's awful at doing that. So, you know, we kind of split it. I don't let him get away with it. (F20 female SINC, earning £38K; female responsibility for housework)

Even the woman with the lowest relative income (20 per cent of the couple's total income) and one of the lowest absolute incomes reported that housework *should* be shared, even though she went on to excuse her partner from not doing his share:

> It should be both equally (laughs). It's just that it's an individual thing, a man, he might be not as, not house-proud but things might not ... matter to him as much. I know I'm very pedantic about things and I'm a bit of a perfectionist so I want things a certain way at home. So I know that he can have his meal and say oh well the dishes can be put in the dishwasher later or tomorrow. Whereas I'm like no, get them out of the way now, so it's that sort of detail where, because I'm pedantic ... and I think it sometimes comes to a head and you think well, no this is not fair, but then it's me wanting it to be that way, so if that's the case, I choose to do it that way.

> (R12, female MEM, earning £23K; female responsibility for housework)

Based on these extracts, it may be suggested that the women, especially those earning the same or more than their partners, are simultaneously challenging or 'undoing' (Deutsch, 2007) as well as 'doing' gender. They are fully aware that their material contribution to the household should be fairly reflected in the sharing of housework, and are often frustrated at their lack of success in changing the situation. At the same time, their frustrations are to some extent mollified by the 'myth of male incompetence' (Tichenor, 2005: 41), echoing the previous respondent's use of gender 'essentialism'[3] to excuse her partner:

> I tried to level it out but it didn't work. He didn't do it to the right standard. I think they do it on purpose, men, don't they? ... Using the cleaner, he'll just clean round things, then all of a sudden you'll move the sofa and you're like, 'What is that under there?' ... or he says, 'Don't clean upstairs now because no one goes up there bar us, you don't need to hoover' is his argument. (F30, female WEM, earning £33K; female responsibility for housework)

Gupta (2007) argues that a woman's absolute, rather than relative, income is a better predictor of her level of housework and therefore, lower-income women do more than higher-income women (see also Gupta and Ash, 2008). However, our data did not support this argument, as there appeared to be a pattern of those earning the highest incomes (£90K or more) *and* those with the lowest incomes (£23K or less) reporting a more equal sharing than women in the middle income groups. There was also no clear association between women's absolute and relative income and male contribution to housework.

The extent, form and success of women's contestation to the gendered nature of domestic work demonstrated some interesting differences. Some have argued that higher-qualified women have higher expectations of equality and are more willing and able to engage in contesting the gender order (e.g. Crompton and Harris, 1999; Pesquera, 1997). However, the examples above suggest that women from all occupational levels expected equal sharing of domestic work with their male partners, with varying degrees of success.

NOTES

1. We used the NS-SEC 3-category classification. Doctors and accountants are professionals, and the majority of finance employees are classified as 'Intermediate'. In retail, the majority of employees would generally be classified as 'routine and manual', although our sample contained a larger proportion of those in managerial posts than anticipated.
2. Defined as working between 40 and 60 per cent of total hours.
3. For more on gender essentialism, see Crompton and Lyonette (2005).

REFERENCES

Acker J (1990) Hierarchies, jobs, bodies: a theory of gendered organisations. *Gender and Society* 4(2): 139–58.

Bianchi SM, Milkie MA, Sayer LC and Robinson JP (2000) Is anyone doing the housework? Trends in the gender division of household labor. *Social Forces* 79(1): 191–228.

Coltrane S (2009) Fatherhood, gender and work–family policies. In: Gornick JC and Meyers MK (eds) *Gender Equality: Transforming Family Divisions of Labor*. London and New York: Verso, 385–409.

Connolly M and Gregory M (2008) The part-time pay penalty: earnings trajectories of British women. *Oxford Economic Papers* 61(Supplement): i76–i97.

Crompton R and Harris F (1999) Attitudes, women's employment and the changing domestic division of labour. In: Crompton R (ed.) *Restructuring Gender Relations and Employment*. Oxford: Oxford University Press, 105–27.

Crompton R and Lyonette C (2005) The new gender essentialism – domestic and family 'choices' and their relation to attitudes. *British Journal of Sociology* 56(4): 601–24.

Crompton R and Lyonette C (2008) Who does the housework? The division of labour within the home. In: Park A, Curtice J, Thomson K, Phillips M, Johnson M and Clery E (eds) *British Social Attitudes: The 24th Report*. London: Sage Publications, 53–80.

Deutsch FM (2007) Undoing gender. *Gender and Society* 21(1): 106–27.

Gatrell CJ (2005) *Hard Labour: The Sociology of Parenthood*. Maidenhead: Open University Press.

Grant L, Yeandle S and Buckner L (2005) *Working below Potential: Women and Part-Time Work*, EOC Working Paper Series no. 40. Manchester: Equal Opportunities Commission.

Gupta S (2007) Autonomy, dependence or display? The relationship between married women's earnings and housework. *Journal of Marriage and Family* 69: 399–417.

Kan MY, Sullivan O and Gershuny J (2011) Gender convergence in domestic work: discerning the effects of interactional and institutional barriers from large-scale data. *Sociology* 45(2): 234–51.

Pesquera B (1997) In the beginning he wouldn't even lift a spoon. In: Lamphere L, Ragone H and Zavella P (eds) *Situated Lives Gender and Culture in Everyday Life*. London: Routledge, 208–22.

Sullivan O (2004) Changing gender practices within the household: a theoretical perspective. *Gender and Society* 18(2): 207–22.

Sullivan O (2011) An end to gender display through the performance of housework? A review and reassessment of the quantitative literature using insights from the qualitative literature. *Journal of Family Theory and Review* 3(March): 1–13.

Thornley C (2007) Working part-time for the state: gender, class and the public sector pay gap. *Gender, Work and Organisation* 14(5): 454–75.

Tichenor VJ (2005) *Earning More and Getting Less: Why Successful Wives Can't Buy Equality.* New Brunswick, NJ and London: Rutgers University Press.

Part 5 – Further reading

Social inequalities are well served across the book, but a few dedicated texts should help. Platt, L. (2019) *Understanding Inequalities: Stratification and Difference* (2nd edn, Cambridge: Polity) is a wide-ranging book and a good starting point. The field of disability studies is outlined in Barnes, C., and Mercer, G. (2010) *Exploring Disability: A Sociological Introduction* (2nd edn, Cambridge: Polity). Race and ethnicity is a thriving field, and a good way into this is with Chattoo, S., Atkin, K., Craig, G., and Flynn, R. (eds) (2019) *Understanding 'Race' and Ethnicity* (2nd edn, Bristol: Policy Press). Then the very large field of gender and sexuality can be approached from Rahman, M., and Jackson, S. (2010) *Gender and Sexuality: Sociological Approaches* (Cambridge: Polity).

Sociology, 9th edition

Chapter 7, 'Gender and Sexuality', chapter 8, 'Race, Ethnicity and Migration', chapter 9, 'Stratification and Social Class', and the relevant sections in chapter 10, 'Health, Illness and Disability', cover sociological research into the various social divisions. Chapter 6, 'Global Inequality', also looks at some of the issues around the world.

Part 6 Relationships and the Life Course

People are born and go through childhood, youth and adulthood before entering a period of old age and, eventually, dying. This common-sense view of a universal human life cycle is not entirely false, but it is a partial description which becomes evident when we think about terms used to describe particular stages of life. There are children, of course, but also adolescents, teenagers, youth, young adults, the 'young old' and the 'old old', to name just a few. The concept of the teenager did not emerge until the 1950s, when rapid economic growth enabled young people to become consumers of pop music and fashion. Similarly, the categories young old (those aged 65 to 74) and old old (aged 75 to 84) make sense only once average life expectancy has risen significantly.

Such changes hint at the social construction of life stages, and sociologists today use the concept of a life course rather than a life cycle, as the latter suggests a universal human lifespan while the former more accurately reflects the shifting experience over generations. Similarly, it is clear that personal relationships, forms of intimacy, and family life also undergo many significant changes over time and across societies. Our readings in this section cover some of these issues, from studies of the social self, personal life and love to generational experience and theories of the life course.

The section opens with an extract from George Herbert Mead's classic work on the formation of the social self. Mead describes himself as a 'social behaviourist', though his ideas have been highly influential in the interactionist tradition of sociology stemming from Max Weber. The significance of Mead's work is that it is a systematic rejection of all notions that the individual's 'self' emerges naturally from human biology or is a function of the developing brain. Instead he argues for a 'fully social' theory of self-formation in which the key is relationships and social interaction, which makes his theory a starting point for further empirical sociological study. Mead argues that what we call the self is actually made up of two parts: the biological 'I' and the social 'me', which, once formed, function together to create self-conscious individuals. The theory views selfhood as slowly developing through childhood play and organized games in which the individual begins to see themselves 'as if from the outside' by taking on the role of a 'generalized other'. The reading extracts some of Mead's central ideas on this process and its consequences for social scientific work.

The wide-ranging feminist intervention in sociology raised some serious issues about families, family relations and domestic abuse. The idealized family of 1950s sociology was a particular target, with a series of studies demonstrating that this was more ideological than factual. The acknowledgement of same-sex relationships and households also challenged the notion of an idealized, heterosexual nuclear family form to which all people should aspire. One consequence is the acceptance that the sociology of the family has to become a sociology of families, a recognition of the diversity of family forms across classes, ethnic groups and many more. However, perhaps the more significant shift has been away from the concept of 'the family' in the direction of a sociology of intimacy and/or personal life. A key proponent of the latter is Carol Smart, and Reading 32 sets out the main terms of this change in focus. Smart argues that the study of personal life is necessarily broader than family sociology, as it explores people's meaningful relationships in total. Some of these may well still fit conventional ideas of 'family', but the extent to which they do becomes the subject of empirical research, not assumed in advance. Smart provides a useful introduction to what personal life studies might entail.

One element of intimate relations that seems to be ever present is love. If pop songs, novels and films are a guide, love should be *the* most significant aspect of all our lives. Yet social historians have provided some convincing evidence that romantic love has not always been at the centre of personal relationships. Far from it. Before modern times, people formed relationships and married for companionship, financial stability, familial cooperation and other perfectly rational reasons. But, by contrast, love appears to be unstable, random and, as some sociologists argue, frankly chaotic. Eva Illouz focuses on an under-reported aspect of intimate relationships, namely the 'misery of love' – painful arguments and agonizing break-ups, divorce, depression and emotional turmoil. The 'quest for love' almost always involves a painful downside. Illouz looks at the changing forms of these agonies along three main dimensions of the self: the will, recognition and desire – in short, how we actually 'want' something, what counts in sustaining our sense of self-worth, what are the things we long for and how do we long for them. Illouz

outlines and takes issue with the psychologization and individualization of love and its miseries, offering, instead, a sociological perspective on the issue.

In Reading 34, Stephen J. Hunt discusses some of the main reasons why sociologists have moved towards the adoption of life-course perspectives rather than continuing with the concept of the life cycle. One advantage of the life-course concept is its ability to connect broad socio-economic change to shifts in the stages of life experienced by successive generations. Sociological thinking would expect that major developments such as post-Fordism, postmodernization, globalization and the digital revolution to impact on many aspects of social life, including the average lifespan and life-stage categorization. The social constructionist approach of life-course studies seems better able to analyse these periods of social change than a biologically oriented, universalist life-cycle position. Hunt provides a reliable and concise account of the emergence of life-course studies and suggests how the latter may be able to contribute to more effective policy-making.

Journalistic commentary often draws on the idea of common generational experience, particularly in its depictions of changing norms of behaviour and values. Commentaries abound on the post-Second World War Baby-Boom Generation (boomers), 1960s Hippy or Beat Generation and, more recently, the technologically savvy but work-insecure Generation X and later Millennials. In such cases the idea conveyed is that these generational groups share certain experiences in common that have shaped their attitudes and behaviour, usually in negative ways as producing new social problems to be solved. Our final reading in this section, from Lorraine Green, rehearses some of the arguments in favour of a sociology of generations, carefully distinguishing the contours of this enterprise from the more politicized and normative writing. Although some of the early sociologists were interested in generations as distinct social groups, notably Karl Mannheim, that interest did not carry forward in a systematic way. As a result, we can find some fascinating individual studies but not a strongly established research tradition. Perhaps the growing interest in life-course studies may lead more sociologists to see that generational change can be a fruitful avenue for understanding social and cultural change.

31. I, Me and the Social Self*

George Herbert Mead

In our statement of the development of intelligence we have already suggested that the language process is essential for the development of the self. The self has a character which is different from that of the physiological organism proper. The self is something which has a development; it is not initially there, at birth, but arises in the process of social experience and activity, that is, develops in the given individual as a result of his relations to that process as a whole and to other individuals within that process. The intelligence of the lower forms of animal life, like a great deal of human intelligence, does not involve a self. In our habitual actions, for example, in our moving about in a world that is simply there and to which we are so adjusted that no thinking is involved, there is a certain amount of sensuous experience such as persons have when they are just waking up, a bare thereness of the world. Such characters about us may exist in experience without taking their place in relationship to the self. One must, of course, under those conditions, distinguish between the experience that immediately takes place and our own organization of it into the experience of the self. One says upon analysis that a certain item had its place in his experience, in the experience of his self. We do inevitably tend at a certain level of sophistication to organize all experience into that of a self. We do so intimately identify our experiences, especially our affective experiences, with the self that it takes a moment's abstraction to realize that pain and pleasure can be there without being the experience of the self. Similarly, we normally organize our memories upon the string of our self. If we date things we always date them from the point of view of our past experiences. We frequently have memories that we cannot date, that we cannot place. A picture comes before us suddenly and we are at a loss to explain when that experience originally took place. We remember perfectly distinctly the picture, but we do not have it definitely placed, and until we can place it in terms of our past experience we are not satisfied. Nevertheless, I think it is obvious when one comes to consider it that the self is not necessarily involved in the life of the organism, nor involved in what we term our sensuous experience, that is, experience in a world about us for which we have habitual reactions.

We can distinguish very definitely between the self and the body. The body can be there and can operate in a very intelligent fashion without there being a self involved in the experience. The self has the characteristic that it is an object to itself, and that characteristic distinguishes it from other objects and from the body. It is perfectly true that the eye can see the foot, but it does not see the body as a whole. We cannot see our backs; we can feel certain portions of them, if we are agile, but we cannot get an experience of our whole body. There are, of course, experiences which are somewhat vague and difficult of location, but the bodily experiences are for us organized about a self. [. . .]

* From Mead, G. H. (1972 [1934]) *Mind, Self, and Society: From the Standpoint of a Social Behaviorist* (Chicago: University of Chicago Press). Extracts from pp. 135–136, 149, 150–152, 154–156, 158.

[. . .]

Another set of background factors in the genesis of the self is represented in the activities of play and the game.

[. . .]

[. . .] In the play period the child utilizes his own responses to these stimuli which he makes use of in building a self. The response which he has a tendency to make to these stimuli organizes them. He plays that he is, for instance, offering himself something, and he buys it; he gives a letter to himself and takes it away; he addresses himself as a parent, as a teacher; he arrests himself as a policeman. He has a set of stimuli which call out in himself the sort of responses they call out in others. He takes this group of responses and organizes them into a certain whole. Such is the simplest form of being another to one's self. It involves a temporal situation. The child says something in one character and responds in another character, and then his responding in another character is a stimulus to himself in the first character, and so the conversation goes on. A certain organized structure arises in him and in his other which replies to it, and these carry on the conversation of gestures between themselves.

If we contrast play with the situation in an organized game, we note the essential difference that the child who plays in a game must be ready to take the attitude of everyone else involved in that game, and that these different rôles must have definite relationship to each other. Taking a very simple game such as hide-and-seek, everyone with the exception of the one who is hiding is a person who is hunting. A child does not require more than the person who is hunted and the one who is hunting. If a child is playing in the first sense he just goes on playing, but there is no basic organization gained. In that early stage he passes from one rôle to another just as a whim takes him. But in a game where a number of individuals are involved, then the child taking one rôle must be ready to take the rôle of everyone else. If

he gets in a ball nine he must have the responses of each position involved in his own position. He must know what everyone else is going to do in order to carry out his own play. He has to take all of these rôles. They do not all have to be present in consciousness at the same time, but at some moments he has to have three or four individuals present in his own attitude, such as the one who is going to throw the ball, the one who is going to catch it, and so on. These responses must be, in some degree, present in his own make-up. In the game, then, there is a set of responses of such others so organized that the attitude of one calls out the appropriate attitudes of the other.

This organization is put in the form of the rules of the game. Children take a great interest in rules. They make rules on the spot in order to help themselves out of difficulties. Part of the enjoyment of the game is to get these rules. Now, the rules are the set of responses which a particular attitude calls out. You can demand a certain response in others if you take a certain attitude. These responses are all in yourself as well. There you get an organized set of such responses as that to which I have referred, which is something more elaborate than the rôles found in play. Here there is just a set of responses that follow on each other indefinitely. At such a stage we speak of a child as not yet having a fully developed self. The child responds in a fairly intelligent fashion to the immediate stimuli that come to him, but they are not organized. He does not organize his life as we would like to have him do, namely, as a whole. There is just a set of responses of the type of play. The child reacts to a certain stimulus, and the reaction is in himself that is called out in others, but he is not a whole self. In his game he has to have an organization of these rôles; otherwise he cannot play the game. The game represents the passage in the life of the child from taking the rôle of others in play to the organized part that is essential to self-consciousness in the full sense of the term.

[. . .]

The organized community or social group which gives to the individual his unity of self may be called "the generalized' other." The attitude of the generalized other is the attitude of the whole community.[1] Thus, for example, in the case of such a social group as a ball team, the team is the generalized other in so far as it enters—as an organized process or social activity—into the experience of any one of the individual members of it.

If the given human individual is to develop a self in the fullest sense, it is not sufficient for him merely to take the attitudes of other human individuals toward himself and toward one another within the human social process, and to bring that social process as a whole into his individual experience merely in these terms: he must also, in the same way that he takes the attitudes of other individuals toward himself and toward one another, take their attitudes toward the various phases or aspects of the common social activity or set of social undertakings in which, as members of an organized society or social group, they are all engaged; and he must then, by generalizing these individual attitudes of that organized society or social group itself, as a whole, act toward different social projects which at any given time it is carrying out, or toward the various larger phases of the general social process which constitutes its life and of which these projects are specific manifestations. This getting of the broad activities of any given social whole or organized society as such within the experiential field of any one of the individuals involved or included in that whole is, in other words, the essential basis and prerequisite of the fullest development of that individual's self: only in so far as he takes the attitudes of the organized social group to which he belongs toward the organized, co-operative social activity or set of such activities in which that group as such is engaged, does he develop a complete self or possess the sort of complete self he has developed. And on the other hand, the complex co-operative processes and activities and institutional functionings of organized human society are also possible only in so far as every

individual involved in them or belonging to that society can take the general attitudes of all other such individuals with reference to these processes and activities and institutional functionings, and to the organized social whole of experiential relations and interactions thereby constituted—and can direct his own behavior accordingly.

It is in the form of the generalized other that the social process influences the behavior of the individuals involved in it and carrying it on, i.e., that the community exercises control over the conduct of its individual members; for it is in this form that the social process or community enters as a determining factor into the individual's thinking. In abstract thought the individual takes the, attitude of the generalized other[2] toward himself, without reference to its expression in any particular other individuals; and in concrete thought he takes that attitude in so far as it is expressed in the attitudes toward his behavior of those other individuals with whom he is involved in the given social situation or act. But only by taking the attitude of the generalized other toward himself, in one or another of these ways, can he think at all; for only thus can thinking—or the internalized conversation of gestures which constitutes thinking—occur. And only through the taking by individuals of the attitude or attitudes of the generalized other toward themselves is the existence of a universe of discourse, as that system of common or social meanings which thinking presupposes at its context, rendered possible.

[. . .]

I have pointed out, then, that there are two general stages in the full development of the self. At the first of these stages, the individual's self is constituted simply by an organization of the particular attitudes of other individuals toward himself and toward one another in the specific social acts in which he participates with them. But at the second stage in the full development of the individual's self that self is constituted not only by an organization of these particular individual attitudes, but also by an organization of the social attitudes of the generalized other or the social group as a whole to which he belongs. These social or group attitudes are brought within the individual's field of direct experience, and are included as elements in the structure or constitution of his self, in the same way that the attitudes of particular other individuals are; and the individual arrives at them, or succeeds in taking them, by means of further organizing, and then generalizing, the attitudes of particular other individuals in terms of their organized social bearings and implications. So the self reaches its full development by organizing these individual attitudes of others into the organized social or group attitudes, and by thus becoming an individual reflection of the general systematic pattern of social or group behavior in which it and the others are all involved—a pattern which enters as a whole into the individual's experience in terms of these organized group attitudes which, through the mechanism of his central nervous system, he takes toward himself, just as he takes the individual attitudes of others.

NOTES

1. It is possible for inanimate objects, no less than for other human organisms, to form parts of the generalized and organized—the completely socialized—other for any given human individual, in so far as he responds to such objects socially or in a social fashion (by means of the mechanism of thought, the internalized conversation of gestures). Any thing—any object or set of objects, whether animate or inanimate, human or animal, or merely physical—toward which he acts, or to which he responds, socially, is an element in what for him is the generalized other; by taking the attitudes of which toward himself

he becomes conscious of himself as an object or individual, and thus develops a self or personality. Thus, for example, the cult, in its primitive form, is merely the social embodiment of the relation between the given social group or community and its physical environment—an organized social means, adopted by the individual members of that group or community, of entering into social relations with that environment, or (in a sense) of carrying on conversations with it; and in this way that environment becomes part of the total generalized other for each of the individual members of the given social group or community.

2. We have said that the internal conversation of the individual with himself in terms of words or significant gestures—the conversation which constitutes the process or activity of thinking—is carried on by the individual from the standpoint of the "generalized other." And the more abstract that conversation is, the more abstract thinking happens to be, the further removed is the generalized other from any connection with particular individuals. It is especially in abstract thinking, that is to say, that the conversation involved is carried on by the individual with the generalized other, rather than with any particular individuals. Thus it is, for example, that abstract concepts are concepts stated in terms of the attitudes of the entire social group or community; they are stated on the basis of the individual's consciousness of the attitudes of the generalized other toward them, as a result of his taking these attitudes of the generalized other and then responding to them. And thus it is also that abstract propositions are stated in a form which anyone—any other intelligent individual—will accept.

32. Towards a Sociology of Personal Life*

Carol Smart

Ever since the interventions of feminist scholarship into the area of families, the private sphere, domestic life and gender relationships, the term 'family' has been rendered problematic. Michèle Barrett and Mary McIntosh (1982) mounted one of the most sustained critiques of the term, identifying it as a form of ideology rather than a descriptive concept, and one which sustained women's subordination while deflecting discontent through appeals to the naturalness of the biological unit of the heterosexual couple and their children. Following this, feminist work not only tried to avoid using the word family, but to strip away the ideological veil that shrouded discussions of families by deploying more neutral terms such as 'household' or 'private sphere'. There was also a body of empirical research which focused on abuses, violence and economic inequality in nuclear families. Following on from such approaches other criticisms were developed, in particular from the viewpoint of same-sex households; in the UK this included reaction to a notorious legal provision which prevented schools from teaching children about 'pretended families' (same-sex relationships) (Weeks, 1991). The grossness of depicting gay and lesbian households as 'pretended' families led to an absolute aversion to the term. However, the concept of families (as opposed to 'the' family) seemed incredibly tenacious and not only refused to be banished from the lexicon, but seemed instead

to expand quite happily to include a range of relationships and households which would never have fitted the original sociological definition of a nuclear family. Thus concepts developed of families of choice (Weston, 1991) or of friends as family (Pahl, 2000) and, although a core notion of family has undoubtedly remained (especially in relation to close biological kin), the term seems to have become more inclusive and more generous in its embrace. David Morgan (1996) has also helped to shift the field conceptually through his development of the idea of family practices, which captures the idea that families are what families do, no longer being defined exclusively by co-residence or even ultimately by kinship and marriage.

The field is therefore going through a very interesting phase as the sociological imagination stretches and reconfigures in order better to grasp and reflect the complexities of contemporary personal life. And this brings me precisely to the concept of 'personal life', a term now increasingly applied to include not only families as conventionally conceived, but also newer family forms and relationships, reconfigured kinship networks, and friendships. But as suggested at the start of this chapter, 'personal life' is intended to be more than a terminological holdall. The terminology of personal life seeks to embrace conceptual shifts as well as empirical changes to social realities and, for the sake of clarity, I shall enumerate the main components of this field before turning to some of its limitations.

1 First, it is vital to specify what is meant by 'personal'. The term is used in contradistinction

---

* From Smart, C. (2007) *Personal Life* (Cambridge: Polity). Extracts from pp. 26–31, 189–190.

to 'individual' because of the problems identified above both with understandings of the individualization thesis and with atomized or disconnected individualism. 'The personal' designates an area of life which impacts closely on people and means much to them, but which does not presume that there is an autonomous individual who makes free choices and exercises unfettered agency. This means that the term 'personal life' can invoke the social, indeed it is conceptualized as always already part of the social. This is because the very possibility of personal life is predicated upon a degree of self-reflection and also connectedness with others. Just as George Herbert Mead (1967, orig. 1934) posited the distinction between the 'I' and the 'me'(where the 'I' is the agentic ego and the 'me' is the social, interconnected person), so I suggest that the field of personal life is the 'me' compared with the 'I' of the individualization thesis. To live a personal life is to have agency and to make choices, but the personhood implicit in the concept requires the presence of others to respond to and to contextualize those actions and choices. Personal life is a reflexive state, but it is not private and it is lived out in relation to one's class position, ethnicity, gender and so on.

2 The idea that personal life is embedded in the social (and cultural, legal, economic etc.) is an analytical statement. It does not mean that ordinary people use the term in colloquial speech in that way, nor does it mean that they always necessarily have a conscious awareness of the social which frames their specific personal lives (Mills, 1940; Brannen and Nilsen, 2005). But the sociologist can map personal lives (revealed through the research process) into their social context and into their specific history or spatial location.

3 The concept of personal life allows for ideas of the life project – particularly significant in the work of Giddens and Beck – in which people have scope for decisions and plans, but it does not incorporate the idea of individually crafted biographies as if people are free-floating agents with sufficient resources to achieve their goals. In Gross's terms 'meaning-constitutive traditions'

are important here, as are such structural factors as social class, ethnicity and gender. So this mode of conceptualizing recognizes the importance of memory and generation or cultural transmission and is alert to the extent to which people are embedded in both sedimented structures and the imaginary.

4 The term is also appropriately neutral in that it does not prioritize relationships with biological kin or marital bonds. Such a landscape of personal life does not have hierarchical boundaries between friends and kin. This means that there is more open conceptual space for families of choice, same-sex intimacies, reconfigured kinship formations and so on.

5 Of particular significance is the way in which the concept contains within it a sense of motion. Personal life is never still or stationary in the way that the old idea of 'the family' appeared to be. While the concept of the life course has injected movement into studies of family life, this adds only a social dimension of generational and cohort ageing, whereas it is equally important to capture other kinds of motion. For example unemployment or divorce can transform personal life, often affecting income, housing and well-being and shifting people into completely different places and spaces, yet these common occurrences are not conceptualized as part of the life course.

6 There is also the potential to overcome the older distinctions made between private and public spheres which have conceptualized family life as a distinct place or institution separate from other social spaces and structures. Personal life is lived in many different places and spaces, it is cumulative (through memory, history and the passage of time) and it forms a range of connections, thus making it flexible rather than brittle and breakable. So personal life is not so concerned with boundary marking and provides the possibility of tracing its flows through systems of education, or work, or elsewhere.

7 The concept also gives recognition to those areas of life which used to be slightly below the sociological radar. Thus personal life includes

issues of sexuality, bodies, emotions, intimacy and can bring them together, creating a whole that is greater than its parts, rather than treating them as separate subfields of the sociological discipline.

8 Finally, personal life as a concept does not invoke the white, middle-class, heterosexual family in the way that, historically at least, the concept of 'the family' has. This means that important dimensions of class, ethnicity, religion, sexuality, gender, and disability can be written through the narrative and given significance through attentiveness not only to difference but by reference to cultural tradition, habitus, memories, generational transmission and emotion. This is not to imply that all these elements can or should be achieved all the time but shifting away from the dominant concept of the family to this broader sphere of social and emotional (inter)relationships opens up new conceptual configurations.

These points are suggestive of the value of reconfiguring the field. But this does not mean that terms such as 'family' or 'family life' should be banned or that the notions of kinship and friendship should be collapsed into a formless sludge. These ideas about personal life are intended to provide a conceptual orientation and potential toolbox rather than a rigid, rule-bound manifesto. Among the inevitable limitations with the concept, the most obvious is that its scope can be seen as too wide and it can appear to include anything and everything that pertains to a person. With more traditional concepts such as the family there were clear conceptual boundaries between 'it' and other institutions. But the comfort achieved by having conceptual boundaries has been at the cost of misrepresenting the ways in which personal life is lived and there are increasing demands for an understanding of fluidity. Morgan (1996) addressed this problem in the development of his ideas about family practices. He argues that 'a growing sense of fluidity' is apparent in a range of sociological fields such that the previously discrete areas of 'family', 'work', 'leisure' and so on are not sealed off from

one another. Rather Morgan suggests that one might start at a given point, but will inevitably cross over these other spaces. He deploys the metaphor of the kaleidoscope with 'the emphasis on shifting patterns of relationships' (1996: 187) to express the kind of realities that sociology seeks to represent and understand. He states:

> The notion of 'family practices' was elaborated to convey a sense of flow and movement between a whole set of overlapping social practices, Practices which were both constructed by the observer and lived by the actual practitioners. Thus 'family', in this account [of family practices], is not a thing but a way of looking at, and describing, practices which might also be described in a variety of other ways. (1996: 199)

Morgan's family practices are therefore fairly unbounded. By inference the idea of personal life is broader still as it does not keep the term 'family' at its core; it is thus an extension of Morgan's original thinking, only slightly wider in scope.

[. . .]

If a term is needed to capture the nature of this project it would be the 'connectedness thesis', which could stand in antithesis to the individualization thesis. Connectedness is not a normative concept and I am not arguing that connection is a human good, nor that it is invariably nourishing and inevitably desirable. On the contrary, I have highlighted some of the problems of connecting with and relating to others. The point about the idea, however, is that it sets the sociological imagination off on a different intellectual trajectory to the one initiated by the individualization thesis. With the latter, one is directed towards gathering information and evidence about fragmentation, differentiation, separation and autonomy. And it also becomes a mindset or inferential framework through which information is interpreted. This tendency needs to be counter-balanced by an awareness of connection, relationship, reciprocal emotion, entwinement, memory, history and so on. Connectedness as a mindset encourages enquiry about all kinds of sociality and seeks to understand how association remains both possible and desirable, as well as how it may take different shapes at different times. But this must not come across as trite, whimsical or contrary. This vision is closely related to my understanding of personal life as derived from the empirical research projects in which I have been involved. In other words, it is grounded sociologically speaking as well as poised to initiate a new intellectual direction.

The approach that I am advocating is also, in some ways, a response to the challenge set by Ulrich Beck (2002). As mentioned above, he argues that the family is now a 'zombie category'; in being so provocative he has sought to prod sociology into waking up from its 'drowsy fixation' with the nucleus of the family (Beck and Beck-Gernsheim, 1995: 147). He implies that as a field of enquiry the sociology of family life has become moribund and dull, quite incapable of grasping much of what is happening to family life and relationships. Beck may be right to acknowledge a lack of theoretical excitement in the field. Where once feminist work turned the whole concept of the family into a site of fruitful intellectual conflict, subsequent work settled into a pattern of empirical research which, in the main, sought to establish or modify those important insights and claims. So Giddens, Beck and Beck-Gernsheim have certainly caused a stir, and their work has, to a large extent, rushed in to fill the theoretical vacuum that they have identified. But what is really needed is an approach that goes beyond their limitations to offer both empirical grounding and a new theoretical orientation, thus initiating a new wave of research and thinking. It is here that the idea of the connectedness thesis comes in, along with the newly designated field of personal life.

REFERENCES

Barrett, M., and McIntosh, M. (1982) *The Anti-Social Family*, London: Verso.

Beck, U., and Beck-Gernsheim, E. (1995) *The Normal Chaos of Love*, Cambridge: Polity.

Beck, U., and Beck-Gernsheim, E. (2002) *Individualization*, London: Sage.

Brannen, J., and Nilsen, A. (2005) 'Individualisation, Choice and Structure: A Discussion of Current Trends in Sociological Analysis', *Sociological Review*, 53 (3): 412–28.

Mead, G. H. (1967, orig. 1934) *Mind, Self, and Society*, Chicago: University of Chicago Press.

Mills, C. W. (1940) 'Situated Actions and Vocabularies of Motive', *American Sociological Review*, 5 (6): 904–13.

Morgan, D. (1996) *Family Connections*, Cambridge: Polity.

Pahl, R. (2000) *On Friendship*, Cambridge: Polity.

Weeks, J. (1991) 'Pretended Family Relationships', in D. Clarke (ed.) *Marriage, Domestic Life and Social Change*, London: Routledge.

Weston, K. (1991) *Families we Choose: Lesbian, Gays and Kinship*, New York: Columbia University Press.

33. Love as a Sociological Problem*

Eva Illouz

Wuthering Heights (1847) belongs to a long literary tradition portraying love as an agonizingly painful emotion.[1] The novel's notorious protagonists, Heathcliff and Catherine, develop a strong love for each other while growing up together, yet Catherine decides to marry Edgar Linton, a socially more appropriate match. Humiliated when he accidentally overhears Catherine claim that she would degrade herself in marrying him, Heathcliff runs away. Catherine looks for him in the fields, and when she does not find him, she falls ill to the point of near-death.

In a far more ironic mode, *Madame Bovary* (1856) describes the unhappy marriage of a romantic woman with a kind-hearted but mediocre provincial doctor, who cannot satisfy his wife's sappily romantic and social fantasies. Its eponymous protagonist thinks she has found the hero she has so frequently read and dreamed about in the figure of Rodolphe Boulanger, a dashing landowner. After a three-year-long affair, they decide to elope. On the fateful day, Emma receives Rodolphe's letter breaking off his promise. Here the narrator dispenses with his usual irony when describing the romantic feelings of his heroine, instead describing her suffering with compassion:

> She leant against the embrasure of the window, and reread the letter with angry sneers. But the more she fixed her attention upon it, the more confused were

her ideas. She saw him again, heard him, encircled him with her arms, and throbs of her heart, that beat against her breast like blows of a sledge-hammer, grew faster and faster, with uneven intervals. She looked about her with the wish that the earth might crumble into pieces. Why not end it all? What restrained her? She was free. She advanced, looking at the paving-stones, saying to herself, "Come! come!"[2]

By our own standards, Catherine and Emma's pain seems extreme, but it is still intelligible to us. Yet, as this book seeks to claim, the romantic agony that both of these women experience has changed its content, color, and texture. First of all, the opposition between society and love which each enacts in her suffering is hardly relevant to modern societies. Indeed, there would be few economic obstacles or normative prohibitions preventing either Catherine or Emma from making their love their first and only choice. If anything, our contemporary sense of appropriateness would command us to follow the dictates of our heart, not of our social milieu. Second, a battery of experts would now be likely to come to the rescue of a hesitant Catherine and of Emma's passionless marriage: psychological counseling, couple therapy, divorce lawyers, mediation specialists, would massively appropriate and adjudicate over the private dilemmas of prospective or bored wives. In the absence of (or in conjunction with) experts' help, their modern counterparts would have shared the secret of their love with others, most likely female friends, or, at the very least, occasional anonymous friends found on the Internet, thus considerably diminishing the

* From Illouz, E. (2012) *Why Love Hurts: A Sociological Explanation* (Cambridge: Polity). Extracts from pp. 1–3, 4–6.

solitude of their passion. Between their desire and their despair, there would have been a thick flow of words, self-analysis, and friendly or expert advice. A contemporary Catherine or Emma would have spent a great deal of time reflecting and talking about their pain and likely found its causes in their own (or their lovers') deficient childhood. They would have derived a sense of glory not from the experience of grief, but precisely from having overcome it, through an arsenal of self-help therapeutic techniques. Modern romantic pain generates an almost endless gloss, the purpose of which is both to understand and extirpate its causes. Dying, committing suicide, and running away to a cloister no longer belong to our cultural repertoires. This is not to say, obviously, that we, "post-" or "late" moderns, do not know something about the agony of love. In fact we may possibly know more about it than our predecessors. But what it does suggest is that the social organization of romantic pain has changed profoundly. This book is about understanding the nature of that transformation through an examination of the changes undergone in three different and crucial aspects of the self: the will (how we want something), recognition (what matters for our sense of worth), and desire (what we long for and how we long for it).

[...]

Despite the widespread and almost collective character of these experiences, our culture insists they are the result of faulty or insufficiently mature psyches. Countless self-help manuals and workshops profess to help us better manage our romantic lives by making us more aware of the ways in which we unconsciously engineer our own defeats. The Freudian culture in which we are steeped has made the forceful claim that sexual attraction is best explained by our past experiences, and that the love preference is formed in early life in the relationship between the child and its parents. For many, the Freudian assertion that the family designs the pattern of

the erotic career has been the main explanation for why and how we fail to find or to sustain love. Undaunted by incoherence, Freudian culture even further claims that whether our partner is opposite or similar to our parents, s/he is a direct reflection of our childhood experiences – themselves the key to explaining our romantic destiny. With the idea of repetition compulsion, Freud went one step further and argued that early experiences of loss, however painful, will be reenacted throughout adult life, as a way to gain mastery over them. This idea had a tremendous impact on the collective view and treatment of romantic misery, suggesting it is a salutary dimension of the process of maturation. More: Freudian culture suggested that, by and large, romantic misery was inevitable and self-inflicted.

[...]

Throughout the twentieth century, the idea that romantic misery is self-made was uncannily successful, perhaps because psychology simultaneously offered the consoling promise that it could be undone. Painful experiences of love were a powerful engine activating a host of professionals (psychoanalysts, psychologists, and therapists of all kinds), the publishing industry, television, and numerous other media industries. The extraordinarily successful industry of self-help was made possible against the backdrop of the deep-seated belief that our miseries are tailor-made to our psychic history, that speech and self-knowledge have healing virtues, and that identifying the patterns and sources of our miseries helps us overcome them. The agonies of love now point only to the self, its private history, and its capacity to shape itself.

Precisely because we live in a time where the idea of individual responsibility reigns supreme, the vocation of sociology remains vital. In the same way that at the end of the nineteenth century it was radical to claim that poverty was the result not of dubious morality or weak character, but of systematic economic exploitation, it is now urgent to claim not that the failures of our private lives are the result of weak psyches, but rather that the vagaries and miseries of our emotional life are shaped by institutional arrangements. The purpose of this book is thus to vastly shift the angle of analysis of what is wrong in contemporary relationships. What is wrong are not dysfunctional childhoods or insufficiently self-aware psyches, but the set of social and cultural tensions and contradictions that have come to structure modern selves and identities. As such, this suggestion is not new. Feminist writers and thinkers have long contested both the popular belief in love as the source of all happiness and the psychological individualist understanding of the miseries of love. Contrary to popular mythology, feminists argue, romantic love is not the source of transcendence, happiness, and self-realization. Rather, it is one of the main causes of the divide between men and women, as well as one of the cultural practices through which women are made to accept (and "love") their submission to men. For, when in love, men and women continue to perform the deep divisions that characterize their respective identities: in Simone de Beauvoir's famous words, even in love men retain their sovereignty, while women aim to abandon themselves.[3] In her controversial *The Dialectic of Sex* [...], Shulamith Firestone went a step further: the source of men's social power and energy is the love women provide for them and continue to provide for men, thus suggesting that love is the cement with which the edifice of male domination has been built.[4] Romantic love not only hides class and sex segregation, but in fact makes it possible. In Ti-Grace Atkinson's striking words, romantic love is the "psychological pivot in the persecution of women."[5] The most arresting claim made by feminists is that a struggle for power lies at the core of love and sexuality, and that men have had and continue to have the upper hand in that struggle because there is a convergence between economic and sexual power. Such sexual male power consists in the capacity to define the objects of love and to set up the rules that govern courtship and the expression of romantic sentiments. Ultimately,

male power resides in the fact that gender identities and hierarchy are played out and reproduced in the expression and experience of romantic sentiments, and that, conversely, sentiments sustain broader economic and political power differentials.[6]

But in many ways, it is also this assumption about the primacy of power that constitutes a flaw in what has become the dominant strand of feminist critique of love. In periods where patriarchy was far more powerful than it is today, love played a much *less* significant role in the subjectivity of men and women. More than that: the cultural prominence of love seems to have been associated with a decline – not an increase – in men's power in the family and with the rise of more egalitarian and symmetrical gender relationships. Moreover, much of feminist theory is premised on the assumption that in love (and other) relationships, power is *the* primary building block of social relationships. It thus must disregard the vast amount of empirical evidence suggesting that love is no less primary than power, and that it is also a powerful and invisible mover of social relationships. In reducing women's love (and desire to love) to patriarchy, feminist theory often fails to understand the reasons why love holds such a powerful sway on modern women *as well as on* men and fails to grasp the egalitarian strain contained in the ideology of love, and its capacity to subvert from within patriarchy. Patriarchy certainly plays a central role in explaining the structure of relationships between the sexes and the uncanny fascination which heterosexuality still exerts on them, but it alone cannot explain the extraordinary grip of the love ideal on modern men and women.

This book thus wants to outline a framework in order to identify the institutional causes for romantic misery, but it takes for granted that the experience of love exerts a powerful hold that cannot be simply explained by "false consciousness."[7] This would be to foreclose the question before it is even asked. My claim here is that the reason why love is so central to our happiness and identity is not far from the reason why it is such a difficult aspect of our experience: both have to do with the ways in which self and identity are institutionalized in modernity. If many of us have "a kind of nagging anxiety, or unease" about love and a sense that matters of love make us "troubled, restless, and dissatisfied with ourselves," to use the words of philosopher Harry Frankfurt,[8] it is because love contains, mirrors, and amplifies the "entrapment" of the self in the institutions of modernity,[9] institutions, to be sure, shaped by economic and gender relations. As Karl Marx famously put it, "Human beings make their history themselves, but they do not do so voluntarily, not under circumstances of their own choosing, rather under immediately found, given and transmitted circumstances."[10] When we love or sulk, we do so by using resources and in situations that are not of our own making, and it is these resources and situations this book would like to study. Throughout the following pages, my overall argument is that something fundamental about the structure of the romantic self has changed in modernity. Very broadly, this can be described as a change in the structure of our romantic will, what we want and how we come to implement what we want with a sexual partner (chapters 2 and 3); as a change in what makes the self vulnerable, that is, what makes one feel unworthy (chapter 4); and, finally, as a change in the organization of desire, the content of the thoughts and emotions which activate our erotic and romantic desires (chapters 5 and 6). How the will is structured, how recognition is constituted, and how desire is activated constitute the three main lines of analysis of the transformations of love in modernity. Ultimately, my aim is to do to love what Marx did to commodities: to show that it is shaped and produced by concrete social relations; to show that love circulates in a marketplace of unequal competing actors; and to argue that some people command greater capacity to define the terms in which they are loved than others.

NOTES

1. E. Brontë, *Wuthering Heights* (Oxford: Oxford University Press, 2008 [1847]).
2. G. Flaubert, *Madame Bovary* (New York: Courier Dover Publications, 1996 [1857]), p. 145.
3. S. de Beauvoir, *The Second Sex* (New York: Vintage Books, 1970 [1949]).
4. S. Firestone, *The Dialectic of Sex: The Case for Feminist Revolution* (New York: Bantam, 1970), p. 129.
5. T.-G. Atkinson, "Radical Feminism and Love" (1974), in Susan Ostrov Weisser (ed.), *Women and Romance: A Reader* (New York: New York University Press, 2001), pp. 138–42.
6. C.A. MacKinnon, *Sexual Harassment of Working Women: A Case of Sex Discrimination* (New Haven: Yale University Press, 1979); A. Rich "Compulsory Heterosexuality and Lesbian Existence," *Signs*, 5(4) (1980), 631–60; S. Schecter, "Towards an Analysis of the Persistence of Violence against Women in the Home," *Aegis: Magazine on Ending Violence against Women* (July/August 1979), p. 47; S. Schecter, *Women and Male Violence: The Visions and Struggles of the Battered Women's Movement* (New York: South End Press, 1983).
7. See A. Swidler, *Talk of Love* (Chicago: University of Chicago Press, 2001) for an excellent answer to that question.
8. H. Frankfurt, *The Reasons of Love* (Princeton: Princeton University Press, 2004), p. 5.
9. E. Chowers, *The Modern Self in the Labyrinth* (Cambridge, MA: Harvard University Press, 2003).
10. Quoted and translated in P. Wagner, *A Sociology of Modernity: Liberty and Discipline* (London: Routledge, 1994), p. xiii.

34. From the Life Cycle to the Life Course*

Stephen J. Hunt

[. . .] Using the example of the United Kingdom, by way of marking increase in longevity, in 1951 there were only 271 centurions (people aged 100 and over), while according to the Office for National Statistics Report (2013) their number was estimated to be 13,780 in 2013; of these, 710 were approximated to be aged 105 or older. By the year 2030, there may well be 30,000 people living beyond their hundredth birthday.

There is some conjecture as to the underlying reasons behind this progressive gain in the lifespan, although broadly speaking they are undeniably related to improved environmental conditions and, to a lesser extent, medical advances which have virtually eliminated infectious diseases in Western societies. What cannot be doubted, however, are the *consequences* of longer life duration. One consideration is that Sociology is obliged to reconsider the familiar 'stages' of life, raising such profound questions as to what exactly constitutes the onset of 'old age'. Is it 65, 75 or 85 years old? As will continuingly be discussed throughout this volume, at the same time as life expectancy increases, the age categories which once formed a primary basis for structuring the life course are arguably disintegrating. At the very least some categories are increasingly shortened, others lengthened, raising further questions such as when does childhood end?; when does mid-life begin?; and indeed,

is 'old age' a meaningful 'stage' in the contemporary life course at all? Given these questions, the sociological tendency has been to practically abandon concepts related to the 'stages' of life. Plansibly they are now better designated as 'phases' or 'transitions' of life, often lacking coherence or direction and open to considerable negotiation.

These developments have, in turn, enforced a growing sociological emphasis on embracing a social constructionist approach that is concerned with deconstructing how such concepts as 'stages' have come to be forged in the first place and what the implications are for designating people into categories such as 'youth', 'mid-life' or 'old'. Nonetheless, it would probably be erroneous to entirely discard these age categories, even if they no longer comprehensively provide guides to life encounters. They do, for the most part, permit a point of departure for discussion over a number of crucial subject matters. That acknowledged, there is little doubt that these categories are increasingly void of their most deterministic qualities and provide only broad signifiers of life course experiences.

If these 'phases' of life are deemed as a starting point for analysis, it is clear that a number have been subject to a radical change. Others, or at least some aspects of them, have endured in fairly time-honoured tradition. The undertaking of this volume, as before, in investigating both change and continuity, is to consider the ongoing deliberations about the repercussions. These deliberations are of more than sociological interest, since they also inform current policy

---

* From Hunt, S. J. (2017) *The Life Course: A Sociological Introduction* (2nd edn, Basingstoke: Palgrave Macmillan). Extracts from pp. 2–4, 10–11, 27–28.

discourses surrounding such topics as the implications of an ageing population, sexual diversity and ethics circumscribing various emergent technologies. It is these discourses which, if a generalisation can be made, inform competing views of the socio-cultural trajectories associated with the life course, literally from (if not before) the cradle to the grave.

While the so-called stages of life might be transformed, how individuals envisage and negotiate them is impacted by the anticipation that, all things being equal, life expectancy will extend into at least the late 70s/early 80s. This is almost certain to influence reflexive thinking in the present. In short, what is unique about Western culture is not just the prevalence of modes of individualism and individual responsibility, but the way in which many people plan ahead and navigate future life and major life events. In this sense, the life course may have become more meaningful and more subjective. Yet, at the same time, the life course now seems less predictable and pre-determined, more infused with calculations of risk and anticipations of possible repercussions of discontinuity.

If such reflexive thinking and life experiences signify a profound shift in how the life course is appraised and comprehended, then this tilt has been accompanied by some notable economic, technological and cultural developments associated with what has come to be alternatively known as late- or postmodernity. The rise of the so-called new technologies, and the move to an economy of consumption rather than production – one accompanied by a distinct culture of choice – have all forged novel modes of social experience and encounter. It follows that the sociological enterprise has attempted to identify and account for the implications which, in turn, have generated fresh theoretical perspectives clearly building upon the growing distinction between the 'life-cycle' and the 'life course', the latter being the current preferred operational framework. As a result, notions of a coherent and inevitable 'life-cycle' are largely redundant and make little sense in a changing world where, as tentatively already

noted, the once assumed 'stages' of life and what they entail for life events are no longer so 'fixed' and predictable.

Yet, it is probably true to say that sociological theory is now betwixt 'n' between. New theories are not quite universally accepted and continue to be ardently deliberated, while older paradigms are by no means entirely redundant. There is still scope to apply conventional sociological suppositions. Many of these are concerned with such issues as structured social inequalities which continue to inform life course chances – class, gender, ethnicity and, of course, age – demographic categories scarcely rendered superfluous by acute changes observable at the end of the twentieth century and the beginning of a new millennium.

To be sure, recent sociological work has thrown light on how social inequalities and demographic variables may have a cumulative impact on the life course and life experiences. In turn, these factors not only impinge on life chances, but forge the very nature and structure of the 'phases' and crucial transitions throughout the life course. Simultaneously, Sociology has come to understand the importance of 'historical generations'. In short, that life experiences are influenced by the historical periods in which an individual's life course takes place. Yet while such factors invariably shape life course experiences, there is increasing recognition that human beings, through conscious personal agency, attempt to make sense of and act in response to situations in which they find themselves. This recognition in respect of the importance of personal agency would seem to be of increasing relevance in a social context that is subject to considerable change and variation.

[. . .]

Undoubtedly, contemporary societies, whether the complex post-industrial societies of the West or the vast variety of cultures which may be placed somewhat awkwardly under the rubric of 'emerging economies' or 'developing nations', are undergoing considerable transformations in a rising global order. Nonetheless, the sociological enterprise, despite changing conceptualisations and contextualisations, continues its erstwhile project in attempting to comprehend the human condition in terms of institutional settings or, as frequently preferred in late/postmodern theorising, the 'processes' which forge the lives of individuals and the life chances and opportunities of particular social constituencies.

These 'processes', be they economic, technological, cultural or political, endure in influencing life in many different respects, and for all of life. Considering the way they have changed in terms of the life course is an attractive one. There remains so much about the life course that is indicative of the nature of contemporary society, at least within the Western environment. Once it would have been almost obligatory to discuss the experiences of the life course, or the concept of the 'life-cycle' as previously preferred, primarily in terms of the impact of social institutions at particular 'stages' of life. This was principally so by way of those institutions which appeared to be universal and enduring. The family is arguably the most obvious human arrangement in this respect. Whether through the nurturing or early socialisation of the child or the institution of marriage and parenting that seemed to provide a marker of adult maturity and social responsibility, kinship structures have historically been central. Much no longer holds, however. The so-called decline of the family and increasing rates of marital break-down, coupled with the emergence of variations in family life, typified by the single parent and 'reconstituted' family, whereby children from previous relationships come together in a new household, ensure that generalisations and predictions regarding experiences of the family during the life course are at least problematic.

Variations in family structure, to which can be added the far-reaching changes in human relationships generally, also beg to be flagged up by the relevance of a social constructionist approach as an essential part of the sociological enterprise.

Above all, the emergence of the post-industrial society provides a reminder that, sociologically speaking, nothing is inevitable and the once taken-for-granted social arrangements are by no means universal. There are patent and palpable implications to be registered for the life course, suggesting that the key 'markers' of life have been subject to cultural variation, if not transmogrification. Here is an acknowledgement that transformations, including those identified with the family, should not necessarily breed apprehension merely because they are novel and unfamiliar.

[...]

As a theoretical perspective, the 'life course' has been characterised as 'a sequence of socially defined events and roles that the individual enacts over time' (Giele and Elder 1998, 221. Whether or not this definition entirely captures the essence of what the concept amounts to remains open to contention. What cannot be doubted, however, is the increasing acceptance of the framework of a 'life course' and its apparent conceptual advantages. At the very least it is able to account for the variety and complexity of 'trajectories' and 'transitions' in life experiences in Western societies. The matter of variety and complexity was suggested by Glen Elder (1994) who detected several prevailing and interrelated themes in the life course approach which point to its conceptual advantages: the interplay of human lives and historical time; 'timing of lives'; linked or interdependent lives; and human agency in making choices. Each of these will be briefly considered in this chapter. At the same time it might be said that a life course perspective allows for a greater historical and cross-cultural comparison, and this seems imperative given the radical changing global order.

Barbara Mitchell (2003) has explored how it is possible to trace the development of a life course approach which became more prevalent by the middle of the twentieth century. She notes that it by no means constituted a single sociological perspective, since a number of themes developed which also saw contributions from other social sciences. This remains the case today. Nonetheless, if any generalisation can be made. Mitchell maintains, it is plausibly that fresh perspectives focus on the importance of social change rather than continuity. This was certainly true of Western society, and the timing of the academic writings on the life course reflected the profound social transformations which were taking place.

The emphasis of the relevant studies varied considerably but the tendency was to throw light on the matter of social change and how it related to age, the cohort effect and the historical period in which the life course was experienced. Mitchell points to the work of Bernice Neugarten in particular who, as noted above, orientated her research to concentrate on the degree of deviation by people from the norms expected of their age group, including the time they decided to marry and begin a family. It was clear in Neugarten's findings that the time of marriage and the commencement of the family were open to numerous variations, and the choice not to engage in either was becoming increasingly commonplace.

It was probably not until the late twentieth century, as Mitchell records, that the life course approach came to be increasingly designated as an 'emerging paradigm' (Rodgers and White 1993) with both distinctive theories and methods. [. . .]

REFERENCES

Elder, G. (1994) 'Time, Human Agency, and Social Change: Perspectives on the Life Course', *Social Psychology Quarterly*, 57(1): 4–15.

Giele, J. and Elder, G. (1998) *Methods of Life Course Research: Qualitative and Quantitative Approaches*, Thousand Oaks, CA: Sage.

Mitchell, B. (2003) 'Life Course Theory', International Encyclopedia of Marriage and Family, www.encyclopedia.com/doc/1G2-34 06900275.html, accessed 4 June 2008.

Office for National Statistics (2013) 'Estimates of the Very Old (including Centenarians) for England and Wales, United Kingdom, 2002 to 2013', www.ons.gov.uk/ons/taxonomy/index.html?nscl=Household+Income+and+Expenditure, accessed 13 July 2014.

Rodgers, R. and White, J. (1993) 'Family Development Theory', in P. Boss, W. Doherty, R. Larossa, W. Schumm and S. Steinmetz (eds.), *Sourcebook of Family Theories and Methods: A Contextual Approach*, New York: Plenum.

35. The Significance of Generational Experience*

Lorraine Green

Two common terms relevant to life course sociology are *cohort* and *generation* – although some psychologists also increasingly deploy these terms, but to study more individualistic issues. 'Cohort' generally refers to a group of people born at the same time or within only a few years of each other, who often share common characteristics, such as going to school together or experiencing a significant event, such as a war, simultaneously. For statistical analysis, people tend to be placed in cohorts five or ten years apart, and cohort analysis is more popular than generational analysis because cohorts are easier to subdivide and specify. 'Generation' tends to indicate kinship lineage, such as parent, child or grandparent generation, assuming a twenty- or thirty-year span between each. This is, however, problematic methodologically and analytically if people bear children at very different ages or have more than one family. 'If one five-year old child has parents in their early twenties, another parents in their forties, and a third has a mother of twenty-two and a fifty-year-old father, clearly not all parents are of the same generation' (Green, 2015: 100).

'Generation' has, however, confusingly been used synonymously with the word 'cohort' to describe a political generation or a generation that selfidentifies in terms of its political, social and cultural differences from other generations

(Braungart and Braungart, 1986). In the 1960s, for example, many young people campaigned for social causes such as women's, black and gay people's rights/equality, and against wars and nuclear weapons, and their political views/activism had endured twenty years later (McAdam, 1989). Clearly, however, not everyone within that generation identified as a peaceloving, egalitarian, hippy flower child, and there are also blurred boundaries between some generations (Alwin and McCammon, 2003). Those born after World War Two, between 1946 and 1964 in the UK, the first generation to experience consumerism and a full welfare state, have been named *the Baby Boomers*, and those between 1964 and the mid-1980s – *Generation X* or *the Xers* – are characterized by growing technological expertise but lower job security and less politicization. The generation following them, born between the mid-1980s and late 1990s, are variously known as *Generation Y*, or *the digital, net, echo boomer* or *IPOD* (insecure, pressurized, over-taxed and debt-ridden) *generation*. They are an increasingly individualistic and technologically savvy, but also a technologically very dependent, generation. The most recent generation born from the late 1990s onwards have been coined *Generation Z* (or *the Post-Millennials, Centennials or iGen*), and these children and young people in 2016 confronted the worst economic recession in the UK since the 1930s, which began in 2008, whilst also being more technology proficient and technology-dependent than any generations preceding them.

The media, politicians and public intellectuals

---

* From Green, L. (2017) *Understanding the Life Course: Sociological and Psychological Perspectives* (2nd edn, Cambridge: Polity). Extracts from pp. 23–25, 230, 231.

also often identify social problems in terms of generations such as the 'Baby Boomers' and the 'Jilted Generation', but deploy these terms in a very subjective, imprecise way, using them to further certain political agendas. For example, the Boomers have sometimes been depicted as a selfish generation, responsible for today's young people being unable to find jobs and an impending drain on societal resources as they age. At other times, younger generations have been depicted as narcissistic and the Boomers as responsible and social justice pioneers. White (2013) ponders whether this 'public imaginary' encourages people to conform to such generational labels, or alternatively what power they might have to repudiate them. One study of fifty-two Canadians aged 24–86 found that ordinary people deployed 'generation' either to demarcate people of different ages, as in 'my generation' or 'the older generations', or alternatively to refer to groups born during specific periods with particular identifying characteristics or shared values or behaviour. These lay respondents, however, acknowledged that not everyone of a similar age or from a certain group behaved in the same ways (Foster, 2013). Pilcher (1994) acknowledges that a group could be both a cohort and a generation simultaneously but suggests *generation* be used when referring to kinship, as in grandparent, parent and child generations, and *social generation* deployed to convey the cohort sense of sharing similar outlooks.

Mannheim, in his seminal article on the sociology of generations (1952), argues that the historical is important socially because, in their youth, individuals attain a generational consciousness, formed out of their experiences and the socio-political climate, which affects their whole lives. However, retrospectively, we may demarcate particular *turning points* in our lives as significant – such as developing a serious illness in young adulthood (Denzin, 1989) – incidents not coinciding with particular ages, stages or social or political cohort or generational experiences. A turning point generally represents one or more critical incidents or experiences leading

to a changed awareness or condition. This results in the initiation of a trajectory which may be perceived positively or negatively, such as unplanned pregnancy leading to single parenthood, involvement in criminal behaviour leading to a criminal career or giving up drugs or alcohol after prior problems (Teruya and Hser, 2010). Easton et al. (2013) also identified a turning point for post-traumatic growth for men sexually abused as children. This occurred often decades later, being triggered by such events as the abuser dying, the survivor hitting 'rock bottom', or being issued an ultimatum by their partners about seeking counselling, and also being more likely if the man was less supportive of highly masculine gender norms.

Other important descriptors include *transitions* and *trajectories*. 'Transitions' refers to changes in status and role which are generally known about and prepared for – such as from being single to being married, or from student to full-time worker. Some transitions may become compressed or conversely dispersed over time, such as the transition from education to first full-time work extending with the expansion of higher education (George, 1993). Others become less common and predictable than before, such as if and when marriage and parenthood might occur. 'Trajectories' are long-term themed pathways, involving an interdependent series of events in different areas of life, such as trajectories of schooling, work, drug use, mental health, criminal behaviour and parenthood, and may include many transitions within them. One study of eighty-six Swiss people with psychiatric disorders revealed diverse and pluralized life course trajectories (Muller et al., 2011). There was much transitioning between situations, such as living with parents and independent living and being employed and unemployed, but, for some, autonomous living, forging a stable intimate relationship, having children or getting a job never happened as they lived indefinitely with parents or in institutions or sheltered housing. Normative transitions were, however, determined not by the disappearance of symptoms but by people's ability to deal with them and still forge a 'normal' life.

[. . .]

The individualized, de-standardized or 'yo-yoization' (Elchardus and Smits, 2006) hypotheses of contemporary life courses, proposed by postmodernist and poststructuralist thinkers, suggest considerable choice for all individuals and the possibility of restructuring many life experiences previously viewed as predetermined and occurring at different ages. Institutional age-defined structuring, such as that related to schooling and careers, biologically imposed age-related restrictions regarding 'natural' reproduction for women, and the far-reaching and cumulative impact of social divisions, such as social class, gender, 'race'/ethnicity and disability (cumulative advantage/disadvantage theory), in opposition to these claims, strongly suggest there is less choice or flexibility than assumed. Social divisions and inequalities impact greatly on identity and the opportunities one has. They interact, accrue and accumulate over the life course, resulting in a significantly more affluent, comfortable and healthy old age for some than for others, alongside significant differences in morbidity, mortality and life expectancy.

There are also vast generational and cohort disparities in transitions into, and the markers associated with, for example, young adulthood or old age. Young adulthood was previously delineated by markers such as spatial, economic and emotional independence from family of origin, full-time employment, and marriage and childbearing, but is currently becoming more difficult to demarcate sequentially and chronologically through these markers. It has consequently been suggested that new markers, such as taking full responsibility for one's actions, autonomous thought and relational factors, such as caring for others, may be more relevant today. Old age is also seen as extending, in tandem with increasing life expectancy, and has been subdivided by some theorists into distinct subcategories such

as the 'young old', 'middle old' and 'old old'. Laslett (1989), for example, subdivided old age into a third age characterized by affluence, reasonably good health and comfort, and a fourth later age when people become increasingly prone to long-term disability and health problems. Laslett, however, unfortunately failed to attend sufficiently to the impact of factors such as social class and poverty on ageing, and these omissions considerably weaken the universal – or even full Western – applicability of his theory.

[. . .]

There are also differences between early and late middle age when 'natural' childbearing becomes ruled out for women, there is less possibility of progressing further up one's occupational ladder, even if this is aspired to, and individuals generally become more reflective and retrospective, focusing more on time lived and time left to live than previously. Social division and cohort and social generational effects, influenced by both historical and contemporary changes, can also impact seriously on one's life during a particular age stage. Therefore, one's social class or gender (social divisions), the impact of social movements (social generation effects) and/or the advent of mass consumption and new technology (period effects) may render the life experiences of two apparently initially similar cohorts, born only a few years apart, immeasurably different. Due to the advent of new reproductive technology, increasing solo living, same-sex partnerships, reconstituted families and the increasing likelihood of later parenthood, family and kinship relationships have considerably diversified. One middle-aged or even older couple may have young children; another could have young children, adult children and even grandchildren. Another couple's children may be completely unrelated to them biologically, or there may be a number of half-siblings and stepsiblings living permanently within one family setting or moving fluidly between different families, or perhaps living half the week with one parent and the rest of the week at the other parent's house. In another scenario a midlife gay man might donate sperm for a friend or relative. Whether he sees himself as a father, uncle or purely a mechanical sperm donor will depend on whether he has any involvement in the parenting of that child and what arrangements he has negotiated with the main carers, and this may also change as he and the child age. Other middle-aged people may be voluntarily single or childless or may have significant caring responsibilities for ageing relatives. The financial and living situations of individuals and couples of a similar age will also vary significantly according to their social class and other factors, and their values may be profoundly different.

REFERENCES

Alwin, D. F. and McCammon, R. J. (2003) 'Generations, Cohorts and Social Change', in J. T. Mortimer and M. J. Shanahan (eds.), *Handbook of the Life Course*, New York: Kluwer Academic / Plenum.

Braungart, R. and Braungart, M. M. (1986) 'Life Course and Generational Politics', *Annual Review of Sociology*, 1: 205–31.

Denzin, N. (1989) *Interpretive Interactionism*, Applied Social Research Methods Series, 16, Newbury Park, CA: Sage.

Easton, S. D., Coohey, C., Rhodes, A. M. and Moorthy, M. V. (2013) 'Posttraumatic Growth among Men with Histories of Child Sexual Abuse', *Child Maltreatment*, 18: 211–20.

Elchardus, M. and Smits, W. (2006) 'The Persistence of the Standardized Life Cycle', *Time and Society*, 15(2/3): 303–26.

Foster, K. (2013) 'Generation and Discourse in Working Life Stories', *The British Journal of Sociology*, 64(2): 195–215.

George, L. K. (1993) 'Sociological Perspectives on Life Transitions', *Annual Review of Sociology*, 19: 353–73.

Green, L. (2015) 'Age and the Life Course: Continuity, Change and the Modern Mirage of Infinite Choice', in M. Holborn (ed.), *Contemporary Sociology*, Cambridge: Polity.

Laslett, P. (1989) *A Fresh Map of Life: The Emergence of the Third Age*, London: George, Weidenfeld and Nicolson Ltd.

Mannheim, K. (1952) 'The Problem of Generations', in K. Mannheim, *Essays on the Sociology of Knowledge*, London: RKP.

McAdam, D. (1989) 'The Biographical Consequences of Activism', *American Sociological Review*, 54: 744–60.

Muller, N. S., Sapin, M., Gauthier, J., Orita, A. and Widemer, E. D. (2011) 'Pluralized Life Courses? An Exploration of the Life Trajectories of Individuals with Psychiatric Disorders', *International Journal of Social Psychiatry*, 58(3): 266–77.

Pilcher, J. (1994) 'Mannheim's Sociology of Generations: An Undervalued Legacy', *The British Journal of Sociology*, 45(3): 481–95.

Teruya, C. and Hser, Y. (2010) 'Turning Points in the Life Course: Current Findings and Future Directions in Drug Usc Research', *Current Drug Abuse Review*, 3(3): 189–97.

White, J. (2013) 'Thinking Generation', *The British Journal of Sociology*, 64(2): 216–46.

Part 6 – Further reading

A general, and very good, introduction to the study of everyday life is Scott, S. (2009) *Making Sense of Everyday Life* (Cambridge: Polity). For life-course debates and the role of generations, Green, L. (2017) *Understanding the Life Course: Sociological and Psychological Perspectives* (2nd edn, Cambridge: Polity) is a reliable source text. The changing specialism of families is well covered in the readings collected in Treas, J., Scott, J., and Richards, M. (eds) (2017) *The Blackwell Companion to the Sociology of Families* (Chichester: Wiley Blackwell). Finally, Smart, C. (2007) *Personal Life* (Cambridge: Polity) was a trailblazer for studies in this area, and this is a very accessible place to begin.

Sociology, 9th edition

Studies of families and personal life are covered in chapter 15, 'Families and Intimate Relationships'. The life course has its own dedicated chapter 14, and issues of self-formation and identity can be found in chapter 12, 'Social Interaction and Daily Life'. Chapter 7 also includes material on love, relationships and sexuality.

Part 7 Interaction and Communication

Complex communication is a fundamental feature of everyday life, from face-to-face conversations and interactions in real time to the one-way transmissions of mass media via television programmes and film and, more recently, synchronous or asynchronous multiuser chatrooms, vlogs and social media. Human communication is more than just the use of vocal language: it also involves reading and interpreting signs, symbols and body language. The interactionist tradition of sociology originating in the work of Max Weber and George Herbert Mead has been the main source of insights in the field of communications. In particular, symbolic interactionism has a long history of research into small-scale interactions and social situations. It was the interactionists who produced micro-level studies of social roles and positions to discover how individuals are able to maintain a sense of self amid the demands and norms of pre-existing roles.

The best-known exponent of interactionism is probably Erving Goffman, whose detailed studies have inspired consecutive generations of sociologists. Reading 36 is extracted from Goffman's *The Presentation of Self in Everyday Life*, a small but nonetheless classic work of sociological research and theorizing. In this text, the author takes us into the complex and surprising ways in which people present or try to present their 'self' in different social settings. Goffman's 'dramaturgical' approach – that is, he draws parallels between stage plays and real life

– employs a range of novel concepts that have become part of the fabric of modern sociology. In this piece, we see how waiters and waitresses comport themselves very differently when *frontstage* in the restaurant and *backstage* in the kitchens, so much so that their performances seem to come from two separate 'characters'. Goffman also discusses the apparently simple fact that, to give a convincing performance, actors must believe in their character, or at least create that belief in others. Seamlessly combining empirical and theoretical material, Goffman demonstrates the extent of the work in which we all have to engage if we are to prevent our selves from being submerged under the welter of expectations of others.

One type of interaction that may not always be thought of as such is violence. Whatever we may think of warfare, conflict, street brawls or domestic abuse, sociologically they are all forms of social interaction, albeit of a specific kind. And, if so, then it ought to be possible for interactionism to provide an explanation of why violence occurs, define the main aspects of each type of violent interaction and, ultimately, identify what we can learn from studying them that may be useful in lessening the harm they inflict. In Reading 37, Randall Collins outlines his very ambitious aim of providing a theoretical framework that may be adopted in the study of all kinds of violent social interaction situations. The extract covers a lot of ground, but it begins by setting out two central points of the approach. First, rather than examining the motives of actors or the psychology of individuals, Collins's theory puts the interaction itself into the centre of the analysis. Second, studies should make comparisons across different kinds of violent interaction in order to assess how situations affect the level of violence that results. Collins also has things to say both about how digitization has led to violence becoming much more readily observable and the resulting consequences.

Since the 1970s, feminist sociologists have explored issues of female beauty practices, eating disorders among girls and young women, and the pressures felt by women to meet the beauty norms emanating from a male gaze and masculine aesthetic. At the same time, some feminist writers have argued that the shifting gender power balance (partly attributable to feminism itself) has actually created more choice for women, and if they choose to engage in certain beauty practices or body modification then they are free to do so. Are these two views compatible? In Reading 38, Sheila Jeffreys forcefully argues that beauty practices, including cosmetic surgery, and beauty norms are a fundamental aspect that sustains male domination of women. Indeed, she argues that things have, in fact, got worse, as many of today's surgical interventions are more harmful and 'cruel' and, alongside female genital mutilation, should be classified as such by the United Nations. Jeffreys's argument takes aim at the fashion industry and online imagery in the production and maintenance of the male gaze and its negative consequences for women. The provocative conclusion in this text is that Western culture cannot be seen as 'progressive' when compared to the cultures in other regions of the world, even though its mechanisms of producing compliance may be less severe.

Although the subject of personal and social identity has been of interest to sociologists for many years, in recent times it has taken on a new significance as societies have become more multicultural and 'identity politics' has risen to prominence. Studying identities takes us into the long-standing structure–agency debate, because, although our perceived identity may feel intensely private and individual, social relations, interactions and structures all help to shape who (we think) we are. Our work roles, familial roles and peer groups all carry expectations which partly shape our identity, and our social identity always exists in relation to other people. Reading 39, from Susie Scott, outlines some of the definitional and theoretical issues that we need to be able to understand how identities 'work'. For example, how does identity differ from identification? How are personal and social identities related? Where does the concept of the social self fit in to processes of identity formation? Scott takes an overtly symbolic interactionist position in relation to these questions, and the book is a reliable guide to the interactionist perspective on identity.

The persistent accusation of 'fake news' made against news reports, reporters and outlets by former US President Donald Trump effectively popularized the concept as part of the political populist critique of mainstream news. Recent years have also seen the widespread dissemination of online material by state actors aimed at undermining democratic elections and sowing confusion about which sources can be trusted for reliable information. Some scholars see these developments as potentially dangerous for democratic systems, eroding trust in the political process and pushing people towards strong leaders with anti-establishment views. In short, we seem to be heading into a 'post-truth' world in which the truth is less valuable and sought after.

Reading 40, from Dominic Malcolm, is a

careful and distinctly sociological analysis of the post-truth phenomenon, which has been dominated by politically loaded assessments. Drawing on Norbert Elias's sociology of knowledge, Malcolm rejects arguments that see post-truth as inevitably destructive of rational debate or even as the 'end of democracy'. Instead, he argues that post-truth is one product of new forms of communication and the shifting relations between knowledge elites and the wider public. What we may be seeing is an emergent form of knowledge rooted in a complicated mix of intense emotional commitments and increasingly rational techniques of debate.

36. Self Presentation and Impression Management*

Erving Goffman

When an individual plays a part he implicitly requests his observers to take seriously the impression that is fostered before them. They are asked to believe that the character they see actually possesses the attributes he appears to possess, that the task he performs will have the consequences that are implicitly claimed for it, and that, in general, matters are what they appear to be. In line with this, there is the popular view that the individual offers his performance and puts on his show 'for the benefit of other people'. It will be convenient to begin a consideration of performances by turning the question around and looking at the individual's own belief in the impression of reality that he attempts to engender in those among whom he finds himself.

At one extreme, one finds that the performer can be fully taken in by his own act; he can be sincerely convinced that the impression of reality which he stages is the real reality. When his audience is also convinced in this way about the show he puts on – and this seems to be the typical case – then for the moment at least, only the sociologist or the socially disgruntled will have any doubts about the 'realness' of what is presented.

At the other extreme, we find that the performer may not be taken in at all by his own routine. This possibility is understandable, since no one is in quite as good an observational position to see through the act as the person who puts it on. Coupled with this, the performer may

be moved to guide the conviction of his audience only as a means to other ends, having no ultimate concern in the conception that they have of him or of the situation. When the individual has no belief in his own act and no ultimate concern with the beliefs of his audience, we may call him cynical, reserving the term 'sincere' for individuals who believe in the impression fostered by their own performance. It should be understood that the cynic, with all his professional disinvolvement, may obtain unprofessional pleasures from his masquerade, experiencing a kind of gleeful spiritual aggression from the fact that he can toy at will with something his audience must take seriously.[1]

It is not assumed, of course, that all cynical performers are interested in deluding their audiences for purposes of what is called 'self-interest' or private gain. A cynical individual may delude his audience for what he considers to be their own good, or for the good of the community, etc. For illustrations of this we need not appeal to sadly enlightened showmen such as Marcus Aurelius or Hsun Tzû. We know that in service occupations practitioners who may otherwise be sincere are sometimes forced to delude their customers because their customers show such a heartfelt demand for it. Doctors who are led into giving placebos, filling station attendants who resignedly check and recheck tyre pressures for anxious women motorists, shoe clerks who sell a shoe that fits but tell the customer it is the size she wants to hear – these are cynical performers whose audiences will not allow them to be sincere. Similarly, it seems that sympathetic patients

* From Goffman, E. (1980 [1959]) *The Presentation of Self in Everyday Life* (London: Penguin). Extracts from pp. 28–32, 114–117.

in mental wards will sometimes feign bizarre symptoms so that student nurses will not be subjected to a disappointingly sane performance.[2] So also, when inferiors extend their most lavish reception for visiting superiors, the selfish desire to win favour may not be the chief motive; the inferior may be tactfully attempting to put the superior at ease by simulating the kind of world the superior is thought to take for granted.

I have suggested two extremes: an individual may be taken in by his own act or be cynical about it. These extremes are something a little more than just the ends of a continuum. Each provides the individual with a position which has its own particular securities and defences, so there will be a tendency for those who have travelled close to one of these poles to complete the voyage. Starting with lack of inward belief in one's role, the individual may follow the natural movement described by Park:

It is probably no mere historical accident that the word person, in its first meaning, is a mask. It is rather a recognition of the fact that everyone is always and everywhere, more or less consciously, playing a role. . . . It is in these roles that we know each other; it is in these roles that we know ourselves.[3]

In a sense, and in so far as this mask represents the conception we have formed of ourselves – the role we are striving to live up to – this mask is our truer self, the self we would like to be. In the end, our conception of our role becomes second nature and an integral part of our personality. We come into the world as individuals, achieve character, and become persons.[4]

This may be illustrated from the community life of Shetland.[5] For the last four or five years the island's tourist hotel has been owned and operated by a married couple of crofter origins. From the beginning, the owners were forced to set aside their own conceptions as to how life ought to be led, displaying in the hotel a full round of middle-class services and amenities. Lately, however, it appears that the managers have become less cynical about the performance that they stage; they themselves are becoming

middle class and more and more enamoured of the selves their clients impute to them.

Another illustration may be found in the raw recruit who initially follows army etiquette in order to avoid physical punishment and eventually comes to follow the rules so that his organization will not be shamed and his officers and fellow soldiers will respect him.

As suggested, the cycle of disbelief-to-belief can be followed in the other direction, starting with conviction or insecure aspiration and ending in cynicism. Professions which the public holds in religious awe often allow their recruits to follow it in this direction not because of a slow realization that they are deluding their audience – for by ordinary social standards the claims they make may be quite valid – but because they can use this cynicism as a means of insulating their inner selves from contact with the audience. And we may even expect to find typical careers of faith, with the individual starting out with one kind of involvement in the performance he is required to give, then moving back and forth several times between sincerity and cynicism before completing all the phases and turning-points of self-belief for a person of his station. Thus, students of medical schools suggest that idealistically oriented beginners in medical school typically lay aside their holy aspirations for a period of time. During the first two years the students find that their interest in medicine must be dropped that they may give all their time to the task of learning how to get through examinations. During the next two years they are too busy learning about diseases to show much concern for the persons who are diseased. It is only after their medical schooling has ended that their original ideals about medical service may be reasserted.[6]

While we can expect to find natural movement back and forth between cynicism and sincerity, still we must not rule out the kind of transitional point that can be sustained on the strength of a little self-illusion. We find that the individual may attempt to induce the audience to judge him and the situation in a particular way, and he may seek this judgement as an ultimate end in itself, and yet he may not completely believe that he deserves the valuation of self which he asks for or that the impression of reality which he fosters is valid. Another mixture of cynicism and belief is suggested in Kroeber's discussion of shamanism:

> Next, there is the old question of deception. Probably most shamans or medicine men, the world over, help along with sleight-of-hand in curing and especially in exhibitions of power. This sleight-of-hand is sometimes deliberate; in many cases awareness is perhaps not deeper than the foreconscious. The attitude, whether there has been repression or not, seems to be as towards a pious fraud. Field ethnographers seem quite generally convinced that even shamans who know that they are frauds nevertheless also believe in their powers, and especially in those of other shamans: they consult them when they themselves or their children are ill.[7]

[. . .]

It was suggested earlier that when one's activity occurs in the presence of other persons, some aspects of the activity are expressively accentuated and other aspects, which might discredit the fostered impression, are suppressed. It is clear that accentuated facts make their appearance in what I have called a front region; it should be just as clear that there may be another region – a 'back region' or 'backstage' – where the suppressed facts make an appearance.

A back region or backstage may be defined as a place, relative to a given performance, where the impression fostered by the performance is knowingly contradicted as a matter of course. There are, of course, many characteristic functions of such places. It is here that the capacity of a performance to express something beyond itself may be painstakingly fabricated; it is here that illusions and impressions are openly constructed. Here stage props and items of personal front can be stored in a kind of compact collapsing of whole repertoires of actions and characters.[8] Here grades of ceremonial equipment, such as different types of liquor or clothes, can be hidden so that the audience will not be able to see the treatment accorded them in comparison with the treatment that could have been accorded them. Here devices such as the telephone are sequestered so that they can be used 'privately'. Here costumes and other parts of personal front may be adjusted and scrutinized for flaws. Here the team can run through its performance, checking for offending expressions when no audience is present to be affronted by them; here poor members of the team, who are expressively inept, can be schooled or dropped from the performance. Here the performer can relax; he can drop his front, forgo speaking his lines, and step out of character. [. . .]

Very commonly the back region of a performance is located at one end of the place where the performance is presented, being cut off from it by a partition and guarded passageway. By having the front and back regions adjacent in this way, a performer out in front can receive backstage assistance while the performance is in progress and can interrupt his performance momentarily for brief periods of relaxation. In general, of course, the back region will be the place where the performer can reliably expect that no member of the audience will intrude.

Since the vital secrets of a show are visible backstage and since performers behave out of character while there, it is natural to expect that the passage from the front region to the back region will be kept closed to members of the audience or that the entire back region will be kept hidden from them. This is a widely practised technique of impression management, and requires further discussion.

Obviously, control of backstage plays a significant role in the process of 'work control' whereby individuals attempt to buffer themselves from the deterministic demands that surround them. If a factory worker is to succeed in giving the appearance of working hard all day, then he must have a safe place to hide the jig that enables him to turn out a day's work with less than a full day's effort.[9] If the bereaved are to be given the illusion that the dead one is really in a deep and tranquil sleep, then the undertaker must be able to keep the bereaved from the workroom where the corpses are drained, stuffed, and painted in preparation for their final performance.[10] If a mental hospital staff is to give a good impression of the hospital to those who come to visit their committed kinfolk, then it will be important to be able to bar visitors from the wards, especially the chronic wards, restricting the outsiders to special visiting-rooms where it will be practicable to have relatively nice furnishings and to ensure that all patients present are well dressed, well washed, well handled and relatively well behaved. So, too, in many service trades, the customer is asked to leave the thing that needs service and to go away so that the tradesman can work in private. When the customer returns for his automobile – or watch, or trousers, or radio – it is presented to him in good working order, an order that incidentally conceals the amount and kind of work that had to be done, the number of mistakes that were first made before getting it fixed, and other details the client would have to know before being able to judge the reasonableness of the fee that is asked of him.

Service personnel so commonly take for granted the right to keep the audience away from the back region that attention is drawn more to cases where this common strategy cannot be applied than to cases where it can. [. . .]

NOTES

1. Perhaps the real crime of the confidence man is not that he takes money from his victims but that he robs all of us of the belief that middle-class manners and appearance can be sustained only by middle-class people. A disabused professional can be cynically hostile to the service relation his clients expect him to extend to them; the confidence man is in a position to hold the whole 'legit' world in this contempt.
2. See Taxel, 'Authority Structure in a Mental Hospital Ward', page 4. Harry Stack Sullivan has suggested that the tact of institutionalized performers can operate in the other direction, resulting in a kind of *noblesse-oblige* sanity. See his 'Socio-Psychiatric Research', *American Journal of Psychiatry*, x, pages 987–98:

   > 'A study of "social recoveries" in one of our large mental hospitals some years ago taught me that patients were often released from care because they had learned not to manifest symptoms to the environing persons; in other words, had integrated enough of the personal environment to realize the prejudice opposed to their delusions. It seemed almost as if they grew wise enough to be tolerant of the imbecility surrounding them, having finally discovered that it was stupidity and not malice. They could then secure satisfaction from contact with others, while discharging a part of their cravings by psychotic means.'

3. Robert Ezra Park, *Race and Culture* (Glencoe, Illinois: The Free Press, 1950), page 249.
4. ibid., page 250.
5. Shetland Isle study.
6. H. S. Becker and Blanche Greer, 'The Fate of Idealism in Medical School', *American Sociological Review*, 23, pages 50–56.
7. A. L. Kroeber, *The Nature of Culture* (Chicago: University of Chicago Press, 1952), page 311.
8. As Métraux ('Dramatic Elements in Ritual Possession', page 24) suggests, even the practice of voodoo cults will require such facilities:

   > Every case of possession has its theatrical side, as shown in the matter of disguises. The rooms of the sanctuary are not unlike the wings of a theater where the possessed find the necessary accessories. Unlike the hysteric, who reveals his anguish and his desires through symptoms – a personal means of expression – the ritual of possession must conform to the classic image of a mythical personage.

9. See Orvis Collins, Melville Dalton, and Donald Roy, 'Restriction of Output and

Social Cleavage in Industry', *Applied Anthropology* (now *Human Organization*), iv, pages 1–14, especially page 9.

10. Mr Habenstein has suggested in seminar that in some states the undertaker has a legal right to prevent relatives of the deceased from entering the workroom where the corpse is in preparation. Presumably the sight of what has to be done to the dead to make them look attractive would be too great a shock for non-professionals and especially for kinfolk of the deceased. Mr Habenstein also suggests that kinfolk may want to be kept from the undertaker's workroom because of their own fear of their own morbid curiosity.

37. Violence in Sociological Perspective*

Randall Collins

There is a vast array of types of violence. It is short and episodic as a slap in the face; or massive and organized as a war. It can be passionate and angry as a quarrel; or callous and impersonal as the bureaucratic administration of gas chambers. It is happy as drunken carousing, fearful as soldiers in combat, vicious as a torturer. It can be furtive and hidden as a rape-murder, or public as a ritual execution. It is programmed entertainment in the form of sporting contests, the plot tension of drama, the action of action-adventure, the staple shocker of the news edition. It is horrible and heroic, disgusting and exciting, the most condemned and glorified of human acts.

This vast array can be explained by a relatively compact theory. A few main processes, in combination and in differing degrees of intensity, give the conditions for when and how the various forms of violence occur.

Two moves will set up the analysis. First, put the interaction in the center of the analysis, not the individual, the social background, the culture, or even the motivation: that is to say, look for the characteristics of violent situations. That means looking for data that gets us as close as possible into the dynamics of situations. Second, compare across different kinds of violence. We need to break down the usual categories—homicides in one research specialty, war in another, child abuse in another, police violence yet elsewhere—and look for the situations that occur within them.

Not that all situations are the same; we want to compare the range of variation in situations, which affects the kind and amount of violence that emerges. This will turn the wide variety of violence into a methodological advantage, giving clues to the circumstances that explain when and in what manner violence unfolds.

Violent Situations

Not violent individuals, but violent situations—this is what a micro-sociological theory is about. We seek the contours of situations, which shape the emotions and acts of the individuals who step inside them. It is a false lead to look for types of violent individuals, constant across situations. A huge amount of research has not yielded very strong results here. Young men, yes, are most likely to be perpetrators of many kinds of violence. But not all young men are violent. And middle-aged men, children, and women are violent too, in the appropriate situations. Similarly with background variables such as poverty, race, and origins in divorce or single-parent families. Though there are some statistical correlations between these variables and certain kinds of violence, these fall short of predicting most violence in at least three aspects:

First, most young men, poor people, black people, or children of divorce do not become murderers, rapists, batterers, or armed robbers; and there are a certain number of affluent persons, white people, or products of conventional families who do. Similarly, the much asserted

* From Collins, R. (2008) *Violence: A Micro-sociological Theory* (Princeton, NJ: Princeton University Press). Extracts from pp. 1–3, 4–6.

explanation that violent offenders are typically past victims of child abuse accounts for only a minority of the cases.

Second, such analysis conveys a plausible picture of the etiology of violence only because it restricts the dependent variable to particular categories of illegal or highly stigmatized violence; it does not hold up well when we broaden out to all kinds of violence. Poverty, family strain, child abuse, and the like do not account for police violence or for which soldiers do the most killing in combat, for who runs gas chambers or commits ethnic cleansing. No one has shown that being abused as a child is likely to make someone a cowboy cop, a carousing drunk, or a decorated war hero. No doubt there are readers who will bridle at the suggestion; for them, violence naturally falls into hermetically sealed sections, and "bad" social conditions should be responsible for "bad" violence, whereas "good" violence—which is not seen as violence at all, when it is carried out by authorized state agents—is not subject to analysis since it is part of normal social order. In this way of thinking, there is an intermediate category of innocuous or "naughty" violence (i.e., carousing that gets out of hand), or violence that is committed by "good" persons; this is explained, or explained away, by another set of moral categories. Such distinctions are a good example of conventional social categories getting in the way of sociological analysis. If we zero in on the situation of interaction—the angry boyfriend with the crying baby, the armed robber squeezing the trigger on the holdup victim, the cop beating up the suspect—we can see patterns of confrontation, tension, and emotional flow, which are at the heart of the situation where violence is carried out. This is another way of seeing that the background conditions—poverty, race, childhood experiences—are a long way from what is crucial to the dynamics of the violent situation.

Third, even those persons who are violent, are violent only a small part of the time. Consider what we mean when we say that a person is violent, or "very violent." We have in mind someone who is a convicted murderer, or has committed a string of murders; who has been in many fights, slashed people with a knife, or battered them with fists. But if we consider that everyday life unfolds in a chain of situations, minute by minute, most of the time there is very little violence. This is apparent from ethnographic observations, even in statistically very violent neighborhoods. A homicide rate of ten deaths per 100,000 persons (the rate in the United States peaking in 1990) is a fairly high rate, but it means that *99,990* out of 100,000 persons do not get murdered in a year; and 97,000 of them (again, taking the peak rate) are not assaulted even in minor incidents. And these violent incidents are spread out over a year; the chances of murder or assault happening to a particular person at any particular moment on a particular day during that year are very small. This applies even to those persons who actually do commit one or more murders, assaults, armed robberies, or rapes (or for that matter, cops who beat up suspects) during the course of the year. Even those persons who statistically commit a lot of crime scarcely do so at a rate of more than once a week or so; the most notorious massacres in schools, workplaces, or public places, carried out by lone individuals, have killed as many as twenty-five persons, but generally within a single episode (Hickey 2002; Newman et al. 2004). The most sustained violent persons are serial killers, who average between six and thirteen victims over a period of years; but these are extremely rare (about one victim per five million population), and even these repeat killers go months between killings, waiting for just the right situation to strike (Hickey 2002: 12–13, 241–42). Another kind of rare cluster of violence, crime sprees, may continue for a period of days, in a chain of events linked closely by emotions and circumstances so as to comprise a tunnel of violence. Leaving these extended sequences of violence aside for the moment, I want to underline the conclusion: even people that we think of as very violent—because they have been violent in more than one situation, or spectacularly violent on some occasion—are violent only in very particular situations.[1] Even the toughest hoodlums are off duty some of the time. Most of the time, the most dangerous, most violent persons are not doing anything violent. Even for these people, the dynamics of situations are crucial in explaining what violence they actually do.

[. . .]

A new era has emerged in recent decades as it has become possible to study violence as recorded on video tape from security systems, police recordings, and news and amateur video photographers. When ordinary observers see such recordings, they are usually shocked. A riot eventually followed the publicity given to a video recording, taken by an amateur with a new camcorder, of the Rodney King arrest in Los Angeles in 1991. Events are always interpreted in terms of prevailing ideological categories; the concepts easily at hand were those of a racially motivated beating. But what was so shocking about the Rodney King video was not its racial aspect; it was the beating itself, which did not look at all like what we think violence is supposed to look like. Visual evidence shows us something about violence that we are not prepared to see. [. . .]

Violence as it actually becomes visible in real-life situations is about the intertwining of human emotions of fear, anger, and excitement, in ways that run right against the conventional morality of normal situations. It is just this shocking and unexpected quality of violence, as it actually appears in the cold eye of the camera, that gives a clue to the emotional dynamics at the center of a micro-situational theory of violence.

We live in an era in which our ability to see what happens in real-life situations is far greater than ever before. We owe this new vision to a combination of technology and sociological method. The ethnomethodologists of the 1960s and 1970s took off as an intellectual movement in tandem with the use of newly portable cassette tape recorders; this made it possible to record at least the audio part of real-life social interactions and to play it back repeatedly, slowing it down and subjecting it to analysis in a way that had

been barely possible with fleeting observations in real time, giving rise to the field of conversation analysis (Sacks, Schegloff, and Jefferson 1974; Schegloff 1992). As video recording devices became more portable and ubiquitous, it has been possible to look at other aspects of microbehavior, including bodily rhythms, postures, and expressions of emotion. Thus it is not surprising that the period from about 1980 onward has been the golden age for the sociology of emotions (Katz 1999, among many others).

[. . .]

This is so also in the micro-sociology of violence. The video revolution has made available much more information about what happens in violent situations than ever before. But real-life recording conditions are not like Hollywood film studios; lighting and composition are far from ideal, and the camera angles and distance may not be just the ones a micro-sociologist would prefer. We need to disengage ourselves from the conventions of dramatically satisfying film (including TV commercials) where the camera cuts to a new angle every few seconds at the most, and a great deal of editing has gone on to juxtapose an interesting and engaging sequence. A micro-sociologist can spot the difference between raw observational recording and artistically or editorially processed film, usually within seconds. Raw conflict is not very engaging, for all sorts of reasons; as micro-sociologists, we are not in it for entertainment.

Other approaches besides live video have opened up the landscape of violence as it really happens. Still photography has gotten better throughout the past century and a half; cameras have become more portable, and lenses and lighting devices have made it possible to capture scenes that previously would have been limited to static posed shots in relatively sheltered conditions. Professional photographers have become more intrepid, particularly in riots, demonstrations, and war zones; the number of photographers killed has gone up drastically in the past ten years, far above any previous period.[2] This too is an opportunity for micro-sociologists, although the aforementioned caveats again apply. Still photos are often better than videos for capturing the emotional aspects of violent interaction. When we analyze a video of a conflict sequence (or indeed any video of interaction), we may slow it down to segments of micro-seconds (frame-by-frame in older camera film) to pull out just those details of bodily posture, facial expression, and sequence of micromovements. In depictions of riots, which I use extensively in this work, still photos dramatically show the division between the active few on the violent front and the supporting mass of demonstrators. The danger is in assuming one can read the still photo without sociological sensibilities. Highly artistic or ideological photographers are less useful here than routine news photographers; some photos of demonstrations or combat have an artistic or political message that governs the whole composition; we need to look from a different vantage point to get at the micro-sociological aspects of conflict.

NOTES

1. I am concerned here chiefly with the violence of individuals and small groups. A different kind of violence, as in war or genocide, is structured by large-scale organizations, and can produce much higher numbers of persons killed and injured, in actions that can go on for much longer periods of time. But even here, the individuals involved are not violent all the time and in all contexts; at other times they generally are surprisingly different from the way they act in the midst of their violent routines.

2. During 2004, between fifty-three and fifty-six journalists and media workers were killed, the highest number since 1994 during the ethnic violence in former Yugoslavia *(San Diego Union Tribune,* Jan. 8, 2005). A considerable proportion of these were photographers and video camera operators.

REFERENCES

Hickey, Eric. W. 2002. *Serial Murderers and Their Victims.* Belmont, Calif.: Wadsworth.

Katz, Jack. 1999. *How Emotions Work.* Chicago: University of Chicago Press.

Newman, Katherine S., Cybelle Fox, David Harding, Jal Mehta, and Wendy Roth. 2004. *Rampage: The Social Roots of School Shootings.* New York: Basic Books.

Sacks, Harvey, Emanuel A. Schegloff, and Gail Jefferson. 1974. "A Simplest Systematics for the Organization of Turn-taking for Conversation." *Language* 50: 696–735.

Schegloff, Emanuel. 1992. "Repair after Last Turn: The Last Structurally Provided Defense of Intersubjectivity in Conversation." *American Journal of Sociology* 97.

38. Misogyny, Beauty and Body Modification*

Sheila Jeffreys

In the 1970s a feminist critique of makeup and other beauty practices emerged from consciousness-raising groups. The American radical feminist theorist Catharine A. MacKinnon called consciousness-raising the "methodology" of feminism (MacKinnon, 1989). In these groups women discussed how they felt about themselves and their bodies. They identified the pressures within male dominance that caused them to feel they should diet, depilate and makeup. Feminist writers rejected a masculine aesthetics that caused women to feel their bodies were inadequate and to engage in expensive, time-consuming practices that left them feeling that they were inauthentic and unacceptable when barefaced (Dworkin, 1974). "Beauty" was identified as oppressive to women.

In the last two decades the brutality of the beauty practices that women carry out on their bodies has become much more severe. Today's practices require the breaking of skin, spilling of blood and rearrangement or amputation of body parts. Foreign bodies, in the form of breast implants, are placed under the flesh and next to the heart, women's labia are cut to shape, fat is liposuctioned out of the thighs and buttocks and sometimes injected into other sites such as cheeks and chins. The new cutting and piercing industry will now split women's tongues in two as well as creating holes in nipples, clitoris hood or bellybuttons, for the placement of "body art"

jewellery (Jeffreys, 2000). These developments are much more dangerous prescriptions for women's health than the practices common in the 1960s and 1970s when the feminist critique was formed. It might be expected, then, that there would have been a sharpening of this critique and a renewed awareness of its relevance in response to this more concerted attack on the integrity of women's bodies. But this is not what happened. Instead, the feminist perspective, which caused many thousands of women to eschew beauty culture and products, came under challenge in the 1980s and 1990s.

The challenge came from two directions. Liberal feminists, such as Natasha Walter (UK) and Karen Lehrman (USA), argued that there was nothing wrong with lipstick or women making themselves look good, with all the products and practices of beauty culture (Walter, 1999; Lehrman, 1997). Feminism itself had created choice for women, they said, and enabled women now to "choose" lipstick where once it might have been thrust upon them. Meanwhile the influence of postmodern ideas in the academy led to some rather similar rhetoric about "choice", usually in the form of "agency", emanating from some feminist theorists and researchers (Davis, 1995). Bolder propositions were made as well, such as the idea that beauty practices could be socially transformative. Postmodern feminist theorists such as Judith Butler (1990), with their ideas on gender performativity, inspired the notion among queer theorists that the beauty practices of femininity adopted by unconventional actors, or outrageously, could

---

* From Jeffreys, S. (2015) *Beauty and Misogyny: Harmful Cultural Practices in the West* (London: Routledge). Extracts from pp. 1–3, 171–173.

be transgressive (Roof, 1998). Other postmodern feminists such as Elizabeth Grosz argued that the body is simply a "text" which can be written on, and that tattooing, cutting, let alone lipstick, are just interesting ways of writing on it (Grosz, 1994). It is in response to this recent defence of beauty practices against the feminist critique that this book has been written.

In *Beauty and Misogyny* I suggest that beauty practices are not about women's individual choice or a "discursive space" for women's creative expression but, as other radical feminist theorists have argued before me, a most important aspect of women's oppression. The feminist philosopher Marilyn Frye has written incisively of what makes a theory feminist, and why it is not enough to rely on women's individual assurances that a practice is OK with them and in their interests:

> One of the great powers of feminism is that it goes so far in making the experiences and lives of women intelligible. Trying to make sense of one's own feelings, motivations, desires, ambitions, actions and reactions without taking into account the forces which maintain the subordination of women to men is like trying to explain why a marble stops rolling without taking friction into account. What feminist theory is about, to a great extent, is just identifying those forces . . . and displaying the mechanics of their applications to women as a group (or caste) and to individual women. The measure of the success of the theory is just how much sense it makes of what did not make sense before.
>
> (Frye, 1983, p. xi)

In this book I attempt to identify some of the "forces which maintain the subordination of women to men" in relation to beauty practices.

I seek to make sense of why beauty practices are not only just as pervasive 30 years after the feminist critique developed, but in many ways are more extreme. To do this I use some new approaches that are suited to explaining this escalation of cruelty in what is expected of women in the twenty-first century. One impetus towards my writing this book lies in my growing impatience with the western bias of the useful United Nations concept of "harmful traditional/cultural

practices". In United Nations (UN) documents such as the Fact Sheet on "Harmful Traditional Practices" (UN, 1995), harmful cultural/traditional practices are understood to be damaging to the health of women and girls, to be performed for men's benefit, to create stereotyped roles for the sexes and to be justified by tradition. This concept provides a good lens through which to examine practices that are harmful to women in the west – such as beauty practices. [. . .]

[. . .]

The practices I have examined in this book show that western culture is not "progressive" in comparison with non-western cultures in the cultural requirements for women's appearance. The enforcement mechanisms are likely, however, to be less severe, as women are not usually beaten in the street or in their families for failure to comply. But in the severity of their impact on women's health and lives the western practices fulfil the United Nations criteria for recognizing harmful traditional/cultural practices very well. Though recognition of these practices as harmful traditional/cultural practices does not offer an immediate solution it can help to clear away those veils of mystification that represent what western women are required to do to their bodies as just fashion, or medicine or choice. A growing understanding that these western practices are both culturally constructed and harmful will found the development of a culture of resistance.

Western beauty practices fulfil the first and most important criterion for a harmful traditional/cultural practice – that they should be harmful to the health of women and girls. There is little doubt, for instance, that cosmetic surgery practices that are becoming more and more brutal, lead to health problems and death. The death of Olivia Goldsmith, the US author of the novel on which the movie *First Wives Club* was based, shows that women are not protected by wealth or social privilege from destruction in the fulfilment of their sexual corvée (Kingston, 2004). She suffered a heart attack from a bad reaction to the anaesthetic during a routine cosmetic surgery procedure to tighten skin on her neck. The US sociologist, Deborah H. Sullivan (2002), explains in her book on American medicine's development of the cosmetic surgery industry that it is hard to establish figures for death and injury. However she describes the research carried out by the *Sun-Sentinel* newspaper in Florida into malpractice insurance claims, lawsuits, autopsy records, and newspaper accounts to establish the numbers of serious incidents of death and injury from cosmetic surgery in that state alone (Sullivan, 2002). They discovered that in the 26 months before the end of their research period, first quarter of 1999, there were 18 deaths. It may not be unreasonable to compare this rate of death and injury with those that result from practices such as female genital mutilation.

Unlike FGM, cosmetic surgery is not universal, but it is becoming more and more common and diverse in its forms. In the twenty-first century cosmetic surgery has become so normalized that a mainstream television show, *Extreme Makeover*, has a large primetime audience. In the American version people compete to have large numbers of severe surgical procedures carried out on their bodies to make their appearance more culturally acceptable (Moran and Walker, 2004). The Australian version is now being planned. There are forms of serious damage from other beauty practices too such as piercing and cutting, and the wearing of high-heeled shoes. Hammer toes, bunions, calf and heel injuries are indisputably harmful. There are likely to be less easily identifiable costs to mental health too from having to carry out everyday beauty practices and wear sexually objectifying costume in the street and at work.

Western beauty practices do not only arise from the subordination of women but should perhaps be seen as the most publicly visible evidence of that subordination. The crippling of feet, for instance, indicates the brutal strength of male dominance. That western beauty practices are for the benefit of men should be clear from the evidence of the innumerable websites on which men scream their demands that women get mutilated and celebrate the sexual stimulation this gives them. Some of the practices are newly savage or even new in kind but they resemble those practices that have traditionally been required of women in many cultures and which demonstrate women's lowly status. They unmistakably create the sexual difference that is such an important function of harmful cultural practices. They are justified by tradition, as in the popular wisdom that women have always wanted to be beautiful and that it is natural for men to be attracted to "beautiful" women. They are blamed on women and the role of men in enforcing and demanding these practices is concealed.

There is, however, a major difference in the way that harmful beauty practices are inscribed in culture and enforced on women in the west. This is the fact that they have been constructed into major industries that make large fortunes for transnational corporations and are a significant force in the global economy. The profitability of these practices to the cosmetics, sex, fashion, advertising and medical industries creates a major obstacle to women's ability to resist and eliminate them. There is so much money in these industries based on commercializing harmful cultural practices that they constitute a massive political force that requires the continuance of women's pain. The cosmetic surgery industry in the USA, for instance, is estimated to be worth US$8 billion yearly (Church *et al.,* 2003). While in non-western cultures harmful practices are enforced by families and communities they are not usually the foundation of huge and immensely profitable industries. They are perhaps therefore easier to identify and easier to target. Education can be used to change attitudes in the campaign to eliminate them. In the west these industries have political and economic clout and education will not be sufficient. In the place of religion and family the full force of powerful capitalist industries occupies cultural space.

A newly confident, mainstreamed and increasingly profitable international sex industry is a relatively new player in the business of beauty.

But it has had very serious effects already in the pornographization of culture and the demand for more savage, invasive and brutal beauty practices. The international sex industry is becoming a more and more important market "sector" and is estimated by a 1998 report from the International Labour Organization to be worth 2–14 per cent of the economies of some Asian countries (Lim, 1998). The pornography and prostitution industries intersect with the entertainment and advertising industries to create images of women in the clothing and poses of prostitution on billboards, music videos, and mainstream television programmes such as *Sex and the City*. This cultural saturation with women as sexual playthings creates a powerful force to compel women to fulfil their sexual corvée. The gloves are off. More and more what is understood to be "beauty" is recognizably the look of prostitution.

In the west women are supposed to be empowered, possessed of opportunities and choices unimaginable only a generation ago, yet these same women are hobbled by clothing and shoes, maimed by surgery in ways that the feminist generation of the 1970s could not have imagined. Indeed much of the surgery is being conducted precisely on women of that 1970s generation as they discover that the sexual corvée knows no age boundaries. There is no longer a retirement age from this arduous, unpaid labour.

The new savagery of beauty practices may result from men having great difficulty adjusting to the change in relations between the sexes that women's new opportunities bring. Men's problems in adapting to women's greater equality are clear from the invigoration of the sex industry. Research on sex tourism shows that the men see their sexual access to obviously unequal unempowered women as a compensation for the dominance they feel they have lost over women in the west (O'Connell Davidson, 1995). Mail order bride company websites offer western men obedient and humble women from countries like Russia and the Philippines where dire poverty can command deference. In the west the threats that men face to their total cultural, political, economic dominance can be compensated for by the invigorated and newly brutalizing sexual corvée that women are having to demonstrate in streets and workplaces. Women may have the right to walk in public, and the right to work outside the home, but they must show their deference through their discomfort and pain. The cost is high.

REFERENCES

Butler, Judith. (1990). *Gender Trouble: Feminism and the Subversion of Identity.* London: Routledge.

Church, Rosemary, Weaver, Lisa Rose and Cohen, Elizabeth. (2003). Plastic Surgery Becoming More Common. Insight. CNN International. Cable News Network. Retrieved 1 March 2004 from http://web.lexis-nexis.com.mate.lib.unimelb.edu.au/universe/document?_m=afd02569d2d87f8b74404858889f4f4e&_docnum=l&wchp=dGLbVtz-zSkVb&_md5=137bf02dfeeb444546f3470e48ae2d0f.

Davis. Kathy. (1995). *Reshaping the Female Body: The Dilemma of Cosmetic Surgery.* New York: Routledge.

Dworkin, Andrea. (1974). *Woman Hating.* New York: E. P. Dutton.

Frye, Marilyn. (1983). *The Politics of Reality.* Trumansburg, New York: The Crossing Press.

Grosz, Elizabeth. (1994). *Volatile Bodies: Toward a Corporeal Feminism.* St. Leonards, NSW: Allen and Unwin.

Jeffreys, Sheila. (2000). Body Art and Social Status: Piercing, Cutting and Tattooing from a Feminist Perspective. *Feminism and Psychology,* November: 409–430.

Kingston, Anne. (2004). Olivia Goldsmith's death offers useful lessons to use all. *Saturday Post,* 24 January. http://permalink.gmane.org/gmane.music.dadl.ot/3616 (accessed 4 November, 2014).

Lehrman, Karen. (1997). *The Lipstick Proviso.* New York: Anchor Books.

Lim, Lin Lean (ed.) (1998). *The Sex Sector: The Economic and Social Bases of Prostitution in*

Southeast Asia. Geneva: International Labour Office.

MacKinnon, Catharine. (1989). *Towards a Feminist Theory of the State*. Cambridge, MA: Harvard University Press.

Moran, Jonathan and Walker, Kylie. (2004). Going to extremes. *Townsville Bulletin/ Townsville Sun*, 17 January.

O'Connell Davidson, Julia. (1995). British sex tourists in Thailand. In Maynard. Mary and Purvis, June (Eds), *(Hetero)Sexual Politics*. London: Taylor and Francis, pp. 42–65.

Roof, Judith. (1998). 1970s lesbian feminism meets 1990s butch-femme. In Munt, Sally R.

(Ed.), *Butch/Femme: Inside Lesbian Gender*. London: Cassell, pp. 27–35.

Sullivan, Deborah A. (2002). *Cosmetic Surgery: The Cutting Edge of Commercial Medicine in America*. New Brunswick, NJ: Rutgers University Press.

United Nations (1995). Fact Sheet No. 23 on Harmful Traditional Practices Affecting the Health of Women and Children. Geneva: United Nations.

Walter, Natasha. (1999). *The New Feminism*. London: Virago.

39. Constructing and Negotiating Social Identity*

Susie Scott

Identity is an evocative and intriguing concept, replete with paradoxes. On the one hand, it refers to something private and personal – our understanding of ourselves – yet, on the other hand, it remains intangible, elusive and resistant to definition (Strauss 1969). We may think we know who we are, but these ideas are constantly changing, shaped by our experiences, relationships and interactions: who I am now is not the same as who I was yesterday or who I will be tomorrow. We also tend to think of identity as something highly individual, which marks us out as unique – yet in forming these self-images we inevitably draw on wider cultural representations, discourses, norms and values, which we share with those who inhabit our social worlds.

Sociologists have always been interested in identity, because it resonates with many of the issues and debates that characterize our discipline. Interpretivist sociology, in particular, is concerned with the relationship between self and society (Hewitt 2007), which is mutually constitutive: the social world is created by people interacting in routinized and orderly ways, while the meanings they attach to these experiences are shaped by those very patterns, in the form of socially constructed structures, institutions and normative frameworks. Max Weber, on whose work this tradition is based, argued that sociology should involve the interpretive study of social action: the process by which individuals organize and make sense of their behaviour by taking into account other people's meanings and motivations (Weber 1904). We think, feel and behave not as isolated individuals, but as social actors with a relational consciousness. Meanwhile, sociology's aims to 'make the familiar strange' (Garfinkel 1967) and relate 'private troubles to public issues' (Mills 1959) are relevant to the study of identity as an aspect of everyday life that we often take for granted, despite its social and political dimensions. The latter have come to prominence since the mid-twentieth century through the rise of identity politics, citizenship debates and civil rights activism, reminding us that, aside from academic theorizing, we have a moral and ethical duty to investigate identities (Wetherell 2009).

What is identity?

Identity can be defined as a set of integrated ideas about the self, the roles we play and the qualities that make us unique. Ostensibly, this implies a relatively stable entity, which we perceive as internally consistent (Allport 1961; Gergen 1968), and use to sustain a boundary between ourselves and others. However, this very image may just be a construction: one that is constantly changing and whose existence is more illusory than real. Lyman and Scott (1970) conceive identity as an aggregate of social roles that one has played across different situations, which together create the impression of something 'trans-situational', or greater than the sum of its

* From Scott, S. (2015) *Negotiating Identity: Symbolic Interactionist Approaches to Social Identity* (Cambridge: Polity). Extracts from pp. 1–3, 5, 20–21.

parts. Turner (1968), similarly, points towards a succession of 'situated selves' that we inhabit as we move between social settings, which are 'averaged out' to create an overall sense of identity. Here we encounter what Lawler (2008) suggests is a central paradox of identity: that it combines notions of sameness and continuity with notions of difference and distinctiveness.

A similar duality is recognized by Williams (2000), who makes a distinction between *identity,* a sense of oneself as a coherent and stable entity, and *identification,* a social process of categorizing ourselves as similar to certain social groups and different from others. Social identity is therefore relational: defined relative to other people or groups. I find out who I *am* by knowing what I am *not*: understanding where and with whom I do (or don't) belong. For example, the Twenty Statements Test, devised by Iowa sociologists Kuhn and McPartland (1954), asked students to write a list of twenty words to describe themselves. The overwhelming majority of these referred to social categories, roles, statuses and group memberships, such as gender, age, ethnicity, occupation and family relationships. Other common descriptors that were found, such as ideological beliefs, interests, ambitions and self-evaluations, can also be seen as socially shaped.

We can distinguish identity from two closely related concepts: *selfhood* and *personhood. Selfhood* is a reflexive state of consciousness about one's internal thoughts and feelings, while *personhood* is a set of publicly presented or externally attributed characteristics that others use to determine our status (Jenkins 2004), with moral, philosophical or political connotations. Cohen (1994) similarly points to the primacy of the *self,* as those aspects of experience which are private, internal and subjective, over *personhood,* as a set of publicly externally attributed characteristics, rights or statuses. Jenkins (2004) suggests that self and personhood are interconnected dimensions of experience which are mutually constitutive. Identity is the dialectical process of their articulation, an umbrella that encompasses them both. Lindesmith et al. (1999: 218) also distinguish

between the *self,* a reflexive, communicative subject who witnesses him- or herself through a succession of transitory moments of interaction, and *identity,* or the meanings individuals give to these experiences as being unified.

Jenkins (2004) suggests four features of identity: *similarity* (a sense of one's uniformity and consistency), *difference* (a sense of one's uniqueness and distinctiveness from others), *reflexivity* (the ability to think about ourselves) and *process* (agency, independence and change over time). Lindesmith et al. (1999) agree that identity is multi-layered, incorporating different types of self: the *phenomenological self* (an internal stream of consciousness about one's current situation), the *interactional self* (as presented and displayed to others), the *linguistic self* (representations of the self to oneself or others through language and biographical stories), the *material self* (the body and externally visible parts of the self, which are potentially commodifiable) and the *ideological self* (broader cultural and historical definitions of what it means to be a good citizen in a particular society).

Then, there are different types of identity, which have been theorized across the social sciences. The social philosopher Harré (1998) saw *social identity* (externally applied categorizations or attributions) as being different from *personal identity* (the belief individuals have in their own self-consistency). In social psychology, Tajfel (1982) defined *social identity* in terms of affiliations with reference groups and the processes to which this gives rise, such as social comparison, in- and out-group relations and prejudice. Meanwhile Hewitt (2007) distinguished between *personal identity* (a sense of uniqueness and difference, together with integrity and consistency), *biographical identity* (the self as recounted through narratives and stories), *social identity* (group memberships and affiliations that forge connections and shared values) and *situational identity* (produced through the presentation or 'announcement' [Stone 1962] of particular versions of the self in specific interaction settings, and the extent to which these are accepted by those we encounter therein). In sociology, Goffman (1963) made a distinction between *personal identity* (the 'single, continuous record of facts' that documents an individual's life, for example in photographs), *social identity* (the 'complement of attributes' seen as ordinary, natural and normal for members of a recognized category) and *ego identity* (a person's subjective sense of their own character, developed over time).

[. . .]

The symbolic interactionist concept of the 'social self' centres on the idea that selfhood is relational, arising through social interaction at the micro level. This is a symbolic and communicative process by which actors understand themselves through their relations with others. It involves reflection and perspective-taking, definitions and judgements; the self is an active agent, capable of manipulating objects in the social world. Hewitt (2007) adds that the social self is processual: it is not a fixed object or entity but, rather, fluid, emergent and mutable. Selfhood is never finished but in a constant state of becoming. Identity, similarly, is 'never gained nor maintained once and for all . . . it is constantly lost and regained' (Erikson 1959: 118) through social negotiation.

These theories stem from the philosophical tradition of pragmatism: the study of human praxis, or meaningful activity. Ontologically, pragmatism teaches that social reality is constructed through human action: we define the social world and the objects within it in terms of their use for us, or practical effects upon situations (Dewey 1922). The term 'object' here incorporates people, and, most crucially, one's own self: we can reflect upon ourselves as social objects in other people's worlds, and imagine their perceptions and judgements of us. James (1890: 295) argued that this is a key means of understanding ourselves, which also suggests multiplicity: an actor has 'as many social selves as there are distinct groups of persons about whose opinions he [*sic*] cares'.

Pragmatism suggests that the self has two sides: it is both subject and object simultaneously. The mind has a reflective capacity: we think, feel and act, but also reflect upon the social consequences of this, and modify our self-image accordingly. Cooley's (1902) concept of the Looking Glass Self had three elements: imagining how we appear to others, imagining how they might judge us, and the resultant self-feelings, such as pride or shame. This in turn shows that the self is a dynamic *process*, which is never complete: we do not simply 'have' selves but rather 'do' or 'make' (and re-make) them, through constant reflection.

[. . .]

To summarize, there are three main features of the symbolic interactionist and dramaturgical approaches to identity. Firstly, identity is a *process*. It is not something that people have, or are ascribed to, or that stays the same throughout their lives, but rather something that continuously unfolds and evolves. This process is mediated by social interaction, as actors perceive and respond to the symbolic meaning of each other's actions, and so identity is negotiated through interaction. Maines (2001: 242) defines identities as the 'social categories through which people may be located and given meaning' in a situational context.

Secondly, identity is *performative*. We have seen from Goffman's dramaturgy how SI envisages social actors working together and alone to display versions of themselves, and using a myriad of strategies to this end: impression management, information control, facework gestures, and so on. Identity is therefore something that is actively accomplished, worked at and 'done' by individuals in the course of interaction, and this is a self-conscious, reflexive process. The SI meaning of 'performance' is different from the word 'performative', used in poststructuralism (e.g. Butler's gender theory), where there is a deconstructionist, anti-essentialist ontology of selfhood. SI puts a more pragmatic emphasis on what actors do and what is shown (the performance that can be observed) rather than the abstract capacities or potentials of subjectivity. This retains the idea of a core self as the agent authoring these choices: there has to be an actor behind the character.

Thirdly, identity is *pragmatic*: something that does not just exist at the abstract level of image and perception, but rather is tangibly expressed through concrete lines of action, which can be observed and analysed. SI research involves empirical studies that illustrate how identities are negotiated, performed and managed in specific interaction contexts, and uses these data as evidence to support or challenge theoretical ideas. Lofland (1970) identifies this as a key strength of the approach, immunizing it against accusations of abstract armchair theorizing. Such empirical studies are exactly the kind of material on which I shall be drawing throughout the book, to bring the theoretical concepts to life and ground them in relatable examples.

These three qualities of process, performance and pragmatism lie at the heart of the SI approach to identity and characterize the shape of its research.

REFERENCES

Allport, G.W. (1961) *Pattern and Growth in Personality*. New York: Holt, Rinehart & Winston.

Cohen, A.P. (1994) *Self Consciousness: An Alternative Anthropology of Identity*. London: Routledge.

Cooley, C.H. (1902) *Human Nature and the Social Order*. New Brunswick, NJ: Transaction, 1992.

Dewey, J. (1922) *Human Nature and Conduct*. New York: Holt & Co.

Erikson, E.H. (1959) *Identity and the Life Cycle*. New York: International Universities Press.

Garfinkel, H. (1967) *Studies in Ethnomethodology*. Englewood Cliffs, NJ: Prentice-Hall.

Gergen, K.J. (1968) 'Personal consistency and the presentation of self.' In C. Gordon & K.J. Gergen (eds), *The Self in Social Interaction*. New York: Wiley, pp. 299–308.

Goffman, E. (1963a) *Stigma: Notes on the Management of Spoiled Identity*. Harmondsworth: Penguin.

Harré, R. (1998) *The Singular Self: An Introduction to the Psychology of Personhood*. London: Sage.

Hewitt, J. (2007) *Self and Society: A Symbolic Interactionist Social Psychology*. New York: Allyn & Bacon.

James, W. (1890) *The Principles of Psychology*. Cambridge, MA: Harvard University Press, 1983.

Jenkins, R. (2004) *Social Identity*. London: Routledge.

Kuhn, M.H. & McPartland, T.S. (1954) 'An empirical investigation of self-attitudes.' *American Sociological Review*, 19, 1, 68–76.

Lawler, S. (2008) *Identity: Sociological Perspectives*. Cambridge: Polity.

Lindesmith, A.R., Strauss, A.L. & Denzin, N.K. (1999) *Social Psychology*. Thousand Oaks, CA: Sage.

Lofland, J. (1970) 'Interactionist imagery and analytic interruptus.' In T. Shibutani (ed.), *Human Nature and Collective Behavior: Papers in Honor of Herbert Blumer*, pp. 35–45.

Lyman, S.M. & Scott, M.B. (1970) *A Sociology of the Absurd* (2nd edition). New York: General Hall, 1989.

Maines, D.R. (2001) *The Faultline of Consciousness: A View of Interactionism in Sociology*. Hawthorne, NY: Aldine de Gruyter.

Mills, C.W. (1959) *The Sociological Imagination*. New York: Oxford University Press.

Stone, G. (1962) 'Appearance and the self.' In A. Rose (ed.), *Human Behavior and Social Processes*. Boston: Houghton-Mifflin, pp. 86–118.

Strauss, A.L. (1969) *Mirrors and Masks*. London: Martin Robertson.

Tajfel, H. (1982) 'Social psychology of intergroup relations.' *Annual Review of Psychology*, 33, 1–39.

Turner, R.H. (1968) 'The self-conception in social interaction.' In C. Gordon & K.J. Gergen (eds), *The Self in Social Interactionism*. New York: Wiley, pp. 93–106.

Weber, M. (1904) '"Objectivity" in social science and social policy.' In his *The Methodology of the Social Sciences* (trans. & ed. E.A. Shils & H.A. Finch). New York: Free Press, 1949, pp. 50–112.

Wetherell, M. (ed.) (2009) *Identity in the 21st Century: New Trends in Changing Times*. Basingstoke: Palgrave.

Williams, R. (2000) *Making Identity Matter*. Durham: sociologypress.

40. Knowledge Production in a Post-Truth World*

Dominic Malcolm

In popular usage, post-truth encapsulates five interconnected ideas. Primarily definitions of post-truth argue that emotion has become more significant than objective fact in shaping personal beliefs and public debates. Second, post-truth includes the relativisation of truth; the idea that political statements, and even empirically grounded scientific positions, are subject to the manipulation of knowledge producers (Lockie, 2017). Correlatively, politicians can apparently contradict their prior assertions without incurring reputational damage and, hence, a third characteristic of post-truth is the decline of shame when one is exposed for being factually wrong or suspected of deception (Blackburn, 2018). Fourth, this phenomenon has seemingly been accompanied by a tendency to polarise views. Finally, the manipulation of knowledge and the polarisation of views tends to fuel 'conspiracy' theories.

Post-truth is generally seen as a matter for concern; born, for instance, 'from a sense of regret by those who worry that truth is being eclipsed' (McIntyre, 2018: xiii). This potential reversal of modernist advances in knowledge production dominant since the scientific revolution of the Renaissance and Enlightenment threatens to undermine human control over social and scientific 'problems'. Post-truth has been associated with a rise in authoritarianism, the blunting of socially progressive movements and the decline

of democratic scrutiny (Biesecker, 2018; Collins et al., 2020).

In response, most post-truth analyses advocate a return to traditional ways of evaluating knowledge; the re-assertion of the primacy of truth, evident for instance in the growth of 'fact-checking' in the (mainstream) media and by specialist organisations (Waisbord, 2018). Such responses thus invoke abstract and essentialist concepts such as 'truth' as 'reality', and the ontological primacy of objectivity over subjectivity. Such philosophical absolutism focuses on the individual purveyor/receiver of truth/falsehood and thus sees knowledge as 'independent of social processes, and definite and certain knowledge as the ideal which can be attained by following certain rules or rationality' (Wilterdink, 2003: 302). Yet, as we will see, this is an approach which is 'expressive of a particular strand of rationality . . . of a particular historical juncture' (Dunning and Hughes, 2013: 148), making it ill-equipped for advancing understanding of what appears to be a historically distinct but relatively dynamic change to the social conceptualisation and mobilisation of knowledge. A sociological re-evaluation is important because of the social significance of the issues raised and, more practically, because recourse to philosophical ideas does not appear to have constrained the development of post-truth.

In contrast, a sociological analysis of post-truth which sought to examine the social conditions in which these historically specific forms of knowledge have emerged provides a more nuanced position from which to respond to post-truth developments. It would, moreover, understand

* From Malcolm, D. (2021) 'Post-Truth Society? An Eliasian Sociological Analysis of Knowledge in the 21st Century', *Sociology*, March: 1–17. Extracts from pp. 1–2, 8–9, 14–15.

post-truth in its own terms, without reducing the debate to the philosophical concepts that, a priori, are being challenged. As discussed in the next section, this account builds on and extends sociological analyses of communication, science and expertise which feed into a more overarching sociology of knowledge. This article provides the first sociological reconsideration of post-truth 'in the round' and, in so doing, seeks to initiate a broader sociological and theoretically oriented discussion of this important social phenomenon.

[. . .]

For Elias, symbol emancipation and the capacity to learn language are both unique to, yet effectively universal among, members of the human species. He argued that: (a) 'knowledge cannot be regarded as such if it cannot be produced in linguistic form' (Elias, 2011 [1991]: 27); and (b) more sophisticated forms of language relatively enable the transmission of knowledge across generations. Language thus facilitates the lengthening of human interdependencies and more sophisticated forms of symbol emancipation enable humans to spread more complex bodies of knowledge across both time and space. Communication and capacities for knowing and remembering are, according to Elias (2011 [1991]), distinguishable but inseparable.

Elias illustrated the interdependence of modes of communication and thinking in his discussion of Renaissance artists. He described how perspectivist painters such as Velazquez developed techniques to both more realistically depict three-dimensional space and evoke nuance and implication rather than 'simple' literal representation (Elias, 2007 [1987]). The techniques stemmed from the artists' greater relative detachment. For instance, Velazquez's *Las Meninas* showed 'at the same time' the painter's 'pride and his humility. It shows how he saw himself and how he wanted to be seen by others', which itself was predicated on 'a high capacity for seeing oneself from a distance as one might be perceived by others' (Elias, 2007 [1987]: 52 and

62). These paintings appealed to the audience's parallel development of sensibilities and thus for Elias these were artistic manifestations of the relatively intensified civilising processes occurring as part of the Renaissance.

Viewed through this lens, we can see that previous post-truth analyses correctly identify the role of social media in the rise of post-truth (Fuller, 2018; Waisbord, 2018). The commonplace linkage to the decline of traditional media is however misguided, partly because the social/mainstream media distinction returns us to the problematic truth/ falsehood dichotomy and partly because it nostalgically venerates the truthfulness of television and newspapers. Postman (1985), for instance, argued that by the 1980s television had normalised discontinuity and fragmentation and thus 'rendered [Americans] insensitive to contradiction' (Hannan, 2018: 217).

Rather, social media is important because it engenders more complex forms of symbol emancipation. While communication has developed from firstly purely physical and oral forms, to pictures and text, and latterly a combination of moving pictures, sound and text (i.e. film), social media extends the progressive development of forms of human expression in three ways. First, the use of filters and hashtags provides a shorthand summary of potentially more complex sets of ideas, and has been shown to help build 'filter bubbles' or 'echo chambers'; '"ad-hoc" publics – spaces where a diversity of experience and expertise can co-exist around a topic of shared interest' (Myrick et al., 2016: 603). Similarly, hyperlinking is understood to have fundamentally changed communication, helping to structure and expand human networks and being 'loaded with symbolic and social power' (De Maeyer, 2012: 737). Third, emoticons, which are mostly used to express emotion, humour or for emphasis (Derks et al., 2008), entail increasingly involved and less detached communication.

Social media also expands the use of pictorial/ film communication via memes, vines and gifs. Van Dijck (2008) argues that the primary function of photography has shifted from representation to self-presentation and social communication; from the sharing of objects to the sharing of experiences. The rise of the 'selfie' has democratised the shifting blend of involvement and detachment evident in Elias's perspectivist painters example, as camera phones enable repeated placement of the self in social context and evoke self-reflection. Van Dijck (2008: 69–70) cites the example of the photographs posted by US military at the Abu Ghraib prison to illustrate how new communication tools explicitly engender the kind of more emotionally oriented forms of communication that characterise post-truth, as 'pictures casually mailed out … meant to be thrown away after reading the message, became permanently engraved on the consciousness of a generation … painful visual evidence of its [the USA's] military hubris'. Social media is therefore important to post-truth because it represents an emerging and more complex stage of symbol emancipation.

The effectiveness of new forms of communication varies as they undergo a relatively rapid phase of development (akin to what Elias termed the 'drag effect'). The symbols humans use for communication 'can become more – but also less – reality congruent than they were at an earlier stage' (Elias, 2011 [1991]: 16). New forms of symbol emancipation require new interpretative skills. Indicatively media researchers talk about the importance of media generations, defined by the dominant media technology of one's formative years, and have even suggested that media relationships should replace the traditional concept of generation (Bolin and Westlund, 2009). Consequently, concerns about the impact of social media can be explained in relation to the relatively unrefined use of new communication technologies and the varying rates at which populations adopt these rapidly developing communication tools (Bolin and Westlund, 2009). In contrast with past developments, contemporary symbol emancipation is a distinctly more widespread movement, illustrative of the 'growing pains of a maturing democratic intelligence' identified by Fuller (2018: 181).

[…]

Following Fuller (2018) this article conceives of post-truth as a change in the socially prevalent styles of debate fuelled by the democratising trends of communication technology developments and changing public perceptions of (scientific) expertise. However, this article goes beyond Fuller to argue that post-truth entails an intensification in the blend of emotion and fact, of involved and detached modes of thinking. Moreover, it positions these technological developments as more fundamentally changing the use of 'language' (or what Elias called symbol emancipation), which, in turn, has shaped and been shaped by the changing nature of human interdependencies. In combination these have served to create a shift in human habitus characterised by the foresight to anticipate multiple audience receptions, and negotiate feelings of shame and embarrassment associated with being challenged over the validity of one's position. Such an explanation is aligned with Elias's desire 'to explore, not just the social contingency of knowledge but also the *different ways* in which knowledge is tied dynamically to different and differently emergent human psyches and figurations' (Dunning and Hughes, 2013: 131, emphasis in original). Seen in this light, post-truth does not so much represent an a priori challenge to Elias's theory of civilising processes but helps us to extend the usefulness of this paradigm by evidencing the more complex rationalities within the development of the social constraint towards greater self-restraint.

As noted in the introduction, the primary way post-truth developments have been viewed is through a prism of potential social disaster. Through a re-conceptualisation of post-truth, and analysis of the incipient social processes, an alternative depiction of contemporary developments emerges. The widespread focus on emotion relative to 'fact' is both an exaggeration and over-simplification, and while a focus on post-truth as the democratisation of long-standing rhetorical strategies is evident (Fuller,

2018), deeper and more significant shifts in the structure of communication, changing human interdependencies and social habitus are occurring. Specifically, we are not simply seeing a relativisation of 'truth' but a new blend of truth and emotion characterised by a deeper and more complex consideration of political and scientific claims than has hitherto been evident. The threats to democracy posed by right-wing populists' dismissal of expertise undoubtedly remain (Collins et al., 2020), but post-truth is perhaps the symptom of these threats rather than the cause.

Elias's sociology of knowledge not only provides the basis for this more adequate understanding of the post-truth phenomenon, but also helps explain why post-truth developments have met with such social concern. Certainly, one of the primary reasons is the ongoing power game (Fuller, 2018) and shifts in the relations between knowledge elites and publics. In post-truth societies knowledge producing subjects have been turned into the objects of study – the news creators have been turned into news and the work of scientists has become subject to empirical questioning. Second, Elias and Scotson (2008 [1965]) noted that while outsiders find relatively little appeal in exercising self-restraint in accordance with dominant social norms (and thus can readily embrace post-truth), the exercise of self-restraint is central to the emotional bonds and unity of established groups. Third, in *The Society of Individuals* Elias (2010 [1991]) noted that people often resort to nostalgic representations of past social order in time of pronounced social change (Crow and Laidlaw, 2019). Elias (2007 [1987]: 25) also suggested that 'from the relative pacification of non-human nature stands out all the more starkly the untamed ferocity of the struggles between human groups themselves'. It is in such a context that ideological (rather than physical) tribal war is predicted, and that the 'death of democracy' might be feared (Biesecker, 2018). (While climate change has been the focus of much post-truth debate in recent years, the central issues are not non-human nature as

such, but the impact of human behaviour on non-human nature.) For these reasons dominant social groups have responded to political and status challenge with emotional appeals highlighting the fundamentally problematic basis of emotively driven debates.

REFERENCES

Biesecker B (2018) Guest editor's introduction: Toward an archaeogenealogy of post-truth. *Philosophy and Rhetoric* 51: 329–341.

Blackburn S (2018) *On Truth*. Oxford: Oxford University Press.

Bolin G and Westlund O (2009) Mobile generations: The role of mobile technology in the shaping of Swedish media generations. *International Journal of Communications* 3: 108–124.

Collins H, Evans R, Durant D, et al. (2020) *Experts and the Will of the People: Society, Populism and Science*. Switzerland: Palgrave Macmillan.

Crow G and Laidlaw M (2019) Norbert Elias's extended theory of community: From established/ outsider relations to the gendered we–I balance. *The Sociological Review* 67(3): 568–584.

De Maeyer J (2012) Towards a hyperlinked society: A critical review of link studies. *New Media & Society* 15(5): 737–751.

Derks D, Bos A and Grumbkow J (2008) Emoticons in computer-mediated communication: Social motives and social context. *CyberPsychology & Behaviour* 11(1): 99–101.

Dunning E and Hughes J (2013) *Norbert Elias and Modern Sociology: Knowledge, Interdependence, Power, Process*. London: Bloomsbury.

Elias N (2007 [1987]) *Involvement and Detachment: The Collected Works of Norbert Elias*, Vol. 8. Ed. Quilley S. Dublin: University College Dublin Press.

Elias N (2010 [1991]) *The Society of Individuals*. Dublin: University College Dublin Press.

Elias N (2011 [1991]) *The Symbol Theory: The Collected Works of Norbert Elias*, Vol. 13. Ed. Kilminster R. Dublin: University College Dublin Press.

Elias N and Scotson J (2008 [1965]) *The Established and the Outsiders: The Collected Works of Norbert Elias*, Vol. 4. Ed. Wouters C. Dublin: University College Dublin Press.

Fuller S (2018) *Post Truth: Knowledge as a Power Game*. London: Anthem Press.

Hannan J (2018) Trolling ourselves to death? Social media and post-truth politics. *European Journal of Communication* 33(2): 214–226.

Lockie S (2017) Post-truth politics and the social sciences. *Environmental Sociology* 3: 1–5.

McIntyre L (2018) *Post-Truth*. Boston, MA: MIT Press.

Myrick J, Holton A, Himelboim I, et al. (2016) #Stupidcancer: Exploring a typology of social support and the role of emotional expression in a social media community. *Health Communication* 31(5): 596–605.

Postman N (1985) *Amusing Ourselves to Death: Public Discourse in the Age of Show Business*. New York: Penguin.

Van Dijck J (2008) Digital photography: Communication, identity, memory. *Visual Communication* 7(1): 57–76.

Waisbord S (2018) Truth is what happens in the news. *Journalism Studies* 19: 1866–1878.

Wilterdink NA (2003) Norbert Elias's sociology of knowledge and its significance for the study of the sciences. In: Dunning E and Mennell S (eds) *Norbert Elias: Sage Masters in Modern Social Thought*, Vol. 1. London: SAGE, 301–316.

Part 7 – Further reading

The symbolic interactionist perspective which has contributed most to microsociology is still best approached via Goffman himself, so Goffman, E. (1990 [1959]) *The Presentation of Self in Everyday Life* (Harmondsworth: Penguin) is an excellent place to start reading. On sociology's contribution to understanding violence, Malešević, S. (2010) *The Sociology of War and Violence* (Cambridge: Cambridge University Press) is very hard to beat. Lorber, J. (2012) *Gender Inequality: Feminist Theories and Politics* (5th edn, Oxford: Oxford University Press) provides an excellent account of the field of gender studies. Finally, a gateway into studies of media is Curran, J., and Hesmondhalgh, D. (2019) *Media and Society* (6th edn, New York: Bloomsbury Academic).

Sociology, 9th edition

Chapter 12, 'Social Interaction and Daily Life', is clearly the place to go for matters relating to social selves and interaction theories. For war and violence, chapter 21, 'Nations, War and Terrorism', covers a lot of ground. Chapter 7, 'Gender and Sexuality', is dedicated to sociological work on gender, sexuality and feminism. And, again, there is a whole chapter covering the field of media sociology.

Part 8

Health, Illness and the Body

After experiencing the first pandemic of the twenty-first century, readers will need no convincing that matters of health and illness are of major concern for sociologists. COVID-19 demonstrated that good health is a prerequisite for an active individual lifestyle but also that promoting public health is one of very few issues that legitimize the imposition of a state of emergency and severe restrictions on individual freedoms and rights. Studies of health and illness were, for many years, dominated by medics and biological scientists, but from the mid-twentieth century sociologists began to take more of an interest. The work of the American sociologist Talcott Parsons effectively opened up the whole field to sociological enquiry with his ideas on how people who are ill are encouraged to play a 'sick role', with numerous expectations attached. Parsons argued that there are clear social aspects to health and illness. Illness has to be confirmed and validated by a medic, who acts as a gatekeeper to the sick role, in which people can be absolved, temporarily, from some duties and responsibilities. Illness is a social as well as a physical or mental condition and, since Parsons, the sociology of health and illness developed into one of sociology's most vibrant specialisms.

Compared to all alternatives, contemporary scientific medicine, known as biomedicine, is seen as the most effective way of dealing with illness and disease. Its impact can be seen in steadily rising life expectancy,

generally better health into later life, and improving health for all social groups in society. Yet, some have argued that biomedicine has been wrongly credited with health improvements that are really the outcome of improved diet, less physically demanding work and healthier environments. Others go further, arguing that scientific medicine is itself the cause of much illness – such as the transmission of MRSA in hospitals – and that an over-reliance on professional medics has effectively deskilled people in relation to their own health, thereby creating a debilitating health dependency. In our reading on this subject, Peter Conrad introduces the concept of *medicalization*, defined as the process through which non-medical problems come to be redefined as medical issues to be treated by medics. Examples include pregnancy and childbirth, alcoholism, sexual dysfunction, menopause, ADHD and even sleep. In these cases the legitimate remit of the medical profession is continually expanded, a situation that Ivan Illich once described as 'medical imperialism'. Conrad explores the current state of the medicalization debate. He also reminds us that the process can ebb and flow, as de-medicalization is always possible and has occurred in some cases.

The experience of health and illness differs across societies as well as across social groups within a society. For instance, women live, on average, longer than men, working-class men in general have poorer health outcomes than middle- and upper-class men, while a very stark contrast can be seen between the Global North and the Global South. The countries of the South suffer from illness and diseases that were brought under control or eliminated in the wealthier North many years ago, while newly developed medicines are not equally shared globally. This situation can be seen in relation to the skewed distribution of antiviral drugs for the treatment of HIV/AIDS and in the novel vaccines for COVID-19. In both cases, Europe and North America successfully laid claim to the bulk of the early supply. Health inequalities such as these have been a major theme of the sociology of health and illness. Our reading from Richard Wilkinson and Kate Pickett outlines their influential work on the connection between health and illness and levels of equality/inequality in the wealthiest societies. In a nutshell, they produce a large volume of data which, they argue, shows that the most significant health problems are more common in the most socio-economically unequal societies. If they are right, then moving in the direction of increasing equality should benefit the health of everyone.

As we noted earlier, modern biomedicine is credited with many spectacular successes in improving the health of nations. When COVID-19 emerged, governments around the world looked to science and biomedicine, not homeopathy or other alternative therapies, for advice, treatments and vaccine development. In Reading 43, Sarah Nettleton pulls together the various strands to present an overview of what we actually mean by 'biomedicine'. Key among these is the separation of mind and body, with medicine focusing on the individual body and its functioning. Arguably, this has led to the relative neglect of mental health in medicine and society that is only recently starting to be rectified. Focusing on the body has also led to doctors being seen very much as engineers who are called on to diagnose

breakdowns and remedy malfunctions in the human machine. Critics suggest this is a denuded model of the human being which fails to grasp the psychological and social aspects of health and illness. Nettleton also provides a useful critique of the biomedical model and introduces some of the main challenges to its continuing dominance from several directions.

The dominant place of biomedicine in societies means that health problems and disease are widely seen as falling within the province of medicine, with little or no role for the social sciences. However, as we have seen above, sociologists have gradually made inroads into this argument, demonstrating empirically and theoretically that there is more to health and illness than individual bodies. For example, the study of health inequalities has consistently shown that both health and illness are socially patterned along lines of the major social divisions of class, gender, race and ethnic group, and disability. This body of work raises questions about the impact of poverty and social inequality but also a more general question: does the social level of reality actually *cause* illness? Our reading from William C. Cockerham argues that it does, and he illustrates the terms of his argument in relation to COVID-19 and smoking. The negative health impacts of smoking on the body are well known, including damage to the lungs, cardiovascular system and blood vessels caused by tar from tobacco. Yet, it is the decision made by people to start and continue smoking that is the causal factor, and those decisions are made in social interactions and contexts. People actually learn how to smoke from others, and they learn how to enjoy the practice, which means they continue to engage in it. In short, smoking is a social activity, and understanding this activity requires sociological concepts and theories. Combining biological and sociological knowledge should therefore lead to more effective policy and interventions and a reduction in illness and disease.

At the time of writing, sociological studies of the COVID-19 pandemic are just beginning to be published and, such has been the disruption and significance of it, undoubtedly there will be many more over the next few years. Our final extract in this section is from Jens O. Zinn and dates from April 2020, around the time that the virus was spreading rapidly across Europe. Drawing on Ulrich Beck's risk theory, this piece traces the factors that led to COVID-19 becoming a 'monstrous threat' to the world's societies. Clearly there was the potential threat from the virus itself, which epidemiologists and modellers presented to governments. But

the media also played a key role, collecting and presenting data on a daily basis, showing desperate images and videos of patients and medical staff in healthcare settings, and in this way contributing to a growing awareness among the public of risk. The pandemic and responses to it also highlighted existing social inequalities, not just in healthcare but more broadly. For example, black and minority ethnic groups had higher death rates than white groups, domestic violence against women increased, and the state-imposed lockdowns tended to affect people in poor-quality and overcrowded housing disproportionately. Zinn's article also examines the idea of a 'new normal' and considers whether the 'old normal' can ever return.

41. The Medical Re-definition of Social Life*

Peter Conrad

When I began teaching medical sociology in the 1970s, the terrain of health and illness looked quite different from what we find in the early twenty-first century. In my classes, there was no mention of now-common maladies such as attention-deficit/hyperactivity disorder (ADHD), anorexia, chronic fatigue syndrome (CFS), post-traumatic stress disorder (PTSD), panic disorder, fetal alcohol syndrome, premenstrual syndrome (PMS), and sudden infant death syndrome (SIDS), to name some of the most prevalent. Neither obesity nor alcoholism was widely viewed in the medical profession as a disease. There was no mention of diseases like AIDS or contested illnesses like Gulf War syndrome or multiple chemical sensitivity disorder. While Ritalin was used with a relatively small number of children and tranquilizers were commonly prescribed for certain problems, human growth hormone (hGH), Viagra, and antidepressants like selective serotonin reuptake inhibitors (SSRIs) were not yet produced.

In the past thirty years or so, medical professionals have identified several problems that have become commonly known illnesses or disorders. In this book I address illnesses or "syndromes" that relate to behavior, a psychic state, or a bodily condition that now has a medical diagnosis and medical treatment. Clearly, the number of life problems that are defined as medical has increased enormously. Does this mean that there is a new epidemic of medical problems or that medicine is better able to identify and treat already existing problems? Or does it mean that a whole range of life's problems have now received medical diagnoses and are subject to medical treatment, despite dubious evidence of their medical nature?

I am not interested in adjudicating whether any particular problem is *really* a medical problem. That is far beyond the scope of my expertise and the boundaries of this book. I am interested in the social underpinnings of this expansion of medical jurisdiction and the social implications of this development. We can examine the medicalization of human problems and bracket the question of whether they are "real" medical problems. What constitutes a real medical problem may be largely in the eyes of the beholder or in the realm of those who have the authority to define a problem as medical. In this sense it is the viability of the designation rather than the validity of the diagnosis that is grist for the sociological mill.

The impact of medicine and medical concepts has expanded enormously in the past fifty years. To take just two common indicators, the percentage of our gross national product spent on health care has increased from 4.5 percent in 1950 to 16 percent in 2006, and the number of physicians has grown from 148 per 100,000 in 1970 to 281 per 100,000 in 2003 (Kaiser Family Foundation, 2005: Exhibit 5–7). The number of physicians per population nearly doubled in that period, greatly extending medical capacity.

* From Conrad, P. (2007) *The Medicalization of Society: On the Transformation of Human Conditions into Treatable Disorders* (Baltimore: Johns Hopkins University Press). Extracts from pp. 3–4, 5–6, 7–8, 13–14.

244   PETER CONRAD

In this same period the jurisdiction of medicine has grown to include new problems that previously were not deemed to fall within the medical sphere.

"Medicalization" describes a process by which nonmedical problems become defined and treated as medical problems, usually in terms of illness and disorders. Some analysts have suggested that the growth of medical jurisdiction is "one of the most potent transformations of the last half of the twentieth century in the West" (Clarke et al., 2003: 161). For nearly four decades, sociologists, anthropologists, historians, bioethicists, physicians, and others have written about medicalization (Ballard and Elston, 2005). These analysts have focused on the specific instances of medicalization, examining the origins, range, and impact of medicalization on society, medicine, patients, and culture (Conrad, 1992; Bartholomew, 2000; Lock, 2001). While some have simply examined the development of medicalization, most have taken a somewhat critical or skeptical view of this social transformation.

[...]

The key to medicalization is definition. That is, problem is defined in medical terms, described using medical language, understood through the adoption of a medical framework, or "treated" with a medical intervention. While much writing, including my own, has been critical of medicalization, it is important to remember that medicalization describes a process. Thus, we can examine the medicalization of epilepsy, a disorder most people would agree is "really" medical, as well as we can examine the medicalization of alcoholism, ADHD, menopause, or erectile dysfunction. While "medicalize" literally means "to make medical," and the analytical emphasis has been on overmedicalization and its consequences assumptions of overmedicalization are not a given in the perspective. The main point in considering medicalization is that an entity that is regarded an illness or disease is not ipso facto a medical problem; rather, it needs to become defined as

one. While the medical profession often has first call on most maladies that can be related to the body and to a large degree the psyche (Zola, 1972), some active agents are necessary for most problems to become medicalized (Conrad, 1992; Conrad and Schneider, 1992).

Many of the earliest studies assumed that physicians were the key to understanding medicalization. Illich (1976) used the catchy but misleading phrase "medical imperialism." It soon became clear, however, that medicalization was more complicated than the annexation of new problems by doctors and the medical profession. In cases like alcoholism, medicalization was primarily accomplished by a social movement (Alcoholics Anonymous), and physicians were actually late adopters of the view of alcoholism as a disease (Conrad and Schneider, 1992). And even to this day, the medical profession or individual doctors may be only marginally involved with the management of alcoholism, and actual medical treatments are not requisite for medicalization (Conrad, 1992; Appleton, 1995).

Although medicalization occurs primarily with deviance and "normal life events," it cuts a wide swath through our society and encompasses broad areas of human life. Among other categories, the medicalization of deviance includes alcoholism, mental disorders, opiate addictions, eating disorders, sexual and gender difference, sexual dysfunction, learning disabilities, and child and sexual abuse. It also has spawned numerous new categories, from ADHD to PMS to PTSD to CFS. Behaviors that were once defined as immoral, sinful, or criminal have been given medical meaning, moving them from badness to sickness. Certain common life processes have been medicalized as well, including anxiety and mood, menstruation, birth control, infertility, childbirth, menopause, aging, and death.

The growth of medicalized categories suggests an increase in medicalization (see chapter 6), but this growth is not simply a result of medical colorization or moral entrepreneurship. Arthur Barsky and Jonathan Boros point out that the public's tolerance of mild symptoms has decreased, spurring a "progressive medicalization of physical distress in which uncomfortable body states and isolated symptom are reclassified as diseases" (1995: 1931). Social movements, patient organizations, and individual patients have also been important advocates for medicalization (Broom and Woodward, 1996). In recent years corporate entities like the pharmaceutical industry and potential patients as consumers have begun to play more significant roles in medicalization.

[. . .]

Medical categories can also expand or contract. One dimension of the degree of medicalization is the elasticity of a medical category. "While some categories are narrow and circumspect, others can expand and incorporate a number of other problems" (Conrad, 1992: 221). For example, Alzheimer disease (AD) was once an obscure disorder, but with the removal of "age" as a criterion (Fox, 1989) there was no longer a distinction between AD and senile dementia. This change in definition to include cases of senile dementia in the population of adults over 60 years old sharply increased the number of cases of AD. As a result, AD has become one of the top five causes of death in the United States (cf. Bond. 1992). Medicalization by diagnostic expansion will be examined in chapter 3.

Medicalization is bidirectional, in the sense that there can be both medicalization and demedicalization, but the trend in the past century has been toward the expansion of medical jurisdiction. For demedicalization to occur, the problem must no longer be defined in medical terms, and medical treatments can no longer be deemed appropriate interventions. A classic example is masturbation, which in the nineteenth century was considered a disease and worthy of medical intervention (Engelhardt, 1974) but by the mid-twentieth century was no longer seen as requiring medical treatment. In a somewhat different vein, the disability movement has advocated, with partial success, for a demedicalization of disability and a reframing of it in terms of

access and civil rights (Oliver, 1996). The most notable example is homosexuality, which was officially demedicalized in the 1970s; in chapter 5 I examine the possibilities of its remedicalization. Childbirth, by contrast, has been radically transformed in recent years with "natural childbirth," birthing rooms, nurse midwives, and a host of other changes, but it has not been demedicalized. Childbirth is still defined as a medical event, and medical professionals still attend it. Birthing at home with lay midwives approaches demedicalization, but it remains care. In general, there are few contemporary cases of demedicalization to examine.

Critics have been concerned that medicalization transforms aspects of everyday life into pathologies, narrowing the range of what is considered acceptable. Medicalization also focuses the source of the problem in the individual rather than in the social environment; it calls for individual medical interventions rather than more collective or social solutions. Furthermore, by expanding medical jurisdiction, medicalization increases the amount of medical social control over human behavior. Early critics warned that medical social control would likely replace other forms of social control (Pitts, 1968; Zola, 1972), and while this has not occurred, it can be argued that medical social control has continued to expand. Although many definitions of medical social control have been offered, I still contend that "the greatest social control power comes from having the authority to define certain behaviors, persons and things" (Conrad and Schneider, 1992:8). Thus, in general, the key issue remains definitional—the power to have a particular set of (medical) definitions realized in both spirit and practice. [. . .]

[. . .]

Following Lupton (1997) and to a lesser degree Armstrong (1995), Williams acknowledges that both approaches focus on medicine as a dominant institution that has expanded its gaze and jurisdiction substantially in the past half-century or more. The Foucauldian view emphasizes more how the discourses of medicine and health become central to the subjectivities of people's lives, manifested as "the wholesale incorporation of the body and disease . . . in the discursive matter via the productive effects of power/knowledge, viewed as socially constructed entities" (Williams, 2001: 148). Without getting into a debate about the differences between a Foucauldian perspective and that presented in most medicalization studies, let me at least note some complementary lines of analysis. Medicalization studies, as I and others engage in them, focus especially on the creation, promotion, and application of medical categories (and treatments or solutions) to human problems and events; while we are certainly interested in the social control aspects of medicalization, we see them as something that goes beyond, but may include, discourse and subjectivity. Numerous studies have emphasized how medicalization has transformed the normal into the pathological and how medical ideologies, interventions, and therapies have reset and controlled the borders of acceptable behavior, bodies, and states of being. The medical gaze, discourse, and surveillance are fundamental elements of this process, even if these writers use a different vocabulary. It is clear that the postmodern critique points to the limits of modernist categorization, but it is the very processes of medical categorization that create medicalization. It is not necessary to adopt postmodern premises to be critical of the categorization of wide swatches of life into medical diagnoses or to adopt some relativist critique of medicals viewpoints and cultural power. Foucault wrote about medicalization in one of his earlier works, *Birth of the Clinic*: "The two dreams (i.e., nationalized medical profession and disappearance of disease) are isomorphic; the first expressing in a very positive way the strict, militant, dogmatic medicalization of society, by way of quasi-religious conversion and the establishment of a therapeutic clergy: the second expressing the same medicalization, but in a triumphant, negative way, that is to say, the volitization of disease in a corrected, organized, and ceaselessly supervised environment, in which medicine itself would finally disappear, together with its object and *raison d'être*" (1966:32).

The medicalization thesis, as it is now constituted, focuses to some degree on both of these dimensions: it examines how medicine and the emerging engines of medicalization develop and apply medical categories, and to a lesser degree it focuses on how the populace has internalized medical and therapeutic perspectives as a taken-for-granted subjectivity (cf. Furedi, 2006). Indeed, most medicalization analysts contend that increasing parts of life have become medicalized and that medical or quasi-medical remedies are often explicitly sought for an expanding range of human difficulties. To put it crudely, medicalization of all sorts of life problems is now a common part of our professional, consumer, and market culture.

REFERENCES

Appleton, Lynn M. 1995. "Rethinking Medicalization: Alcoholism and Anomalies." Pp. 59–80 in Joel Best (ed.), *Images of Issues*, 2nd ed. New York: Aldine de Gruyter.

Armstrong, David. 1995. "The Rise of Surveillance Medicine." *Sociology of Health and Illness* 17: 393–404.

Ballard, Karen, and Mary Ann Elston. 2005. "Medicalization: A Multi-Dimensional Concept." *Social Theory and Health* 3: 228–41.

Barsky, Arthur J., and Jonathan F. Boros. 1995. "Somatization and Medicalization in the Era of Managed Care." *Journal of the American Medical Association* 274: 1931–34.

Bartholomew, Robert E. 2000. *Exotic Deviance: Medicalizing Cultural Idioms from Strangeness to Illness*. Boulder: University Press of Colorado.

Bond, John. 1992. "The Medicalization of Dementia." *Journal of Aging Studies* 6: 397–403.

Broom, Dorothy H., and Roslyn V. Woodward. 1996. "Medicalization Reconsidered: Toward a Collaborative Approach to Care." *Sociology of Health and Illness* 19: 357–78.

Clarke, Adele E., Janey K. Shim, Laura Mamo, et al. 2003. "Biomedicalization: Technoscientific Transformations of Health Illness, and U.S. Biomedicine." *American Sociological Review* 68: 161–94.

Conrad, Peter. 1992. "Medicalization and Social Control." *Annual Review of Sociology* 18: 209–32.

Conrad, Peter, and Joseph W. Schneider. 1992. *Deviance and Medicalization: From Badness to Sickness.* Expanded ed. Philadelphia: Temple University Press.

Engelhardt, H. Tristan. 1974. "The Disease of Masturbation: Values and the Concept of Disease." *Bulletin of the History of Medicine* 48: 234–48.

Foucault, Michel. 1966. *Birth of the Clinic.* New York: Vintage.

Fox, Patrick. 1989. "From Senility to Alzheimer's Disease: The Rise of the Alzheimer's Movement." *Milbank Quarterly* 67: 58–101.

Furedi, Frank. 2006. "The End of Professional Dominance." *Society* 43 (6): 14–18.

Illich, Ivan. 1976. *Medical Nemesis.* New York: Pantheon.

Kaiser Family Foundation. 2005. "Non-Federal Physicians per 100,000 Civilian Population, 1970–2003" (Exhibit 5–7). *Trends and Indicators in the Changing Health Care Marketplace.* www.kff.org/insurance/7031/ti20045-7.cfm.

Lock, Margaret. 2001. "Medicalization: Cultural Concerns." Pp. 9534–39 in Neil J. Smelser and Paul B. Baltes (eds.), *International Encyclopedia of the Social and Behavioral Sciences.* New York: Elsevier.

Lupton, Deborah. 1997. "Foucault and the Medicalization Critique." Pp. 94–112 in Alan Peterson and Robin Bunton (eds.), *Foucault: Health and Medicine.* London: Routledge.

Oliver, Mike. 1996. *Understanding Disability: From Theory to Practice.* Basingstoke: Macmillan.

Pitts, Jesse. 1968. "Social Control: The Concept," *International Encyclopedia of Social Sciences* 14. New York: Macmillan.

Williams, Simon J. 2001. "Sociological Imperialism and the Profession of Medicine Revisited: Where Are We Now?" *Sociology of Health and Illness* 23 (2):135–58.

Zola, Irving Kenneth. 1972. "Medicine as an Institution of Social Control." Pp. 404–14 in Peter Conrad (ed.), *The Sociology of Health and Illness: Critical Perspectives*, 6th ed. New York: Worth.

42. Does Inequality Cause Poor Health Outcomes?*

Richard Wilkinson and Kate Pickett

The last nine chapters have shown, among the rich developed countries and among the fifty states of the United States, that most of the important health and social problems of the rich world are more common in more unequal societies. In both settings the relationships are too strong to be dismissed as chance findings. The importance of these relationships can scarcely be overestimated. First, the differences between more and less equal societies are large – problems are anything from three times to ten times as common in the more unequal societies. Second, these differences are not differences between high- and low-risk groups within populations which might apply only to a small proportion of the population, or just to the poor. Rather, they are differences between the prevalence of different problems which apply to whole populations.

Dysfunctional Societies

One of the points which emerge from Chapters 4–12 is a tendency for some countries to do well on just about everything and others to do badly. You can predict a country's performance on one outcome from a knowledge of others. If – for instance – a country does badly on health, you can predict with some confidence that it will also imprison a larger proportion of its population,

have more teenage pregnancies, lower literacy scores, more obesity, worse mental health, and so on. Inequality seems to make countries socially dysfunctional across a wide range of outcomes.

Internationally, at the healthy end of the distribution we always seem to find the Scandinavian countries and Japan. At the opposite end, suffering high rates of most of the health and social problems, are usually the USA, Portugal and the UK. The same is true among the fifty states of the USA. Among those that tend to perform well across the board are New Hampshire, Minnesota, North Dakota and Vermont, and among those which do least well are Mississippi, Louisiana and Alabama.

Figure 13.1 summarizes our findings. It is an exact copy of Figure 2.2. It shows again the relationship between inequality and our combined Index of Health and Social Problems. This graph also shows that the relationship is not dependent on any particular group of countries – for instance those at either end of the distribution. Instead it is robust across the range of inequality found in the developed market democracies. Even though we sometimes find less strong relationships among our analyses of the fifty US states, in the international analyses the USA as a whole is just where its inequality would lead us to expect.

Though some countries' figures are presumably more accurate than others, it is clearly important that we do not cherry-pick the data. That is why we have used the same set of inequality data, published by the United Nations, throughout. In the analyses of the American states we have used

* From Wilkinson, R. and Pickett, K. (2010) *The Spirit Level: Why Equality is Better for Everyone* (London: Penguin). Extracts from pp. 173–175, 177–180, 181–182, 195.

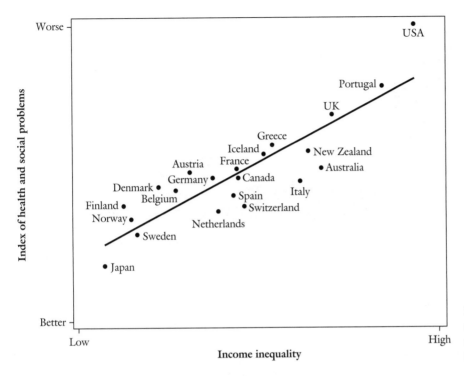

Figure 13.1 Health and social problems are more common in more unequal countries.

the US census data as published. However, even if someone had a strong objection to the figures for one or other society, it would clearly not change the overall picture presented in Figure 13.1. The same applies to the figures we use for all the health and social problems. Each set is as provided at source – we take them as published with no ifs or buts.

The only social problem we have encountered which tends to be more common in more equal countries (but not significantly among more equal states in the USA) is, perhaps surprisingly, suicide. The reasons for this are twofold. First, in some countries suicide is not more common lower down the social scale. In Britain a well-defined social gradient has only emerged in recent decades. Second, suicide is often inversely related to homicide. There seems to be something in the psychological cliché that anger sometimes goes in and sometimes goes out: do you blame yourself or others for things that go wrong? In Chapter 3 we noted the rise in the tendency to blame the outside world – defensive narcissism – and the contrasts between the US and Japan. It is notable

that in a paper on health in Harlem in New York, suicide was the only cause of death which was less common there than in the rest of the USA.[1]

[. . .]

Comparisons of health in different groups of the population in more and less equal societies show that the benefits of greater equality are very widespread. Most recently, a study in the *Journal of the American Medical Association* compared health among middle-aged men in the USA and England (not the whole UK).[2] To increase comparability the study was confined to the non-Hispanic white populations in both countries. People were divided into both income and educational categories. In Figure 13.2 rates of diabetes, hypertension, cancer, lung disease and heart disease are shown in each of three educational categories – high, medium and low. The American rates are the darker bars in the background and those for England are the lighter ones in front. There is a consistent tendency for rates of these conditions to be higher in the US

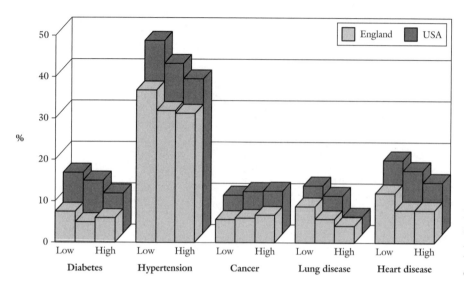

Figure 13.2 Rates of illness are lower at both low and high educational levels in England compared to the USA.[2]

than in England, not just among the less well-educated, but across all educational levels. The same was also true of death rates and various biological markers such as blood pressure, cholesterol and stress measures.

Though this is only just apparent, the authors of the study say that the social class differences in health tend to be steeper in the USA than in England regardless of whether people are classified by income or education.[3]

In that comparison, England was the more equal and the healthier of the two countries.

But there have also been similar comparisons of death rates in Sweden with those in England and Wales. To allow accurate comparisons, Swedish researchers classified a large number of Swedish deaths according to the British occupational class classification. The classification runs from unskilled manual occupations in class V at the bottom, to professional occupations in class I at the top. Figure 13.3 shows the differences they found in death rates for working-age men.[4] Sweden, as the more equal of the two countries, had lower death rates in all occupational classes;

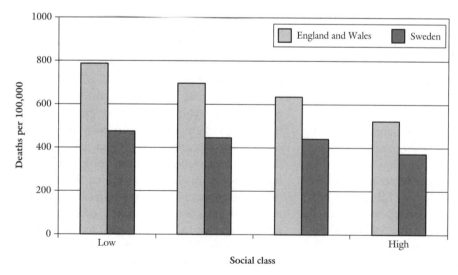

Figure 13.3 Death rates among working-age men are lower in all occupational classes in Sweden compared to England and Wales.[4]

so much so that their highest death rates – in the lowest classes – are lower than the highest class in England and Wales.

Another similar study compared infant mortality rates in Sweden with England and Wales.[5] Infant deaths were classified by father's occupation and occupations were again coded the same way in each country. The results are shown in Figure 13.4. Deaths of babies born to single parents, which cannot be coded by father's occupation, are shown separately. Once again, the Swedish death rates are lower right across the society. (Note that as both these studies were published some time ago, the actual death rates they show are considerably higher than the current ones.)

Comparisons have also been made between the more and less equal of the fifty states of the USA. Here too the benefits of smaller income differences in the more equal states seem to spread across all income groups. One study concluded that 'income inequality exerts a comparable effect across all population subgroups', whether people are classified by education, race or income – so much so that the authors suggested that inequality acted like a pollutant spread throughout society.[6] In a study of our own, we looked at the relationship between median county income and death rates in all counties of the USA. We compared the relationship between county median income and county death rates according to whether the counties were in the twenty-five more equal states or the twenty-five less equal states. As Figure 13.5 shows, in both the more and less equal states, poorer counties tended – as expected – to have higher death rates. However at all levels of income, death rates were lower in the twenty-five more equal states than in the twenty-five less equal states. Comparing counties at each level of income showed that the benefits of greater equality were largest in the poorer counties, but still existed even in the richest counties. In its essentials the picture is much like that shown in Figures 13.3 and 13.4 comparing Sweden with England and Wales. Just as among US counties, where the benefits of greater state equality extended to all income groups, so the benefits of Sweden's greater equality extended across all classes, but were biggest in the lowest classes.

Figure 8.4 in Chapter 8, which compared young people's literacy scores across different countries according to their parents' level of education (and so indirectly according to the social status of their family of upbringing) also showed that the benefits of greater equality extend throughout society. In more equal Finland and Belgium the benefits of greater equality were, once again, bigger at the bottom of the social ladder than in less equal UK

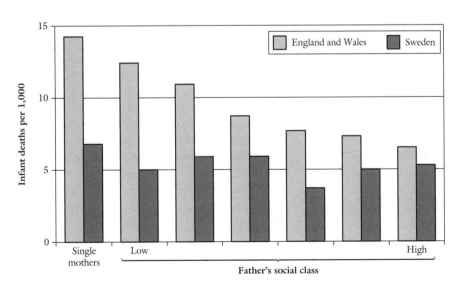

Figure 13.4 Infant mortality rates are lower in all occupational classes in Sweden than in England and Wales.[7]

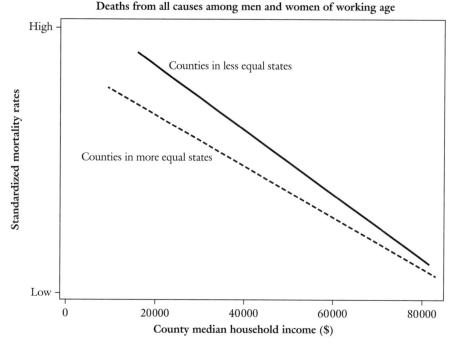

Figure 13.5 The relation between country median income and county death rates according to whether the counties are in the twenty-five more equal states or the twenty-five less equal states.

and USA. But even the children of parents with the very highest levels of education did better in Finland and Belgium than they did in the more unequal UK or USA.

[...]

As the research findings have come in over the years, the widespread nature of the benefits of greater equality seemed at first so paradoxical that they called everything into question. Several attempts by international collaborative groups to compare health inequalities in different countries suggested that health inequalities did not differ very much from one country to another. This seemed inconsistent with the evidence that health was better in more equal societies. How could greater equality improve health unless it did so by narrowing the health differences between rich and poor? At the time this seemed a major stumbling block. Now, however, we can see how the two sets of findings are consistent, Smaller income differences improve health for everyone, but make a bigger difference to the health of

the poor than the rich. If smaller income differences lead to roughly the same percentage reduction in death rates across the whole society then, when measured in relative terms, the differences in death rates between rich and poor will remain unchanged. Suppose death rates arc 60 per 100,000 people in the bottom class and only 20 per 100,000 in the top one. If you then knock 50 per cent off death rates in all groups, you will have reduced the death rate by 30 in the bottom group and by 10 at the top. But although the poor have had much the biggest absolute decline in death rates, there is still a threefold relative class difference in death rates. Whatever the percentage reduction in death rates, as long as it applies right across society, it will make most difference to the poor but still leave relative measures of the difference unchanged.

We can now see that the studies which once looked paradoxical were in fact telling us something important about the effects of greater equality. By suggesting that more and less equal societies contained similar relative health differentials within them, they were telling us that everyone receives roughly proportional benefits from greater equality. There are now several studies of this issue using data for US states,[8, 6, 7] and at least five international ones, which provide consistent evidence that, rather than being confined to the poor, the benefits of greater equality are widely spread.[1, 2, 4, 5, 8]

[...]

[...] A successful theory is one which predicts the existence of previously unknown phenomena or relationships which can then be verified. The theory that more equal societies were healthier arose from one set of international data. There have now been a very large number of tests (about 200) of that theory in different settings. With the exception of studies which looked at inequality in small local areas, an overwhelming majority of these tests confirmed the theory. Second, if the link is causal it implies that there must be a mechanism. The search for a mechanism led to the discovery that social relationships (as measured by social cohesion, trust, involvement in community life and low levels of violence) are better in more equal societies. This happened at a time when the importance of social relationships to health was beginning to be more widely recognized. Third, the theory that poor health might be one of a range of problems with social gradients related to inequality has been tested (initially on cause-specific death rates as described earlier in this chapter) and has since been amply confirmed in two different settings as we have described in Chapters 4–12. Fourth, at a time when there was no reason to think that inequality had psychosocial effects, the relation between health and equality seemed to imply that inequality must be affecting health through psychosocial processes related to social differentiation. That inequality does have powerful psychosocial effects is now confirmed by its links (shown in earlier chapters) with the quality of social relations and numerous behavioural outcomes.

It is very difficult to see how the enormous variations which exist from one society to another in the level of problems associated with low social status can be explained without accepting that inequality is the common denominator, and a hugely damaging force.

NOTES

1. C. McCord and H. P. Freeman, 'Excess mortality in Harlem', *New England Journal of Medicine* (1990) 322 (3): 173–7.
2. J. Banks, M. Marmot, Z. Oldfield and J. P. Smith, 'Disease and disadvantage in the United States and in England', *Journal of the American Medical Association* (2006) 295 (17): 2037–45.
3. J. Banks, M. Marmot, Z. Oldfield and J. P. Smith, 'The SES Health Gradient on Both Sides of the Atlantic'. NBER Working Paper 12674. Cambridge, MA: National Bureau of Economic Research, 2007.
4. D. Vagero and O. Lundberg, 'Health inequalities in Britain and Sweden', *Lancet* (1989) 2 (8653): 35–6.
5. D. A. Leon, D. Vagero and P. O. Olausson, 'Social class differences in infant mortality in Sweden: comparison with England and Wales', *British Medical Journal* (1992) 305 (6855): 687–91.
6. S. V. Subramanian and I. Kawachi, 'Whose health is affected by income inequality? A multilevel interaction analysis of contemporaneous and lagged effects of state income inequality on individual self-rated health in the United States', *Health and Place* (2006) 12 (2): 141–56.
7. M. Wolfson, G. Kaplan, J. Lynch, N. Ross and E. Backlund, 'Relation between income inequality and mortality: empirical demonstration', *British Medical Journal* (1999) 319 (7215): 953–5.
8. S. J. Babones, 'Income inequality and population health; correlation and causality', *Social Science and Medicine* (2008) 66 (7): 1614–26.

43. Challenging the Dominance of Biomedicine*

Sarah Nettleton

The development of the sociology of health and illness has to be understood in terms of its relation to the dominant paradigm of Western medicine: *biomedicine*. Many of the central concerns of the sociology of health and illness have emerged as reactions to, and critiques of, this paradigm. [. . .]

Medicine and the Biomedical Model

Modern Western medicine rests upon what has become known as the biomedical model. This model is based on six assumptions. First, that the mind and the body can be treated separately; this is referred to as medicine's *mind/body dualism*. Second, that the body can be repaired like a machine; thus, medicine adopts a *mechanical metaphor*, presuming that doctors can act like engineers to mend that which is dysfunctional. Third, and consequently, the merits of technological interventions are sometimes overplayed, which results in medicine adopting a *technological imperative*. Fourth, biomedicine is *reductionist*, in that explanations of disease focus on biological changes to the relative neglect of social psychological and political factors. Fifth, such reductionism was accentuated by the development of the 'germ theory' of disease in the nineteenth century, which assumed that every disease is caused by a specific, identifiable agent – namely a 'disease entity' (such as a parasite, virus or bacterium). This is referred to as the *doctrine of specific aetiology*. Finally, this biomedical approach was *universalized*. Originally developed in the global metropole (Connell, 2007), it was imposed throughout the world as the legitimate way of approaching the treatment of disease, the management of illness and the education of doctors. The assumption that biomedicine is objective and universal was bound up in the colonial projects whereby populations were exploited by clinical researchers in the name of science (Anderson, 2014; Good et al., 2008).

The biomedical model, which has dominated formal medical care in the global North since the end of the eighteenth century, is neatly summed up by Paul Atkinson (1988: 180) in the following way:

> It is reductionist in form, seeking explanations of dysfunction in invariant biological structures and processes; it privileges such explanations at the expense of social, cultural and biographical explanations. In its clinical mode, this dominant model of medical reasoning implies: that diseases exist as distinct entities; that those entities are revealed through the inspection of 'signs' and 'symptoms'; that the individual patient is a more or less passive site of disease manifestation; that diseases are to be understood as categorical departures or deviations from 'normality'.

[. . .]

During the decades leading up to the start of the new millennium, the institution of medicine and the biomedical model were challenged

* From Nettleton, S. (2021) *The Sociology of Health and Illness* (4th edn, Cambridge: Polity). Extracts from pp. 2–4, 5–7.

by critiques emerging from both popular and academic sources. These criticisms have been intensified within the context of the escalating costs of health care. Medicine is not a homogeneous institution, and criticisms of the biomedical model and medical practice are voiced within medicine as well as outside it. Striking at the heart of biomedicine is the challenge to its effectiveness. It has been argued, from within both medicine (Engel, 1981) and sociology, that medicine's *efficacy* has been overplayed. Thomas McKeown (1976), a professor of social medicine, for example, demonstrated by way of historical demographic studies that the decline in mortality that has occurred within Western societies has had more to do with nutrition, hygiene and patterns of reproduction (essentially social phenomena) than it has to do with vaccinations, treatments or other modes of medical interventions (see Chapter 9). Drawing on this type of evidence, authors have pointed to the fact that pouring resources into medical technologies has resulted in diminishing returns (Powles, 1973). Taking this further, Ivan Illich (1976) has argued that biomedicine does more harm than good. Rather than curing and healing, medicine actually contributes to illness through the iatrogenic effects of its interventions, such as the side-effects of drugs and the sometimes negative clinical consequences of surgery. This is evident in the history of mental health services, where pharmacological and surgical interventions, as well as other treatments such as lobotomies and electro convulsive therapy (ECT), which to our eyes might seem barbaric, were presented as innovative and progressive during the 1950s through to the late 1980s. Joanna Moncrieff is one of a number of critical psychiatrists who detail the political expediency of the adoption of drugs that have, or are presented as having, specific solutions to common illnesses such as depression. Writing on the history of the 'antidepressant', Moncrieff (2008: 2346) argues that when, for instance, the drug imipramine was proposed as being effective in depression, 'it was presented solely as acting in a disease specific way and it was soon referred to as an "antidepressant"', and its widespread use was established 'before any evidence was available to support this view'. And indeed, the jury is still out concerning the harms and benefits of antidepressants (Moncrieff, 2018). The forces that drove the widespread use of antidepressant drugs included psychiatry's ambition to be better integrated into mainstream medicine, and be recognized as treating rather than just managing disease. This ambition, alongside the shift of psychiatric care from the asylum to the community, helped to create a wider market for medications for mental health problems (see Chapter 5).

Antibiotic resistance is a further contemporary example of iatrogenic medicine (Podolsky, 2015; Will, 2018). Seen as a wonder drug in the 1940s – a 'magic bullet' that contributed to the control of infectious diseases and made surgery safer – today the overuse of antibiotics has led to an increase in antibiotic-resistant organisms. Despite a growing consensus that there is an urgent need to reduce use of antibiotics, their global human consumption increased by a third between 2000 and 2010 (Van Boeckel et al., 2014). Antimicrobial resistance is now at the centre of a political storm, tapping into and amplifying anxieties that map on to debates relating to responsibility, culpability and blame of patients, practitioners and pharmaceutical companies, all of whom are variously fingered as contributing to overuse or compliancy (Brown and Nettleton, 2017). As Charlotte Humphrey (2000: 355) puts it: 'Looked at through Illich's eyes, resistance can be seen as the Aesclepian thunderbolt – the inevitable dark side of the miraculous treatment, hastened in its release by the medical profession's use of the antibiotic miracle.'

[. . .]

A second criticism of biomedicine is that it fails to locate the body within its socioenvironmental context. In fact, an alternative to the biomedical model is often referred to as the 'socio-environmental model' of medicine (Engel, 1981). Focusing on the biological changes within the body, biomedicine has underestimated the links between people's material circumstances and illness. The privileging of the biological over the social is evident in our contemporary preoccupation with genetic influences on health and illness. Genetic explanations, for example, are popular and compelling. Peter Conrad (2002) draws on René Dubos's (1959) influential book, *Mirage of Health*, to suggest that, like the germ theory of disease, which was privileged in the nineteenth century, contemporary genetic theories rest on the assumptions of the doctrine of specific aetiology, a focus on the internal rather than the external environment, and the metaphor of the body as a machine. As such, 'the public depiction of the new genetics aligns perfectly with the old germ theory model' (Conrad, 2002: 78). He reminds us of the dangers inherent in presuming that the causes and treatment of disease reside within the body of the individual. Patterns of mortality and morbidity, or a person's 'life chances', are related to social structures, and vary according to gender, social class, 'race' and age; the biomedical model fails to account for the *social inequalities in health* (see Chapter 9).

Medicine has also been taken to task for the way in which it treats patients as passive objects rather than 'whole' persons. Critiques of biomedicine have argued that it is essential to recognize that lay people have their own valid interpretations and accounts of their experiences of health and illness. For example, medical practitioner and editor of the prestigious medical journal *The Lancet*, Richard Horton, presents a powerful argument in his book *Second Opinion* (2003), which calls on medicine to place the concept of 'human dignity' at its core. For treatment and care to be effective, Horton argues, health practitioners need to be sensitive to the perceptions, feelings and concerns of their patients. The sociology of health and illness argues that sociocultural factors influence people's perceptions and experiences of health and illness, which cannot be presumed to be simply reactions to physical bodily changes (see Chapters 4 and 5).

Perhaps the most powerful criticism in this respect has come from women, especially from the women's health movement in reaction to medicine's approach to childbirth. The institution of medicine took control of childbirth out of the hands of women in the nineteenth century (Oakley, 1976; Donnison, 1977; Kent, 2000) and managed to ensure, despite the lack of any sound evidence of benefit (Tew, 1990), that by the 1970s virtually all babies were born in hospital. Thus, what is fundamentally a woman's experience was removed from the domestic domain to the public one of the hospital, wherein a male-dominated branch of medicine – obstetrics – had control. Moreover, what is perhaps more remarkable is the way in which pregnancy and childbirth came to be treated as 'illness' and were therefore subjected to a whole array of technological interventions. In this respect, the experience of having a baby was *medicalized*; that is, a normal life event came to be treated as a medical problem that required medical regulation and supervision (see Chapter 6). Medical discourse has contributed to the construction of women's bodies as fragile, passive vessels that routinely require medical monitoring and interventions (Martin, 1989). Health literature by women and for women (Boston Women's Health Book Collective, 2011) and medical care based on alternative philosophies to those espoused by the dominant institutions of medicine (Annandale, 2009) were established.

A fifth challenge to biomedicine is the assumption that, through its scientific method, it identifies the truth about disease. By contrast, sociologists have suggested that disease and the body, medicine's prime objects of study, are *socially constructed* (see Chapter 2). It is argued, therefore, that disease categories are not accurate descriptions of anatomical malfunctions, but are socially created; that is, they are created as a result of reasonings that are socially imbued. Medical belief systems are contingent upon the society which produces them. Furthermore, there is a correspondence between modes of organization, technological forms and medical knowledge. It is evident that technology and practices co-construct knowledge of the body (Jewson, 1976; see also Chapter 7). Indeed, the apparent 'facticity' of medicine means that values may be transformed into apparent facts (White, 2009). This gives rise to hierarchies of 'normal' and 'pathological' bodies, 'fit' and 'abject' bodies. For example, the belief in the nineteenth century that women's bodies were medically unsuited to education was supported by anatomical 'evidence' (Laqueur, 1990).

A corollary to challenging biomedicine's scientific basis is to question its presumed superiority in relation to other forms of healing. Medicine has questioned the basis of healing that does not match its own paradigm, positioning it as 'alternative' or 'complementary' medicine. Diverse and established forms of healing are castigated as 'unscientific' (BMA, 1992). However, another view, which suggests that all knowledge is contingent, would imply that alternative medicines are of equal validity and that many people are successfully treated by alternative practitioners (BMA, 1993; Cooper et al., 2013; see also Chapter 10).

The further challenge is the claim that the boundaries of the medical profession are best viewed as the outcome of sociopolitical struggles rather than being based on the demarcations of scientific knowledge, as the traditional progressive Whig histories imply. That is, what counts as legitimate medical knowledge and practice is decided through social processes rather than being shaped by natural objects of which the profession has an accurate knowledge. Similarly, the division of labour between health professions is socially negotiated and is mediated by gender, 'race' and class (see Chapter 10). It is these sociopolitical processes, mediated by social structures, that have permitted the continuation of *professional medical dominance*. In turn, this medical dominance has contributed to the perpetuation of capitalist, colonial and patriarchal structures, and led to the eclipse of healing activities which take place beyond the boundaries of formal health care.

As sociologists, we must be critical but not smug. Indeed, accusations of medical imperialism are reflected in sociological imperialism (Strong, 1979). Sociological concepts, like those in medicine, emerged in the global North – what Raewyn Connell (2007) calls the 'global metropole' – and were then applied to the global periphery. 'The biomedical sciences and the social sciences, as we know them today, were constructed in the global metropole, the group of rich capitalist countries of western Europe and north America, formerly the centres of overseas empires and now the "core" of the global economy' (Connell, 2011: 1371).

Social movements and voices in the global South, in concert with a growing body of scholars in the global North, are effectively challenging the epistemological, theoretical and methodological frameworks that comprise the metropole sociological canon. Reworking orthodox sociological histories of 'modernity' and articulating 'epistemologies of the south' (Bhambra and Santos, 2017) encourages social scientists to critically reflect on their key concepts, categories and theories. These developments are relevant to a final significant challenge to conventional biomedicine, which can be found in postcolonial studies of medicine that examine the historical formation and perpetuation of scientific categories in the context of colonial relations. Frantz Fanon's classic work on medicine and colonialism, *A Dying Colonialism*, describes how the French medical service in Algeria was inextricably entangled with the French colonial system (1965: 122–3) and how this played out in everyday power relations in the context of medical practice and health care, where Algerians distrusted the occupying medical workforce. Fanon's writings remain influential today and have been taken up by postcolonial scholars who reveal how biomedical practices were, and still are, both sustained and supported by colonial relations, institutional structures and violence (Good et al., 2008). Biomedicine describes what bodies are, what bodies are capable of, how bodies should be managed and treated. If biomedicine is assumed to be objective, neutral and universal, then we can see that it is politically potent. Medical sociologists have tended to be provincial and ethnocentric in their approaches. Nevertheless, the canon of this field of study attempts to upset categories and epistemologies, decipher the social construction of knowledge, explore relations of power and analyse embodied social movements, and there is therefore much in common with postcolonial approaches. This means there is ample scope and a pressing need for further research into health and illness from these perspectives (Seth, 2017), not least because they encourage us to ask onto-logical questions relating to categorizations and classifications of health, disease, illness, disability and the body.

REFERENCES

Anderson, W. (2014). 'Making Global Health History: The Postcolonial Worldliness of Biomedicine', *Social History of Medicine*, 27(2), 372–384.

Annandale, E. (2009). *Women's Health and Social Change*. Abingdon: Taylor & Francis.

Atkinson, P. (1988). 'Discourse, Descriptions and Diagnoses: Reproducing Normal Medicine', in M. Lock and D. Gordon (eds), *Biomedicine Examined*. London: Kluwer Academic Publishers.

Bhambra, G. K. and Santos, B. D. S. (2017). 'Introduction: Global Challenges for Sociology', *Sociology*, 51(1), 3–10.

BMA (1992). 'Report on an Alternative Medicine', in M. Saks (ed.), *Alternative Medicine in Britain*. Oxford: Clarendon Press. (Partially reproduced version of BMA, *Alternative Therapy*. London: British Medical Association, 1986.)

BMA (1993). *Complementary Medicine: New Approaches to Good Practice*. London: British Medical Association.

Boston Women's Health Book Collective (2011 [1970]). *Our Bodies, Ourselves, for the New Century*. Boston, MA: Simon and Schuster Inc.

Brown, N. and Nettleton, S. (2017). 'There Is Worse to Come': The Biopolitics of Traumatism in Antimicrobial Resistance (AMR)', *Sociological Review*, 65(3), 493–508.

Connell, R. (2007). *Southern Theory: The Global Dynamics of Knowledge in Social Science*. London: Allen & Unwin.

Connell, R. (2011). 'Southern Bodies and Disability: Re-thinking Concepts', *Third World Quarterly*, 32(8), 1369–1381.

Conrad, P. (2002). 'A Mirage of Genes', in S. Nettleton and U. Gustafsson (eds), *The Sociology of Health and Illness Reader*. Cambridge: Polity.

Cooper, K. L., Harris, P. E., Relton, C. and Thomas, K. J. (2013). 'Prevalence of Visits to Five Types of Complementary and Alternative Medicine Practitioners by the General Population: A Systematic Review', *Complementary Therapies in Clinical Practice*, 19(4), 214–220.

Donnison, J. (1977). *Midwives and Medical Men: A History of Inter-Professional Rivalries and Women's Rights*. London: Heinemann.

Dubos, R. (1959). *Mirage of Health*. New York: Harper & Row.

Engel, G. L. (1981). 'The Need for a New Medical Model: A Challenge to Bio-medicine', in A. L. Kaplan, H. T. Engelhardt and J. J. McCartney (eds), *Concepts of Health and Disease: Interdisciplinary Perspectives*. London: Addison-Wesley.

Fanon, F. (1965) *A Dying Colonialism*. New York: Grove Press.

Good, M.-J. D., Hyde, S. T., Pinto, S. and Good, B. J. (2008). *Postcolonial Disorders*. Berkeley: University of California Press.

Horton, R. (2003). *Second Opinion: Doctors, Diseases and Decisions in Modern Medicine*. London: Granta Books.

Humphrey, C. (2000). 'Antibiotic Resistance: An Exemplary Case of Medical Nemesis', *Critical Public Health*, 10(3), 353–358.

Illich, I. (1976). *Limits to Medicine*. London: Marion Boyars.

Jewson, N. (1976). 'The Disappearance of the

Sick Man from Medical Cosmology 1770–1870', *Sociology*, 10, 225–44.

Kent, J. (2000). *Social Perspectives on Pregnancy and Childbirth for Midwives, Nurses and the Caring Professions*. Buckingham: Open University Press.

Laqueur, T. (1990). *Making Sex: Body and Gender from the Greeks to Freud*. Cambridge, MA: Harvard University Press.

Martin, E. (1989). *The Woman in the Body: A Cultural Analysis of Reproduction*. Milton Keynes: Open University Press.

McKeown, T. (1976). *The Role of Medicine: Dream, Mirage, or Nemesis?*. London: Nuffield Provincial Hospitals Trust.

Moncrieff, J. (2008). 'The Creation of the Concept of an Antidepressant: An Historical Analysis', *Social Science & Medicine*, 66(11), 2346–2355.

Moncrieff, J. (2018). 'What Does the Latest Meta-Analysis Really Tell Us about Antidepressants?', *Epidemiology and Psychiatric Sciences*, 27(5), 430–432.

Oakley, A. (1976). 'Wisewoman and Medicine Man: Changes in the Management of Childbirth', in J. Mitchell and A. Oakley (eds), *The Rights and Wrongs of Women*. Harmondsworth: Penguin.

Podolsky, S. H. (2015). *The Antibiotic Era: Reform, Resistance, and the Pursuit of a Rational Therapeutics*. Baltimore, MD: Johns Hopkins University Press.

Powles, J. (1973). 'On the Limitations of Modern Medicine', *Science, Medicine and Man*, 1, 1–30.

Seth, S. (2017). 'Colonial History and Postcolonial Science Studies', *Radical History Review*, 127, 63–85.

Strong, P. M. (1979). Sociological Imperialism and the Profession of Medicine: A Critical Examination of the Thesis of Medical Imperialism', *Social Science & Medicine*, 13, 199–215.

Tew, M. (1990). *Safer Childbirth: A Critical History of Maternity Care*. London: Chapman Hall.

Van Boeckel, T. P, Gandra, S., Ashok, A., Caudron, Q., Grenfell, B. T. . . . Laxminarayan, R. (2014). 'Global Antibiotic Consumption 2000 to 2010: An Analysis of National Pharmaceutical Sales Data', *Lancet Infectious Diseases*, 14(8), 742–750.

White, K. (2009). *An Introduction to the Sociology of Health and Illness*, 2nd edn. London: Sage.

Will, C. M. (2018). 'Beyond Behavior? Institutions, Interactions and Inequalities in the Response to Antimicrobial Resistance', *Sociology of Health & Illness*, 40(3), e1–e9.

44. Health and Illness in Sociological Perspective*

William C. Cockerham

Ask people if they think society can make them sick, and the probabilities are high they will answer in the affirmative. Stress, poverty, low socioeconomic status, unhealthy lifestyles, and unpleasant living and work conditions are among the many inherently social variables typically regarded by lay persons as causes of ill health. However, with the exception of stress, this view is not expressed in much of the research literature. Studies in public health, epidemiology, behavioral medicine, and other sciences in the health field typically minimize the relevance of social factors in their investigations. Usually social variables are characterized as distant or secondary influences on health and illness, not as direct causes (Link and Phelan 1995, 2000; Phelan and Link 2013). Being poor, for example, is held to produce greater exposure to something that will make a person sick, rather than bring on sickness itself. However, social variables have been found to be more powerful in inducing adversity or enrichment in health outcomes than formerly assumed. Society may indeed make you sick or, conversely, promote your health.

It is the intent of this book to assess the evidence indicating that this is so. It is clear that most diseases have social connections. That is, the social context can shape the risk of exposure, the susceptibility of the host, and the disease's course and outcome – regardless of whether the disease is infectious, genetic, metabolic,

malignant, or degenerative (Holtz et al. 2006). This includes major afflictions like heart disease, Type 2 diabetes, stroke, cancers like lung and cervical neoplasms, HIV/AIDS and other sexually-transmitted infections, pulmonary diseases, kidney disease, and many other ailments. Even rheumatoid arthritis, which might at first consideration seem to be exclusively physiological, is grounded in socioeconomic status, with lower-status persons having a significantly greater risk of becoming arthritic than individuals higher up the social scale (Bengtsson et al. 2005; Pederson et al. 2006). Consequently, the basic thesis of this book is that social factors do more than influence health for large populations and the lived experience of illness for individuals; rather, such factors have a direct causal effect on physical health and illness.

How can this be? Just because most diseases have a social connection of some type does not necessarily mean that such links can actually cause a disease to occur – or does it? Social factors such as living conditions, lifestyles, stressors, norms, social values, and attitudes are obviously not pathogens like germs or viruses, nor are they cancer cells or coagulated clots of blood that clog arteries. Yet, quarantined in a laboratory, viruses, cancers, and the like do not make a person sick. They need to be exposed to a human host and assault the body's physiological defenses in order to be causal. However, assigning causation solely to biological entities does not account for all of the relevant factors in a disease's pathogenesis, especially in relation to the social behaviors and conditions that bind the person to the disease in

---

* From Cockerham, W. (2021) *Social Causes of Health and Disease* (2nd edn, Cambridge: Polity). Extracts from pp. 1–5, 211–212, 213.

the first place. Social factors can initiate the onset of the pathology and, in this way, serve as a direct cause for several diseases. Two of many examples are the coronavirus and smoking tobacco.

Coronavirus

Coronavirus (COVID-19) unleashed itself on the world in the fall of 2019 in Wuhan, China, a city of 11 million. It subsequently spread across the globe as the most widely contagious pandemic yet to come since the Spanish flu of 1918. By the summer of 2020, over 10 million people were confirmed to have been infected, more than 500,000 were thought to have died, and trade and travel were severely disrupted on a global basis. Final tallies on the disease's deadly and varied effects are not available as the pandemic is ongoing as this book goes to press. However, it was nevertheless clear at the time that COVID-19 ranks as an event of historic proportions. Nearly every country in the world was affected, air travel and cruise ships were shut down, public gatherings cancelled, businesses and schools closed, stay-at-home orders issued, unemployment soared, and the 2020 Olympics postponed for a year.

Does the "social" have a causation role with respect to COVID-19? The answer is clearly yes," as seen in the stringent requirement for "social distancing" (keeping away from other people) and the likely causal trail. Early information indicated that the coronavirus originated in bats in China that likely infected an anteater-like creature known as a pangolin. The evidence comes from testing the genome sequence of the coronavirus in bats and pangolins, which was found to be almost identical with the virus's genome in infected humans (Andersen et al. 2020; Zhou et al. 2020). If the coronavirus had stayed isolated among bats and pangolins in the wild, it would have remained a biological anomaly. But it didn't. As a result of urbanization, globalization, and climate change in recent decades, wildlife habitats have been affected and exposed

various species to greater contact with humans (Armelagos and Harper 2016; Cockerham and Cockerham 2010).

At the point pangolins became infected, the "social" began to take over as a cause of the pandemic. Pangolins are a desired food delicacy in China and sold in Wuhan's Huanan Seafood Wholesale Market where live wild animals can be purchased for human consumption. Just as the SARS (severe acute respiratory syndrome) pandemic of 2002–3 began in China's live wild animal "wet" markets, coronavirus apparently took a similar transmission path from bats through animals (pangolins instead of civets and raccoon dogs) to reach humans in a crowded marketplace. Lax health and safety regulations, combined with ineffective local government inspections in such markets, likely made transmission easier. Regardless of where it originated, a human became sick. The first case (the so-called patient "zero"?) was allegedly a 55-year-old Chinese man in Hubei Province where Wuhan is located. He was hospitalized in mid-November 2019 with a previously unknown pneumonia. By December 8, there were more patients.

No public alarm was sounded until December 30, 2019, when Dr. Li Wenliang, a 34-year-old ophthalmologist at Wuhan Central Hospital, began noticing some of his patients had a viral infection. He thought it was a reoccurrence of SARS and began alerting his colleagues through social media. The Wuhan police took Dr. Li into custody the first week of January 2020 for spreading a false rumor. They required him to sign a confession admitting his alleged deception before releasing him. A month later (February 7), he died from the coronavirus after catching it from a patient he was treating for glaucoma, becoming one of the real heroes of the pandemic.

A travel ban to and from Wuhan was issued on January 23, 2020, but by that time, infected Chinese had traveled to cities throughout the country and abroad. The Wuhan Municipal Health Commission informed the World Health Organization on January 31 of an epidemic caused by a new virus that was initially named the severe acute respiratory syndrome coronavirus 2 (SARS-CoV-2). WHO changed the name to COVID-19 on February 12. By mid-February, the coronavirus had erupted into a full-scale epidemic, centered in Wuhan, infecting some 90,000 people and killing at least 4,600 in China while dispersing worldwide through tourism, business travel, and community spread. The Chinese government took Draconian measures to restrict people inside their homes, close whole regions of the country to travel, and mobilize medical resources to test for the virus and treat it as best they could since no cure was available. By mid-March, the situation in China improved.

Yet other countries began having severe problems, especially Iran in the Middle East and Spain and Italy in Europe. The problem in Italy, as it was in China, was a late start in isolating affected areas and restricting movement. The first known patient, a 38-year-old man in the Lombardy region in northern Italy, had not been to China and was thought to have contracted the virus from another European. He refused hospitalization and went home before returning a second time, infecting several people at the hospital and others he visited, conducting an active social life and playing on a soccer team while contagious. The spread of the disease was so quick that in the next 24 hours some 36 additional patients were admitted to the hospital, none of whom had any direct contact with the first patient. Out of some 234,000 confirmed cases in Italy in late spring 2020, more than 34,000 died. Spain had even more cases, nearly 287,000, with fewer than 30,000 deaths. Britain later moved to the top in deaths in Europe and then Russia.

The United States, with its large number of international visitors and travelers, was impacted the most. Nearly 2.5 million people were confirmed as infected by late June with over 126,000 deaths. However, the number of cases changes daily as the pandemic is ongoing and are likely to be even higher by the time this book is published. The coronavirus first appeared on the West coast in the state of Washington, and soon after that, California. The hardest-hit state was New York, with more than 30 percent of all cases nationwide. COVID-19 apparently arrived there by way of a traveler from Europe. By late June, New York's more than 395,000 confirmed cases were greater than those of most countries except the US as a whole, Brazil, Russia, and India. Males were more likely to be infected than females and older people age 65 and above with pre-existing health problems such as obesity, hypertension, heart disease, diabetes, dementia, atrial fibrillation, and chronic obstructive pulmonary disease (COPD) were especially subject to infection and death. Nursing homes were major sites for infection, with about 20 percent of all deaths nationwide. Fortunately, children were the least affected. One reason Italy had such a high mortality rate was because of its large, disproportionately elderly population. The final story on the 2019–20 coronavirus pandemic has yet to be written at this time, but it serves as an example of the social causation of disease as "social distancing" and "stay at home" measures become the primary means of preventing infection, or conversely, acquiring it through close social proximity.

[. . .]

[. . .] Recognition of the causal properties of social variables in health matters has been slow in coming, but there is growing evidence that this is indeed the case. This development will require a paradigm shift away from methodological individualism to a more balanced conceptual approach that includes a renewed focus on structural effects. As discussed, methodological individualism refers to research centered on the individual's attitudes and behaviors, thereby making the individual the focal point of the researcher's attention. Variables beyond the level of individuals and small groups in determining health outcomes are thus ignored, even though people can find their health and longevity directly influenced – either positively or negatively – by social structures. A comprehensive understanding of health and disease is therefore impossible without considering the role of macro-level structures.

The Return of Structure

As Bryan Turner (2003) points out, one might argue that much of the influential research in medical sociology in the second half of the twentieth century, namely symbolic interaction and the vast volume of literature on stress, has been predominately social psychological. Turner finds that even Parsons, who attempted to develop a sociology of sickness with his concept of the sick role, produced an area of research that became typically psychological. Durkheim's theory of suicide is depicted as a self-consciously sociological theory as it locates the causes of suicide in social forces rather than the psychology of individuals. But, as we have seen, Durkheim did not become a strong influence in medical sociology and theories of causal structures in health matters have languished.

Acknowledgment of the causal role of social factors and conditions in sickness and mortality has been slowed not only because of the priority given to the individual in social science research, but also results from prior methodological difficulties in determining the direct effects of macro-level variables on the health of individuals. With the increasing use of multilevel forms of statistical analysis in medical sociology, like hierarchical linear modeling, random coefficient models, and mixed models, the way is open to simultaneously determine the effects of sequentially higher and multiple structures on health.

[. . .]

Overlooking the influence of social structures on people removes an ever present and vital variable from the analysis of their social behavior. Moreover, when the relative strengths of structure and agency are considered it is the case that the effects of structure cannot only outweigh agency, but render it relatively powerless (G. Williams 2003). People with jobs carrying high risks to their health, for example, may have little or no choice or option about exercising agency because they need the money the jobs pay.

Agency, in turn, does not seem to be capable of exerting a similar smothering effect on structure, although agency may at times be more important than structure in particular social scenarios than in others. For instance, an individual may decide to change physicians when the attending doctor is uncommunicative, brusque, or makes a mistake and this behavior may have little or nothing to do with structure. Everyday human social behavior incorporates the exercise of both agency and structure in its calculation and researchers need to do likewise. They also need to recognize that agency and structure are not equal in their influence on that behavior – as one or the other is likely to be dominant.

REFERENCES

Andersen, Kristian G., Andrew Rambaut, W. Ian Lipkin, Edward C. Holmes, and Robert L. Garry. 2020. "The Proximal Origin of SARS-CoV-2." *Nature Medicine* 26:450–55.

Armelagos. George J. and Kristen N. Harper. 2016. "Emerging Infectious Diseases, Urbanization, and Globalization in the Time of Global Warming." In *The New Blackwell Companion to Medical Sociology*, ed. William Cockerham, 290–311. Oxford, UK: Wiley-Blackwell.

Bengtsson, C., B. Nordmark, L. Klareskog, I. Lundberg, L. Alfredsson, and the EIRA Study Group. 2005. "Socioeconomic Status and the Risk of Developing Rheumatoid Arthritis: Results from the Swedish EIRA Study." *Annals of the Rheumatic Diseases* 64:1588–94.

Cockerham, Geoffrey B. and William C. Cockerham. 2010. *Health and Globalization.* Cambridge, UK: Polity.

Holtz, Timothy H., Seth Holmes, Scott Stonington, and Leon Eisenberg. 2006. "Health is Still Social: Contemporary Examples in the Age of Genome." *PLoS Medicine* 3:e419–25.

Link, Bruce G. and Jo Phelan. 1995. "Social Conditions as Fundamental Causes of Disease."

Journal of Health and Social Behavior (Extra Issue):80–94.

Link, Bruce G. and Jo Phelan. 2000. "Evaluating the Fundamental Cause Explanation for Social Disparities in Health." In *The Handbook of Medical Sociology*, 5th ed., ed. Chloe Bird, Peter Conrad, and Allen Fremont, 33–46. Upper Saddle River, NJ: Prentice Hall.

Pederson, M., S. Jackson, M. Klarlund, and M. Frisch. 2006. "Socioeconomic Status and Risk of Rheumatoid Arthritis." *Journal of Rheumatology* 33:1069–74.

Phelan, Jo C. and Bruce G. Link. 2013. "Fundamental Cause Theory." In *Medical Sociology on the Move: New Directions in Theory*, ed. William Cockerham, 105–26. Dordrecht: Springer.

Turner, Bryan S. 2003. "Social Capital, Inequality and Health: The Durkheimian Revival." *Social Theory & Health* 1:4–20.

Williams, Gareth. 2003. "The Determinants of Health: Structure, Context and Agency." *Sociology of Health & Illness* 25:131–54.

Zhou, Peng et al. 2020. "A Pneumonia Outbreak Associated with a New Coronavirus of Probable Bat Origin." *Nature* 579:270–3.

45. The Exceptional and the Normal after COVID-19*

Jens O. Zinn

As other corona viruses before, SARS-CoV-2 emerged from the ways how we live and work and used the opportunity to jump the boundary between animals and humans (NIH 2020). COVID-19 developed first unobserved, was quickly transferred and carried by human bodies to distant places and, when finally discovered, it had already developed into a major social threat not mainly due to its ability to kill but by challenging our way of living and the social institutions, which have been developed to protect and manage human health and well-being.

COVID-19 got a head start with China first silencing her concerned doctors. When recognising the ability of the coronavirus to spread quickly and to cause a severe illness, Chinese authorities responded with the relentless power of totalitarian regime, by isolating Wuhan, a major travel hub of more than 11 million population from China and the world. They also applied rigid mobility restrictions and enforced behavioural changes. Similarly, the World Health Organisation (WHO), as well as other national governments, when being informed about the discovery of a new coronavirus were initially slow to respond, allowing the virus to spread further and developing into a major force.

* From Zinn, J.O. (2020) '"A Monstrous Threat": How a State of Exception Turns Into a "New Normal"', *Journal of Risk Research*, 23(7–8): 1083–1091. Extracts from pp. 1084–1085, 1086–1088.

The media

During March 2020, with infection rates and deaths soaring, and the media reporting about an overloaded health care system, first in Italy and soon after in Spain, the originally Chinese virus had become a powerful global agent. The daily press briefings of the director general of the WHO, Tedros Adhanom Ghebreyesus and experts from national institutes responsible for disease control and prevention were given prime time in television news to promote the most recent data and advice on how to protect against the virus. Similarly online platforms such as the 'worldometer' provided regular updates on coronavirus infection rates and fatalities worldwide.[1]

The media complemented data with pictures of desperate nurses and doctors being overwhelmed by the number of patients, the lack of protective gear, the traumatised relatives just having lost a loved one, the piling of coffins, the death of famous people, and the sense that everyone could become infected and die. Thus, COVID-19 had most characteristics necessary for becoming a major news event (Kitzinger 1999), and the media played its part to spread the news, inform the public and provide pictures and reports sharing what it means and feels like to be in the centre of a crisis. Sometimes, martial language that compared hospitals with 'war zones' and political measures with a 'war against the virus' heightened the feeling of urgency and disaster. At the same time, they played a vital role in promoting the message of the medical experts, which are commonly amongst the most trustworthy professional groups (IPSOS MORI 2020; Funk et al. 2019), emphasising the lack of cure, the deadly danger we are facing, and the need to act fiercely to stop the virus spreading.

Thereby, the media reporting from people experiencing the virus as well as the experts' judgements, amplified risk consciousness in the public sphere (Pidgeon, Kasperson, and Slovic 2003). This consciousness was the backdrop providing politicians with legitimacy for extraordinary measures and restrictions, thus distracting debate from political negligence (e.g. savings in the health care system, slow response to the virus), secondary risks and deeper socio-structural issues (Ribeiro et al. 2018; Wallis and Nerlich 2005).

Psychological mechanisms

The social acceptance of highly restricted measures was also supported by psychological mechanisms of risk perception. When risks are experienced as catastrophic, people tend not to accept any likelihood of a potentially catastrophic event occurring (e.g. death of a loved one, high number of fatalities). The degree of unfamiliarity with a risk as well as the involuntary exposure increases the perceived risk (Slovic 2000; Starr 1969) and fosters the acceptance of even highly restricting measures of social distancing. Many might feel even more vulnerable as intuitive responses to crisis, such as sticking together with the loved one at times of crisis, became itself a source of high risk, thereby eroding feelings of ontological security (Giddens 1991).

Socio-historical dynamics

The experts' authority in the debate builds on the institutionalisation and spread of epidemiological knowledge that had become increasingly influential within the medical profession (Skolbekken 1995) and the public sphere since World War Two (Zinn 2020). The proliferation of risk language, the reporting of medical research in the news and the authority of medical research in the definition and management of health risk are connected (Zinn and McDonald 2018). For a long time, experts have warned that it is not a question of if but when a next deadly pandemic would strike (DW 2019). While in many cases it is possible to geographically contain a virus (e.g. Ebola and MARS), the H1N1 swine flu in 2009 mobilised fantasies of the next Spanish flu threatening humanity (Shaban 2020). Such concerns of how to prepare for the next pandemic have been nourished by a growing body of expert knowledge.

The political power of coronavirus

These different factors combined provided the virus with political power that pressured governments such as in the UK and recently Sweden with an initially relatively relaxed approach to controlling the spread to engage in more rigid approaches (Boseley 2020; Nikel 2020). Equally, at the outset hesitant leaders, who tried to oppose the evidence such as Donald Trump in the US joined the global fight. In contrast, in Brazil Jair Bolsonaro's resistance to acknowledge the threat triggered growing resistance and opposition, destabilising his leadership (Londoño, Andreoni, and Casado 2020).

Governments of different countries restricted people's freedoms to different degrees by shutting down businesses, imposing lockdowns and further social distancing measures, often enforced by punishing noncompliance. Despite varying in their degree of restrictions, these measures where regularly introduced as "without alternative", prompting the impression that the more restrictive the means the better. Measures were legitimised by a continuous stream of numbers – such as on daily new numbers of infected persons or deaths – that was employed to illustrate the severity of the threat and how well countries managed the spread of the virus.

[...]

The experiences of the COVID-19 pandemic have shown that social inequalities surface in different ways and therefore require different approaches to identify and tackle them. Inequalities can directly relate to the resources available to manage (i) the pandemic, (ii) the structure and organisation of care and health care necessary to look after vulnerable populations, and (iii) the impact of the means to manage the virus such as social distancing measures, on everyday life, which may intensify the experience of disadvantage. These inequalities are visible on a global level as well as nationally and within the social structure of society.

COVID-19 has challenged the national resources available to accommodate the large number of patients in need of intensive care. When Italy and Spain struggled under the demand it became clear that they both had relatively low numbers of intensive care beds available (Spain: 9.7 per 100,000 population; Italy 8.6) in contrast to other countries (Germany: 33.9; Austria: 28.9 and the US: 25.8). The picture was similar for acute care hospital beds that are important to manage a higher load at times of crisis with the exception of the US, which is amongst the lowest (2.4 beds per 1000 population, OECD 2020: 11–2) and Japan (7.8) and Korea (7.1) leading the table. These and other data highlight differences both in investments in the health sector, inequalities in national wealth but there are also significant differences in who has access to health care with the US being known for being more exclusive. With COVID-19 spreading to countries with large parts of their population living in poverty and health care systems already struggling, there are growing concerns to what extent they will manage the pandemic (WHO. 2020).

Inequalities are also observable in the affectedness of the virus drawing attention to differences in the health status of different populations within a society. The higher COVID-19 fatality rates of African Americans in the US (Evelyn 2020) are a telling example suspected to reflect deep social inequalities of the US characterised by differences in health status, access to health support and average life expectancy (Wilkinson and Pickett 2009). Similarly, the overproportionate number of non-white COVID-19 patients in intensive care in the UK asks for explanations (Booth 2020).

The means to manage COVID-19 can also bring to light unsolved social issues in the care system of a society. For example, aging societies such as Germany require and attract a large number of foreign care workers from Eastern Europe, which profit from the comparatively high income. Since foreign care workers are essential for the underfunded and understaffed elderly care system in Germany, they are exempt from the travel ban for foreigners but must prove their work contract at the border. However, since adhering to legal home care arrangements is expensive, many people in need of care revert to work arrangements in the grey or black market (Horn et al. 2019). These estimated 150,000 to 300,000 carers (Löffelholz 2017) cannot continue their work during the travel ban, losing income and leaving vulnerable people and their relatives without support, and adding additional problems to the coronavirus crisis. In this way, the means managing the COVID-19 worsens unsolved social issues and further exposes vulnerable people.

The lockdowns many governments have imposed cause additional stress for the mental well-being of both single people living in as well as people living together under cramped conditions. For already disadvantaged people being required to stay at home for an unknown time span may have negative effects on a number of levels. This situation has been linked to a worldwide surge in domestic violence (Townsend 2020; Taub 2020). Children's opportunities to continue their education also vary during lockdown. Some might get support from their middle-class parents while others lack the supportive environment needed to successfully learn from home (e.g. educated or available parents, hardware/internet access). The longer the lockdown, the more negative these effects are.

Economic costs equally have been high as social lockdown directly influences one's opportunity for gainful employment. Particularly employees in unprotected and casual work who are not system relevant and who may not be able to work from home are affected by a sudden loss of income, jeopardizing them and their families. The expected economic downturn and recession following from the closure of businesses as part of the coronavirus lockdown will have negative effects for large social groups. There are already soaring numbers of people looking for work in many countries (UN News 2020), while there are warnings that half a billion people worldwide could be pushed into poverty by the corona virus (Oxfam 2020) likely to have long term effects on their overall well-being.

Considering and balancing such risks when responding to a pandemic can improve outcomes, but general socio-structural risks, which might 'silently kill' are more difficult to judge and to balance against immediate threats of an illness. Therefore, significant interventions into the social and economic life have not only immediate but also long-term negative effects for a large proportion of the members of a society important to take into account.

[. . .]

From an epidemiological perspective, COVID-19 is a test case for even more serious infectious diseases spreading globally. It has exposed weaknesses in national health systems and of governments' responses as well as national and international inequalities. It also evidenced the influence of global lifestyles with high mobility patterns and global dependencies. The response is framed by the sense that no one should be exposed to the risk of dying by a virus if preventable, supported by subjective risk perceptions and institutional zero-risk priorities. However, such ethical standards tend to neglect the reality of competing risks and favour more immediate over socio-structural and individualised risks such as ill health and reduced life-expectancies,

which tend to kill more 'silently'. Indeed, the case of COVID-19 has proved the importance of governments responding swiftly in face of a pandemic to prevent viruses becoming a monstrous agent. Nevertheless, the undifferentiated top down approach proves a lack of confidence in the public to respond reasonably in the face of crisis. Prioritising the epidemiological measures to control the spread of a deadly virus such as comprehensive lockdown of social life affects social groups unequally and produces secondary risks. It is rather questionable whether compelling people to stay at home over a lengthy time improves population health. School closures will affect the children of the already disadvantaged people most, thereby further dividing social groups. The application of broader ethical standards to evaluate and take into account the social and economic implications are the basis for developing more flexible tools, which combine effective disease control with the application of self-responsible hygiene and social distancing measures to keep social and economic costs low. Because of these costs, in many countries where the infection rates slow down, the social pressure increases to scale down the COVID-19 restrictions (EU 2020).

NOTE

1.   https://www.worldometers.info/

REFERENCES

Booth, R. 2020. "BAME groups hit harder by Covid-19 than white people, UK study suggests". *The Guardian online*, 7 April 2020. Accessed 14/04/2020 at https://www.theguardian.com/world/2020/apr/07/bame-groups-hit-harder-covid-19-than-white-people-uk.

Boseley, S. 2020. "Coronavirus: health experts fear epidemic will 'let rip' through UK." *The Guardian online*, 15 March 2020. Accessed 14/04/2020 at https://www.the

guardian.com/world/2020/mar/15/coro
navirus-health-experts-fear-epidemic-will-let-
rip-through-uk.

DW 2019. 'Next flu pandemic 'a matter of when,
not if' says WHO." *DW*, 11 March 2019.
Accessed 14/04/2020 at https://www.dw
.com/en/next-flu-pandemic-a-matter-of-when
-not-if-says-who/a-47853367.

EU 2020. "COVID-19: EU Commission Suggests
Gradual Return to Normalcy." *Schengen visa
info*, 12 Apr 2020. Accessed 15/04/2020 at
https://www.schengenvisainfo.com/news/co
vid-19-eu-commission-suggests-gradual-retur
n-to-normalcy/.

Evelyn, K. 2020. "'It's a racial justice issue':
Black Americans are dying in greater numbers from Covid-19." *The Guardian online.*
Accessed 14/04/2020 at https://www.the
guardian.com/world/2020/apr/08/its-a-raci
al-justice-issue-black-americans-are-dying-in-gr
eater-numbers-from-covid-19.

Funk, C., M. Hefferon, B. Kennedy, and C.
Johnson. 2019. "Trust and Mistrust in
Americans' Views of Scientific Experts",
August 2, *PEW Research Centre, Science and
Society*, accessed 10/04/2020 at: https://
www.pewresearch.org/science/2019/08/02/
trust-and-mistrust-in-americans-views-of-scien
tific-experts/.

Giddens, A. 1991. *Modernity and Self-Identity.
Self and Society in the Late Modern Age.*
Cambridge: Polity.

Horn, V., C. Schweppe, A. Böcker, and M.
Bruquetas-Callejo. 2019. "Live-in Migrant
Care Worker Arrangements in Germany and
The Netherlands: motivations and Justifications
in Family Decision-Making." *International
Journal of Ageing and Later Life* 13 (2):
83–113. doi:10.3384/ijal.1652-8670.18410.

IPSOS MORI. 2020. "Trust in Professions:
Long-term trends". Accessed 10/04/2020 at:
https://www.ipsos.com/ipsosmori/en-uk/tr
ust-professions-long-term-trends?view=wide.

Kitzinger, J. 1999. "Researching Risk and the
Media." *Health, Risk & Society* 1 (1): 55–69.
doi:10.1080/13698579908407007.

Löffelholz, J. 2017. "Schwarzarbeit ab 800
Euro". *Süddeutsche Zeitung*, 23 Jan 2017.
Accessed 14/04/2020 at https://www.suedd
eutsche.de/wirtschaft/illegal-schwarzarbeit-ab-
800-euro-1.3345286.

Londoño, E., M. Andreoni, and L. Casado.
2020. "Bolsonaro, Isolated and Defiant,
Dismisses Coronavirus Threat to Brazil." *The
New York Times.* Accessed 14/04/2020 at
https://www.nytimes.com/2020/04/01/wo
rld/americas/brazil-bolsonaro-coronavirus.html.

NIH (National Institute of Allergy and Infectious
Diseases). 2020. *COVID-19, MERS & SARS.*
Accessed 12/04/2020 at https://www.niaid.
nih.gov/diseases-conditions/covid-19.

Nikel, D. 2020. "Sweden: 22 Scientists Say
Coronavirus Strategy Has Failed As Deaths
Top 1,000." *Forbes.* Accessed 14/04/2020 at
https://www.forbes.com/sites/davidnikel/20
20/04/14/sweden-22-scientists-say-coronavir
us-strategy-has-failed-as-deaths-top-1000/#7d
fa8f047b6c.

OECD. 2020. "Beyond Containment: health
systems responses to COVID-19 in the
OECD". Updated 31 March 2020. Accessed
10/04/2020 at: https://read.oecdilibrary.
org/view/?ref=119_119689ud5comtf84&Titl
e=Beyond%20Containment:Health%20systems
%20responses%20to%20COVID-19%20in%20t
he%20OECD.

Oxfam. 2020. "Half a billion people could be
pushed into poverty by coronavirus, warns
Oxfam". Accessed 15/04/2020 at https://
www.oxfam.org/en/press-releases/half-billion
-people-could-be-pushed-poverty-coronavirus-
warns-oxfam.

Pidgeon, N., R. E. Kasperson, and P. Slovic.
2003. *The Social Amplification of Risk.*
Cambridge: CUP.

Ribeiro, B., S. Hartley, B. Nerlich, and R. Jaspal.
2018. "Media Coverage of the Zika Crisis in
Brazil: "the Construction of a 'War' Frame
That Masked Social and Gender Inequalities."
Social Science & Medicine 200: 137–144.
doi:10.1016/j.socscimed.2018.01.023.

Shaban, A. R. A. 2020. "Throwback: Bush,

Obama pandemic warning, Gadaffi's vaccine caution." *africanews.com.* Accessed 14/04/2020 at https://www.africanews.com/2020/04/11/throwback-bush-obama-pandemic-warning-gadaffi-s-vaccine-caution/.

Skolbekken, J.-A. 1995. "The Risk Epidemic in Medical Journals." *Social Science & Medicine* 40 (3): 291–305. doi:10.1016/0277-9536(94)00262-R.

Slovic, P. 2000. *The Perception of Risk.* Earthscan, London.

Starr, C. 1969. "Social Benefits versus Technological Risk." *Science* 165 (3899): 1232–1238. doi:10.1126/science.165.3899.1232.

Taub, A. 2020. "A New Covid-19 Crisis: Domestic Abuse Rises Worldwide." *The New York Times.* Accessed 14/04/2020 at https://www.nytimes.com/2020/04/06/world/coronavirus-domestic-violence.html.

Townsend, M. 2020. "Revealed: surge in domestic violence during Covid-19 crisis." *The Guardian online.* Accessed 14/04/2020 at https://www.theguardian.com/society/2020/apr/12/domestic-violence-surges-seven-hundred-percent-uk-coronavirus.

UN News. 2020. "COVID-19. impact could cause equivalent of 195 million job losses, says ILO chief." 8 April 2020. Accessed 14/04/2020 at https://news.un.org/en/story/2020/04/1061322.

Wallis, P., and B. Nerlich. 2005. "Disease Metaphors in New Epidemics: The UK Media Framing of the 2003 SARS Epidemic." *Social Science & Medicine* 60 (11): 2629–2639. doi:10.1016/j.socscimed.2004.11.031.

WHO. 2020. "WHO concerned as COVID-19 cases accelerate in Africa". WHO regional office for Africa, Brazzaville, 2 April 2020. Accessed 04/04/2020 at https://www.afro.who.int/news/who-concerned-covid-19-cases-accelerate-africa.

Wilkinson, R., and K. Pickett. 2009. *The Spirit Level.* London: Allen Lane.

Zinn, J. O. 2020. *The UK 'at Risk'. A Corpus Approach to Historical Social Change 1785–2009.* Cham, Switzerland: Palgrave Macmillan.

Zinn, J. O., and D. McDonald. 2018. *Risk in the New York Times (1987–2014). A Corpus-Based Exploration of Sociological Theories.* Cham, Switzerland: Palgrave Macmillan.

Part 8 – Further reading

The sociology of health and illness is a very broad field and a few overview texts are needed to get to grips with it. Hence readers could try Nettleton, S. (2020) *The Sociology of Health and Illness* (4th edn, Cambridge: Polity). Barry, A.-M. and Yuill, C. (2016) *Understanding the Sociology of Health: An Introduction* (4th edn, London: Sage) is very reliable and comprehensive. On the subject of medicalization, Conrad, P. (2007) *The Medicalization of Society: On the Transformation of Human Conditions into Treatable Disorders* (Baltimore: Johns Hopkins University Press) is as good as it gets – an engaging and fascinating book. Finally, given the times we are living in, it would be well worth reading Horton, R. (2021) *The COVID-19 Catastrophe: What's Gone Wrong and How to Stop it Happening Again* (2nd edn, Cambridge: Polity).

Sociology, 9th edition

Chapter 10, 'Health, Illness and Disability', covers all of the issues in this section, but a search of the index will reveal numerous places where health inequalities are discussed throughout the book.

Part 9

Crime and Social Control

Crime and deviance are probably the most common subjects of all television drama series, movies and news output today. And the bulk of these representations are rooted in the individualization of criminality, exploring the psychological make-up and motivation of individuals to commit crimes. In sociology, our interest shifts to the examination of broad patterns of crime and victimization in order to gain a better understanding of which social groups are more and less likely to be victims and lawbreakers. For sociologists, crime is just a smaller subset of the more general category of deviance. While deviance may be defined as non-conformity to generally accepted rules and norms, crime refers only to behaviour that breaks society's laws. Hence, there is a difference between criminology, which focuses on criminality, and the much broader sociology of crime and deviance. Our readings reflect this broader remit.

One of the defining studies of the sociology of deviance is Howard Becker's 1963 book *Outsiders*. Working in the symbolic interactionist tradition, Becker's work explicitly rejects all individualistic notions of deviant behaviour, carefully setting out his alternative sociological account of deviance as it arises within social networks and social interactions. Becker's famous definition of deviance – that it is created by social groups who make the rules, whose infraction is then defined as 'deviance' – retains its radicalism even today. This process of rule-making and

redefining actions effectively marks the rule-breakers as deviants and outsiders. Hence, Becker arrives at his sociological conclusion: 'deviance is not a quality of the act the person commits, but rather a consequence of the application by others of rules and sanctions to an "offender"' (1963: 9). The actual process of deviance construction is considerably more complex than this pithy outline, and Becker goes on to discuss his thesis in detail, using the examples of marijuana use, musical cultures and occupational groups. Becker's ideas have things to tell us about how social control operates within social life.

Many criminal justice systems today make widespread use of prison sentences for a range of very different types of offence, and many prison populations around the world – notably in the UK and USA – are at their highest recorded levels. Our reading by David Garland was written at the turn of the twenty-first century to launch a new journal, *Punishment and Society*. Garland summarizes some of the key trends in punishment and penal policy, including the increasing recourse in democratic societies to incarceration for criminal behaviour and the introduction of commercial companies into the penal system. He notes that such developments may mark a significant shift towards a new focus on 'penal control' that ought to be the subject of renewed academic interest and a more systematic research effort. Since this article was published, there has been more interest in the sociology of punishment, though arguably the populist politics of being seen to be 'tough on crime' is as influential as ever.

Criminal justice systems operate on the basis that everyone is 'equal before the law', with each case dealt with on its own merits regardless of the status of the individuals charged with offences. Yet even a cursory look at the prison statistics of the industrialized countries shows that some social groups are disproportionately represented in the prison population. For example, men are far more likely to be imprisoned than women, while people from black and minority ethnic groups are over-represented in the prison population. Our reading here explores the role of prisons and the penal regime in the racialization of justice in the USA. Loïc Wacquant outlines the history of racialized justice since the 1860s, when penal institutions supported and helped to stabilize the system of white domination. Today, he argues that the intertwining of carceral institutions with US ghettos has become central to the process of 'race-making' by reviving a very old linkage between 'blackness' and criminality or violence. This can be observed in opinion surveys which show that many white people are fearful of becoming victims of crime committed by black youth, especially street crimes in the larger cities. But it also emerges in the disproportionate stop-and-search statistics, which are heavily skewed towards black people, and the prohibition on voting for former prisoners, who are disproportionately from black and other minority groups. In Wacquant's terms, blackness has become a form of 'civic felony' that exacerbates existing racial divisions.

Since the mass take-up of the internet and the facilitation of a full range of online activities, from shopping and banking to social media, the social world has effectively expanded to include cyberspace. Unsurprisingly, criminal activity has also moved online, taking in a range of crimes from push-payment and romance frauds to account hacking and identity theft. A first step in making sociological sense of online crime is to define what is meant by 'cybercrime' and to analyse how its various forms may be different from, or similar to, conventional crime. For example, many conventional crimes, such as financial fraud, may use digital technology to achieve their aim, but are they really 'true' cybercrimes? Reading 49, from David S. Wall, presents a typology of cybercrimes using examples of each type, looking to differentiate those that could not have been committed without networked information technology. He argues that the first generation of cybercrimes are those that, in some way, involve computers. Second-generation cybercrime is undertaken by hackers who are able to find ways of getting into computer networks. But third-generation or *true* cybercrimes involve 'botnets' used to administer a computer user's machine remotely in order to commit crime. Because they are based within computer networks, cybercrimes have an extensive, even global reach, making law enforcement more difficult. Wall argues that cyber crimewaves can now be measured 'in hours and minutes rather than months and years', and understanding them better should help to create more effective regulation and prevention.

Densely populated large cities and urban environments have been at the forefront of numerous crime prevention and control initiatives, especially those which target 'street crimes', such as bike and car theft and anti-social behaviour. For example, urban areas were testbeds for an approach known as situational crime prevention, which aimed not to reform offenders but to build crime-resistant environments. Katherine Beckett and Steve Herbert analysed the associated policing practices of dispersal orders, exclusion zones and other measures in Seattle, USA, though similar tactics have been adopted elsewhere. They argue that the increasing use of spatial exclusion to deal with 'undesirables' and undesirable behaviour amounts to the return of the much older punishment of exile or banishment. The latter can be traced back to ancient times, and it seems odd to describe modern methods in these terms. Yet the authors contend that to be legally compelled to leave an area, and to stay away for specified periods of time, does amount to a form of banishment. They also note that many of the offending behaviours are not strictly 'crimes' but forms of deviance or civil offences that are nonetheless punished as if they were crimes. The reading outlines some of these and makes the case for reintroducing the concept of banishment into sociological and criminological studies.

46. The Social Construction of Outsiders*

Howard S. Becker

All social groups make rules and attempt, at some times and under some circumstances, to enforce them. Social rules define situations and the kinds of behavior appropriate to them, specifying some actions as "right" and forbidding others as "wrong." When a rule is enforced, the person who is supposed to have broken it may be seen as a special kind of person, one who cannot be trusted to live by the rules agreed on by the group. He is regarded as an *outsider*. But the person who is thus labeled an outsider may have a different view of the matter. He may not accept the rule by which he is being judged and may not regard those who judge him as either competent or legitimately entitled to do so. Hence, a second meaning of the term emerges: the rulebreaker may feel his judges arc *outsiders*.

[. . .]

The sociological view I have just discussed defines deviance as the infraction of some agreed-upon rule. It then goes on to ask who breaks rules, and to search for the factors in their personalities and life situations that might account for the infractions. This assumes that those who have broken a rule constitute a homogeneous category, because they have committed the same deviant act.

Such an assumption seems to me to ignore the central fact about deviance: it is created by society. I do not mean this in the way it is ordinarily understood, in which the causes of deviance are located in the social situation of the deviant or in "social factors" which prompt his action. I mean, rather, that social groups *create deviance by making the rules whose infraction constitutes deviance,* and by applying those rules to particular people and labeling them as outsiders. From this point of view, deviance is *not* a quality of the act the person commits, but rather a consequence of the application by others of rules and sanctions to an "offender." The deviant is one to whom that label has successfully been applied; deviant behavior is behavior that people so label.[1]

Since deviance is, among other things, a consequence of the responses of others to a person's act, students of deviance cannot assume that they are dealing with a homogeneous category when they study people who have been labeled deviant. That is, they cannot assume that these people have actually committed a deviant act or broken some rule, because the process of labeling may not be infallible; some people may be labeled deviant who in fact have not broken a rule. Furthermore, they cannot assume that the category of those labeled deviant will contain all those who actually have broken a rule, for many offenders may escape apprehension and thus fail to be included in the population of "deviants" they study. Insofar as the category lacks homogeneity and fails to include all the cases that belong in it, one cannot reasonably expect to find common factors of personality or life situation that will account for the supposed deviance.

* From Becker, H. S. (1963) *Outsiders: Studies in the Sociology of Deviance* (New York: The Free Press). Extracts from pp. 1–2, 8–10, 12–13, 15–17, 24–25.

What, then, do people who have been labeled deviant have in common? At the least, they share the label and the experience of being labeled as outsiders. I will begin my analysis with this basic similarity and view deviance as the product of a transaction that takes place between some social group and one who is viewed by that group as a rule-breaker. I will be less concerned with the personal and social characteristics of deviants than with the process by which they come to be thought of as outsiders and their reactions to that judgment.

[...]

The degree to which other people will respond to a given act as deviant varies greatly. Several kinds of variation seem worth noting. First of all, there is variation over time. A person believed to have committed a given "deviant" act may at one time be responded to much more leniently than he would be at some other time. The occurrence of "drives" against various kinds of deviance illustrates this clearly. At various times, enforcement officials may decide to make an all-out attack on some particular kind of deviance, such as gambling, drug addiction, or homosexuality. It is obviously much more dangerous to engage in one of these activities when a drive is on than at any other time. (In a very interesting study of crime news in Colorado newspapers, Davis found that the amount of crime reported in Colorado newspapers showed very little association with actual changes in the amount of crime taking place in Colorado. And, further, that people's estimate of how much increase there had been in crime in Colorado was associated with the increase in the amount of crime news bur not with any increase in the amount of crime.)[2]

The degree to which an act will be treated as deviant depends also on who commits the act and who feels he has been harmed by it. Rules tend to be applied more to some persons than others. Studies of juvenile delinquency make the point clearly. Boys from middle-class areas do not get as far in the legal process when they are apprehended as do boys from slum areas. The middle-class boy is less likely, when picked up by the police, to be taken to the station; less likely when taken to the station to be booked; and it is extremely unlikely that he will be convicted and sentenced.[3] [...]

[...]

I have been using the term "outsiders" to refer to those people who are judged by others to be deviant and thus to stand outside the circle of "normal" members of the group. But the term contains a second meaning, whose analysis leads to another important set of sociological problems: "outsiders," from the point of view of the person who is labeled deviant, may be the people who make the rules he had been found guilty of breaking.

Social rules are the creation of specific social groups. Modern societies are not simple organizations in which everyone agrees on what the rules are and how they are to be applied in specific situations. They are, instead, highly differentiated along social class lines, ethnic lines, occupational lines and cultural lines. These groups need not and, in fact, often do not share the same rules. The problems they face in dealing with their environment, the history and traditions they carry with them, all lead to the evolution of different sets of rules. Insofar as the rules of various groups conflict and contradict one another, there will be disagreement about the kind of behavior that is proper in any given situation.

Italian immigrants who went on making wine for themselves and their friends during Prohibition were acting properly by Italian immigrant standards, but were breaking the law of their new country (as, of course, were many of their Old American neighbors). Medical patients who shop around for a doctor may, from the perspective of their own group, be doing what is necessary to protect their health by making sure they get what seems to them the best possible doctor; but, from the perspective of the physician, what they do is wrong because it breaks down the trust the patient ought to put in his physician. The lower-class delinquent who fights for his "turf" is only doing what he considers necessary and right, but teachers, social workers, and police see it differently.

While it may be argued that many or most rules are generally agreed to by all members of a society, empirical research on a given rule generally reveals variation in people's attitudes. Formal rules, enforced by some specially constituted group, may differ from those actually thought appropriate by most people.[4] Factions in a group may disagree on what I have called actual operating rules. Most important for the study of behavior ordinarily labeled deviant, the perspectives of the people who engage in the behavior are likely to be quite different from those of the people who condemn it. In this latter situation, a person may feel that he is being judged according to rules he has had no hand in making and does not accept, rules forced on him by outsiders.

To what extent and under what circumstances do people attempt to force their rules on others who do not subscribe to them? Let us distinguish two cases. In the first, only those who are actually members of the group have any interest in making and enforcing certain rules. If an orthodox Jew disobeys the laws of kashruth only other orthodox Jews will regard this as a transgression; Christians or nonorthodox Jews will not consider this deviance and would have no interest in interfering. In the second case, members of a group consider it important to their welfare that members of certain other groups obey certain rules. Thus, people consider it extremely important that those who practice the healing arts abide by certain rules; this is the reason the state licenses physicians, nurses, and others, and forbids anyone who is not licensed to engage in healing activities.

To the extent that a group tried to impose its rules on other groups in the society, we are presented with a second question: Who can, in fact, force others to accept their rules and what are the causes of their success? This is, of course, a question of political and economic power. Later we will consider the political and economic process through which rules are created and enforced. Here it is enough to note that people are in fact always *forcing* their rules on others, applying them more or less against the will and without the consent of those others. By and large, for example, rules are made for young people by their elders. Though the youth of this country exert a powerful influence culturally – the mass media of communication are tailored to their interests, for instance – many important kinds of rules are made for our youth by adults. Rules regarding school attendance and sex behavior are not drawn up with regard to the problems of adolescence. Rather, adolescents find themselves surrounded by rules about these matters which have been made by older and more settled people. It is considered legitimate to do this, for youngsters are considered neither wise enough nor responsible enough to make proper rules for themselves.

[...]

A useful conception in developing sequential models of various kinds of deviant behavior is that of *career*.[5] Originally developed in studies of occupations, the concept refers to the sequence of movements from one position to another in an occupational system made by any individual who works in that system. Furthermore, it includes the notion of "career contingency," those factors on which mobility from one position to another depends. Career contingencies include both objective facts of social structure and changes in the perspectives, motivations, and desires of the individual. Ordinarily, in the study of occupations, we use the concept to distinguish between those who have a "successful" career (in whatever terms success is defined within the occupation) and those who do not. It can also be used to distinguish several varieties of career outcomes, ignoring the question of "success."

The model can easily be transformed for use in the study of deviant careers. In so transforming it, we should not confine our interest to those who follow a career that leads them into ever-increasing deviance, to those who ultimately take on an extremely deviant identity and way of life. We should also consider those who have a more fleeting contact with deviance, whose careers lead them away from it into conventional ways of life. Thus, for example, studies of delinquents who fail to become adult criminals might teach us even more than studies of delinquents who progress in crime.

NOTES

1. The most important earlier statements of this view can be found in Frank Tonnenbaum, *Crime and the Community* (New York: McGraw Hill Book Co., Inc., 1951), and E. M. Lemert, *Social Pathology* (New York: McGraw Hill Book Co., Inc., 1951). A recent article stating a position very similar to mine is John Kitsuse, "Societal Reaction to Deviance: Problems of Theory and Method," *Social Problems*, 9 (Winter, 1962), 247–256.

2. F. James Davis, "Crime News in Colorado Newspapers" *American Journal of Sociology*, LVII (January, 1952), 325–330.

3. See Albert K. Cohen and James F. Short, Jr., "Juvenile Delinquency," in Robert K. Merton and Robert A. Nisbet, editors, *Contemporary Social Problems* (New York: Harcourt, Brace and World, Inc., 1961), p. 87.

4. Arnold M. Rose and Arthur E. Prell, "Does the Punishment Fit the Crime? – A Study in Social Valuation," *American Journal of Sociology*, LXI (November, 1955), 247–259.

5. See Everett C. Hughes, *Men and Their Work* (New York: The Free Press of Glencoe, 1958), pp. 56–67, 102–115, and 157–168; Oswald Hall, "The Stages of the Medical Career," *American Journal* of *Sociology*, LUI (March, 1948), 243–253; and Howard S. Becker and Anselm L. Strauss, "Careers, Personality, and Adult Socialization," *American Journal of Sociology*, LXII (November, 1956), 253–263.

47. The Shifting Politics of Punishment*

David Garland

Punishment has always presented practical challenges and moral dilemmas for social organization, just as it has always exerted a profound fascination for the literary and popular imagination. Penal institutions of some kind are necessary features of any orderly society, but their necessity and universality does nothing to prevent them being deeply problematic aspects of social life. The modern institutions of punishment are especially prone to conflicts and tensions that tend to undermine their effectiveness and legitimacy as instruments of social policy. These conflicts – between condemnation and forgiveness, vengeance and mercy, the sanctity of law and the humanity of compassion, social defense and individual rights, the urge to exclude and the dream of rehabilitation – set up complex, ambivalent sentiments that colour the day-to-day experience of those caught up in penal relations, whether as administrators and officers, inmates and clients, or as members of the public in whose name penal sanctions are nowadays imposed. Little wonder, then, that the history of penality has been one of reform and reaction, of false dawns and disappointed optimism, particularly in the modern period when the state's institutions of punishment have been viewed not just as instruments of retribution and political power but also as mechanisms of reform and crime control. The modern criminal justice state, developing in the wake of the Enlightenment as one of the pillars of the liberal democratic polity, established an ambitious set of expectations: not just 'doing justice', enforcing the law and punishing wrongdoers, but also reducing crime rates by reforming convicted offenders and deterring those others who might be tempted. The recurring failure to fulfill these expectations has ensured that, for most of the modern period, penal questions have periodically troubled policymakers and, from time to time, have become a focus for public concern and involvement.

At the present time, penal issues have taken on a significance for politics and for popular culture that makes the question of crime and punishment one of the most pressing problems of our age. This is true of much of the developed world, not least the new democracies that have grown up in the wake of the Soviet Union's collapse, many of which are struggling to free themselves of the repressive penal practices of the past era while simultaneously facing the challenge of rapidly increasing crime rates and chronic economic instability. The most egregious signs of the new urgency of penal matters are to be found, however, not in the world's newest democracies and most fragile nationstates, but in the older, more stable ones, like Britain, the Netherlands and Sweden, and above all in the world's leading super-power, the USA. In the last two decades, the US prison population has grown to unprecedented levels and the death penalty has come to be imposed and executed at a rate not seen since the 1950s. The fact that these penal developments coincide roughly in time (if not always in place – state-to-state trends being much more

* From Garland, D. (1999) 'Editorial: Punishment and Society Today', *Punishment and Society*, 1(1): 5–10. Extracts from pp. 5–6, 7–9.

various) with a falling off in national crime rates, together with the continuing effectiveness of 'populist punitiveness' as a form of political appeal, has produced a welter of penal legislation, much of it concerned to increase sentencing levels, to diminish the entitlements of convicted offenders, and generally to give expression to a public sentiment that appears increasingly hostile and punitive, at least as it is relayed through the media and the political process.

No one yet knows what kind of impact these new levels of incarceration and penal control will have upon the communities most affected by them – in this case, black, inner city neighborhoods. It seems likely, though, that the generalization and 'normalization' of penal experience among these social groups is liable to affect everything from child rearing, family stability and labor markets in these communities to the character of race relations and the legitimacy of the law. The question of whether or not mass incarceration and capital punishment reduce crime rates is a legitimate and important issue for penologists and policy-makers, and is the focus of much research in the US and elsewhere. But so too are questions of the ethical status and political effects of such policies, and there is a danger that these wider, deeper questions will be ignored in the current enthusiasm for expressive punishments and the appealing simplicity of the idea that 'prison works'.

The rapid and sustained increase in the US prison population has been accompanied – and to some extent made possible – by the appearance of a small but rapidly expanding private sector providing prison construction, prison management and various other 'correctional services' on a commercial basis. Once again, no one knows just what effects this commercialization of penal provision will have in the future. Some commentators warn that the emerging 'penal-commercial complex' will sustain and escalate a war against crime just as the military-industrial complex of the 1950s and 1960s underwrote the cold war and its arms race. Others are more sanguine, more willing to risk the experiment and more inclined to point to the recurring failures of state

institutions as a reason not to preclude novel ways of 'delivering' punishment. Whoever is right in this, we will all have to come to terms with the fact that the appearance of this commercial sector introduces a new dynamic into the development of penal policy and penal politics, creates new problems (and perhaps opportunities) in the administration of penal institutions, and raises altogether new issues of an ethical and legal kind. It also raises difficult technical and political issues in respect of the regulatory regimes and enforcement mechanisms that these new arrangements will require if they are to be subjected to public scrutiny and accountability. [. . .]

[. . .]

Punishment and penal control are thus firmly on the policy agenda, often in ways that link these issues with broader attempts to reform the welfare state, to promote family values and to reinvigorate 'individual responsibility'. 'Tough on crime' rhetoric has come to be a standard feature of political discourse across the whole political spectrum, even of supposedly left-of-centre parties, and there is no sign that this emphasis is diminishing in the face of falling crime rates. Whatever its validity, the claim that punishment – and penal protection – are what the people want, what they demand, is part of contemporary political orthodoxy, and few politicians are motivated to challenge this new common sense. In this new context, penal issues have become highly emotive and extensively politicized and they now form a staple element of political debate. In consequence, the effectiveness of imprisonment, the ethics of the death penalty, the scope for restorative sanctions, or the appropriate framework for governing sentencing behavior cease to be matters purely for specialists and become relevant to everyone.

The politics of many of the developed western democracies in the last few decades have been a politics of reaction and reconstruction in which the institutional structures and political understandings of the post-war welfare state have been challenged and to some extent transformed. There is reason to believe that our penal institutions are currently undergoing a similar structural transformation that is changing the meaning of criminal justice in ways that we are only beginning to understand. The erosion of correctionalist ideologies; the turn to expressive justice and punitive measures; the return of the victim; the stress upon public protection and the management of risk; the changing objectives of community corrections and custodial institutions; the politicization of penal policy discourse; the commercialization of penality; the drift towards mass imprisonment . . . all of these converging trends seem to suggest a field that is being extensively reconfigured, though no singular logic appears to explain quite how. While sociologists of punishment debate the meaning of these transformations, and seek to understand the forces that are bringing them about, these same developments change the policy environment in fundamental ways, and present practitioners with practical problems and ethical issues quite unlike those they have dealt with in the past. (A vivid example of these changed times is the new status of prison or probation-based treatment programs which are now so overlaid with contradictory concerns about public security, victim-satisfaction, individual responsibility and the avoidance of authoritarianism – not to mention effectiveness and value-for-money – that they have become altogether more problematic than they ever appeared in the heyday of the rehabilitative ideal.)

Thirty years ago, academics, practitioners and informed commentators shared a set of assumptions about the correctionalist framework that shaped criminal justice and penal practice. There was a relatively settled, self-conscious, institutional field and the debates and disagreements that occurred operated within a set of established discursive parameters. Penological text-books and practitioner training manuals could articulate the premises that guided penal practice and confidently transmit this culture from one generation to the next. Today, for better or for worse, we

lack any such agreement, or any clear sense of the big picture. Penal systems across the western world appear to be in a state of rapid transition in which the old penological frameworks have broken down but new ones have not yet emerged to take their place. Policy development appears volatile and contradictory, with a great deal of legislative activity, much dissension in the ranks of practitioner groups, and a good deal of conflict between penal experts and politicians. A sure sign that we are indeed in a state of transition, occupying the unsettled terrain betwixt and between different policy regimes, is the uncertain character of today's penal politics. The battle lines of penal debate are blurred and constantly changing. No one today is quite sure what is radical and what is reactionary. Private prisons, victim impact statements, community notification laws, sentencing guidelines, electronic monitoring, punishments in the community – these and dozens of other issues take us into unfamiliar territory where the ideological lines are far from clear and where the old assumptions are an unreliable guide.

The collapse of a long-established institutional framework tends to prompt intellectual ferment and innovation as old habits of thought and recipes for action lose their epistemological privileges and institutional supports. It is not, then, surprising that the traditional assumptions of a correctionalist, technicist penology have been increasingly disrupted over the past two decades by more critical and diverse ways of thinking about penality. From the mid 1970s onwards, penal institutions and ideas have become a focus for path-breaking work in numerous fields as scholars have come to question the practices of mid-century penality and probe further into the social, political and cultural rationales upon which these were based. Our understanding of modern imprisonment has been completely transformed by the historical work of Rothman, Ignatieff, Foucault, Beattie, Spierenburg and others, just as our moral intuitions about punishment have been altered by the philosophical work of the likes of Joel Feinberg and Herbert Morris. The same period saw the forceful emergence of sociological studies of punishment, beginning with the rediscovery of Rusche and Kirchheimer's work and the revival of interest in Émile Durkheim. More recently, significant work has begun to appear in political science, cultural studies and feminist scholarships, as writers in these disciplines turn their attention to ways in which penal issues have come to function in the political life and cultural imagination of modern societies. The intellectual event that we are witnessing – no doubt linked to the institutional changes described above – is the formation of a critical interdisciplinary exchange in the conceptual space that used to be occupied by a single 'disciplinary' discourse. Practical penology has converged with historical, sociological and philosophical work in a way that has produced a whole new level of intellectual debate, and a whole new literature of scholarship in the penal realm, as scholars have tried to make sense of the changing terrain, and the social and historical dynamics that lie beneath it.

48. Race, Blackness and Exclusion in the USA*

Loïc Wacquant

[...] The etymology of felony, descended from the medieval Latin *fello* meaning villain or wicked and designating an evil person before it came to mean perpetrator of an infamous crime, reminds us that felon disenfranchisement is quintessentially 'a symbolic act of political banishment, an assertion of the state's power to exclude those who violated prevailing norms' (Keyssar 2000, p. 163).

But then one must ask, what prevailing norms and how are they infringed upon? Here one comes upon what, in the opening lines of *The Souls of Black Folk*, W.E.B. Du Bois (1903, p. 3) wistfully calls 'the strange meaning of being black here' in America. From the birth of the colony to the present day, albeit with variations in intensity and scope, blacks have been cast in the role of the living antithesis to the 'model American', even when, given the opportunity, they have embraced that nation's core values and myths with more zest and abandon than any other group. After the social and symbolic separation of European servants and African slaves crystallised in the closing decades of the seventeenth century, slaves were merged into a compact faceless mass deemed untrustworthy, dissipated, and slothful – in short, the walking-and-breathing despoliation of the Protestant ideal, at once civic and religious, of the 'dependable, orderly, and industrious worker that the Puritans sought to create by creating the Republic, and vice versa (Kolchin 1993, p. 68).

During the revolutionary period, citizens of the new nation were taught to equate the term 'freeman' with political freedom and economic independence, again by contraposition to the dark-skinned slave, who was forcibly denied these twin prerogatives of membership on the spurious grounds that (s)he was congenitally incapable of assuming them. By the mid-nineteenth century, working-class formation operated via racial consolidation by fusing blackness and servility as the reviled antonym of genuine Americanness, 'the perils and pride of Republican citizenship' being defined by opposition to a black population pictured as the embodiment of 'the preindustrial, erotic, careless style of life the white worker hated and longed for' as he was being pressed into the ambit of wage work and subjected to crushing industrial discipline (Roediger 1991, pp. 11, 14). Throughout most of the twentieth century, the racialist strain of Americanism that construes the nation 'as a people held together by common blood and skin color and an inherent fitness for self-government' prevailed even as the universalistic forces of civic nationalism gained strength (e.g., the 1790 law limiting US naturalisation to 'free white persons' was formally abrogated only in 1952, even as a law of 1870 included 'persons of African nativity and African descent' among eligible categories). The slow and begrudging acceptance of Southern and Eastern European immigrants into 'God's melting pot' confirmed and reinforced the continued socio-symbolic marginality of African Americans, as liberal leaders committed on principle to colour-blind inclusiveness 'periodically reinscribed

* From Wacquant, L. (2005) 'Race as Civic Felony', *International Social Science Journal*, 57(183): 127–142. Extracts from pp. 135–139.

racialist notions in their rhetoric and policies' (Gerstle 2001, p. 5).

Race or, to be more precise, *blackness* – for, since the origins, it is the presence of dishonoured dark-skinned persons brought in chains from Africa that has necessitated the (re)invention and perpetuation of racial vision and division – is properly understood as America's *primeval civic felony*. Not in a rhetorical or metaphorical sense but in full accord with the Durkheimian conception of crime as 'an act' that 'offends strong and definite states of the collective conscience' of the society (Durkheim [1893] 1930, p. 47),[1] in this case imputed ways of being and behaving that breach America's idealised representation of itself as the promised land of freedom, equality, and self-determination. For nearly four centuries, blacks have been consistently constructed symbolically and handled institutionally, not merely as noncitizens laying outside of the inaugural social compact of the republic, but as veritable 'anti-citizens' (Roediger 1991, p. 57) standing over and against it. This explains the recurrence of schemes and movements aimed at extirpating them from the societal body by migrating them back to Africa, from Thomas Jefferson's advocacy of deportation after eventual emancipation to the creation by white philanthropists of the American Colonization Society in 1816 to the popular success of the Universal Negro Improvement Association of Marcus Garvey with its plan to repatriate African Americans to Liberia a century later. It also accounts for the prohibition against blacks enlisting in the US military until 1862 and for the cataclysmic socio-symbolic impact of their service under the flag during the two world wars of the twentieth century, which did more to shake the social and mental foundations of the US caste order than all the internal movements of protest until then by eroding the divide between Negroes and whites inside the most honorific organ of the state apparatus, the military (Gerstle 2001, chapters 5–6; Klinkner & Smith 1999, pp. 200–201, McAdam 1989).

Blacks were not part of this 'We the People' that formed 'a more perfect Union' to 'secure

the Blessings of Liberty to [them]selves and [their] posterity', to quote the preamble of the US Constitution. The African and African-American slave, later the Negro sharecropper and the black industrial proletarian, and today the heinous member of the inner-city 'underclass' have been persistently pictured and processed in national discourse and public policy as enemies of the nation – as slaves have been throughout world history.[2] Richard Wright vividly captured this sense of combined strangerhood and nefariousness in *Native Son*, the signal allegorical portrait of the black-American condition at mid-twentieth century, torn between the glorious profession of democracy and the gruesome reality of caste domination. In the scene of the trial of Bigger Thomas, a clumsy black youth who, out of broiling racial confusion and resentment, accidentally kills a young white beauty, the bohemian daughter of an upstanding patrician family from Chicago, Thomas's attorney utters this plea on behalf of the murderer and alleged rapist (for whites cannot imagine that the slaying was not sexually motivated) who, because of the very enormity of his offence (after smothering his victim in panic, he cuts her head off to throw her body into the furnace of her parents' mansion), is made to stand for every black person in America:

> Excluded from, and unassimilated in our society, yet longing to gratify impulses akin to our own but denied the objects and channels evolved through long centuries for their socialized expression, every sunrise and sunset makes him guilty of subversive actions. Every movement of his body is an unconscious protest. Every desire, every dream, no matter how intimate or personal, is a plot or a conspiracy. Every hope is a plan for insurrection. Every glance of the eye is a threat. *His very existence is a crime against the state.* (Wright 1939, p. 821; emphasis in original)

Thus the routine resort, particularly pronounced in periods of transition between regimes of racial rule, to the penal apparatus to ensure that 'the swarthy specter sits in its accustomed seat at the Nation's feast' (Du Bois 1903, p. 10).[3] Thus also the persistent refusal, in the administration of penal law as in public discourse more generally, to individualise blacks, resulting in their lumping into a collective type defined by the status and deeds not of the average member but of the lowest and most fearsome (Walton 1992, pp. 397–401) – such that blacks are always liable to be treated as *humiliores* whenever they fail to furnish tangible proof, by appearance, conduct, or title, that they deserve to be accorded the minimal dignities of civic membership, as in the urban tale of the black Harvard professor who cannot flag down a city taxicab at night. Save for the qualifier 'impermissible', legal scholar George Fletcher is on the right track, then, when he argues that 'categorical divestment of voting rights introduces an impermissible element of caste into the American political system' insofar as it treats former convicts 'as inherently unreliable not only for purposes of voting but also in giving sworn testimony at trial', as persons whose social standing is terminally impaired by prior convictions. With the accelerating conflation of blackness and criminality, felon disenfranchisement is indeed a 'continuation of *infamia*' (Fletcher 1999, pp. 1895–1908) tapping the discredit of slavery and the subsequent sullying of caste separation via Jim Crow and the urban ghetto as reactivated by indelible penal sanction.

[. . .]

The penal alienation of today's convicts makes them social similes if not legal replicas of antebellum slaves in yet another respect: although they are barred from civic participation, they nonetheless weigh on the political scale at the behest and to the benefit of those who control their bodies, much as bondspeople benefited their plantation masters under the 'three-fifths' clause of the US Constitution. Because inmates are tallied by the census as residents of the counties where they serve their sentence, they artificially inflate the population count as well as lower the average income level of the rural towns that harbour most prisons. As a result, these towns accrue added political power in terms of representation in their state legislature as well as garner extra federal funding intended to remedy poverty: public monies that would go to providing services such as education, medical care, and transportation and housing subsidies to poor blacks in the inner city are diverted to the benefit of the predominantly white population of prison municipalities. It is estimated that Cook County will lose $88 million in federal funding during the current decade because of the 26,000-odd Chicagoans (78% of them black) reckoned as residents of the downstate districts where they are incarcerated (Dugan, 2000).

Similarly, the enumeration of convicts transfers political influence from their home to their host county, thereby diluting the electoral strength of blacks and Latinos living in the metropolitan districts from which most prisoners stem – and the more so as detention facilities are located further away from major cities. Thus 80% of New York state prisoners are African-American and Hispanic and two-thirds come from New York City; but 91% of them are housed upstate, in the conservative lily-white districts where all of the new penitentiaries built since 1982 are located. Counting urban prisoners as rural dwellers for purposes of representation (even though the state constitution specifies that penal confinement does not entail loss or change of residence) violates the one-man, one-vote rule, and translates into a net loss of 43,740 residents for New York City, which is computed to have cost urban Democrats two seats in each of the state house and senate (Wagner 2002, p. 10–12). And, just as counting slaves boosted the political power of Southern states and allowed them to entrench slavery by controlling the national agenda, the 'phantom' population of black and brown prisoners enhances the political influence of white politicians who pursue social and penal platforms antithetical to the interests of ghetto residents. In particular, these elected officials have acquired a vested interest in the punitive policies of criminalisation of poverty and carceral escalation suited to replenishing the supply of unruly black bodies that guarantee correctional jobs, taxes, subsidies, and political pull to their communities, to the direct detriment of the segregated urban districts that furnish these convicts.

In light of the fiasco capping the 2000 presidential contest, it is ironic as well as iconic of the increasingly constrictive impact of American electoral codes regarding felons to note that Florida leads the nation with 827,000 disenfranchised convicts and ex-convicts, distributed among 71,200 prison inmates, 131,100 probationers, a paltry 6,000 parolees (testifying to the strictness of correctional policy in that state), and a staggering *613,500 former felons* who, though they have fully repaid their debt to society, will never cast a ballot for the remainder of their lives. In November of 2000, over 256,000 of these potential voters kept from the rolls were black. Had Albert Gore, Jr., the Democratic candidate, collected the vote of a mere one per cent of these electors – many of whom were *illegally* barred from the booth due to data recording and processing errors by the private firm contracted by the Florida Election Board to verify the eligibility of former felons who migrated across state lines[4] – he would have handily won the Sunshine state and conquered the presidency. But there is a measure of poetic justice in his court-ordered defeat in that for eight years Gore served as Vice-President in an administration that worked to increase the number of convicts and ex-convicts with a zeal and efficiency unmatched by any other in American history (Wacquant 2005).

The debarment of ex-felons from the ballot years after they have served their sentence constituted a far more potent bias than all of the 'hanging chads' and misdesigned 'butterfly ballots' of Broward County that consumed public attention during the weeks and months after the aborted Florida election. This episode has reenergised social activists and analysts alike in their denunciation of the seeming infringement on the sanctity of the democratic compact it entails. In a systematic study of the impact of felon disenfranchisement laws on electoral outcomes over the past three decades, Uggen and Manza (2002) have confirmed that, because they strike primarily black and poor potential voters, criminal

disqualifications subtract more votes from the Democratic than from the Republican camp and have likely reversed the results of seven US Senate elections in addition to the 2000 presidential race by curtailing the minority vote. But this justifiable concern for the skewing of electoral *outcomes* skirts the deeper significance of the *process* of felon exclusion, which is to enforce and communicate the degraded status of convicts by turning them into a quasi-outcaste of the American civic community, irrespective of its influence on this or that vote. It is instructive here to recall that, during the phase of imposition of the racial restrictions that gradually erected the Jim Crow regime, opposition to the Negro vote in the segregationist South was not proportional to the actual or potential weight of blacks at the polls. Rather, it was a principled opposition based on the racial syllogism (or, rather, paralogism): voting signifies political equality, which implies social equality, which in turn incites sexual assaults on white women, i.e., threatens the societal myth of the racial purity of whites (Litwack 1998, p. 221). It was not political expediency so much as caste necessity that mandated the political exclusion of the descendants of slaves. The same may well be true today about felons as they have been made over into the latest historical avatar of the 'bad [n***er]'.

NOTES

1. Durkheim goes on to elaborate: 'We must not say that an act offends the common conscience because it is criminal, but that it is criminal because it offends the common conscience. We do not reprove of it because it is a crime; rather, it is a crime because we reprove of it' (1930, p. 48; my translation).

2. 'No master, whether in Ancient Rome, medieval Tuscany, or seventeenth-century Brazil, could forget that the obsequious servant might also be a 'domestic enemy' bent on theft, poisoning, or arson. Throughout history it has been said that

slaves, if occasionally as loyal and as faithful as good dogs, were for the most part lazy, irresponsible, cunning, rebellious, untrustworthy, and sexually promiscuous' (Davis 1976, p. 40–1). Note that this litany of adjectives contains the qualifiers most commonly applied to the urban 'underclass' in the America of the 1980s.

3. Remember that, for Durkheim, punishment is a social function that arises 'wherever a commanding power establishes itself' whose 'primary and principal function is to (. . .) defend the common conscience against all the enemies of the interior as of the exterior' (1930, p. 51; my translation).

4. The state Election Division purged from the rolls voters whose names and birthdate merely *resembled* those of people listed in felony databases in spite of warnings from its own experts that this would automatically result in the unlawful elimination of thousands of eligible voters. A recent study disclosed that black voters were thus expurgated at ten times the rate of whites (Donziger 2002, p. 2).

REFERENCES

DAVIS, D. B. 1976. *The Problem of Slavery in the Age of Revolution, 1770–1823*. Oxford: Oxford University Press.

DONZIGER, S. 2002. *America's Modern Poll Tax: How Structural Disenfranchisement Erodes Democracy*. Washington, DC: Advancement Project.

DU BOIS, W. E. B. 1903. *The Souls of Black Folk*. New York: Vintage/The Library of America, 1990.

DUGAN, M. Census Dollars Bring Bounty to Prison Towns, *Chicago Reporter*, 29, 7 (July–August 2000), pp. 10–11.

DURKHEIM, E. [1893] 1930. *De la division du travail social*. Tenth edition. Paris: Presses Universitaires de France.

FLETCHER, G. 1999. Disenfranchisement as punishment: reflections on the race uses of infamia, *UCLA Law Review*, 46, 1895–1908.

GERSTLE, G. 2001. *American Crucible: Race and Nation in the Twentieth Century*. Princeton, NJ: Princeton University Press.

KEYSSAR, A. 2000. *The Right to Vote: The Contested History of Democracy in the United States*. New York: Basic Books.

KLINKNER, P. A., AND SMITH, R. M. 1999. *The Unsteady March: The Rise and Decline of Racial Equality in America*. Chicago, IL: University of Chicago Press.

KOLCHIN, P. 1993. *American Slavery: 1619–1877*. New York: Hill and Wang.

LITWACK, L. F. 1998. *Trouble in Mind: Black Southerners in the Age of Jim Crow*. New York: Knopf.

MCADAM, D. 1989. *Political Process and the Development of Black Insurgency 1930–1970*. Chicago, IL: University of Chicago Press.

ROEDIGER, D. R. 1991. *The Wages of Whiteness: Race and the Making of the American Working Class*. London: Verso.

UGGEN, C., AND MANZA, J. 2002. Democratic reversal? The political consequences of felon disenfranchisement in the United States, *American Sociological Review*, 67(6), 777–803.

WACQUANT, L. 2005. The great carceral leap backward: incarceration in America from Nixon to Clinton, In: Pratt, J. et al., eds. *The New Punitiveness: Current Trends, Theories, Perspectives*. London: Willan.

WAGNER, P. 2002. *Importing Constituents: Prisoners and Political Clout in New York*. Springfield, MA: Prison Policy Initiative.

WALTON, A. 1992. Willie Horton & Me, In: Early, G., ed., *Speech and Power: The African-American Essay and its Cultural Content, from Polemics to Pulpit*. Saint Paul, MN: Ecco Press, 397–401.

WRIGHT, R. 1939. *Native Son*. Unexpurgated text, in *Early Works*. New York: Vintage/The Library of America, 1991.

49. The Digital Transformation of Criminality*

David S. Wall

Individually, cybercrimes may not be particularly serious and surveys of individual victimizations, police actions and prosecutions show the figures to be quite low, despite expectations to the contrary. However, these local statistics tend not to grasp the global picture as their true seriousness lies in their aggregate impact. We have now entered the world of low-impact, multiple victim crimes where bank robbers no longer have to plan meticulously thefts of millions of dollars; new technological capabilities mean that one person can now commit millions of robberies of $1 each. This 'de minimism' creates a number of important challenges for law enforcement and the policing of offenders. On the one hand, criminal justice systems are not geared up to deal with such offences. On the other hand, the realism, indeed digital realism, of cybercrime is such that the more a behaviour is mediated by new technology, the more it can be governed by that same technology. So, in addition to the prospect of being faced with 'ubiquitous' and automated victimization, we also – simultaneously – face the prospect of being exposed to ubiquitous law enforcement and prevention and the potential problems it creates, such as a potential 'pre-crime' agenda.

[. . .]

* From Wall, D. (2007) *Cybercrime: The Transformation of Crime in the Information Age* (Cambridge: Polity). Extracts from pp. 3–4, 8–9, 10–11, 22–24, 26.

The primary aim of this book is to contribute to our knowledge and understanding of cybercrimes. It is not a manual of computer crimes and the methods by which to resolve them; others do that far better. Rather, it is a critical exploration of the transformations that have taken place in criminal activity and its regulation as a result of networked technologies. Central to the arguments put forward in the forthcoming chapters is a 'transformation thesis' which views cybercrimes as criminal or harmful activities that are informational, global and networked. They are the product of networked technologies that have transformed the division of criminal labour to provide entirely new opportunities for, and indeed, new forms of crime which typically involve the acquisition or manipulation of information and its value across global networks. This notion of transformation is important because it offers the prospect of reconciling seemingly different accounts of cybercrime by representing them as different phases in the process of change. The transformation concept is also important because its flip-side, as indicated above, is that the same technologies which create cybercrimes also provide unique opportunities for their regulation and policing. However, while this may provide a solution, it also stimulates an important debate about the framework for maintaining order and law enforcement on the internet.

[. . .]

Although few would deny that the internet has had a major impact upon criminal behaviour, there is much less consensus as to what that impact has been. Even when nations agree that cybercrimes are a problem there appears to be no overall consensus about how to deal with them collectively (Goodman and Brenner, 2002: 89). All too often claims about the prevalence of cybercrimes lack clarification as to what it is that is particularly 'cyber' about them. Indeed, when so-called cases of cybercrime come to court they often have the familiar ring of the 'traditional' rather than the 'cyber' about them. These offences typically comprise hacking, fraud, pornography, paedophilia, etc., which are already part of existing criminal justice regimes. Perhaps more confusing is the contrast between the many hundreds of thousands of incidents that are supposedly reported each year and the relatively small number of known prosecutions. Is this a case of the absence of evidence not being evidence of its absence, to paraphrase former US Secretary of State, Donald Rumsfeld (Barone, 2004). Or, should we be asking if there are actually such things as cybercrimes? (Brenner, 2001: para. 1). Other authors have questioned whether cybercrimes are actually categories of crime in need of new theory, or whether they are understood better by existing theories (Jones, 2003: 98).

These contrasting viewpoints expose a large gap in our understanding of cybercrimes and beg a number of important questions about the quality of the production of information about cybercrimes. They fall into two groups. The first relate to the reliability and partiality of the informational sources that mould opinion. Has, for example, the cybercrime problem simply been blown up out of all proportion? If so, how has this happened? Has, for example, the media news gathering process effectively fabricated an apparent crime wave out of a few novel and dramatic events? Alternatively, are we experiencing a calculated attempt to peddle 'Fear, Uncertainty and Doubt' by the cyber-security industry – which has been described as a 'self-dramatizing and fear mongering world of security pundits' (Schneier, 2003) with a stake in sensationalizing cybercrimes. 'FUDmongering', as this process has

become known, claims Green (1999), 'is a tactic often used by vendors within a monopoly market in order to propagate their monopoly'. The second group of questions relates to the conceptual basis upon which information is gathered and assumptions are made. Could it be the case that the criminal justice processes are just woefully inefficient at bringing wrongdoers to justice? Indeed, can we realistically expect criminal justice processes designed to counter the social effects of urban migration to respond to an entirely new set of globalized 'virtual' problems? There again, could it be that we are perhaps simply failing to understand the epistemological differences between the various legal, academic, expert and popular (lay) constructions of cybercrime.

[. . .]

Why call it 'cybercrime'?

First coined by William Gibson (1982) and then popularized in his 1984 novel *Neuromancer*, the term 'cyberspace' became a popular descriptor of the mentally constructed virtual environment within which networked computer activity takes place. 'Cybercrime' broadly describes the crimes that take place within that space and the term has come to symbolize insecurity and risk online. By itself, cybercrime is fairly meaningless because it tends to be used metaphorically and emotively rather than scientifically or legally, usually to signify the occurrence of harmful behaviour that is somehow related to the misuse of a networked computer system (Wall, 1997; NCIS, 1999). Largely an invention of the media, 'cybercrime' originally had no specific reference point in law in the UK or US[1] and the offending that did become associated with the term was a rather narrow legal construction based upon concerns about hacking. In fact, many of the so-called cybercrimes that have caused concern over the past decade are not necessarily crimes in criminal law. If we could turn the clock back in time then perhaps the term 'cyberspace crime' would have been a more precise and accurate descriptor. However, regardless of its merits and demerits, the term 'cybercrime' has entered the public parlance and we are stuck with it (Wall, 2005). It is argued here and elsewhere in this book that the term has a greater meaning if we construct it in terms of the transformation of criminal or harmful behaviour by networked technology, rather than simply the behaviour itself. As stated earlier, cybercrimes are understood here to be criminal or harmful activities that involve the acquisition or manipulation of information for gain.

Not only has the term 'cybercrime' acquired considerable linguistic agency, but over the past decade 'cybercrimes' have become firmly embedded in public crime agendas as something that must be governed. This is an interesting happenstance within the context of the transformation thesis, because although the contemporary meaning of 'cyber' is firmly linked to technological innovation, its origins lie in the Greek *kubernetes*, or steersman, which is also the root of the word 'govern'. See, for example, the French usage of the term 'cybernétique' – the art of governing (*Oxford English Dictionary*). The word 'cyber' entered the English language in 'cybernetics', which is the study of systems of control and communications (linked with computers). More by coincidence than design, the words cyber and crime actually sit well together linguistically. This linkage becomes more significant if we understand cybercrimes as crimes which are mediated (governed if you like) by networked technology and not just computer.

[. . .]

The ongoing power struggle for control over cyberspace

The increasing political and commercial power of the internet is forging new power relationships that are gradually shaping and reshaping what is and what is not a cybercrime. This political economy of information capital is marked by an ongoing power play, or 'intellectual land grab', for market control and protection (see Boyle, 1996). Consequently, definitions of acceptable and deviant cyber-behaviour are being shaped by the interests of the 'new' powerful – those who gain a commercial and legal hold on the upper ground. The rising intolerance of the new powerful towards 'risk groups' they perceive as a threat to their own interests is causing concern, especially when 'the problem', as it becomes regarded, is reconstructed within a criminal, rather than civil, law discourse that contrasts competing interests in an adversarial good guys/ bad guys binary. See, for example, the debates over MP3 and MP4s and also the threats of prosecution (typically 'letters before action') and actual prosecutions brought by the Recording Industry Association of America (RIAA) and British Phonographic Industry (BPI) (see Carey and Wall, 2001: 36; Marshall, 2002: 1) and the Motion Picture Associations. Alternatively, see the technological and legal tactics employed to control spammers that are outlined in chapter 9.

It would be wrong, however, simply to assume that the construction of deviance is one-sided. Even if definitions of crime and deviance are originated by the social activity of elites or powerful groups, they have to be embedded in the lives and understandings of ordinary members of society as well as offenders themselves for them to translate into social action. On this, Melossi has observed that 'the struggle around the definition of crime and deviance is located within the field of action that is constituted by plural and even conflicting efforts at producing control' (1994: 205). The key issue here is therefore about whether reliable information flows freely to form reliable viewpoints.

Competing expert claims

Very influential in the production of knowledge about cybercrimes and in shaping public and governmental opinion are the claims of 'experts'. Without reliable knowledge, especially recognized metrics, it is not only hard to validate expert claims, especially when they compete, but it is also difficult to counter inaccurate claims with factual information. The cyber-security industry, which comprises security consultants and aspects of private and public law enforcement agencies, has an economic interest in cybercrime that can shape the focus of any claims made. While claims may be grounded in good information, industry members will tend to present views that favour their own particular interests. There has, for example, been a historical tendency to overestimate the extent of crime on the internet by inflating the importance of low-level automated intrusion statistics.

Levi argues that this is systemic and that the potential impacts of cybercrime may simply be 'talked up' by 'experts', who may deliberately or paranoically inflate the threat, conflating 'experience of with theoretical risk from computer crime' (Levi, 2001: 50) for their own gain, particularly when competing for government resources. Levi has argued that the conflation of experience with theoretical risk is part of the broader 'intelligence threat-assessment mental set' that is perpetuated by 'the self-serving PR of security consultants whose income depends on shocking ... or ... "creating awareness among" ... senior executives and government agencies who complacently fail to spend "enough" money on security' (Levi, 2001: 50). The same PR also feeds the media's current lust for internet-related news and subsequently shapes public knowledge about, and attitudes towards, the internet and drives the resulting debate over crime, providing the regulatory bodies with a mandate for taking action (Wall, 2002: 190). [...]

[...]

What this chapter has illustrated is that cybercrime is not a given, incontrovertible fact. Our understandings of it have been constructed over the past two decades from various countervailing discourses and their attendant epistemologies. Some are concerned with risk assessment (what ought), others with reality (what is). In acknowledging the respective strengths and weaknesses of these discourses we increase our understanding of cybercrimes. To ignore their origins lays us open to confusing risk assessment with reality and its accompanying dangers, particularly the way that it can 'corrupt systems' by creating mindsets in which the only way to combat cybercrimes is thought to be an increase in resources for the enforcement of law and/or to introduce stringent technological countermeasures. This confusion can be further compounded by the over-reliance by the media on contestable statistical 'guesstimates' produced by the cyber-security industry (see above, Leyden, 2005) and the media's dependence upon so-called 'experts' for confirmation.

NOTE

1. There are a few exceptions, such as in Australia, where a Cybercrime Act was introduced in 2001, and in Nigeria, where a Draft Cybercrime Act has been proposed.

REFERENCES

Barone, M. (2004) 'The national interest: absence of evidence is not evidence of absence', *US News & World Report*, 24 March, at www.usnews.com/usnews/opinion/baroneweb/mb_040324.htm.

Boyle, J. (1996) *Shamans, Software and Spleens: Law and the Construction of the Information Society*, Cambridge, MA: Harvard University Press.

Brenner, S. (2001) 'Is there such a thing as "virtual crime"?', *California Criminal Law Review*, 4 (1): 11.

Carey, M. and Wall, D. S. (2001) 'MP3: more beats to the byte', *International Review of Law, Computers and Technology*, 15 (1): 35–58.

Gibson, W. (1982) 'Burning chrome', *Omni Magazine*, July.

Gibson, W. (1984) *Neuromancer*, London: HarperCollins.

Goodman, M. and Brenner, S. (2002) 'The emerging consensus on criminal conduct in cyberspace', *UCLA Journal of Law and Technology*, 3, at www.lawtechjournal.com/articles/2002/03_020625_goodmanbrenner.pdf.

Green, E. (1999) *FUD 101 v1.0*, November 15, at http://badtux.org/home/eric/editorial/fud101-1.0.0.html.

Jones, R. (2003) '"Review of Crime in The Digital Age" by P. Grabosky and R. Smith', *International Journal of Law and Information Technology*, 11: 98.

Levi, M. (2001) '"Between the risk and the reality falls the shadow": evidence and urban legends in computer fraud', in D. S. Wall (ed.), *Crime and the Internet*, London: Routledge, 44–58.

Leyden, J. (2005) 'Webroot guesstimates inflate UK spyware problem', *The Register*, 20 October, at www.theregister.co.uk/2005/10/20/webroot_uk_spyware_guesstimates/.

Marshall, L. (2002) 'Metallica and morality: the rhetorical battleground of the Napster Wars', *Entertainment Law*, 1 (1): 1.

Melossi, D. (1994) 'Normal crimes, élites and social control', in D. Nelken (ed.), *The Futures of Criminology*, London: Sage, pp. 202–19.

NCIS (1999) *Project Trawler: Crime On The Information Highways*, London: National Criminal Intelligence Service.

Schneier, B. (2003) *Beyond Fear: Thinking Sensibly about Security in an Uncertain World*, New York: Springer-Verlag.

Wall, D. S. (1997) 'Policing the virtual community: the internet, cybercrimes and the policing of cyberspace', in P. Francis, P. Davies and V. Jupp (eds), *Policing Futures*, London: Macmillan, 208–36.

Wall, D. S. (2002) 'Insecurity and the policing of cyberspace', in A. Crawford (ed.), *Crime and Insecurity*, Cullompton: Willan, 186–210.

Wall, D. S. (2005) 'The Internet as a conduit for criminals', in A. Pattavina (ed.), *Information Technology and The Criminal Justice System*, Thousand Oaks, CA: Sage, 77–98.

50. Back to the Future: The Return of Banishment*

Katherine Beckett and Steve Herbert

Seattle is arguably one of the most progressive cities in the United States. Its political leaders are almost uniformly Democratic. It boasts one of the most robust efforts at forward-thinking environmental policies. It is home to several icons of the postindustrial economy, such as Microsoft, Amazon.com, Starbucks, and Costco. It sits in a region of stunning natural beauty. As James Fallows once wrote about the city. "If the climate were not so dark and rainy, everyone would want to live there."[1] Yet Seattle is not an urban utopia for everyone. As the stories of Rhonda, Tom, and Jose reveal, the city currently deploys a social control regime that lies in sharp contrast to its progressive image.[2]

At the core of this regime lie practices of banishment. Increasing swaths of urban space are delimited as zones of exclusion from which the undesirable are banned. The uniformed police are marshaled to enforce and often delineate these boundaries; they use their powers to monitor and arrest in an attempt to clear the streets of those considered unsightly or "disorderly."

Seattle is not alone in its deployment of social control tactics that entail banishment. In many other U.S. cities, exclusion orders that make mere presence in public space a crime are regularly imposed. Although it is not well known, New York City, Los Angeles, Portland, Las Vegas, Cincinnati, Honolulu, and many other municipalities employ one or more banishment

strategies. These new legal tools are rarely debated publicly; they are largely deployed without much fanfare against individuals, such as the homeless, whose daily travails are not especially well chronicled. This lack of attention to banishment is unfortunate, because it is an increasingly consequential reality in the lives of many.

For example, public housing authorities across the United States regularly employ trespass enforcement to address concerns about crime and disorder. Specifically, newly created trespass programs permit authorities to trespass admonish unwanted individuals for extended periods of time. Such programs are in operation in New York City,[3] Boston,[4] Richmond (Virginia),[5] and many other cities.[6] Some public housing trespass programs ban those who have been arrested for or convicted of particular crimes from public housing buildings and grounds; this can even include residents. Other no-trespass policies ban nearly all nonresidents.[7]

The adoption of new trespass policies in New York City is increasingly controversial. New York state law explicitly prohibits trespassing in public housing and other locations. Yet prior to 1991, public housing was considered a public space; no one could be arrested for entering lobbies or public hallways in these buildings. In the early 1990s, however, the trespass statute was amended to give public housing authorities the same capacity to exclude unwanted members of the public that is enjoyed by owners of private dwellings.[8] Moreover, a recent executive order enables housing authorities and police officers to *permanently* exclude people from public housing

* From Beckett, K. and Herbert, S. (2010) *Banished: The New Social Control in Urban America* (Oxford: Oxford University Press). Extracts from pp. 8–12.

property for a variety of reasons. Although the city's Operation Safe Housing program specifies that only those arrested for selling drugs on public housing property may be excluded indefinitely, others—including residents and their guests—may be excluded for significant periods of time as well.[9] This policy is enforced through vertical sweeps. Such sweeps are now also conducted in private buildings as a consequence of the Trespass Affidavit Program (TAP).[10] TAP allows building owners in private buildings to sign an affidavit that gives police permission to enter buildings and arrest individuals who are not tenants for trespassing. As a result, trespass arrests have skyrocketed in New York City.[11]

Off-limits orders are also increasingly popular. In numerous U.S. cities, including Cincinnati. Portland, and Fort Lauderdale, judges and correctional officers regularly require those convicted of certain offenses to stay out of particular sections of the city as a condition of their community supervision sentence.[12] In some cases, off-limits orders are imposed on defendants who are not convicted of a crime. In Portland, for example, orders to remain outside drug-free zones and prostitution-free zones may be imposed by police officers at the time of arrest or in lieu of arrest.[13]

Many U.S. cities now deploy other new social control tools that involve spatial exclusion and, like the innovations just described, fuse civil and criminal law. These include gang injunctions, juvenile curfews, and "no contact orders."[14] Civil gang injunctions, widely used by such California cities as Los Angeles, mobilize the civil power of the injunction to address what is typically thought of as a crime problem.[15] In these municipalities, prosecutors and other officials request that judges use injunctive power to prohibit alleged gang members from, among other things, being within a specified target area.[16] In many cases, judges comply with these requests. As is the case with trespass exclusions, a violation of these civil orders is a criminal offense.[17]

In short, cities across the United States increasingly employ novel social control mechanisms that entail spatial exclusion and fuse civil and

criminal legal authority. Other cities of the global North deploy similar tactics.[18] In the United Kingdom, for example, new control measures are increasingly employed to reduce "antisocial" behavior and thereby enhance "security." In particular, Anti-Social Behavioral Contracts and Anti-Social Behavioral Orders cover a wide range of unwanted behaviors, fuse civil and criminal law, and often lead to the imposition of place-based restrictions.[19]

It thus appears that Seattle is on the leading edge of an emerging trend. [. . .]

Banishment is hardly new; imposing exile to encourage conformity dates back to ancient times. Banishment was featured extensively in the Old Testament and was employed in ancient Babylon. Greece, and Rome, as well as by British authorities throughout the colonial empire.[20] In the new republic of the United States, banishment was thought by many to be repulsive but was nonetheless practiced widely. When miscreants proved troublesome, many towns forced them away.

As a result of this history, today banishment is considered an archaic and even primitive form of punishment by many scholars and legal experts.[21] Although the appeal of banishment to people living thousands of years ago and lacking alternative mechanisms for dealing with disruptive behavior makes retrospective sense, most countries now prohibit the banishment of their citizens.[22] In the United States, too, most states disallow interstate banishment. As one legal scholar noted, banishment "would seem more appropriate to *Romeo and Juliet* or *Great Expectations* than to the solution of problems in a modern society."[23]

Nonetheless, the new legal tools we analyze here entail banishment: the legal compulsion to leave specified geographic areas for extended periods of time. Banishment's return raises a number of questions. Why is it reemerging with such blunt force in Seattle and many other cities of the global North? How is it justified? How is it practiced? Who are its targets? How are they targeted? What does it mean for them to be banished?

What does its practice suggest about Seattle as a city? What does it reveal about the contemporary politics of public space and democratic inclusion? Can banishment be justified, or should it be rejected as a solution to urban social problems? Our task in this book is to address these questions by chronicling and assessing the return of banishment in one of America's iconic cities.

Of course, some might object to our use of the term banishment. After all, to the banished historically meant to be excluded from a town, county, state, or country. In the common law tradition, banishment is defined as "a punishment inflicted upon criminals, by compelling them to quit a city, place or country for a specified period of time.[24] Understood this way, banishment, is rarely allowed. Courts now prohibit interstate banishment, and only five states permit intrastate banishment, that is, the legal expulsion of a citizen from a town or county.[25] Furthermore, courts generally do not consider expulsion from a neighborhood or area within a city to constitute banishment.[26]

Given this, our use of *banishment* to describe the exclusion of persons from relatively small geographic areas requires some explanation. It is certainly the case that some of the spaces from which people are banned in Seattle are small in scale—city parks from which expulsions spring can be minuscule, as are some private businesses from which one may be trespassed. It is thus perhaps better to use the term *exclusion* to describe the practices we evaluate.

We prefer to use the term *banishment* for four reasons. First, we want to underscore the strong role of the coercive power of the state in accomplishing this form of spatial segregation.[27] The word *exclusion* often describes more informal practices, such as ostracism from a peer group. Banishment, by contrast, provides a stronger implication of overt state policy, as a policy emerging by dint of "official decree."

This leads to a second motivation behind our use of *banishment*. Banishment is a punishment, meted out to those condemned as deviant or criminal. The practices that entail banishment

rest on the assumption that the social problems to which they are frequently a response—homelessness, addiction, mental illness—may be understood and treated as criminal problems. This is true even to the extent that banishment results from the application of civil rather than criminal law. For reasons we explore later, basing expulsion in civil law only enhances the scope and authority of criminal law and does not alter the fact that these exclusions compel their targets to "quit" a place or risk arrest and incarceration.

Indeed, the deployment of the new control tools—touted by proponents as alternatives to arrest and punishment—has a "net-widening" effect: it creates crimes and criminal cases that would not otherwise exist. Taken together, these techniques represent a dramatic extension of the state's authority and surveillance capacity throughout the urban landscape. The punitive city of twenty-first-century America is one in which an increasing number of acts are regulated and criminalized: the state's ability to search, detain, regulate, and monitor is expanded; and a system of invisible yet highly consequential gates and barriers increasingly constrains the movement of some urbanites in public space.[28]

Third, we believe the term best describes what the ostracized say they experience. Historically, banishment imposed social separation and deprived the exiled of the rights that accompany membership in a political community. Similarly, those who experience banishment in Seattle describe their social and spatial marginalization in sharp terms, not just as a complication in their everyday lives but an expulsion from the body politic. They understand themselves to be cast aside and punished daily for their transgressions, no matter how minor. They also report that their rights as citizens and community members are severely weakened as a result of their banishment, and their exclusion order serves as a kind of "master status"[29] that govern their interactions with authorities, As Bauman writes,

Estrangement is the core function of spatial separation. Estrangement reduces, thins down, and compresses the view of the other; individual qualities and circumstances which tend to be vividly brought within sight thanks to the accumulated experience of daily intercourse, seldom come into view when the intercourse is emaciated or prohibited altogether.[30]

Fourth, through the use of the term *banishment*, we wish to highlight the extent to which the zoning logic is expansionary. Although any given zone of exclusion may be small, some zones are not, and the cumulative effect of creating multiple exclusion zones is to render much of the city a "no go" area for many residents. Those who are homeless or otherwise considered disreputable are quite likely to be the subject of numerous exclusionary bans, to the point where their mobility through the city is severely limited.

Granted, people today are not banned from extensive areas as in the past. We are nevertheless compelled to use the term *banishment* to describe the consequence of the legal tools we analyze. These exclusionary practices rest on the coercive capacity of the state, create crimes and punishments that would not otherwise exist, and deprive their targets of political rights. Moreover, the spaces from which people are banished are growing. Although it may look different from previous iterations, banishment is indisputably back.

NOTES

1. James Fallows, "Saving Salmon or Seattle," *Atlantic Monthly*. 286 (2000): 20–24.
2. The term "social control" refers generally to the process by which social order is maintained, but it has been defined in a number of ways. We define it here more narrowly to refer to the process by which actors undertake concerted efforts to manage or regulate deviant behavior. This definition closely parallels that of Stanley Cohen (*Visions of Social Control*, Cambridge: Polity, 1985) and Donald Black (*The Behaviour of Law*, New York: Academic Press, 1976), and can be differentiated from approaches that are so broad as to equate social control with socialization. For extended discussion of the debate around these various conceptions, see Martin Innes, *Understanding Social Control: Deviance, Crime and Social Order* (New York: McGraw Hill International, 2003).
3. See www.nyc.gov/html/nycha/html/residents/trespass.shtml.
4. See www.bostonhousing.org/pdfs/Trespassing%20Draft%20Policy.pdf.
5. Don Mitchell, "Property Rights, the First Amendment, and Judicial Anti-Urbanism: The Strange Case of *Hicks v. Virginia*," *Urban Geography* 26, no.7 (2005): 565–586. See also dls.state.va.us/pubs/briefs/brief31.htm.
6. Elena Goldstein, "Kept Out: Responding to Public Housing No-Trespass Policies," *Harvard Civil Rights-Civil Liberties Journal* 38 (2003): Mitchell, "Property Rights, the First Amendment, and Judicial Anti-Urbanism."
7. Ibid.
8. *People v. Carter.* 169 Misc.2d 230, 234 (Kings City, 1996).
9. Jaime Adame, "Operation Safe Housing," *Gotham Gazette*, August 17, 2004; Goldstein, "Kept Out."
10. See New York Country District Attorney's Office, Trespass Affidavit and Narcotics Eviction Programs, available at manhattanda.org/officebrochures/TAP.NEP.pdf.
11. Adame, "Operation Safe Housing"; Manny Fernandez, "Barred from Public Housing Even to See Family," *New York Times*, October I. 2007, AI; New York City, "Mayor Michael R. Bloomberg Announces Operation Safe Housing." June 24, 2004; Cara Tabachnick, "Jump in Trespassing Arrests Draws Anger," *Newsday*, April 10, 2007; Rocco Parascandola, "Trespass Arrests under Attack," *Newsday*, April 13, 2007.

12. Peter M. Flanagan, "Trespass-Zoning: Ensuring Neighborhoods a Safer Future by Excluding Those with a Criminal Past," *Notre Dame Law Review* 79 (2003): 327–379; Gordon Hill, "The Use of Pre-Existing Exclusionary Zones as Probationary Conditions for Prostitution Offenses: A Call for the Sincere Application of Heightened Scrutiny," *Seattle University Law Review* 28 (2005); Sandra Moser, "Anti-Prostitution Zones: Justifications for Abolition," *Journal of Criminal Law and Criminology* 91 (summer 2001): 1101; Lisa Sanchez. "Enclosure Acts and Exclusionary Practices: Neighborhood Associations, Community Police, and the Expulsion of the Sexual Outlaw," chapter 6 in *Between Law and Culture: Relocating Legal Studies,* edited by David Theo Goldberg Michael Musheno, and Lisa C. Bower (Minneapolis: University of Minnesota Press, 1997).

13. American Prosecutors Research Institute, *Unwelcome Guest: A Community Prosecution Approach to Street Level Drug Dealing and Prostitution* (2004): Sanchez, Enclosure Acts and Exclusionary Practices"; Abby Sewell, "How Well Do Drug-Free" Zones Really Work?" *Portland Alliance,* November 2005. As Sewell notes in Portland exclusion orders say on a person's record even in the absence of conviction. Other Oregon municipalities appear to be following suit See www.cascade-locks.or.us/leftmenus/ordinance/ord354.pdf. A similar ordinance was in effect in Cincinnati, Ohio, from 1996 to 2000 but was overturned in the Sixth circuit. Three spatial restrictions are now imposed on those convicted as a condition of probation in Cincinnati (Associated Press. "High Court Refuses to Review Cincinnati's Anti-Trespass Law," April 29, 2002).

14. For a critical appraisal of the increased use of no-contact orders, see Jeannie Suk, "Criminal Law Comes Home," *Yale Law Journal* 116, no. 2 (2006): 2–70. For an empirical assessment of the growth and effects of juvenile curfews, see Kenneth Adams. "The Effectiveness of Juvenile Curfews at Crime Prevention." *Annals of the American Academy of Political and Social Science* 587 (2003): 136–159.

15. The use of nuisance statutes, civil injunctions, and abatement proceedings in the war on disorder is not new. Nuisance abatement statutes were an important part of nineteenth and twentieth centuries in campaigns against prostitution and vice. Indeed, some historians suggest that injunctions against brothels and houses of prostitution, in combination with the enforcement of criminal prohibitions against vagrancy, loitering, and prostitution, ultimately sealed the fate of many Progressive era red-light districts. See William J. Novak. *The People's Welfare: Law and Regulation in Nineteenth Century America* (Chapel Hill: University of North Carolina Press, 1996), 165–166. See also Charles S. Ascher and James M. Wolf. "'Red Light' Injunction and Abatement Acts," *Columbia Law Review* 20 (1920): 605–608; Robert McCurdy. "The Use of the Injunction to Destroy Commercialized Prostitution in Chicago," *Journal of Criminal Law* 19 (1929): 515–517. With the development of gang injunctions, however, nuisance laws now place civil restrictions on the movement of people as well as on the uses of property. Moreover, the legal hybridity of the gang injunctions and other legal tools described here does appear to be novel.

16. Edward L. Allan, *Civil Gang Abatement: The Effectiveness and Implications of Policing by Injunction* (New York: LFB Scholarly Publications. 2004); Gary Stewart. "Black Codes and Broken Windows: The Legacy of Racial Hegemony in Anti-Gang Civil Injunctions," *Yale Law Journal* 107, no. 7 (May 1998): 2249–2280.

17. Like the new control mechanisms now deployed in Seattle, civil gang injunctions

raise a number of constitutional issues, like civil trespass admonishments and parks exclusions, these gang injunctions proscribe otherwise legal behaviors (such as associating with others and being in public spaces). They also create personal criminal codes that attach to particular individuals as a result of that person's alleged status as a gang member. Finally, gang injunctions offer very little in the way of due process protections. In particular, only a preponderance of evidence is required to sustain a determination that the injunction has been violated; the accused does not enjoy the right to legal representation; and challenging the constitutionality of the law that makes it a crime for the accused to engage in otherwise legal behavior is quite difficult. See Christopher S. Yoo, "The Constitutionality of Enjoining Street Gangs as Public Nuisances," *Northwest University Law Review* 89 (1994): 212. Stewart, "Black Codes and Broken Windows"; Mathew Mickle Werdegar, "Enjoining the Constitution: The Use of Public Nuisance Abatement Injunctions against Urban Street Gangs," *Stanford Law Review* 51, no. 2 (January 1999): 409–448.

18. On the United Kingdom, see Adam Crawford, "From the Shopping Mall to the Street Corner: Dynamics of Exclusion in the Governance of Public Space," presented to the World University Network. University of Leeds, June 2008; Adam Crawford and Stuart Lister, *The Use and Impact of Dispersal Orders* (Bristol: Policy Press, 2007; Andrew Millie. "Anti-Social Behaviour, Behavioural Expectations and an Urban Aesthetic," *British Journal of Criminology* 48 (2008): 379–394: Elizabeth Burney, *Making People Behave: Anti-Social Behaviour, Politics, and Policy* (Cullompton: Willan, 2005) and *Crime and Banishment: Nuisance and Exclusion in Social Housing* (Winchester Waterside Press. 1999); John Flint and Judy Nixon, "Governing

Neighbours: Anti-Social Behaviour Orders and New Forms of Regulating Conduct in the UK," *Urban Studies* 43 (2006): 939–956: Mike Raco, "Remaking Place and Securitizing Space: Urban Regeneration and the Strategies, Tactics and Practices of Policing in the UK," *Urban Studies* 40 (2005): 1869–1887: Peter Ramsay. "The Theory of Vulnerable Autonomy and the Legitimacy of the Civil Prevention Order." Law, Society and Economy Working Papers, 1/2008. On Germany, see Bernd Belina, "From Disciplining to Dislocation: Area Bans in Recent Urban Policing in Germany," *European Urban and Regional Studies* 14 (2007): 321–336; Jurgen von Mahs, "The Sociospatial Exclusion of Single Homeless People in Berlin and Los Angeles," *American Behavioral Scientist* 48 (2005): 928–960.

19. Crawford. "From the Shopping Mall to the Street Corner."

20. See Michael F. Armstrong. "Banishment: Cruel and Unusual Punishment," *University of Pennsylvania Law Review* 111, no.6 (April 1963): 758–786; Matthew D. Borrelli, "Banishment: The Constitutional and Public Policy Arguments against this Revived Ancient Punishment," 36 *Suffolk University Law Review* 470 (2002–2003); William Garth Snider, "Banishment: The History of its Use and a Proposal for its Abolition under the First Amendment," 24 *Northeast Journal on Criminal And Civil Confinement* 455 (summer 1998).

21. Ibid.

22. Of course, migrants without papers are often banished; this process is referred to as deportation.

23. Armstrong, "Banishment: Cruel and Unusual Punishment."

24. The more complete legal definition is as follows: banishment is the "expulsion, or deportation by the political authority on the ground of expediency: punishment by forced exile, either for years or for life; a

punishment inflicted on criminals, by compelling them to quit a city, place or country, for a specified period of time, or for life," 8 C.J.S. *Banishment* §593 (1930). See also Black, *Law Dictionary* 183 (4th ed., 1951).

25. Snider, "Banishment: The History of Its Use."

26. Ibid.

27. The legal definition of *banishment* similarly underscores the role of political authorities in effecting banishment orders (see note 24). Similarly, the *American Heritage Dictionary*'s first definition of *banishment* is this: "To force to leave a country or place by *official decree*" (emphasis added).

28. Elsewhere, we argue that these conclusions are largely consistent with Stanley Cohen's dystopian account of the net-widening impact of efforts to reform criminal justice practices and institutions. See Katherine Beckett and Steve Herbert, "The Punitive City Revisited: The Transformation of Urban Social Control," pp. 106–122 in *After the War on Crime: Race, Democracy, and a New Reconstruction*, edited by Mary Louise Frampton, Ian Haney Lopez, and Jonathan Simon (New York: New York University Press, 2008); Cohen, *Visions of Social Control*.

29. Howard S. Becker, *Outsiders: Studies in the Sociology of Deviance* (New York: Free Press, 1963).

30. Zygmunt Bauman, "Social Issues of Law and Order," *British Journal of Criminology* 40 (2000): 205–221, 208.

Part 9 – Further reading

A good way into the sociology of deviance is with Atkinson, R. (ed.) (2014) *Shades of Deviance: A Primer on Crime, Deviance and Social Harm* (Abingdon: Routledge). From here, probably the most comprehensive account of theories, even after seven editions, remains Downes, D., Rock, P., and McLaughlin, E. (2016) *Understanding Deviance* (7th edn, Oxford: Oxford University Press). A good dictionary would be a help for this subject, and McLaughlin, E., and Muncie, J. (eds) (2019) *The Sage Dictionary of Criminology* (4th edn, London: Sage) is that book. Finally, Wall, D. (2007) *Cybercrime: The Transformation of Crime in the Information Age* (Cambridge: Polity) is both systematic and engaging.

Sociology, 9th edition

Chapter 22, 'Crime and Deviance', is the obvious place to look, while chapter 12, 'Social Interaction and Daily Life', covers the subject of deviance too. Chapter 13, 'Cities and Urban Life', also has a useful discussion of urban, inner-city issues.

Part 10 Political Sociology

The interest of political sociology has conventionally been in electoral issues, social class and political affiliation, and the nature of power and how it is exercised. In practice this has meant comparing democracies and authoritarian regimes, voting patterns, shifting party political allegiances and the role of political ideologies, as well as the expression of dissent through non-established channels such as through lobbying and social movements. More recent work in political sociology has examined warfare, genocide and ethnic cleansing, and terrorism, and social movement studies have increased during a period of deep dissatisfaction with formal party politics and mistrust of politicians. We have selected readings that reflect these shifting interests.

The section opens with Steven Lukes's programmatic and influential study of power, a basic concept in political sociology. The original book was published in 1975, though a revised edition dates to 2005, where Lukes also reflects on his thesis. The original work (and this reading) sets out his ideas on three competing perspectives on the nature of power. One-dimensional views see power as the ability to get one's own way even in the face of opposition. This is very much the kind of approach adopted by Max Weber and is influenced by a state-centred politics. The main problem here is that this is an 'intentional' view of power as a deliberate attempt to exert influence over others. A two-dimensional view includes the main

tenets of the first position but adds the idea of power as often exercised simply by virtue of existing social arrangements. For example, feminists have long maintained that men have power because they have distinct advantages over women in patriarchally organized societies. However, Lukes argues for a three-dimensional view, which also adds the internal constraints and beliefs through which people willingly acquiesce to structures of domination, which are acquired through the internalization of ideological beliefs. In this version, people may act in ways that are in opposition to their interests and may not realize it. The reading discusses these three forms in much more detail.

With a few notable exceptions, sociologists have not paid enough attention to war, civil conflicts and peacekeeping, despite the discipline having a long-established conflict tradition that deals with class and intra-society conflicts. Yet the consequences of war have been shown to have far-reaching impacts in the (re)shaping of social and international relations, and today there is increasing interest in understanding wars and their aftermath. One form of conflict that has attracted attention is *ethnic cleansing*, the expulsion or intentional killing of people from a specific ethnic group in an attempt to remove or eliminate it from a given territory. Our reading is from Michael Mann's systematic study of what he calls *murderous* cleansing – those episodes that involve mass murder. Mann argues that ethnic cleansing is a modern phenomenon, at least in terms of the number of instances and the sheer extent of the killing. It is also an example of the 'dark side' of democratic systems, because they always carry at least the possibility of tyranny by the majority over minorities, especially in multi-ethnic situations. And ethnic cleansing is made more likely where ethnic identification is stronger than class identification, channelling perceptions of being exploited into ethnic categories. In our extract, Mann explains his thesis and illustrates this with numerous recent conflicts.

The election of Donald Trump as US president in 2016 was perhaps the most notable success from a wave of political populism that includes the UK's 'Brexit' vote to leave the EU and the electoral successes of Viktor Orbán in Hungary, Narendra Modi in India, and numerous others. Although most of the recent wave has tended to have a 'right-wing' character, historically populism has been both left and right wing. But what is populism? A main theme of populist politics is the claim that it represents the interests of 'the people' against the 'elites' or the political establishment. Framed in this way, populism therefore appeals to those who are frustrated or disillusioned with the mainstream political system and its operation. For example, when there seems to be little policy difference between the major parties, citizens may feel they are not well served and opportunities arise for political parties to disrupt 'business as usual'. The reading from Bart Bonikowski aims to clarify the differences and similarities between this kind of populism and ethno-nationalism or authoritarianism. He argues that various social changes have acted to generate a perception among some national 'ethnocultural' majority populations that their status is under threat. This anxiety is then channelled into resentment towards political and cultural elites, minority ethnic groups and migrants,

and populists find that their arguments now fall onto more fertile ground. Bonikowski's analysis provides insights into contemporary populism and helps to explain why it tends to be on the political right.

Anti-Muslim racism, or 'Islamophobia', today still tends to draw on very old ideas and misrepresentations that circulated widely during the era of colonialism, but the form that Islamophobia takes may also depend on the national context in which it operates. For example, the ideology of 'Eurocentrism', which marks 'Western-identified' people as superior, justifies and defends their privileges and advantages against those identified as 'the other'. Reading 54, by Elizabeth Poole and Milly Williamson, looks at the possibility that major events, such as the Brexit campaign and vote or the COVID-19 pandemic, can disrupt these longstanding ideas, providing an opportunity to reshape established racialized narratives. They examine press reports of the first wave of the pandemic, in particular the way that early evidence that key workers were disproportionately affected was covered. The researchers looked at ways in which newspapers that previously focused on negative stories involving Muslims handled the fact that many of the NHS and other key workers, widely described as 'heroes', were also Muslims.

In our final reading we turn to the phenomenon of the social movement, which has become an important part of political sociology. Social movements used to be considered marginal to the sociological mainstream, but that changed with the emergence of a wave of 'new social movements' in the 1960s and 1970s based on non-violence and direct action. Environmentalism, student movements, LGBTQ+ movements, disabled people's movements, and anti-nuclear and peace movements brought many new issues into political systems, thereby expanding the remit of political sociology. In our extract from Marcia Mundt, Karen Ross and Charla

M. Burnett's paper, the authors seek to understand how movements are using the new digital media and devices in their activities. Taking the example of recent Black Lives Matter (BLM) activism, Mundt and her colleagues discuss the various opportunities and risks involved when activists use social media platforms. Social media offer a clear avenue for recruitment and organization of mobilizations and can be used in building coalitions with other groups. They also enable ongoing discussions and can help in the process of making movement messaging more effective in its engagement with the non-committed public. The research was conducted by analysing several hundred social media accounts that used #blacklivesmatter, and the article nicely demonstrates how sociologists themselves now make use of social media in the pursuit of knowledge.

51. Conceptualizing Power in Sociological Theory*

Steven Lukes

Thirty years ago I published a small book enti-tled *Power: A Radical View* (hereafter *PRV*). It was a contribution to an ongoing debate, mainly among American political scientists and sociologists, about an interesting question: how to think about power theoretically and how to study it empirically. But underlying that debate another question was at issue: how to character-ize American politics – as dominated by a ruling elite or as exhibiting pluralist democracy – and it was clear that answering the second question required an answer to the first. My view was, and is, that we need to think about power broadly rather than narrowly – in three dimensions rather than one or two – and that we need to attend to those aspects of power that are least accessible to observation: that, indeed, power is at its most effective when least observable.

[...]

[...] I shall argue for a view of power (that is, a way of identifying it) which is radical in both the theoretical and political senses (and I take these senses in this context to be intimately related). The view I shall defend is, I shall suggest, ine-radicably evaluative and 'essentially contested' (Gallie 1955–6)[1] on the one hand; and empiri-cally applicable on the other. I shall try to show why this view is superior to alternative views. I shall further defend its evaluative and contested

character as no defect, and I shall argue that it is 'operational', that is, empirically useful in that hypotheses can be framed in terms of it that are in principle verifiable and falsifiable (despite cur-rently canvassed arguments to the contrary). And I shall even give examples of such hypotheses – some of which I shall go so far as to claim to be true.

In the course of my argument, I shall touch on a number of issues – methodological, theoretical and political. Among the methodological issues are the limits of behaviourism, the role of values in explanation, and methodological individual-ism. Among the theoretical issues are questions about the limits or bias of pluralism, about false consciousness and about real interests. Among the political issues are the famous three key issue areas studied by Robert Dahl (Dahl 1961) in New Haven (urban redevelopment, public edu-cation and political nominations), poverty and race relations in Baltimore, and air pollution. These matters will not be discussed in their own right, but merely alluded to at relevant points in the argument. That argument is, of its very nature, controversial. And indeed, that it is so is an essential part of my case.

The argument starts by considering a view of power and related concepts which has deep historical roots (notably in the thought of Max Weber) and achieved great influence among American political scientists in the 1960s through the work of Dahl and his fellow pluralists. That view was criticized as superficial and restric-tive, and as leading to an unjustified celebration of American pluralism, which it portrayed as

* From Lukes, S. (2005) *Power: A Radical View* (2nd edn, Basingstoke: Palgrave Macmillan). Extracts from pp. 1, 14–16, 25–29.

meeting the requirements of democracy, nota-bly by Peter Bachrach and Morton S. Baratz in a famous and influential article, 'The Two Faces of Power' (1962) and a second article (Bachrach and Baratz 1963), which were later incorporated (in modified form) in their book *Power and Poverty* (1970). Their argument was in turn subjected to vigorous counter-attack by the pluralists, espe-cially Nelson Polsby (1968), Raymond Wolfinger (1971a, 1971b) and Richard Merelman (1968a, 1968b); but it has also attracted some very inter-esting defences, such as that by Frederick Frey (1971) and at least one extremely interesting empirical application, in Matthew Crenson's book *The Un-Politics of Air Pollution* (Crenson 1971). My argument will be that the pluralists' view was indeed inadequate for the reasons Bachrach and Baratz advance, and that their view gets further, but that it in turn does not get far enough and is in need of radical toughening. My strategy will be to sketch three conceptual maps, which will, I hope, reveal the distinguishing features of these three views of power: that is, the view of the pluralists (which I shall call the one-dimensional view); the view of their critics (which I shall call the two-dimensional view); and a third view of power (which I shall call the three-dimensional view). I shall then discuss the respective strengths and weaknesses of these three views, and I shall try to show, with examples, that the third view allows one to give a deeper and more satisfac-tory analysis of power relations than either of the other two.

[...]

There is no doubt that the two-dimensional view of power represents a major advance over the one-dimensional view: it incorporates into the analysis of power relations the question of the control over the agenda of politics and of the ways in which potential issues are kept out of the political process. None the less, it is, in my view, inadequate on three counts.

In the first place, its critique of behaviourism is too qualified, or, to put it another way, it is still too committed to behaviourism – that is, to the study of overt, 'actual behaviour', of which 'concrete decisions' in situations of conflict are seen as paradigmatic. In trying to assimilate all cases of exclusion of potential issues from the political agenda to the paradigm of a decision, it gives a misleading picture of the ways in which individuals and, above all, groups and institu-tions succeed in excluding potential issues from the political process. Decisions are choices con-sciously and intentionally made by individuals between alternatives, whereas the bias of the system can be mobilized, recreated and rein-forced in ways that are neither consciously chosen nor the intended result of particular individu-als' choices. As Bachrach and Baratz themselves maintain, the domination of defenders of the status quo may be so secure and pervasive that they are unaware of any potential challengers to their position and thus of any alternatives to the existing political process, whose bias they work to maintain. As 'students of power and its con-sequences', they write, 'our main concern is not whether the defenders of the status quo use their power consciously, but rather if and how they exercise it and what effects it has on the politi-cal process and other actors within the system' (Bachrach and Baratz 1970: 50).

[...]

The second count on which the two-dimensional view of power is inadequate is in its association of power with actual, observable conflict. In this respect also the pluralists' critics follow their adversaries too closely[2] (and both in turn again follow Weber, who, as we have seen, stressed the realization of one's will, *despite the resistance of others*). This insistence on actual conflict as essential to power will not do, for at least two reasons.

The first is that, on Bachrach and Baratz's own analysis, two of the types of power may not involve such conflict: namely, manipulation and authority – which they conceive as 'agreement based upon reason' (Bachrach and Baratz 1970:

20), though elsewhere they speak of it as involving a 'possible conflict of values' (p. 37).

The second reason why the insistence on actual and observable conflict will not do is simply that it is highly unsatisfactory to suppose that power is only exercised in situations of such conflict. To put the matter sharply, *A* may exercise power over *B* by getting him to do what he does not want to do, but he also exercises power over him by influencing, shaping or determining his very wants. Indeed, is it not the supreme exercise of power to get another or others to have the desires you want them to have – that is, to secure their compliance by controlling their thoughts and desires? One does not have to go to the lengths of talking about *Brave New World*, or the world of B. F. Skinner, to see this: thought control takes many less total and more mundane forms, through the control of information, through the mass media and through the processes of socialization. Indeed, ironically, there are some excellent descriptions of this phenomenon in *Who Governs?* Consider the picture of the rule of the 'patricians' in the early nineteenth century: 'The elite seems to have possessed that most indispensable of all characteristics in a dominant group – the sense, shared not only by themselves but by the populace, that their claim to govern was legitimate' (Dahl 1961: 17). And Dahl also sees this phenomenon at work under modern 'pluralist' conditions: leaders, he says, 'do not merely *respond* to the preferences of constituents; leaders also *shape* preferences' (p. 164), and, again, 'almost the entire adult population has been subjected to *some* degree of indoctrination through the schools' (p. 317), etc. The trouble seems to be that both Bachrach and Baratz and the pluralists suppose that because power, as they conceptualize it, only shows up in cases of actual conflict, it follows that actual conflict is necessary to power. But this is to ignore the crucial point that the most effective and insidious use of power is to prevent such conflict from arising in the first place.

The third count on which the two-dimensional view of power is inadequate is closely linked to the second: namely, its insistence that nondecision-making power only exists where there are grievances which are denied entry into the political process in the form of issues. If the observer can uncover no grievances, then he must assume there is a 'genuine' consensus on the prevailing allocation of values. To put this another way, it is here assumed that if people feel no grievances, then they have no interests that are harmed by the use of power. But this is also highly unsatisfactory. In the first place, what, in any case, is a grievance – an articulated demand, based on political knowledge, an undirected complaint arising out of everyday experience, a vague feeling of unease or sense of deprivation? (See Lipsitz 1970.) Second, and more important, is it not the supreme and most insidious exercise of power to prevent people, to whatever degree, from having grievances by shaping their perceptions, cognitions and preferences in such a way that they accept their role in the existing order of things, either because they can see or imagine no alternative to it, or because they see it as natural and unchangeable, or because they value it as divinely ordained and beneficial? To assume that the absence of grievance equals genuine consensus is simply to rule out the possibility of false or manipulated consensus by definitional fiat.

In summary, the three-dimensional view of power involves a *thoroughgoing critique of the behavioural focus*[3] of the first two views as too individualistic and allows for consideration of the many ways in which potential issues are kept out of politics, whether through the operation of social forces and institutional practices or through individuals' decisions. This, moreover, can occur in the absence of actual, observable conflict, which may have been successfully averted – though there remains here an implicit reference to potential conflict. This potential, however, may never in fact be actualized. What one may have here is a *latent conflict*, which consists in a contradiction between the interests of those exercising power and the *real interests* of those they exclude.[4] These latter may not express or even be conscious of their interests, but, as I shall argue, the identification of those interests ultimately always rests on empirically supportable and refutable hypotheses.

The distinctive features of the three views of power presented above are summarized below.

One-Dimensional View of Power

Focus on

(a) behaviour
(b) decision-making
(c) (key) issues
(d) observable (overt) conflict
(e) (subjective) interests, seen as policy preferences revealed by political participation

Two-Dimensional View of Power

(Qualified) critique of behavioural focus
Focus on

(a) decision-making and nondecision-making
(b) issues and potential issues
(c) observable (overt or covert) conflict
(d) (subjective) interests, seen as policy preferences or grievances

Three-Dimensional View of Power

Critique of behavioural focus
Focus on

(a) decision-making and control over political agenda (not necessarily through decisions)
(b) issues and potential issues
(c) observable (overt or covert), and latent conflict
(d) subjective and real interests

NOTES

1. Contrast Parsons's lament that 'Unfortunately, the concept of power is not a settled one in the social sciences, either in political science or in sociology' (Parsons 1957: 139).

2. This association is made most clearly in *Power and Poverty* (Bachrach and Baratz 1970: esp. pp. 49–50) in reaction to the pressure of pluralist criticisms of the (potentially three-dimensional) implications of the article on nondecisions (Bachrach and Baratz 1963). See Merelman (1968b) and Bachrach and Baratz 1968.

3. I use the term 'behavioural' in the narrow sense indicated above, to refer to the study of overt and actual behaviour – and specifically concrete decisions. Of course, in the widest sense, the three-dimensional view of power is 'behavioural' in that it is committed to the view that behaviour (action and inaction, conscious and unconscious, actual and potential) provides evidence (direct and indirect) for an attribution of the exercise of power.

4. This conflict is latent in the sense that it is assumed that there would be a conflict of wants or preferences between those exercising power and those subject to it, were the latter to become aware of their interests. (My account of latent conflict and real interests is to be distinguished from Dahrendorf's account of 'objective' and 'latent' interests as 'antagonistic interests conditioned by, even inherent in, social positions', in imperatively co-ordinated associations, which are 'independent of [the individual's] conscious orientations' (Dahrendorf 1959: 174, 178). Dahrendorf assumes as sociologically given what I claim to be empirically ascertainable.)

REFERENCES

Bachrach, P. and Baratz, M. S. (1962) 'The Two Faces of Power', *American Political Science Review*, 56: 941–52; reprinted in Bachrach and Baratz 1970, Bell et al. 1969, and Scott (ed.) 1994.

Bachrach, P. and Baratz, M. S. (1963) 'Decisions and Nondecisions: An Analytical Framework', *American Political Science Review*, 57: 641–51; reprinted in Bachrach and Baratz 1970, Bell et al. 1969, and Scott (ed.) 1994.

Bachrach, P. and Baratz, M. S. (1968) Communication to the Editor, *American Political Science Review*, 62: 1268–9.

Bachrach, P. and Baratz, M. S. (1970) *Power and Poverty: Theory and Practice*. New York: Oxford University Press.

Bell, R., Edwards, D. V. and Harrison Wagner, R. (1969) *Political Power: A Reader in Theory and Research*. New York: Free Press.

Crenson, M. A. (1971) *The Un-Politics of Air Pollution: A Study of Non-Decisionmaking in the Cities*. Baltimore, MD: Johns Hopkins Press.

Dahl, R. A. (1961) *Who Governs? Democracy and Power in an American City*. New Haven, CT: Yale University Press.

Dahrendorf, R. (1959) *Class and Class Conflict in Industrial Society*. London: Routledge & Kegan Paul.

Gallie, W. B. (1955–6) 'Essentially Contested Concepts', *Proceedings of the Aristotelian Society*, 56: 167–98.

Lipsitz, L. (1970) 'On Political Belief: the Grievances of the Poor', in P. Green and S. Levinson (eds), *Power and Community: Dissenting Essays in Political Science*. New York: Random House, Vintage Books.

Merelman, R. (1968a) 'On the Neo-elitist Critique of Community Power', *American Political Science Review*, 62: 451–60.

Merelman, R. (1968b) Communication to the Editor, *American Political Science Review*, 62: 1269.

Mills, C. Wright (1956) *The Power Elite*. New York: Oxford University Press; republished in 2000 with a new Afterword by Alan Wolfe.

Parsons, T. (1957) 'The Distribution of Power in American Society', World Politics, 10: 123–43 (a review article of Mills 1956).

Polsby, N. W. (1968) 'Community: the Study of Community Power', in D. Sills (ed.), *International Encyclopedia of the Social Sciences*. New York: Macmillan and Free Press, 3: 157–63.

Scott, J. (ed.) (1994) *Power: Critical Concepts*. 3 vols. London: Routledge.

Wolfinger, R. E. (1971a) 'Nondecisions and the Study of Local Politics', *American Political Science Review*, 65: 1063–80.

Wolfinger, R. E. (1971b) 'Rejoinder to Frey's "Comment"', *American Political Science Review*, 65: 1102–4.

52. Ethnic Cleansing and the Dark Side of Democracy*

Michael Mann

[...] The world's genocides remain thankfully few, but they are flanked by more numerous cases of less severe but nonetheless murderous cleansing.

This book offers an explanation of such terrible atrocities. For the sake of clarity, I lay it out up front now, in the form of eight general theses. These proceed from the very general to the particular, from the macro to the micro, successively adding parts of an overall explanation. I hope to prove these in the course of the book by examining in detail the very worst cases of cleansing, those that have involved mass murder.

1. My first thesis concerns the broad historical era in which murderous cleansing became common. *Murderous cleansing is modern, because it is the dark side of democracy.* Let me make clear at the outset that I do not claim that democracies routinely commit murderous cleansing. Very few have done so. Nor do I reject democracy as an ideal – I endorse that ideal. Yet democracy has always carried with it the possibility that the majority might tyrannize minorities, and this possibility carries more ominous consequences in certain types of multiethnic environments.

This thesis has two parts, concerning modernity and democracy. Ethnic cleansing is essentially modern. Though not unknown in previous history (and probably common among the very small groups who dominated prehistory), it became more frequent and deadly in modern

times. The 20th-century death toll through ethnic conflict amounted to somewhere over 70 million, dwarfing that of previous centuries. Additionally, conventional welfare increasingly targeted entire peoples as the enemy. Whereas civilians accounted for less than 10 percent of deaths in World War I, they rocketed to over half in World War II and to somewhat above 80 percent in wars fought in the 1990s. Civil wars, mostly ethnic in nature, were now taking over from interstate wars as the main killers. Perhaps 20 million have died in them, though it is impossible to be precise (figures have been hazarded by Chesterman, 2001: 2; Fearon & Laitin, 2003; Gurr, 1993, 2000; Harff, 2003; Markusen & Kopf, 1995: 27–34).

Ethnic and religious conflicts continue to simmer as I write in 2003 – in Northern Ireland, the Basque Country, Cyprus, Bosnia, Kosovo, Macedonia, Algeria, Turkey, Israel, Iraq, Chechnya, Azerbaijan, Afghanistan, Pakistan, India, Sri Lanka, Kashmir, Burma, Tibet, Chinese Xinjiang, Fiji, the southern Philippines, various islands of Indonesia, Bolivia, Peru, Mexico, the Sudan, Somalia, Senegal, Uganda, Sierra Leone, Liberia, Nigeria, Congo, Rwanda, and Burundi. Over half of these cases involve substantial killing. As you read these words, one ethnic crisis probably will be exploding into violence on your television screen or newspaper, while several other explosions will not be deemed newsworthy. The 20th century was bad enough. Perhaps the 21st will be even worse.

[...]

* From Mann, M. (2005) *The Dark Side of Democracy: Explaining Ethnic Cleansing* (New York: Cambridge University Press). Extracts from pp. 2–3, 5, 6–10.

2. *Ethnic hostility rises where ethnicity trumps class as the main form of social stratification, in the process capturing and channeling classlike sentiments toward ethnonationalism.* Cleansing was rare in the past because most big historic societies were class-divided. Aristocracies or other small oligarchies dominated them, and they rarely shared a common culture or ethnic identity with the common people. In fact they despised the people, often considering them barely human. The people did not exist across class lines – class trumped ethnicity.

Even the first modern societies were dominated by the politics of class. Liberal representative states first emerged as a way of compromising class conflict, giving them a plural sense of people and nation. They tolerated some ethnic diversity. But where the modern struggle for democracy involved a whole people struggling against rulers defined as foreign, an ethnic sense of the people arose, often capturing class resentments. The people was seen as a proletarian nation asserting fundamental democratic rights against upper-class imperial nations, which retorted that they were bringing civilization to their backward peoples. Today the Palestinian cause is decidedly proletarian in its tone, seeing its oppressor as an exploiting and colonial Israel – backed up by American imperialism – while Israelis and Americans claim they are defending civilization against primitive terrorists. The arguments are similar to those of class enemies of former times.

Ethnic differences entwine with other social differences – especially of class, region and gender. Ethnonationalism is strongest where it can capture other senses of exploitation. The most serious defect of recent writing on ethnonationalism has been its almost complete neglect of class relations (as in Brubaker, 1996; Hutchinson, 1994; Smith, 2001). Others wrongly see class as materialistic, ethnicity as emotional (Connor, 1994: 144–64; Horowitz, 1985:105–35). This simply inverts the defect of previous generations of writers who believed that class conflict dominated while ignoring ethnicity. Now the reverse is true, and not only among scholars. Our media are

dominated by ethnic strife while largely ignoring class struggles. Yet in actuality these two types of conflict infuse each other. Palestinians, Dayaks, Hutus, and so on believe they are being materially exploited. Bolsheviks and Maoists believed that landlord and Kulak classes were exploiting the nation. To neglect either ethnicity or class is mistaken. Sometimes one or the other may come to dominate, but this will involve the capturing and channeling of the other. The same can be said of gender and regional sentiments.

[. . .]

3. *The danger zone of murderous cleansing is reached when (a) movements claiming to represent two fairly old ethnic groups both lay claim to their own state over all or part of the same territory and (b) this claim seems to them to have substantial legitimacy and some plausible chance of being implemented.* Almost all dangerous cases are bi-ethnic ones, where both groups are quite powerful and where rival claims to political sovereignty are laid on top of quite old senses of ethnic difference – though not on what are generally called *ancient hatreds.* Ethnic differences are worsened to serious hatreds, and to dangerous levels of cleansing, by persistent rival claims to political sovereignty. I characteristically identify four major sources of power in societies: ideological, economic, military, and political. Murderous ethnic conflict concerns primarily *political power relations,* though as it develops it also involves ideological, economic, and finally military power relations too. Mine is essentially a political explanation of ethnic cleansing.

4. *The brink of murderous cleansing is reached when one of two alternative scenarios plays out. (4a). The less powerful side is bolstered to fight rather than to submit* (for submission reduces the deadliness of the conflict) *by believing that aid will be forthcoming from outside* – usually from a neighboring state, perhaps its ethnic homeland state (as in Brubaker's, 1996, model). In this scenario both sides are laying political claim to the same territory, and both believe they have

the resources to achieve it. This was so in the Yugoslav, Rwandan, Kashmiri, and Chechen cases, for example. The current U.S. war against terrorism aims at eliminating such outside support, labeling it *terrorism* (see Chapter 17). *(4b) The stronger side believes it has such overwhelming military power and ideological legitimacy that it can force through its own cleansed state at little physical or moral risk to itself.* This is so in colonial settler cases, as in the North American, Australian, and Circassian cases considered later. The Armenian and Jewish cases mixed these two scenarios together, since the dominant Turkish and German sides believed they had to strike first in order to prevent the weaker Armenian and Jewish sides from allying with far more threatening outsiders. All these terrible eventualities were produced by interaction between the two sides. We cannot explain such escalation merely in terms of the actions or beliefs of the perpetrators. We need to examine the interactions between the perpetrator and victim groups – and usually with other groups as well. For few even bi-ethnic situations lead to murderous cleansing. One or both sides must first decide to fight rather than conciliate or manipulate, and that choice is unusual.

5. *Going over the brink into the perpetration of murderous cleansing occurs where the state exercising sovereignty over the contested territory has been factionalized and radicalized amid an unstable geopolitical environment that usually leads to war.* Out of such political and geopolitical crises radicals emerge calling for tougher treatment of perceived ethnic enemies. In fact, where ethnic conflict between rival groups is quite old, it is usually somewhat ritualized, cyclical, and manageable. Truly murderous cleansing, in contrast, is unexpected, originally unintended, emerging out of unrelated crises like war. Conversely, in cases where states and geopolitics remain stable, even lesser levels of violence – as we see in Chapter 16 in present-day India. But where political institutions are unstable and affected by war, violence may lead to mass murder – as Harff's (2003) study of political cleansings across the world confirms.

[. . .]

6. *Murderous cleansing is rarely the initial intent of perpetrators.* It is rare to find evil geniuses plotting mass murder from the very beginning. Not even Hitler did so. Murderous cleansing typically emerges as a kind of Plan C, developed only after the first two responses to a perceived ethnic threat fail. Plan A typically envisages a carefully planned solution in terms of either compromise or straightforward repression. Plan B is a more radically repressive adaptation to the failure of Plan A, more hastily conceived amid rising violence and some political destabilization. When these both fail, some of the planners radicalize further. To understand the outcome, we must analyze the unintended consequences of a series of interactions yielding escalation. These successive Plans may contain both logical and more contingent escalations. The perpetrators may be ideologically determined from quite early on to rid themselves of the ethnic out-group, and when milder methods fail, they almost logically seem to escalate with resolute determination to overcome all obstacles by more and more radical means. This was true of Hitler and his myrmidons: the Final Solution of the Jewish question seems much less of an accident than the logical escalation of an ideology ruthlessly overcoming all obstacles in its path. For the Young Turks, however, the final solution to the Armenian problem seems much more contingent, flowing out of what they saw as their suddenly desperate situation in 1915.

[. . .]

7. *There are three main levels of perpetrator: (a) radical elites running party-states; (b) bands of militants forming violent paramilitaries; and (c) core constituencies providing mass though not majority popular support.* Elites, militants, and core constituencies are all normally necessary for murderous cleansing to ensue. We cannot simply blame malevolent leaders or ethnic groups en masse. That would be to credit leaders with

truly magical powers of manipulation or whole peoples with truly remarkable single-mindedness. Both assumptions are at odds with everything sociologists know about the nature of human societies. In all my cases particular elites, militants, and core constituencies are linked together in quite complex ways, forming social movements that (like other social movements) embody mundane power relations. Power is exercised in three distinct ways: top-down by elites, bottom-up popular pressures, and coercively sideways by paramilitaries. These pressures interact and so generate mundane relations like those found in all social movements – especially of hierarchy, comradeship, and career. This has a big impact on perpetrators' motives, as we will see in a moment.

The notion of core constituencies reveals that murderous cleansing resonates more in environments favoring combinations of nationalism, statism, and violence. The main core constituencies are ethnic refugees and people from threatened border districts; those more dependent on the state for their subsistence and values: those living and working outside of the main sectors of the economy that generate class conflict (who are more likely to favor class over ethnonationalist models of conflict); those socialized into acceptance of physical violence as a way of solving problems or achieving personal advancement – like soldiers, policemen, criminals, hooligans, and athletes; and those attracted to machismo ideology – young males striving to assert themselves in the world, often led by older males who were socialized as youths in an earlier phase of violence. So the main axes of stratification involved in cleansing movements are region, economic sector, gender, age. Radical ethnonationalist movements tend to contain a normal class structure: leaders come from the upper and middle classes, the rank-and-file from lower down – with the real dirty work often performed by the working class. I explore all these groups' motivations, careers, and interactions.

8. Finally, *ordinary people are brought by normal social structures into committing murderous ethnic*

cleansing, and their motives are much more mundane. To understand ethnic cleansing, we need a sociology of power more than a special psychology of perpetrators as disturbed or psychotic people – though some may be. As the psychologist Charny (1986: 144) observes, "the mass killers of humankind are largely everyday human beings – what we have called normal people according to currently accepted definitions by the mental health profession."

Placed in comparable situations and similar social constituencies, you or I might also commit murderous ethnic cleansing. No ethnic group or nation is invulnerable. Many Americans and Australians committed murderous cleansing in the past; some Jews and Armenians – the most victimized peoples of the 20th century – have perpetrated recent atrocities against Palestinians and Azeris (and, in turn, some of these victim groups are also perpetrators). There are no virtuous peoples. Religions tend to stress the presence in all humans of original sin, the human capacity for evil. Indeed, placed in the right circumstances and constituencies, we are almost all capable of such evil – perhaps even of enjoying it. But original sin would be an insufficient explanation for this, since our capacity for evil becomes realized only in the circumstances explored in this book. In the case of cleansing, these circumstances are less primitive or ancient than modern. There is something in modernity releasing this particular evil on a mass scale. [. . .] Mass murder has been ubiquitous if uncommon throughout most of human history. But murder in order to remove ("cleanse") a people was rare in earlier centuries. Things became more dangerous with the rise of salvation religions and then with the rise of rule by the people. The empirical core of the book then consists of a series of studies of the worst outbursts of modern murderous cleansing. In all of them I go from the most general causes of danger zones to the events that precipitated going over the brink to the actual processes and perpetrators of murderous cleansing.

REFERENCES

Brubaker, R. 1996. *Nationalism Reframed: Nationhood and the National Questions in the New Europe.* Cambridge: Cambridge University Press.

Charny, I. 1986. "Genocide and Mass Destruction: Doing Harm to Others as a Missing Dimension in Psychopathology." *Psychiatry*, vol. 49.

Chesterman, S. (ed.) 2001. *Civilians in Wars.* Boulder, Colo.: Lynne Reinner.

Connor, W. 1994. *Ethnonationalism: The Quest for Understanding.* Princeton, N.J.: Princeton University Press.

Fearon, J., & Laitin, D. 2003. "Ethnicity, Insurgency, and Civil War." *American Political Science Review*, vol. 97.

Gurr, T. 1993. *Minorities at Risk: A Global View of Ethnopolitical Conflicts.* Washington, D.C.: United States Institute of Peace.

Gurr, T. 2000. *Peoples versus States: Minorities at Risk in the New Century.* Washington, D.C.: United States Institute of Peace.

Harff, B. 2003. "No Lessons Learned from the Holocaust? Assessing Risks of Genocide and Political Mass Murder since 1995." *American Political Science Review*, vol. 97.

Horowitz, D. 1985. *Ethnic Groups in Conflict.* Berkeley: University of California Press.

Hutchinson, J. 1994. *Modern Nationalism.* London: Fontana.

Markusen, E., & Kopf, D. 1995. *The Holocaust and Strategic Bombing: Genocide and Total War in the Twentieth Century.* Boulder, Colo.: Westview.

Smith, A. 2001. *Nationalism.* Cambridge: Polity.

53. Populist Politics and Mobilization*

Bart Bonikowski

'Populism' has become the favoured label for a constellation of radical right-wing political parties and movements in Europe, and more recently, the United States. Even though this term is typically used as shorthand for a number of interrelated features of the radical right, its frequent use implies that populism is either the most important among these components or that it is most effective at distinguishing radical-right actors from their mainstream counterparts.[1] While convenient, the casual use of populism as an analytical category risks misunderstanding what populism is – thereby inhibiting the ability to recognize the phenomenon's causes and consequences – and downplaying the other co-constitutive elements of radical-right politics, particularly ethno-nationalism and authoritarianism (Mudde 2007).

This article will demonstrate that greater analytical clarity about the meaning and conceptual boundaries of populism, nationalism[2] and authoritarianism not only leads to a more complete theoretical understanding of contemporary radicalism, but also enables systematic inquiry into the basis of support for this ascendant form of politics. In particular, I argue that neither changes in the supply of populist, ethno-nationalist and authoritarian claims nor aggregate trends in the popular attitudes mobilized by such politics sufficiently explain the recent successes of

radical-right campaigns. Instead, what is needed is attention to the contextual factors that increase the resonance between perennial discursive frames and pre-existing attitudes.[3] By reorienting future empirical inquiry around the concept of resonance – long established in political sociology (Snow and Benford 1988; Schudson 1989) but elaborated in recent work (McDonnell, Bail and Tavory 2017) – scholars can gain better analytical purchase on why the potent ideational mix of populism, ethno-nationalism and authoritarianism has rallied large numbers of supporters in established democracies behind a radical-right agenda.[4]

The three components of contemporary radical politics

More precisely defining the constitutive elements of radical-right politics requires engagement with research traditions that rarely intersect. Populism has been the province of comparative scholars of party politics in Europe and political development in Latin America, while nationalism research has been a primarily historical enterprise, and more recently an object of survey analysis, at the intersection of sociology and political science. Authoritarianism, in turn, has occupied students of European history and the developing world, but less frequently those of contemporary democratic politics. With the emergence of the radical right in Western democracies, however, it is no longer appropriate to think of nationalism and authoritarianism as problems belonging to

* From Bonikowski, B. (2017) 'Ethno-Nationalist Populism and the Mobilization of Collective Resentment', *The British Journal of Sociology*, 68(S1): S181–S213. Extract from pp. S182–S187.

a bygone era or to geographically distant cases, nor is it reasonable to view populism as confined to the fringes of the European and American political fields. If we are to grasp the origins and implications of Brexit, Trump, Le Pen, Wilders, Orbán or Kaczyński, we must leverage the insights of each of these research traditions without conflating their objects of inquiry. Populism, nationalism and authoritarianism are all relevant in the recent upsurge of radical politics, but they are relevant in analytically distinct ways.

Indeed, the coincidence of these three elements was among the most valuable, but also the least appreciated, contributions of Mudde's (2007) classic book on the populist radical right (for elaborations, see Golder 2016; Rooduijn 2014). Mudde argues that nativism is at the core of this emerging party family and that it is its combination with populism and authoritarianism that makes the radical right's political position unique. Yet, most subsequent research has conflated these distinct elements, treating them as part and parcel of a coherent ideology of a pre-determined set of parties. Mudde's own reliance on 'nativism' in place of the broader category of nationalism (particularly its exclusionary forms) and his static operationalization of populism stem from his interest in defining a relatively coherent party family rather than analysing the ideational systems that connect party mobilization strategies with the cultural and cognitive orientations of their supporters. This party-driven approach ends up prioritizing the demand side of radical-right politics at the expense of a '"sociological approach" [. . .] that treat[s] the populist radical right as a passive consequence of macro-level socioeconomic developments', as Mudde critically puts it (2007: 4). Ignoring parties is a mistake, to be sure, but so is reducing all aspects of politics to party ideology. In this paper, I intend to bring back a sociological approach to populism, nationalism and authoritarianism – one that takes seriously the cultural content and structural context of political preferences – while drawing on the wealth of knowledge about radical-right populism in political science.

To that end, I will consider the role of each of the three constitutive elements in fuelling the support for radical-right politics and the consequences they may have when such politics become mainstream. In so doing, I will demonstrate that neither populism nor nationalism is confined to the ideological space occupied by the nexus of nativism, Islamophobia, economic isolationism and welfare chauvinism that has become the hallmark of the radical right. Broadening our understanding of populism and nationalism beyond these ideological confines can help us identify the mechanisms that have contributed to the success of the most exclusionary varieties of these phenomena. Furthermore, I will argue – with the support of evidence from the relevant literatures – that populism and nationalism are not phenomena in public opinion or political discourse. On the contrary, both have figured prominently on the supply and demand sides of politics for decades, which suggests that their recent political effectiveness must be understood contextually.[5] Specifically, these long-standing political repertoires have gained renewed resonance because of the unique confluence of political, economic, cultural and demographic changes – amplified in media and political discourse – that have unfolded in Europe and the United States over the past decade and a half, with deeper roots dating back to the 1970s. By targeting political elites and ethnic, religious and racial minorities, opportunistic political actors on the radical right have been able to mobilize unprecedented support among ethnic majorities experiencing an acute sense of collective status threat, whether actual or perceived.

The resulting politics of resentment are not only upending the existing political balance of power within countries – typically against established parties – but they have the potential to alter the very foundations of the political consensus on which liberal democracies depend. By violating established norms of political practice, radical-right actors are calling into question the integrity of democratic institutions, from judicial autonomy to fair elections. In some cases, such normative threats are accompanied by concrete legal strategies for the authoritarian capture of institutions, as has been the case in Hungary and Poland. It is these long-term consequences of the politics of resentment that are potentially the most dangerous. The interaction between populism, ethno-nationalism, authoritarianism and public anxiety may set into motion dynamic cultural processes that will reshape taken-for-granted political beliefs and erode established institutions, thereby creating future conditions of success for anti-democratic politics.

What Is Populism?

There is an ongoing debate among political scientists studying Latin America, Western and Eastern Europe, and the United States concerning the most appropriate conceptualization of populism. At issue is whether populism is primarily an ideology, a form of political mobilization, or a discursive frame (Alsanidis 2016; Gidron and Bonikowski 2013; Bonikowski and Gidron 2016b). Yet, despite important differences between these three traditions, there is a fair amount of consensus concerning populism's most central features. Fundamentally, populism is a form of politics predicated on the moral vilification of elites and the veneration of ordinary people, who are seen as the sole legitimate source of political power. The specific elites targeted by populists vary depending on the populists' ideological predilections. While elected politicians are often the immediate targets, populism just as often focuses on economic leaders, civil servants and intellectuals, who are seen as exercising undue influence on politics in the pursuit of their own self-interest.

Even though populists tend to define the corrupt elite in explicit terms, the definition of the people is often less clear (Rooduijn and Pauwels 2011). In principle, anyone who is not a member of the elite is included in this category, as suggested by the frequent usage of first-person plural and vague references to 'taxpayers,'

'working people,' or simply 'the people' in populist campaigns. At the same time, however, more exclusionary forms of populism—that is, those that infuse populism with ethno-nationalist content—often employ more restrictive definitions of the polity, based on ethnic, racial, or religious criteria. In such formulations, which Judis (2016) refers to as triadic populism, it is not only elites who are vilified, but also various scapegoated minority groups, who are seen as having co-opted the elites for their own nefarious ends. It is in contrast with these unwelcome groups that the identity of the 'true' people becomes crystallized.

Populism has one more feature around which there is some agreement in the literature: its scepticism toward representative institutions. Because established institutions of the state, such as the courts and legislative bodies, are seen as serving the interests of the elites, populism tends to dismiss them (at least in principle if not in practice) in favour of direct contact between leaders and the populace, typically in the form of rallies, referenda, and other modes of plebiscitarian politics. This tendency contains the potential seeds of authoritarianism, because it suggests that power should be concentrated in the executive, which is seen as the most direct embodiment of the political will of a homogeneous polity. In this respect, populism is seen by some as inherently tied to anti-pluralist politics (Müller 2016).

Even though these core characteristics are present in most varieties of populism, scholars disagree about populism's ontological status and the level of analysis at which it should be investigated. The source of the quandary is the observation that populism is not a complete ideology, in the same vein, for instance, as liberalism or conservatism, because it does not offer a coherent theory of state-society relations with substantive implications for how governance and policy problems should be addressed. Moreover, few practitioners of populism identify with the label and there are no intellectual advocates of a 'populist ideology'. Instead, populism is at best an oppositional moral framework, which allows for a forceful critique of particular social groups.

The question then becomes whether populism is most appropriately understood as an attribute of parties, politicians, political claims, or relations between voters and their representatives. The answers vary across the three traditions to populism research (Gidron and Bonikowski 2013).

For some, populism is a thin-centred ideology: a set of interrelated ideas – even if limited in scope and coherence – that hang together and express a general orientation toward politics (Mudde 2007). Because it is incomplete as a policy perspective, populism is usually combined with a wide range of thicker ideologies, from socialism to ethno-nationalism. Despite its narrowness, however, populism is a perspective to which political candidates and parties subscribe, and thus, it is in these actors' core statements of principles – party manifestos, campaign platforms, and so on – that populism should be observed. It follows then that populism is understood in this tradition as an essential political trait, so that a party or political candidate is either populist or not.

This perspective is subsumed and elaborated by the mobilization tradition, which locates populism not just in ideas, but also in the manner in which political actors interact with voters. This definition of populism involves not only a binary moral logic, but also a number of additional features, including a personalistic political style typical of charismatic leaders, priority placed on voters' unmediated access to political candidates, and attempts to include underrepresented groups in the political process. This approach has been particularly effective in research on Latin American populism (Jansen 2011; Levitsky and Roberts 2011; Weyland 2001). Its portability to other settings, however, has been limited by its 'thick' definition of the phenomenon. Outside Latin America, populism does not always depend on personalistic appeals, charisma, or appeals to marginalized groups. The translation of the concept to Europe and the United States, therefore, requires the stripping away of some of its ancillary features specific to Latin American politics.

To address the comparative and analytical shortcomings of the ideological and mobilization approaches, I have advocated for a more minimalist conceptualization of populism, one that treats it as a form of political discourse (Bonikowski and Gidron 2016b; for a related approach, see Hawkins 2010; Jagers and Walgrave 2007; Poblete 2015; Rooduijn & Pauwels 2011). From this perspective, populism is a political strategy, a way of formulating political claims that is more likely to be employed by the same actors in some circumstances and not others. Rather than treating populism as a property of parties and candidates, it becomes more useful to measure it at the level of political speeches, or even speech elements. This frees populism from the encumbrance of country-specific attributes and it makes it possible to observe populism's dynamics, that is, the mechanisms that increase the probability that political actors will frame their appeals in populist terms in specific circumstances. We can ask, for example, who typically relies on populist claims (political outsiders), when they are most likely to do it (in early stages of campaigns), and how ideology shapes the content of these claims (they are typically economic on the left and focused on nationalism on the right) (Bonikowski and Gidron 2016a).We can also track populism over time to gain a better understanding of trends in its supply-side prevalence.

The discursive approach to populism is parsimonious and flexible and I will rely on it in this paper, but it is not distinctive in one sense: it shares with the other two conceptual approaches a similar answer to the question of what populism is not: it is not a highly structured ideology synonymous with nationalism and illiberal democracy. Some varieties of populism may have affinities with these phenomena and, in practice, may be interconnected with them, but there is no inherent reason why this should be so. It follows then that populism is merely one element in radical-right politics, rather than its defining feature. What is more, the structural logic of populism and the predictors and consequences of its prevalence are not limited to the radical right but are observable across the full ideological spectrum. The challenge for scholars, therefore, is to identify the unique mechanisms that influence populism itself rather than the ideologies with which populism is sometimes associated. Otherwise, if populism is conflated with nationalism, authoritarianism, conservatism, or any other ideology, it risks becoming an analytically vacuous category.

NOTES

1. Though difficult to define without reference to its constituent ideational components, in general terms, the 'radical right' comprises those parties and candidates who advocate for a fundamental reorganization of the political system, typically in a manner that favors dominant ethnic, religious, or racial groups and undermines the power of existing elites (Golder 2016).

2. When referring to the exclusionary claims of the radical right, I rely on the more specific term 'ethno-nationalism,' which signals that this form of politics favors ascriptive ethno-cultural criteria of national membership. As I will argue, however, ethno-nationalism cannot be fully understood without being placed in the context of other varieties of nationalism, with which it competes within modern nations.

3. For the purposes of this paper, I use the concept of 'demand' as shorthand for the mean level of attitudes corresponding to the primary ideational features of radical-right politics. I recognize that the concept of demand could be expanded to account for relative levels of 'resonance' or 'salience' of particular beliefs, but I refrain from doing so to underscore the analytical difference between the distribution and resonance of attitudes.

4. My primary focus in this article is on the radical right, but the ideational elements I examine here, and the contextual changes that affect their resonance, may help explain aspects of radical-left support as well (of course, contemporary radical-left parties rely less on ethno-nationalism than on class-based appeals and economic nationalism). In the discussion section, I briefly attend to the possible similarities and differences between these two varieties of radicalism.

5. My analysis of the supply and demand of radical politics focuses solely on the cultural aspects of political mobilization. I consider structural changes, including those affecting the political field, to be part of the context within which political claims fluctuate in relative resonance. For a review of 'supply-side' institutional changes that may help translate political demand for the radical right into electoral outcomes, see Golder (2016).

REFERENCES

Alsanidis, P. 2016 'Is Populism an Ideology? A Refutation and a New Perspective', *Political Studies* 64: 88–104.

Bonikowski, B. and Gidron, N. 2016a 'The Populist Style in American Politics: Presidential Campaign Discourse, 1952–1996', *Social Forces* 94(4): 1593–621.

Bonikowski, B. and Gidron, N. 2016b 'Multiple Traditions in Populism Research: Toward a Theoretical Synthesis', *Comparative Politics Newsletter*, American Political Science Association 26(2): 7–14.

Gidron, N. and Bonikowski, B. 2013 'Varieties of Populism: Literature Review and Research Agenda', Working Paper, Weatherhead Center for International Affairs, Harvard University, Cambridge, MA.

Golder, M. 2016 'Far Right Parties in Europe', *Annual Review of Political Science* 19: 477–97.

Hawkins, K.A. 2010 *Venezuela's Chavismo and Populism in Comparative Perspective*. New York: Cambridge University Press.

Jagers, J., and Walgrave, S. 2007 'Populism as Political Communication Style: An Empirical Study of Political Parties' Discourse in

Belgium', *European Journal of Political Research* 46:319–45.

Jansen, R.S. 2011 'Populist Mobilization: A New Theoretical Approach to Populism', *Sociological Theory* 29(2): 75–96.

Judis, J.B. 2016 *The Populist Explosion: How the Great Recession Transformed American and European Politics*, New York: Columbia Global Reports.

Levitsky, S. and Roberts, K.M. (eds) 2011 *The Resurgence of the Latin American Left*, Baltimore, MD: Johns Hopkins University Press.

McDonnell, T.E., Bail, C.A. and Tavory, I. 2017 'A Theory of Resonance', *Sociological Theory* 35(1): 1–14.

Mudde, C. 2007 *Populist Radical Right Parties in Europe*, New York: Cambridge University Press.

Müller, J.W. 2016 *What Is Populism?* Philadelphia, PA: University of Pennsylvania Press.

Norris, P. 2011 *Democratic Deficit: Critical Citizens Revisited*, Cambridge: Cambridge University Press.

Poblete, M.E. 2015 'How to Assess Populist Discourse Through Three Current Approaches', *Journal of Political Ideologies* 20: 201–18.

Rooduijn, M. 2014 'Vox Populismus: A Populist Radical Right Attitude among the Public?' *Nations and Nationalism* 20(1): 80–92.

Rooduijn, M. and Pauwels, T. 2011 'Measuring Populism: Comparing Two Methods of Content Analysis', *West European Politics* 34(6): 1272–83.

Schudson, M. 1989 'How Culture Works: Perspectives from Media Studies on the Efficacy of Symbols', *Theory and Society* 18(2): 153–80.

Snow, D.A. and Benford, R.D. 1988 'Ideology, Frame Resonance, and Participant Mobilization', *International Social Movement Research* 1(1): 197–217.

Weyland, K. 2001 'Clarifying a Contested Concept: Populism in the Study of Latin American Politics', *Comparative Politics* 34(1): 1–22.

54. Representations of British Muslims during the COVID-19 Pandemic*

Elizabeth Poole and Milly Williamson

A well-established trajectory of research demonstrates that the UK's news media represents Muslims within a narrow and largely negative framework (Ahmed and Matthes, 2017; Baker et al., 2013; Poole, 2019; Khiabany and Williamson, 2012). This has been exacerbated in a period of tumultuous politics characterized by the rise of populism using racialized immigration narratives to bolster a nationalist project. Pro-Brexit propaganda seized on the refugee crisis as an opportunity to further normalize right-wing narratives claiming that migrating Muslims represent both a security and cultural threat. However, racist discourse has a flexibility that enables it to stretch over new situations and can, thus, be understood as a 'floating signifier' (Lentin and Titley, 2011). Different racialized communities are targeted by mainstream media and the state in ways that ebb and flow historically. Racist narratives can become disrupted by protest movements and other historical events, leaving right-wing politicians and media grasping to readjust racist ideologies. This paper investigated whether the second shockingly abnormal event of the last decade (following Brexit), the COVID crisis, destabilized what have become dominant narratives about Muslims. As it became obvious

that ethnic minority hospital staff and communities were being disproportionately affected by the Coronavirus, alongside the UK media's more widespread recognition of NHS staff, we asked, have we witnessed the emergence of an alternative framework of reporting on Muslims or will the contours of racist ideologies reshape and reanimate old ideas of 'good immigrant' versus 'bad immigrant' as Muslim key workers are distinguished in the reporting from other Muslims? This article addresses these questions by analysing the reporting in four UK newspapers (*Daily Mail*, *The Telegraph*, *The Sun* and *The Mirror*) over a month's coverage at the initial peak time of the crisis (April, 2020). [. . .]

It is essential to understand the reporting of Muslims in Britain during the COVID pandemic in 2020 in the context of prevalent anti-Muslim racism in the UK and across Europe, the wider racist political climate amplified by the 'hostile environment' in the UK introduced by Theresa May as Home Secretary in 2012, and vigorously pursued by successive Conservative administrations, the spread and legitimation of racist ideas through the Brexit campaigns, the ongoing political and media scapegoating of migrants, linking migration to Muslims, and a worrying growth and normalization of extreme right-wing politics across Western countries (Farris, 2017; Khiabany, 2017). The way that Muslims and Islam are reported in the UK media is shaped by the immediate political environment and the historical circumstances that produced it.

* From Poole, E. & Williamson, M. (2021) 'Disrupting or Reconfiguring Racist Narratives about Muslims? The Representation of British Muslims during the COVID Crisis', *Journalism*, 2 July: 1–21. Extracts from pp. 2–3, 8–10, 14–15.

[. . .]

Today in the UK there is a crucial link between the issue of the welfare state, the politics of austerity (which are to be renewed with vigour in subsequent years as inadequate government responses to the pandemic damage economic growth, for which the public sector, workers, and the poor will be expected to pay) and overlapping attacks on multiculturalism, immigration and anti-Muslim racism. For a number of years, the future of the welfare state and the question of immigration have been linked foci of key policy debates in western democracies and their combination has produced a toxic atmosphere – from the EU referendum in Britain and the rise of Trumpism in the US (which looks set to outstay Trump himself) – immigration has been targeted as a central issue, where concerns over a "demographic crisis" (Huntington, 2004) justify the exclusion of migrant and other ethnic minority populations from citizenship and basic rights. This is not a product of Trump and Brexit – but the other way around.

[. . .]

It quickly became apparent that the first casualties of COVID working in the NHS were from a minority ethnic background. Four of the first doctors to die in the UK were also Muslims, followed by another four doctors and two nurses in the coming weeks. The alarming and disproportionate death rate amongst ethnic minority populations was quickly noted and debated by mainstream media.[1] Although this debate initially focused on 'racial' and cultural differences, the scale of the issue forced the media to discuss structural inequalities. Such reportage is not a consequence of media plurality, but rather demonstrates the contradictions that face news media during times of crises, whose 'usual' explanations, as Freedman (2009: 12) puts it, are 'found wanting' when confronted by unprecedented circumstances. Newspapers need to maintain both legitimacy and circulation amongst

readers politically engaged by a new climate. The increased visibility of sources and voices from ethnic minorities was a notable disruption to news as normal, and alongside coverage that appeared to offer a genuine recognition of the NHS and its staff, and other key workers, where ethnic minority populations are overrepresented, had the potential to disrupt what have become fairly standardized tropes about Muslims in the UK. The everyday contribution of Muslims (and more widely ethnic minorities and immigrants) to the social and economic fabric of UK society, which has largely been ignored by mainstream media, could have been redressed. However, the impact of the overwhelming accumulation of stories about Muslims as irreducible other was not undone here, not least because the Muslim identity of the doctors and nurses was left largely unremarked upon.

While it should be noted that the press regulator's (IPSO) Editor's code of practice stipulates that any references to ethnic and religious identity should be avoided 'unless genuinely relevant to the story' (12.2) (this regulation is regularly flouted in 'opinion pieces' (Petley, 2006)), it is noteworthy to examine those instances when the signifier 'Muslim' is considered *not* to be of significance in press discourse. The lack of reference to the religious identity of the casualties of COVID is a striking absence in these press reports and speaks volumes about the ideological function of the signifier 'Muslim'; the culturalization and racialization of religion is a central trope in contemporary Western racist discourses, which are no longer simply couched in terms of superiority and inferiority but on the basis of assumed cultural difference. Amrit Wilson points out that populations that were once identified by language or geography are now identified above all else by their religion (Wilson, 2007: 31). Fortier (2008) argues that this 'taxonomic shift' in Britain is now the site for marking difference (p. 5). Cultural racism has become the norm and acts as a functional equivalent where biological forms of racism are seen to be outmoded (Banton, 2004). Islamophobia is an example of this. However,

Muslimness, unable to function as a marker of difference in this context, is rendered irrelevant.

Of the eight cases where Muslim NHS workers died in this sample, references to their religious identity were minimal and incidental, and only in four cases. This was only included when mentioned by a source (usually towards the end of an article) or was identifiable through another religious signifier such as the headscarf worn by Muslim nurse Areema Nasreen. For example, following the death of Dr Abdul Mabud Chowdhury, *The Telegraph* and *Daily Mail* both included a quote from the Muslim Doctors Association, the single reference to his religious affiliation. And in a story that grabs the media's attention of two brothers dying in the same intensive care unit just weeks after their father, the only clue to their Muslimness is through a reference to the Islamic Mosque Society for Wales (Burrows, 2020). It is not the intention of this article to suggest that religion *should* be a central aspect of reporting, thus essentializing Muslims by reducing them to a singular aspect of identity, overriding intersectional aspects of this. However, by demonstrating the contexts in which the signifier is and is not applied can show how it operates discursively to apply racialized meanings. For example, coverage of these Muslim key workers is in contrast to the first reported COVID-related death of a Sikh doctor, Manjeet Riyat, whose identity is a central part of the story which describes 'the principle of 'seva' which means 'selfless service' and is one of the tenets of the Sikh faith' (Chaudhary et al., 2020). Areema Nasreen received the most coverage of anyone identified as 'Muslim' by the press. Alongside several reports about her, she is also mentioned in each newspaper's regular updates on, and tributes to, NHS workers dying from COVID (such as *The Telegraph* report, Lyons et al., 2020). All newspapers quote her aspirations to be a nurse and, *The Telegraph*, to influence those from Muslim backgrounds, saying "I would like to think that I could inspire others; particularly within Muslim communities" (22 March 2020). As part of a process of retaining legitimacy in the face of huge public outpourings

of gratitude for the NHS, these articles emphasize the positive qualities of these health workers including quotes from family and friends about their sacrifice and dedication, and in doing so, reveal the tensions that confront news media in times of crisis, facing contradictory dynamics in new situations (Freedman, 2009). But the reports reinforce a common dualism of aggressor/victim and borrow from an ideological tradition of separating out 'good' from 'bad' Muslims, which is predicated on the extent to which Muslims distance themselves from the (ideologically constructed) assumed inherently violent tendencies of Islam (Kundnani, 2008). While it is strikingly different to see Muslims celebrated as heroes rather than demonized in articles such as the *Daily Mail's* 'They came to join the NHS and made the 'ultimate sacrifice': Syrian GP becomes the 10th doctor from overseas who has died of coronavirus' (Tingle, 2020), such sentimentalized hero narratives not only omit reference to Muslim identity, but stand in for critical approaches to racial equality and discrimination by implying exceptionalism (upon which the good/bad Muslim-migrant dichotomy depends). By referring to nationality, these health care workers were clearly marked individually as hero-immigrants, while ignoring the collective contribution that migrants make to the UK, further reinforcing that binary. In addition, these more 'positive' stories were set alongside two related articles in the *Daily Mail* on the same day that reanimate the 'otherness' of Muslims by incorrectly suggesting the number of deaths amongst Muslims are low because they may be protected by cultural practices (described as the 'Muslim lifestyle') such as handwashing and lack of Muslim women in employment (Blanchard, 2020; Williams, 2020). And those articles that were critical of the government over lack of PPE drew on the authority of doctors while also omitting their Muslim ethnicity/religion – 'Doctor, 53, who warned Boris Johnson about 'urgent' need for more protective equipment for NHS workers dies from coronavirus after 15 day battle' (Pyman, 2020).

The erasure of Muslim identity in the recognition of NHS staff contributes to a negative set of associations of Muslims by omission, underlying which are the racialized politics of integrationism which condemns multiculturalism. For instance, Liddle (2020) whose column in *The Sun* regularly demonizes Muslims (Khiabany and Williamson, 2008), duplicitously celebrates this 'loss of identity' since the virus began, using a direct form of address to state 'we're all this together – identity politics simply causes unnecessary divisions between us'. In doing so, he also erases the unequal impacts of the pandemic.

[. . .]

It appeared initially that the COVID crisis might provide an opportunity to challenge norms and reframe news discourses about Muslims in the UK; coverage which generally cast healthcare workers as 'heroes' (another binary which needs unpacking) included Muslim healthcare workers and seemed to offer the potential to shift heavily sedimented negative coverage of Muslims in the UK. However, the signifier 'Muslim', so heavily imbued with negative connotations and functioning to signify 'otherness' in the UK news media, was often left unremarked up on the COVID coverage; its absence a reflection that the meaning of 'Muslim' is still anchored to an 'us and them' binary in the UK press. The coverage ultimately reinforced the hegemonic representational framework that has developed since 9/11 by drawing on and reworking wider longstanding tropes in which marginalized groups are 'othered', subject to moral panics, and accused of refusing to integrate.

NOTE

1. Coronovirus: Risk of death is higher for ethnic minorities, BBC, 2 June, https://www.bbc.co.uk/news/health-52889106.

REFERENCES

Ahmed S and Matthes J (2017) Media representation of Muslims and Islam from 2000 to 2015: A meta-analysis. *International Communication Gazette* 79(3): 219–244.

Baker P, Gabrielatos C and McEnery T (2013) *Discourse Analysis and Media Attitudes: The Representation of Islam in the British Press.* Cambridge: Cambridge University Press.

Banton M (2004) Cultural racism. In: Cashmore E (ed.) *Encyclopedia of Race and Ethnic Studies.* London: Routledge, pp.96–98.

Blanchard S (2020) Trevor Phillips asks whether lack of Muslims in England's coronavirus hotspots may be down to their rigorous handwashing practice five times a day. *MailOnline.* 20 April.

Burrows T (2020) Two brothers, 53 and 59, die of coronavirus within hours of one another and just three weeks after their dad passed away. *The Sun.* 28 April.

Chaudhary V, Martin H and Riley E (2020) Family of Britain's first ever Sikh A&E consultant, 52, tell of devastation after 'selfless pioneer' died of coronavirus. *Daily Mail.* 20 April.

Farris S (2017) *In the Name of Women's Rights: The Rise of Femonationalism,* Durham, NC: Duke University Press.

Fortier AM (2008) *Multicultural Horizons: Diversity and the Limits of the Civil Nation.* London: Routledge.

Freedman DJ (2009) 'Smooth operator?' The propaganda model and moments of crisis. *Westminster Papers in Communication* 6(2): 59–72.

Huntington SP (2004) *Who Are We? The Challenges to America's National Identity.* New York, NY: Simon & Schuster.

Khiabany G and Williamson M (2008) Veiled bodies - naked racism: Culture, politics and race in the Sun. *Race and Class* 50(2): 69–88.

Khiabany G and Williamson M (2012) Terror, culture and anti-Muslim racism. In: Freedman

D and Thussu D (eds) *Media and Terrorism: Global Perspectives*. London: Sage, pp.134–150.

Khiabany G (2017) The visible hand of the state. In: Titley G, Freedman D, Khiabany G, et al. (eds) *After Charlie Hebdo: Terror, Racism and Free Speech*, London: Zed.

Kundnani A (2008) Islamism and the roots of liberal rage. *Race and Class* 50(2): 40–68.

Lentin A and Titley G (2011) *The Crisis of Multiculturalism in a Neoliberal Age*. New York, NY: Zed Books.

Liddle R (2020) Loss of identity. *The Sun*. 2 April.

Lyons I, Penna D, Ward V, et al. (2020) These are the health workers who have died from coronavirus. *The Telegraph*. 20 May.

Petley J (2006) Still no redress from the PCC. In Poole E and Richardson JE (eds) *Muslims and the News Media*. London: I. B. Tauris, pp.53–62.

Poole E (2019) Covering diversity. In: Wahl-Jorgensen K and Hanitzsch T (eds) *The Handbook of Journalism Studies*. London: Routledge, pp.469–486.

Pyman T (2020) Doctor, 53, who warned Boris Johnson about 'urgent' need for more protective equipment for NHS workers dies from coronavirus after 15 day battle. *MailOnline*. 9 April.

Tingle R (2020) They came to join the NHS and made the 'ultimate sacrifice'. *MailOnline*. 9 April.

Williams T (2020) Senior NHS nurse claims ethnic minority health workers are being pressured to work on coronavirus wards more than their white colleagues. *MailOnline*. 20 April.

Wilson A (2007) The forced marriage debate and the British state. *Race & Class* 49(1): 25–38.

55. Social Media Use in Black Lives Matter Activism*

Marcia Mundt, Karen Ross and Charla M. Burnett

An under-explored area of social movement research is the role social media can play in broadening movement impact. We address that issue in this article by exploring opportunities and challenges that social media creates for movements to *scale up*, which we define as the process of expansion and/or internal strengthening that broadens movement impact (Ross et al., under review). Drawing on the case of Black Lives Matter (BLM), we use a mixed methods research design to explore how social media platforms, in particular Facebook and Twitter, can provide opportunities for activist groups to broaden movement impact. We contribute to existing social movement literature by highlighting the importance of social media as a scaling tool that simultaneously facilitates *strengthening* the movement by facilitating collective meaning-making and the creation of support networks and *expanding* the movement, specifically by enabling local BLM groups to form coalitions and to amplify and disseminate non-dominant discourses about police brutality and Black liberation. Our research also illustrates the challenges created by social media usage, which extend beyond limitations outlined in existing empirical scholarship.

[. . .]

To address this gap, we focus on the role of social media in the context of BLM, a movement inextricably tied to the digital sphere. Since its inception in 2014, BLM has grown into a national network, part of the broader movement for Black Lives that includes more than 50 organizations with a shared vision and platform for Black liberation and an end to police brutality.[1] BLM is characterized by its explicit rejection of hierarchy and centralized leadership, instead billing itself as "leader-ful," horizontally structured, and characterized by an intersectional approach that lifts up queer women of color (Milkman, 2017). As Ransby (2017) notes, "The suggestion that the organizations that have emerged from the Black Lives Matter protests are somehow lacking because they have rejected the old style of leadership misses what makes this movement most powerful."

Existing research focusing on BLM largely attempts to contextualize the spread of the #blacklivesmatter hashtag. Gallagher, Reagan, Danforth, and Dodds (2018) compare the discourse of BLM and All Lives Matter, based on Twitter usage of hashtags associated with each. They find that the diversity of topics related to BLM is greater than that associated with the #AllLivesMatter hashtag, which is more tightly intertwined with conservative perspectives. Further to this point, Ince, Rojas and Davis (2016) focus on how the public interacts with BLM, highlighting to the potential of broad audiences, rather than just central movement activists, to "alter and manipulate the movement's construction of meaning" (p.

* From Mundt, M., Ross, K. and Burnett, C. M. (2018) 'Scaling Social Movements through Social Media: The Case of Black Lives Matter', *Social Media + Society*, October–December: 1–14. Extracts from pp. 1, 3–4, 6–7, 8–10, 12.

1827). Finally, Yang (2016) illustrates that use of #blacklivesmatter provides an opportunity for users to engage in narrative agency, that is, to create their own stories and discourse around the term and its meaning (see also Bonilla & Rosa, 2015). In contrast, however, Duncan-Shippy, Murphy, and Purdy's (2017) exploration of variation in the intensity and topical breadth of the coverage of BLM by mainstream media finds that mainstream media tends to frame BLM through a relatively narrow lens. Thus, the literature suggests potential tensions between a possible lack of focus on movement messaging on one hand and a media (and public) perception of BLM as narrowly focused on the other hand.

Existing research points to the significance of BLM as an emerging movement in the United States, but also illustrates potential contradictions and gaps in our understanding of the way it is shaped by social media platforms. Our study seeks to address some of these gaps by focusing specifically on how social media creates opportunities and challenges for BLM to broaden its impact. Drawing primarily on interview data from social media–based groups that use the BLM frame, we explore the complexity of scaling through social media in the context of a largely, but not solely, digital movement. We address both possibilities and challenges of using social media as a tool for broadening the impact of BLM as a network and as individual groups.

[...]

Although use of social media by BLM organizers was not described as consciously designed or contrived for the specific purpose of fueling growth, it was identified as central in their organizing efforts in three ways: (1) for mobilizing internal and external resources, (2) for building coalitions among and between BLM groups and other social movements, and (3) for controlling the narrative of the movement. We describe each of these in turn below.

Social Media as a Mobilization Tool: Building Internal Connections

For a number of BLM groups, social media was referenced as a tool for building direct, personal ties within the community of BLM activists. Several group administrators talked about the immense value of having other BLM group leaders online to talk with about personal highs and lows as movement organizers, share ideas, and informally coordinate efforts locally and nationally. For them, social media served as a tool for mobilizing resources in the form of support networks. One BLM organizer shared that "before December 2014, I only knew one other person in this [BLM] community, directly. And since then, I now know a good, I want to say a good 10–15 people, I'm quite sure more than that, that I can actually call and say, 'Look this is what's happening, I need your support'." Moreover, a recurring challenge cited by leaders of BLM groups was leadership attrition due to burn-out. As such, having others to commiserate with and share experiences was recounted as key to maintaining pace and enthusiasm for the cause. One group administrator reflected,

> [Social media] also allows us to be able to network, it allows people in another region to be like, "Okay, I send solidarity," to say, "I feel you." That gives you the extra push and rejuvenation that you need sometimes in this organizing field. And also, you are doing all this work but a lot of folks are not doing the work with you, right? But then a lot of people are having similar problems and doing similar work around the world and so it allows you to be like, 'Okay, I see what you are doing. How did you get through that? Alright, okay. I'm gonna do that over here.' And it allows us to be a whole network without being right in front of each other's faces.

An additional, and important, benefit highlighted in this quote is the possibility for conversations among leadership online, leading to new initiatives or expansion of existing programming or events between locations. For example, if a vigil or speaker series showed success in one city or town with a BLM presence, leaders disseminated success stories to other BLM coordinators or administrators. This indicates the importance of access to one another's work and highlights how social media can open a path for transmission of ideas and knowledge among widely dispersed activists within a given movement. The strong connections forged among BLM activists also suggests that social media can strengthen connections among activists in ways that greatly exceed the creation of "weak ties" indicated in existing scholarship (Hwang & Kim, 2015; Nien, 2017).

[. . .]

Social Media as a Coalition Building Tool

Among the recurrent themes that emerged among BLM group administrators was the significance of social media for building connections and coalitions with other groups in the movement to facilitate strategic action. This kind of coalition building occurred in the form of the development of partnerships between groups, in contrast with the creation of relationships among individual leaders characterizing what we describe as building internal connections. Administrators of a group in the Southwest noted,

> We are in contact with other BLM organizations throughout the country, so we use it just by inviting them on Facebook, or, like, they like our page, we like their page. It allows us to link up with other people who are doing the same work as us.

Administrators of a Midwestern BLM group likewise noted, "All the chapters [in our State]. . . we get together often, and we all do events together." Their statement speaks to the way that social media facilitates connections between groups that can move beyond a purely online presence and in some cases can further increase event turnout.

It is important to note that while connecting with other groups on social media occurred widely, there did not seem to be a single set of criteria for developing partnerships. For instance, some connections took the form of *within movement* coalitions between other groups using the #BlackLivesMatter banner or group name. Groups talked about how this sort of partnership was facilitated by a simple search for "Black Lives Matter" online. For example, one Midwestern group discussed a message they had received from an activist who was looking for connections to local groups in her area, but had been unable to locate these groups on her own. She contacted this group because of its public social media presence and apparent association with the movement: "We had someone down from Louisiana who was very worried about the police, asking us for help. [. . .] She just happened to find us somewhere on Facebook, so she inboxed us and asked us for help, because she saw that we were Black Lives Matter." Social media in this instance helped this individual connect to a BLM group elsewhere that, through their own connections, was able to link her into the movement. Another group administrator noted that she happened to meet some members of another BLM group at one of their events, and "we connected and so then we became Facebook friends and then I stayed connected that way [with what they were doing]." In addition, several administrators spoke about connecting with multiple groups through conference calls hosted by national BLM leadership and using these connections to learn new strategies or about the kinds of events undertaken around the country. In other words, social media facilitated both the initial process of connecting to BLM or specific BLM groups and the possibility of learning from BLM activists in different places.

[. . .]

Social Media as a Narrative Amplification Tool

Coalition building, personal networking, and resource mobilization all speak to significant roles social media can play in scaling movements such as BLM. However, according to our interviewees, perhaps the most notable function of social media is providing activists with the ability to control their own narrative, thus creating awareness and visibility for the issues that the movement addresses. This stands in contrast with the way BLM activists discussed portrayal of the movement in traditional and mainstream forms of media. For instance, one group shared, "Social media provides us a platform to tell our story as real, as raw, and as relevant as it may be, without the worry of a filter being put on, or someone else's perspectives and biases." Moreover, social media tools facilitate amplification of preferred narratives through functions such as "repost" or "share" options.

Groups also noted that social media provides an open source venue for a direct counter narrative. A BLM group administrator in the Mid-Atlantic region spoke about social media as being more credible than traditional news media, using the example of reporting from a protest:

> I actually went to Baltimore when the Freddie Gray uprisings happened. And I could see how accurate Twitter was, versus what the media was saying. Like, I was standing beside the person who was doing the Tweeting. And then I see what the media says . . . Well now, all the sudden, that's another thing. Now you know, before you didn't, before you were taught to trust the media, to trust the source like the Washington Post, like the New York Times. You couldn't cite the internet before . . . you can actually cite Twitter, now you can actually cite Facebook, and it's because now there's more credibility, there's more exposure. You can actually find the people, the grassroots activists and be there and watch and see and their videotaping and then I can read the same article [in the mainstream media], or an article of accounts of the same day and I can say, "That did not happen."

As these quotations show, the use of social media for presenting and amplifying non-dominant narratives highlights an important function of digital platforms in contributing to shifts in public discourse. Indeed, this suggests a far more significant

role for social media in movement scaling than the existing literature on meaning making indicates (e.g., Kavada, 2015; Milan, 2015), because social media use enables movements not only to create a shared narrative, but to easily and quickly disseminate that narrative as a contrast to existing, mainstream discourse. Given the significance of discursive or cultural shifts for movement scaling (Authors, submitted), this further illustrates the role social media can play in broadening movement impact.

NOTE

1. see https://policy.m4bl.org/about/

REFERENCES

Bonilla, Y., & Rosa, J. (2015). #Ferguson: Digital protest, hashtag ethnography, and the racial politics of social media in the United States. *American Ethnologist, 42*, 4–17.

Duncan-Shippy, E. M., Murphy, S. C., & Purdy, M. A. (2017). An examination of mainstream media as an educating institution: The Black Lives Matter movement and contemporary social protest. *Advances in Education in Diverse Communities: Research, Policy and Praxis (The Power of Resistance: Culture, Ideology and Social Reproduction in Global Contexts), 12*, 99–142.

Gallagher, R. J., Reagan, A. J., Danforth, C. M., & Dodds, P. S. (2018). Divergent discourse between protests and counterprotests: #BlackLivesMatter and #AllLivesMatter. *PLoS ONE, 13*, e0195644.

Hwang, H., & Kim, K. (2015). Social media as a tool for social movements: The effect of social media use and social capital on intention to participate in social movements. *International Journal of Consumer Studies, 39*, 478–488.

Ince, J., Rojas, F., & Davis, C. A. (2016). The social media response to Black Lives Matter: How Twitter users interact with Black Lives

Matter through hashtag use. *Ethnic and Racial Studies*, *40*, 1814–1830.

Kavada, A. (2015). Creating the collective: Social media, the occupy movement and its constitution as a collective actor. *Information, Communication & Society*, *18*, 872–886.

Milan, S. (2015). From social movements to cloud protesting: The evolution of collective identity. *Information, Communication & Society*, *18*, 887–900.

Milkman, R. (2017). A new political generation: Millennials and the post-2008 wave of protest. *American Sociological Review*, *82*, 1–31.

Nien, W. L. (2017). What is the role of social media in establishing a chain of equivalence between activists participating in protest movements? *Online Journal of Communication and Media Technologies*, *7*, 182–215.

Ransby, B. (2017, October 21). Black Lives Matter is democracy in action. *The New York Times*. Retrieved from https://www.nytimes.com/2017/10/21/opinion/sunday/black-lives-matter-leadership.html?_r=0

Ross, K., Burnett, C., Raschupkina, Y., & Kew, D. (under review). Scaling up peace building and social justice work: A conceptual model.

Yang, G. (2016). Narrative agency in hashtag activism: The case of #BlackLivesMatter. *Media and Communication*, *4*, 13–17.

Part 10 – Further reading

A very useful introduction to political sociology is Clemens, E. S. (2016) *What is Political Sociology?* (Cambridge: Polity), which answers its title question. Dobratz, B. A., Waldner, L. K., and Buzzell, T. (2019) *Power, Politics and Society: An Introduction to Political Sociology* (2nd edn, New York: Routledge) is also an excellent text and a good place to open your reading. On social movements, one of the best introductory texts is Della Porta, D., and Diani, M. (2020) *Social Movements: An Introduction* (3rd edn, Hoboken, NJ: Wiley). Finally, to get a handle on the origins and development of populism, try Mudde, C., and Kaltwasser, C. R. (2017) *Populism: A Very Short Introduction* (Oxford: Oxford University Press).

Sociology, **9th edition**

Chapter 21, 'Politics, Government and Social Movements', covers all of the key issues and debates, while political issues crop up in almost every chapter. The best strategy, therefore, is to work with the book's index to locate specific subjects of interest.

Index